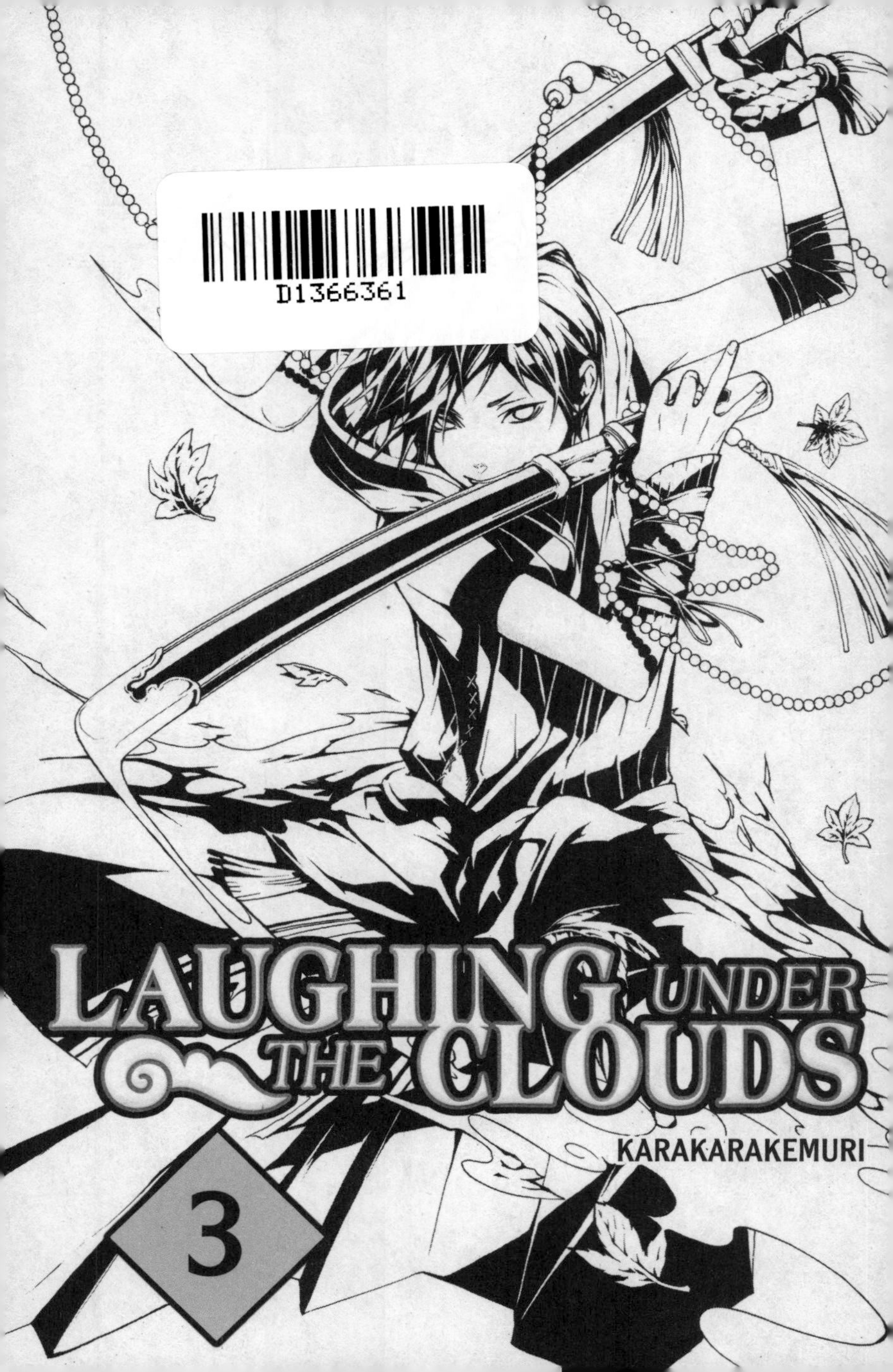
LAUGHING UNDER THE CLOUDS
KARAKARAKEMURI
3

Table of Contents

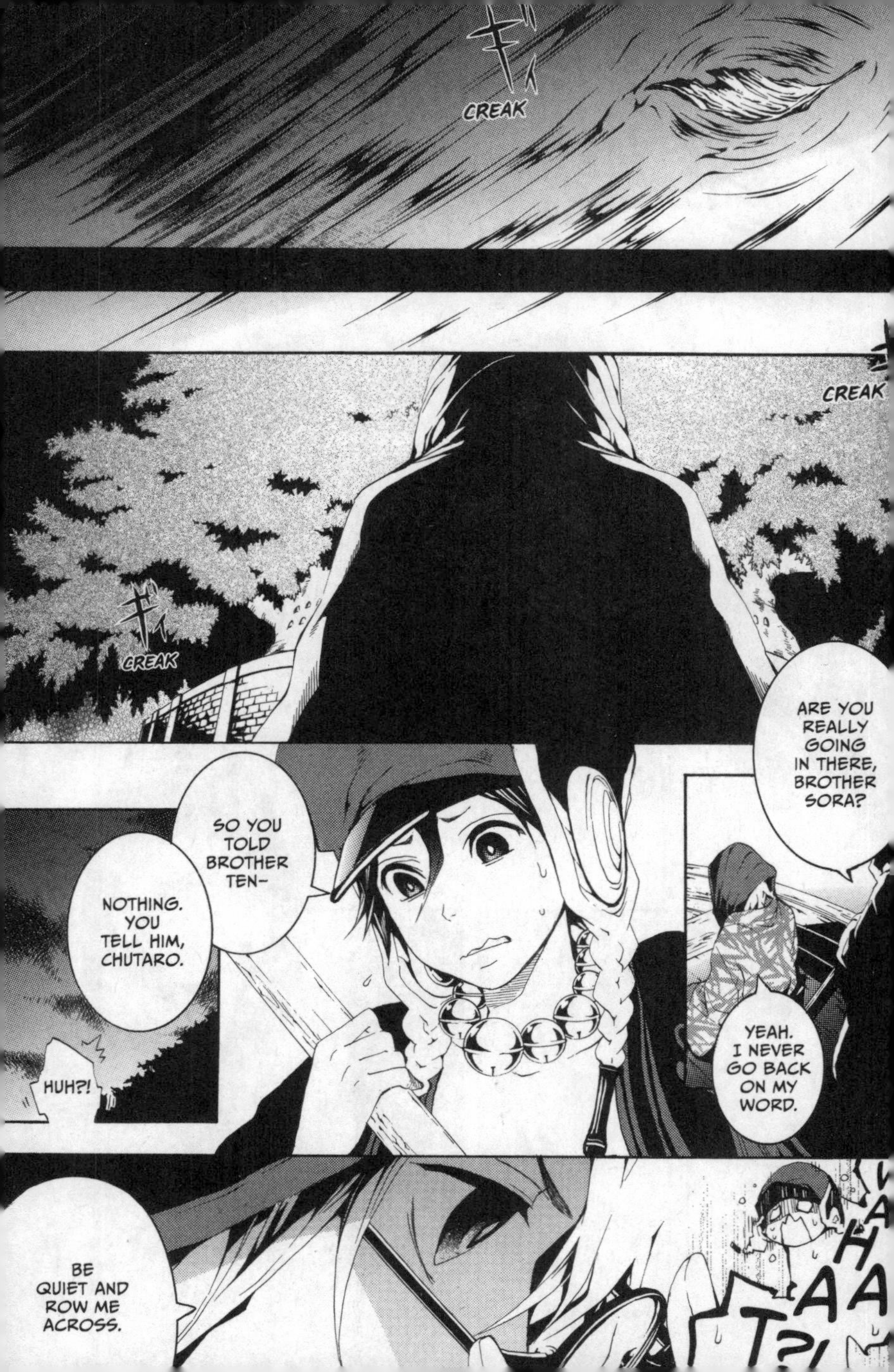
CREAK
CREAK
CREAK
ARE YOU REALLY GOING IN THERE, BROTHER SORA?
YEAH. I NEVER GO BACK ON MY WORD.
SO YOU TOLD BROTHER TEN-
NOTHING. YOU TELL HIM, CHUTARO.
HUH?!
WHAAAT?!
BE QUIET AND ROW ME ACROSS.

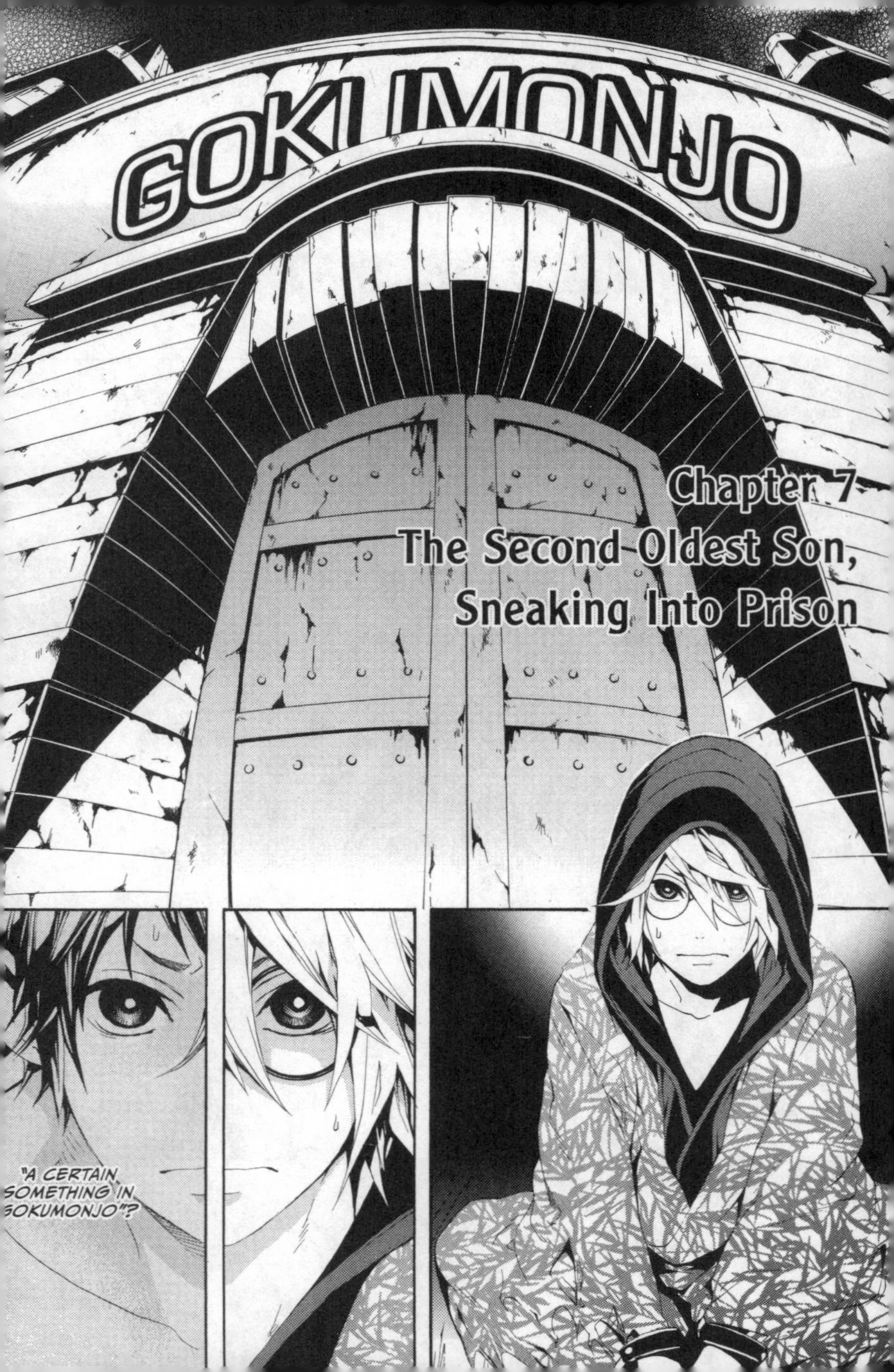
GOKUMONJO
Chapter 7
The Second Oldest Son, Sneaking Into Prison
"A CERTAIN SOMETHING IN GOKUMONJO"?

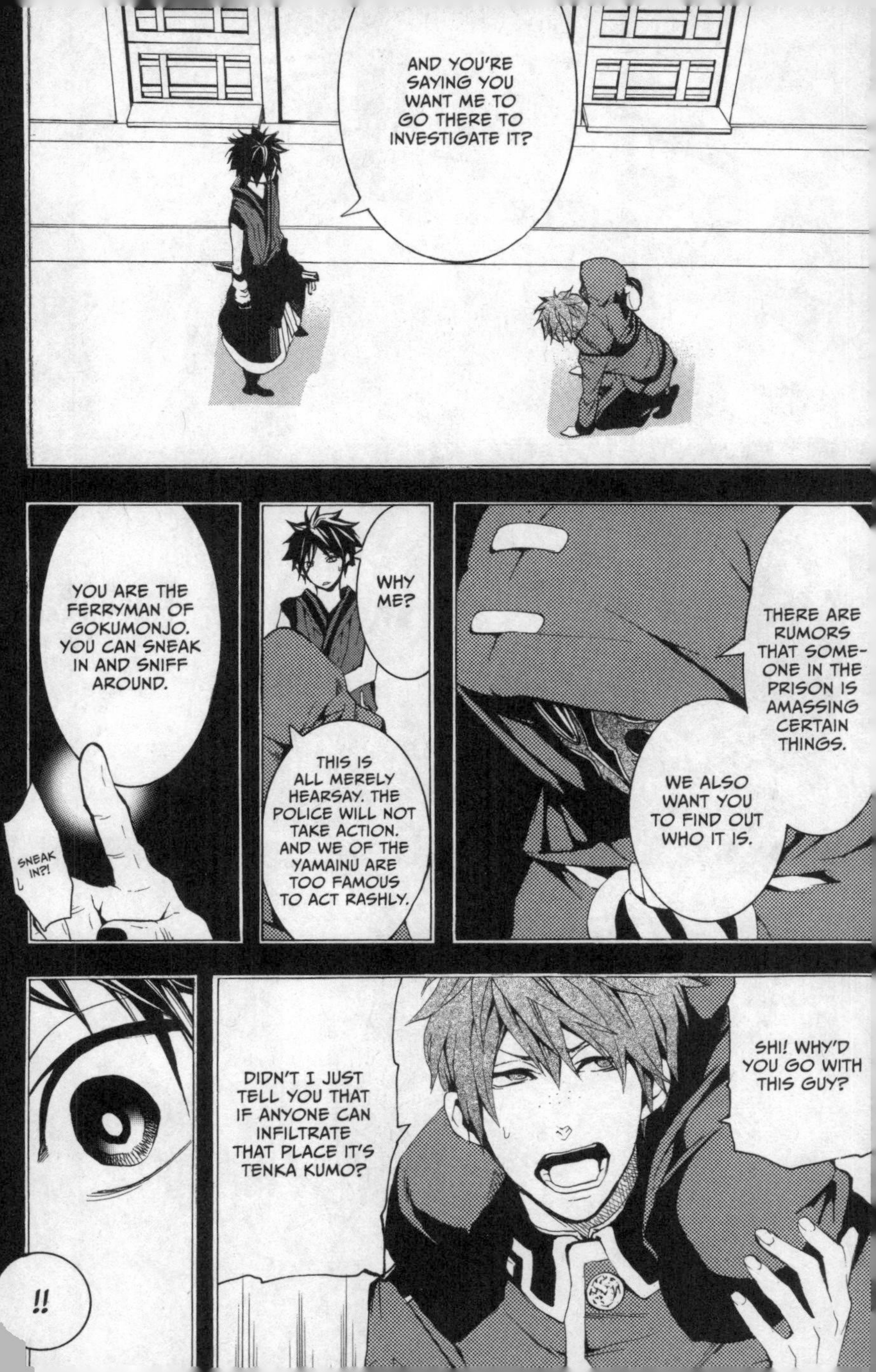
AND YOU'RE SAYING YOU WANT ME TO GO THERE TO INVESTIGATE IT?
THERE ARE RUMORS THAT SOME-ONE IN THE PRISON IS AMASSING CERTAIN THINGS.
WE ALSO WANT YOU TO FIND OUT WHO IT IS.
WHY ME?
THIS IS ALL MERELY HEARSAY. THE POLICE WILL NOT TAKE ACTION. AND WE OF THE YAMAINU ARE TOO FAMOUS TO ACT RASHLY.
YOU ARE THE FERRYMAN OF GOKUMONJO. YOU CAN SNEAK IN AND SNIFF AROUND.
SNEAK IN?!
SHI! WHY'D YOU GO WITH THIS GUY?
DIDN'T I JUST TELL YOU THAT IF ANYONE CAN INFILTRATE THAT PLACE IT'S TENKA KUMO?
!!

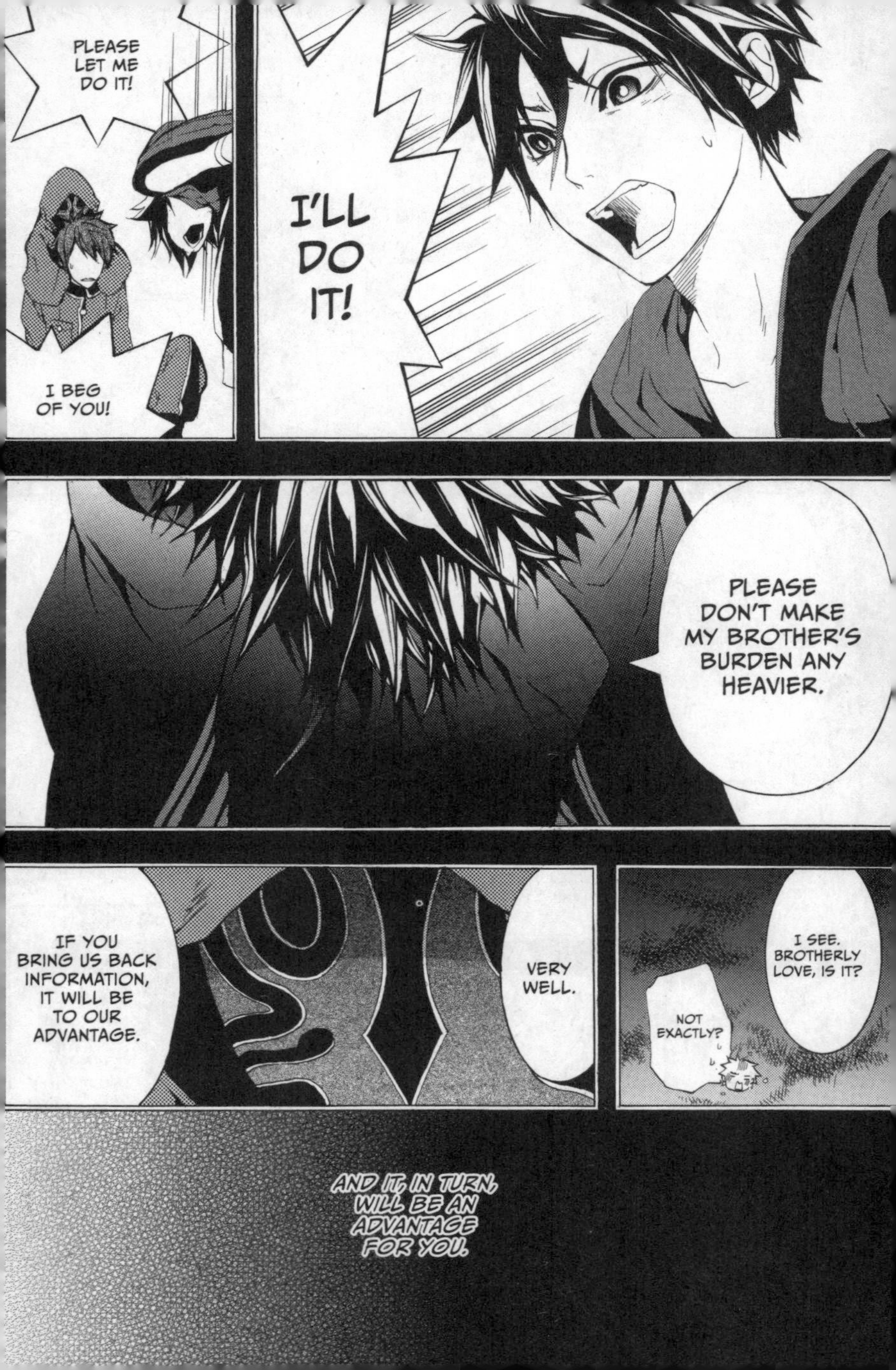
I'LL DO IT!
PLEASE LET ME DO IT!
I BEG OF YOU!
PLEASE DON'T MAKE MY BROTHER'S BURDEN ANY HEAVIER.
I SEE. BROTHERLY LOVE, IS IT?
NOT EXACTLY?
VERY WELL.
IF YOU BRING US BACK INFORMATION, IT WILL BE TO OUR ADVANTAGE.
AND IT, IN TURN, WILL BE AN ADVANTAGE FOR YOU.

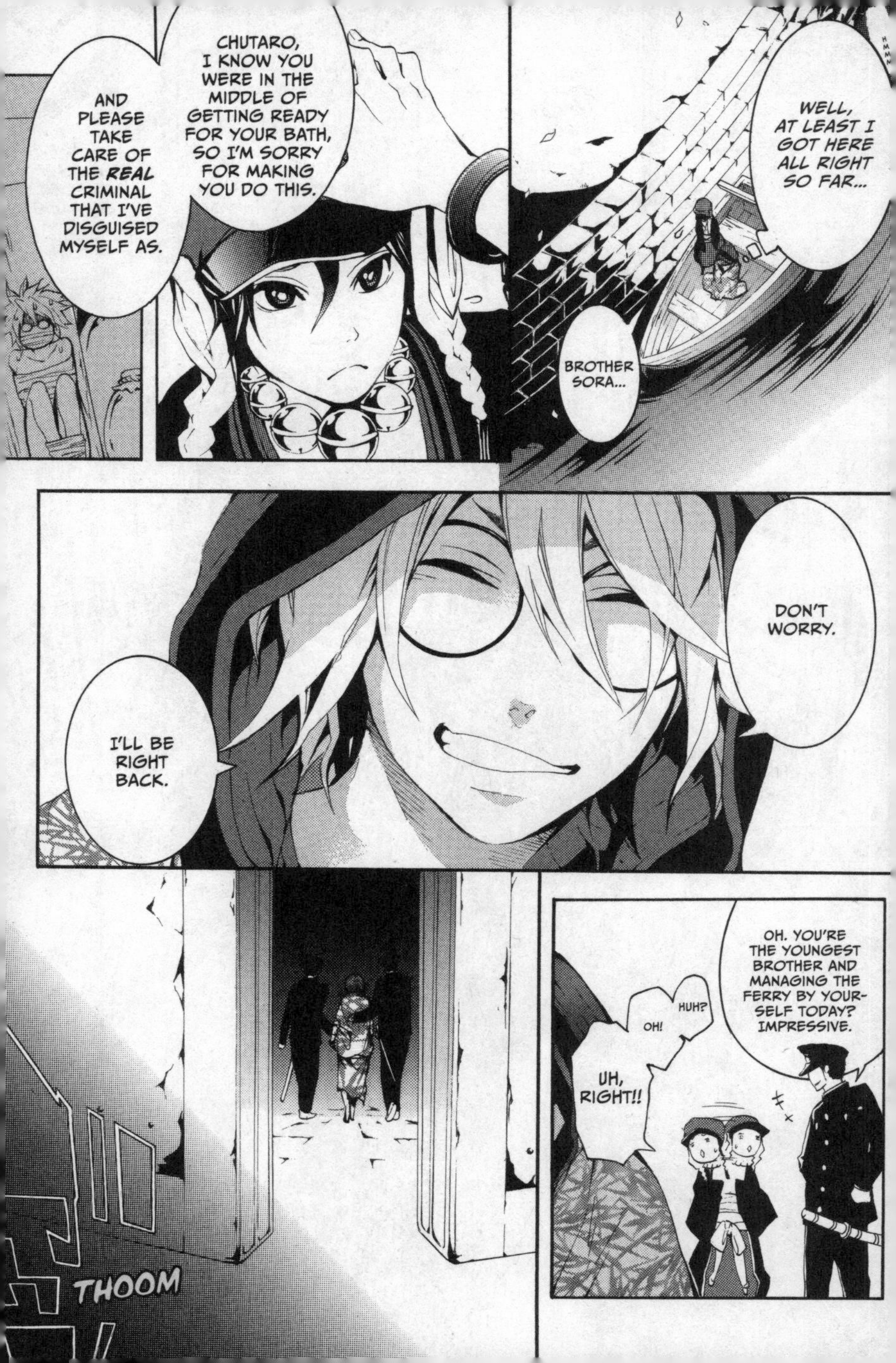
WELL, AT LEAST I GOT HERE ALL RIGHT SO FAR...
BROTHER SORA...
CHUTARO, I KNOW YOU WERE IN THE MIDDLE OF GETTING READY FOR YOUR BATH, SO I'M SORRY FOR MAKING YOU DO THIS.
AND PLEASE TAKE CARE OF THE *REAL* CRIMINAL THAT I'VE DISGUISED MYSELF AS.
DON'T WORRY.
I'LL BE RIGHT BACK.
OH. YOU'RE THE YOUNGEST BROTHER AND MANAGING THE FERRY BY YOURSELF TODAY? IMPRESSIVE.
HUH?
OH!
UH, RIGHT!!
THOOM

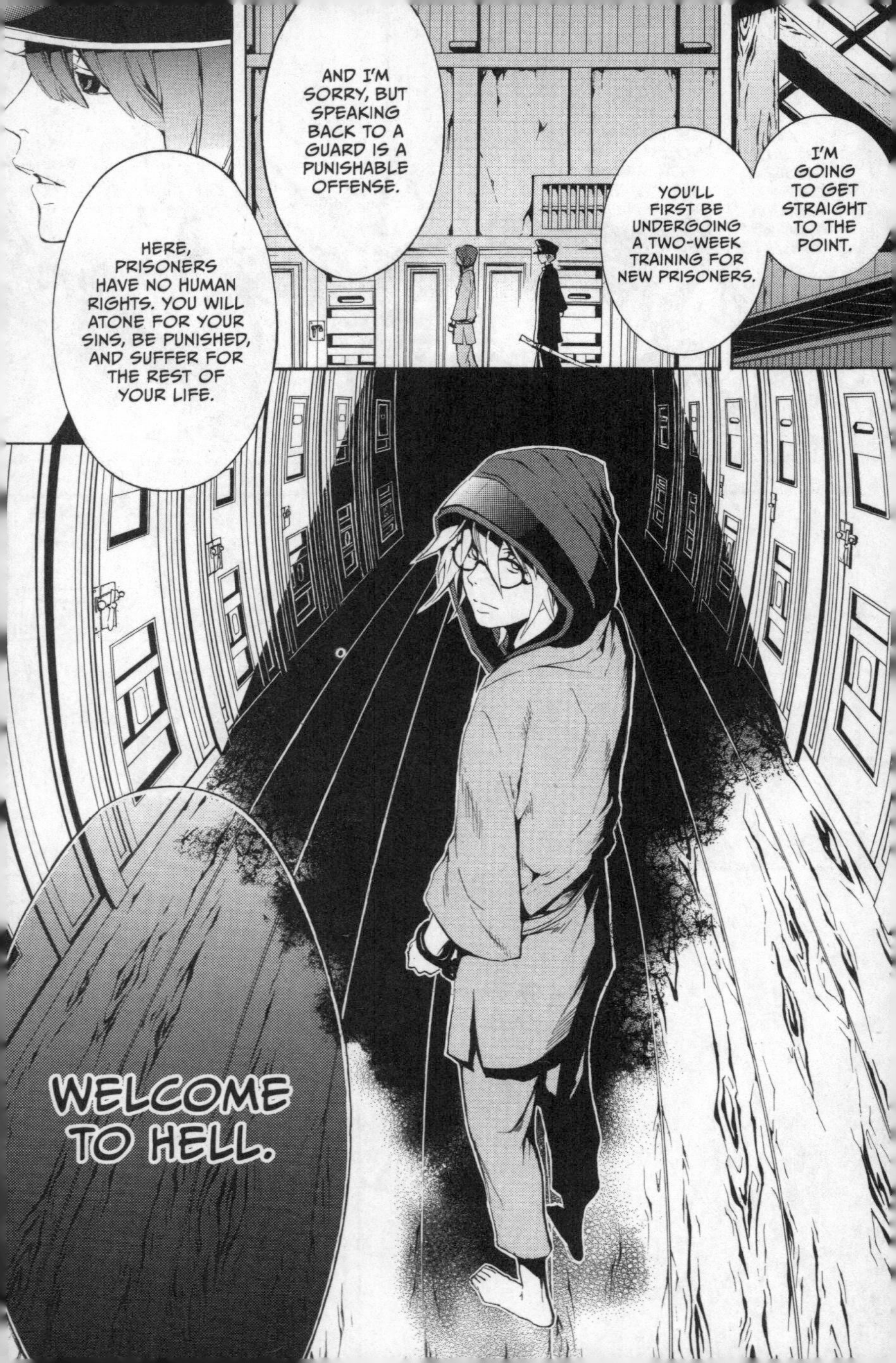
I'M GOING TO GET STRAIGHT TO THE POINT.
YOU'LL FIRST BE UNDERGOING A TWO-WEEK TRAINING FOR NEW PRISONERS.
AND I'M SORRY, BUT SPEAKING BACK TO A GUARD IS A PUNISHABLE OFFENSE.
HERE, PRISONERS HAVE NO HUMAN RIGHTS. YOU WILL ATONE FOR YOUR SINS, BE PUNISHED, AND SUFFER FOR THE REST OF YOUR LIFE.
WELCOME TO HELL.

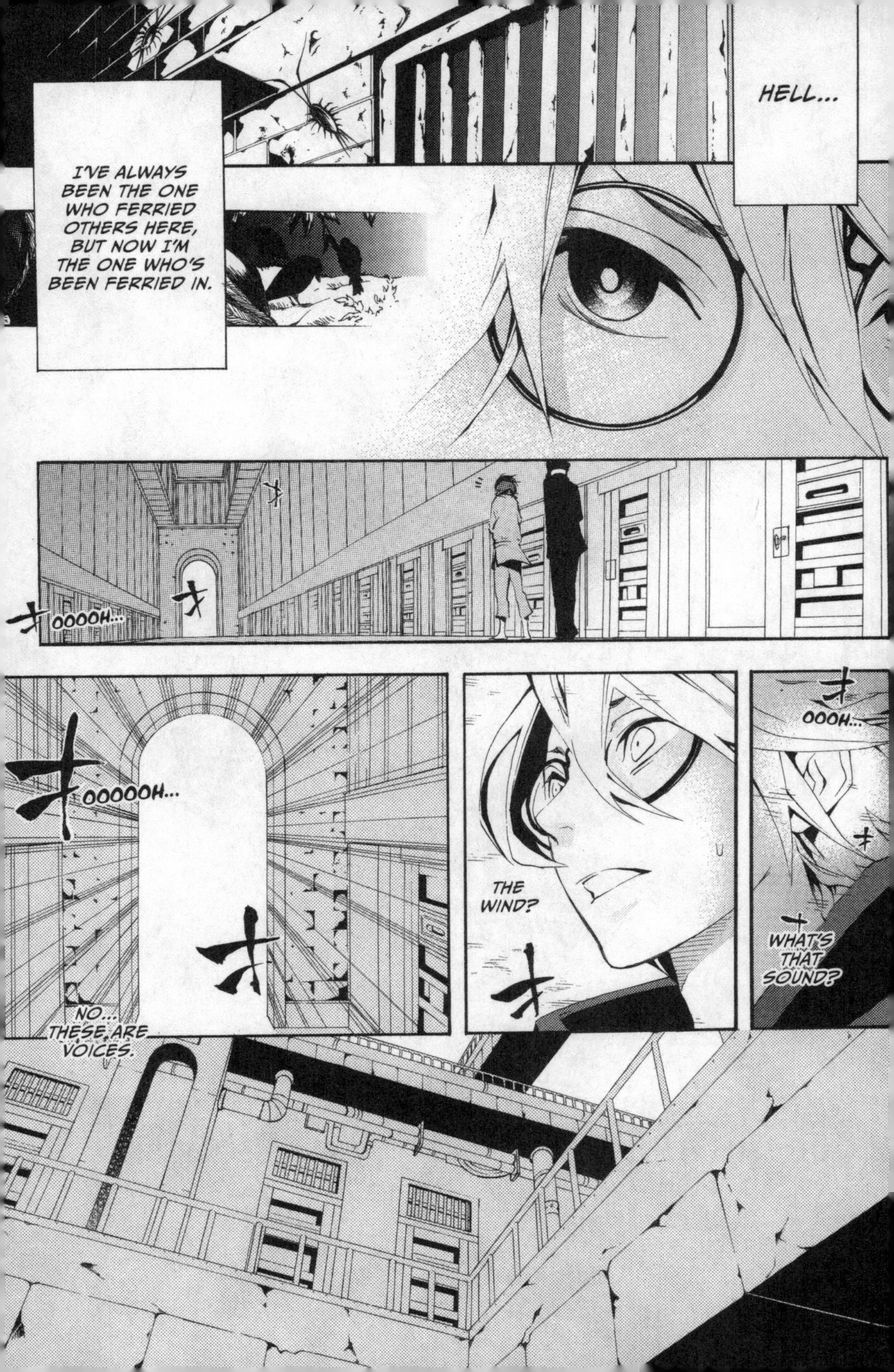
HELL...
I'VE ALWAYS BEEN THE ONE WHO FERRIED OTHERS HERE, BUT NOW I'M THE ONE WHO'S BEEN FERRIED IN.
OOOOH...
OOOH...
WHAT'S THAT SOUND?
THE WIND?
OOOOOH...
NO... THESE ARE VOICES.

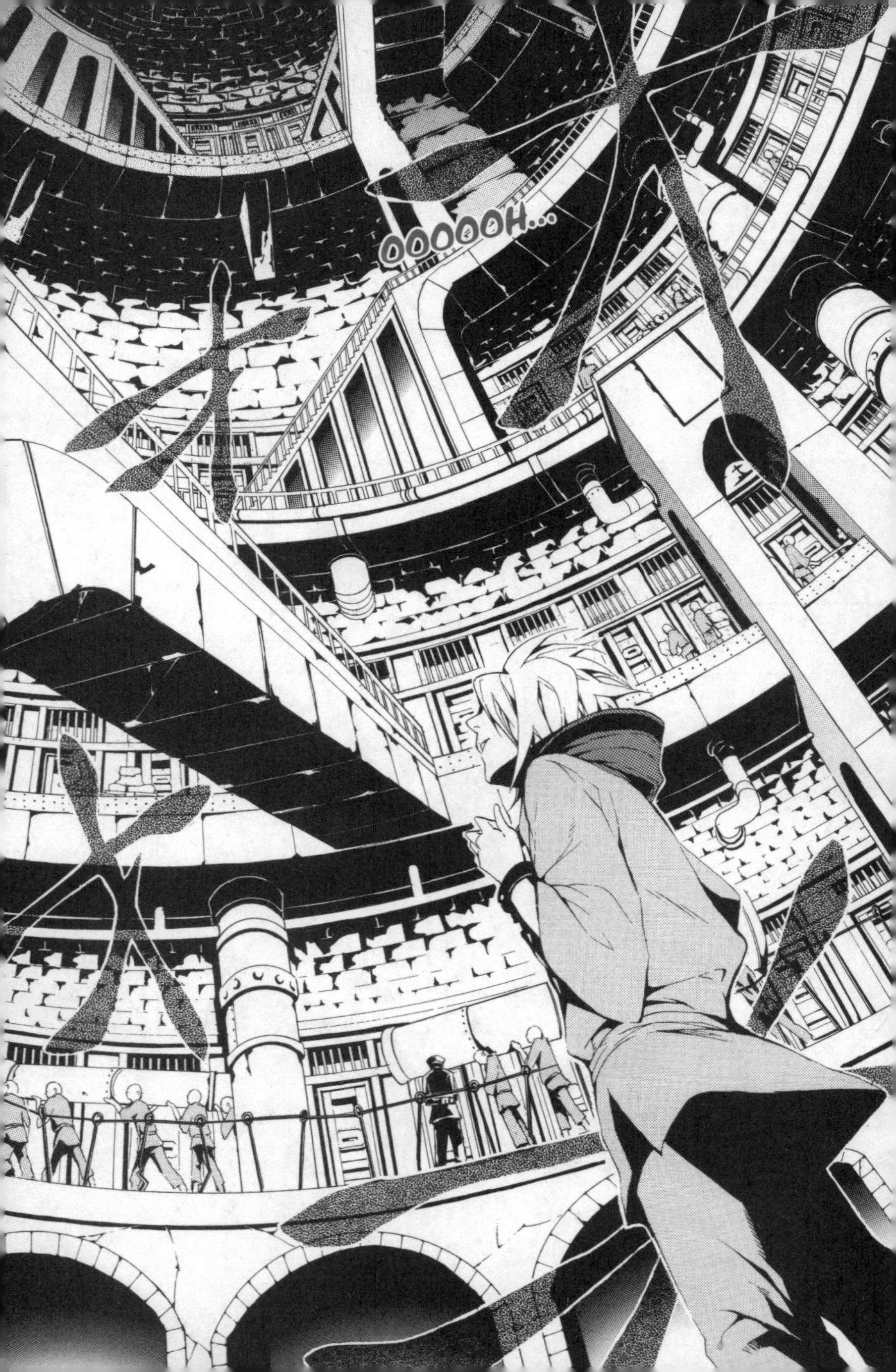
OOOOOH...

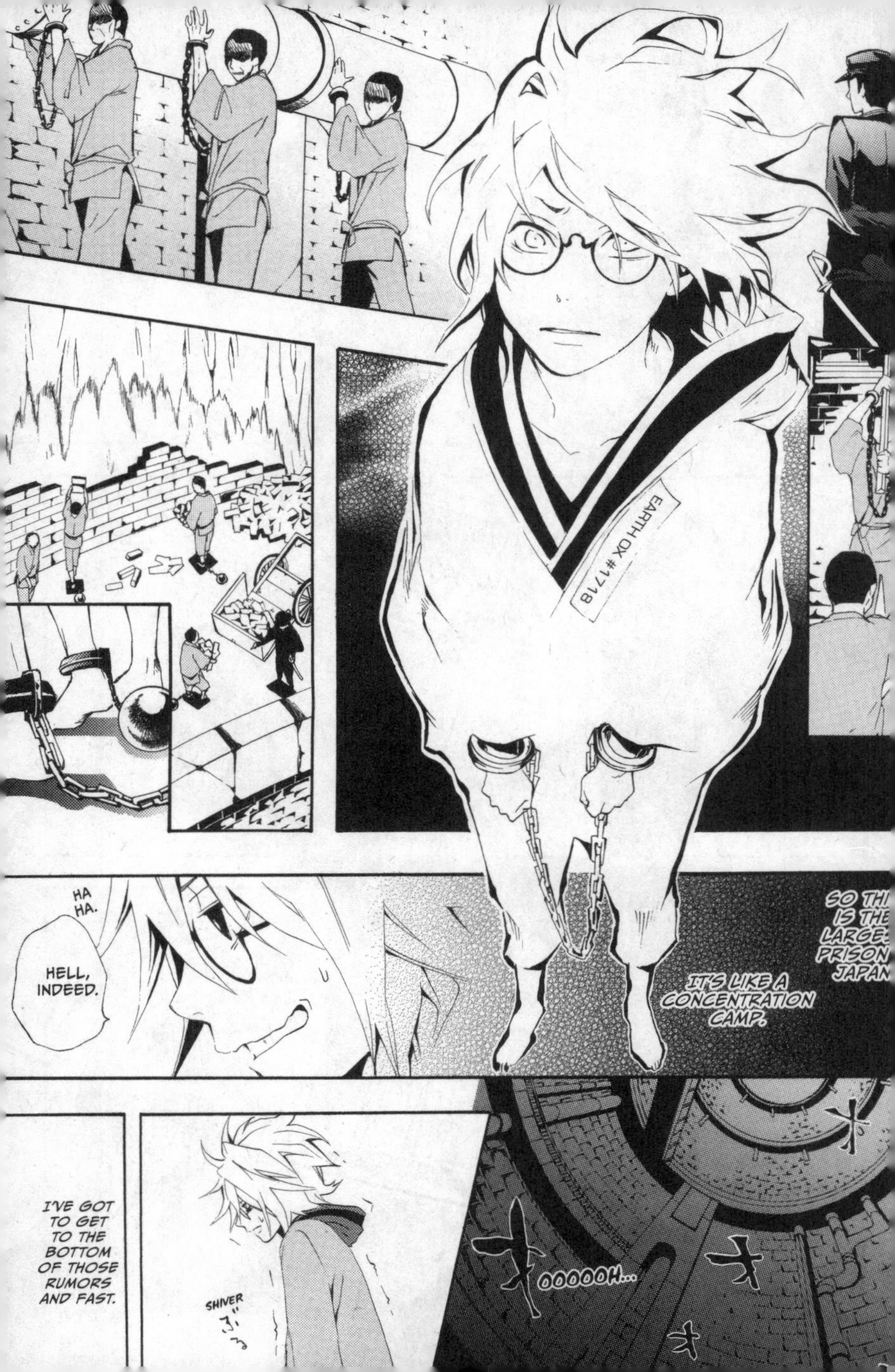
EARTH OX #17718
SO THI IS THE LARGE- PRISON JAPAN
IT'S LIKE A CONCENTRATION CAMP.
HA HA.
HELL, INDEED.
OOOOOH...
I'VE GOT TO GET TO THE BOTTOM OF THOSE RUMORS AND FAST.
SHIVER

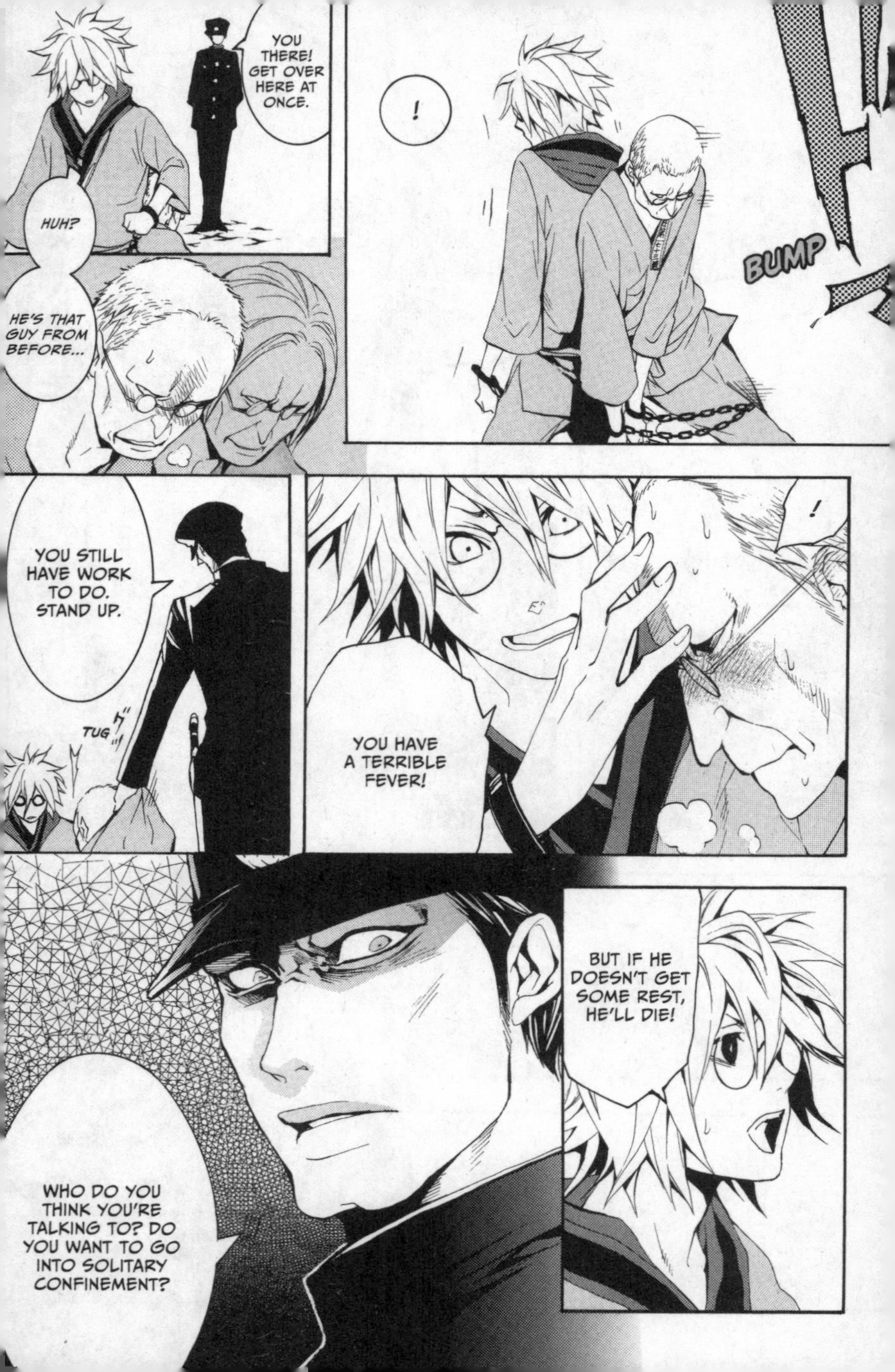
!
BUMP
YOU THERE! GET OVER HERE AT ONCE.
HUH?
HE'S THAT GUY FROM BEFORE...
!
YOU HAVE A TERRIBLE FEVER!
YOU STILL HAVE WORK TO DO. STAND UP.
TUG
BUT IF HE DOESN'T GET SOME REST, HE'LL DIE!
WHO DO YOU THINK YOU'RE TALKING TO? DO YOU WANT TO GO INTO SOLITARY CONFINEMENT?

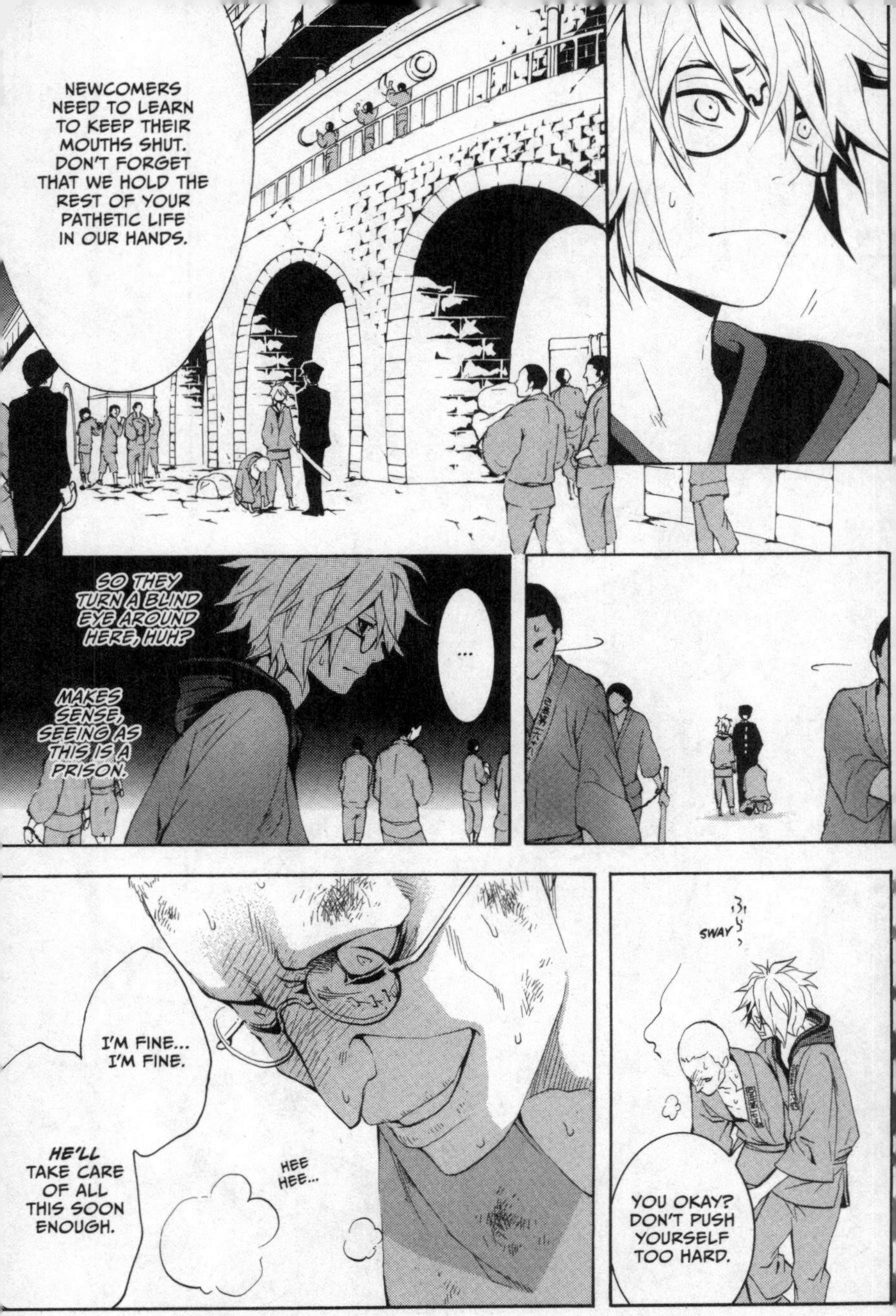
NEWCOMERS NEED TO LEARN TO KEEP THEIR MOUTHS SHUT. DON'T FORGET THAT WE HOLD THE REST OF YOUR PATHETIC LIFE IN OUR HANDS.
...
SO THEY TURN A BLIND EYE AROUND HERE, HUH?
MAKES SENSE, SEEING AS THIS IS A PRISON.
SWAY
YOU OKAY? DON'T PUSH YOURSELF TOO HARD.
I'M FINE... I'M FINE.
HEE HEE...
HE'LL TAKE CARE OF ALL THIS SOON ENOUGH.

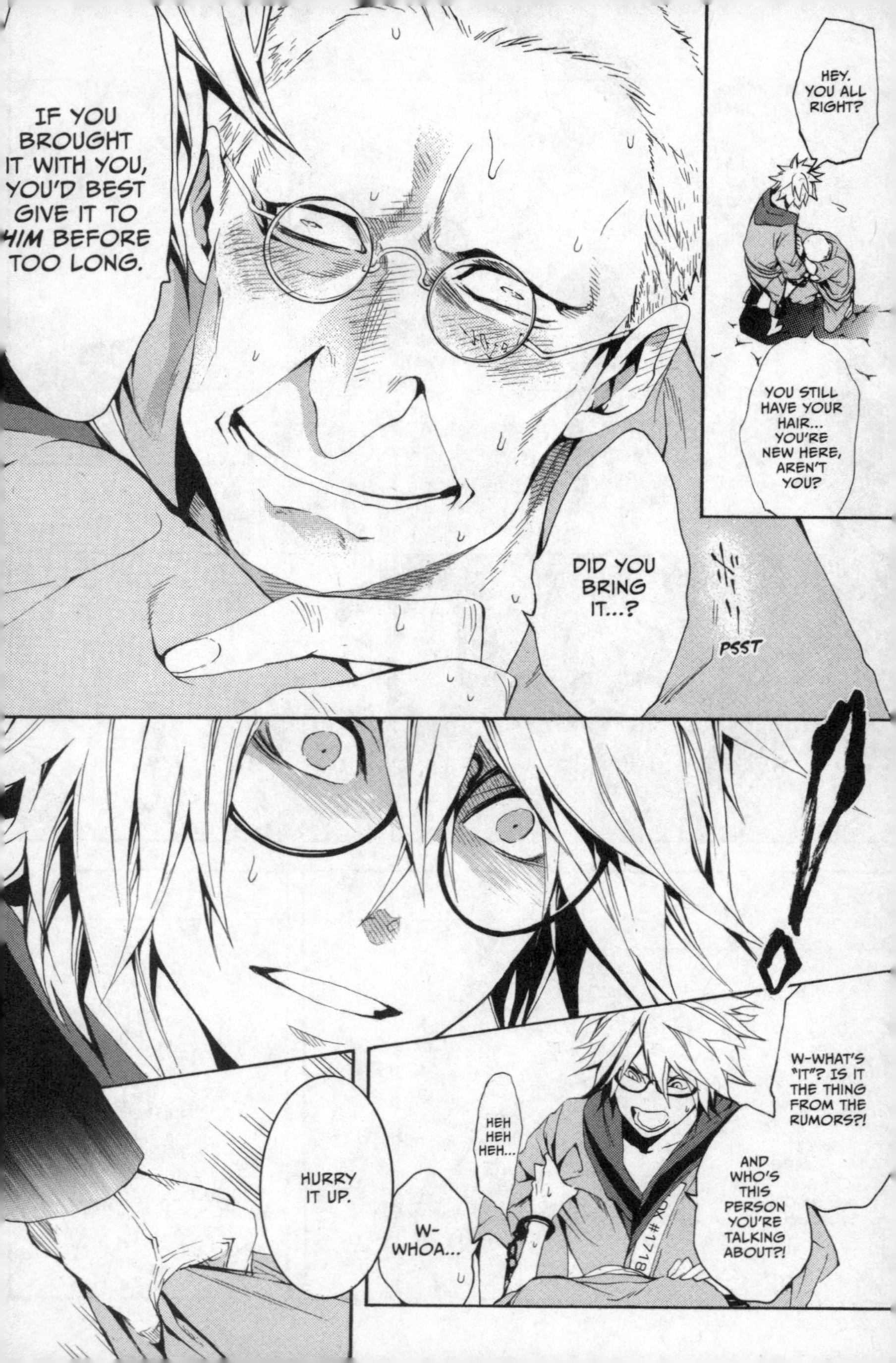
HEY. YOU ALL RIGHT?
YOU STILL HAVE YOUR HAIR... YOU'RE NEW HERE, AREN'T YOU?
PSST
DID YOU BRING IT...?
IF YOU BROUGHT IT WITH YOU, YOU'D BEST GIVE IT TO *HIM* BEFORE TOO LONG.
W-WHAT'S "IT"? IS IT THE THING FROM THE RUMORS?!
AND WHO'S THIS PERSON YOU'RE TALKING ABOUT?!
HEH HEH HEH...
W- WHOA...
HURRY IT UP.

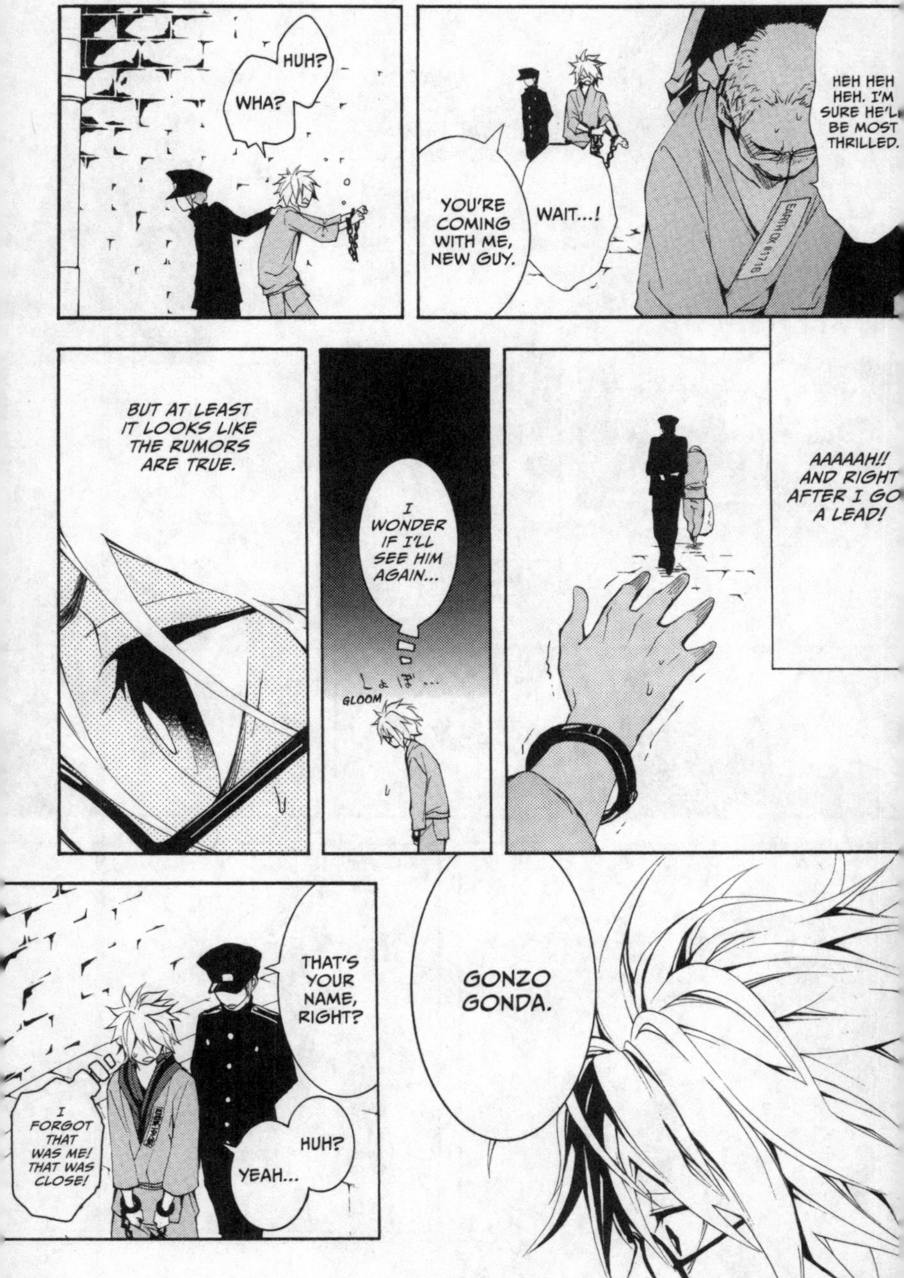
HEH HEH HEH. I'M SURE HE'L BE MOST THRILLED.
YOU'RE COMING WITH ME, NEW GUY.
WAIT...!
HUH?
WHA?
AAAAAH!! AND RIGHT AFTER I GO A LEAD!
I WONDER IF I'LL SEE HIM AGAIN...
しょぼ…
GLOOM
BUT AT LEAST IT LOOKS LIKE THE RUMORS ARE TRUE.
GONZO GONDA.
THAT'S YOUR NAME, RIGHT?
HUH?
YEAH...
I FORGOT THAT WAS ME! THAT WAS CLOSE!

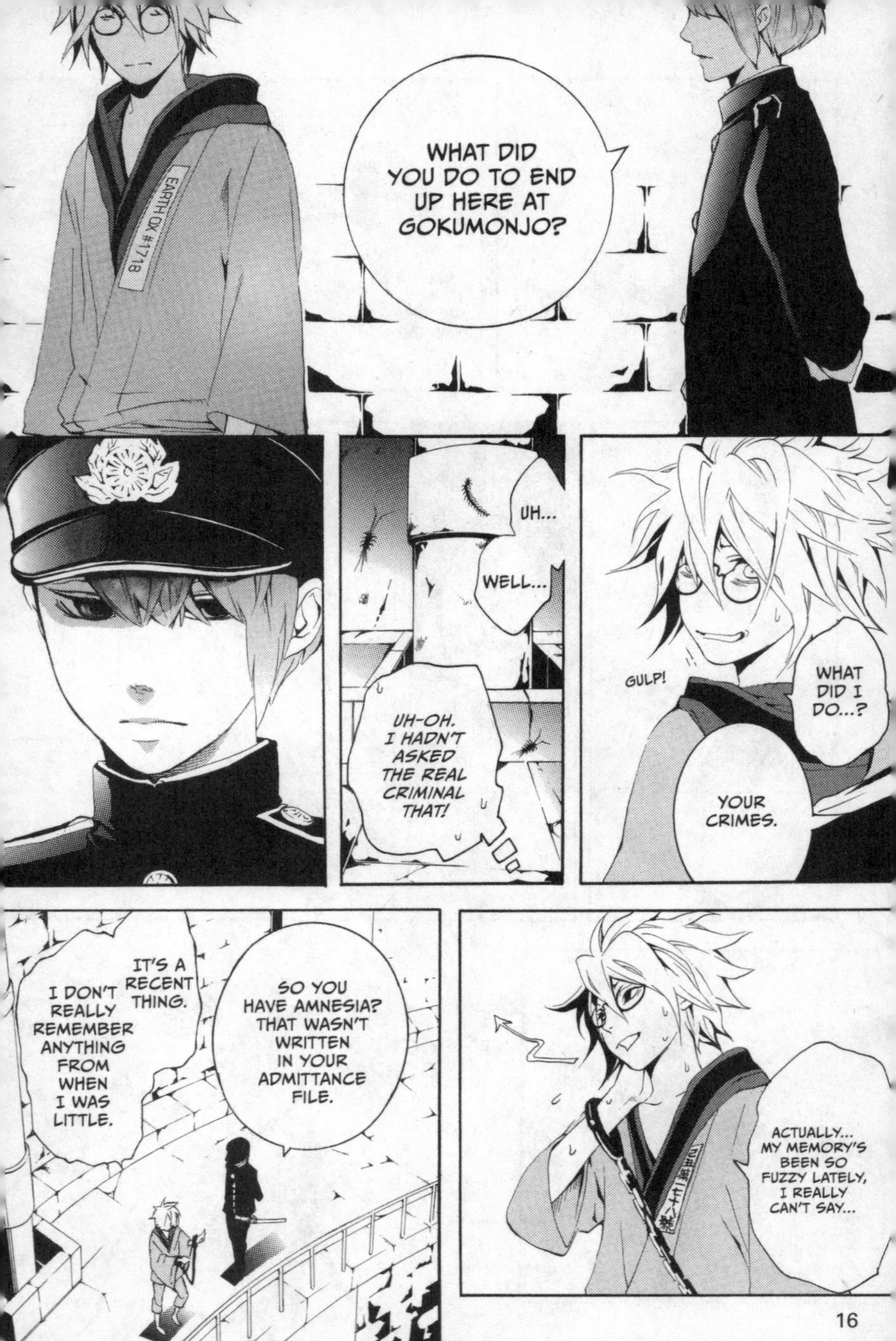
WHAT DID YOU DO TO END UP HERE AT GOKUMONJO?
EARTH OX #1718
WHAT DID I DO...?
GULP!
YOUR CRIMES.
UH...
WELL...
UH-OH. I HADN'T ASKED THE REAL CRIMINAL THAT!
ACTUALLY... MY MEMORY'S BEEN SO FUZZY LATELY, I REALLY CAN'T SAY...
SO YOU HAVE AMNESIA? THAT WASN'T WRITTEN IN YOUR ADMITTANCE FILE.
IT'S A RECENT THING.
I DON'T REALLY REMEMBER ANYTHING FROM WHEN I WAS LITTLE.

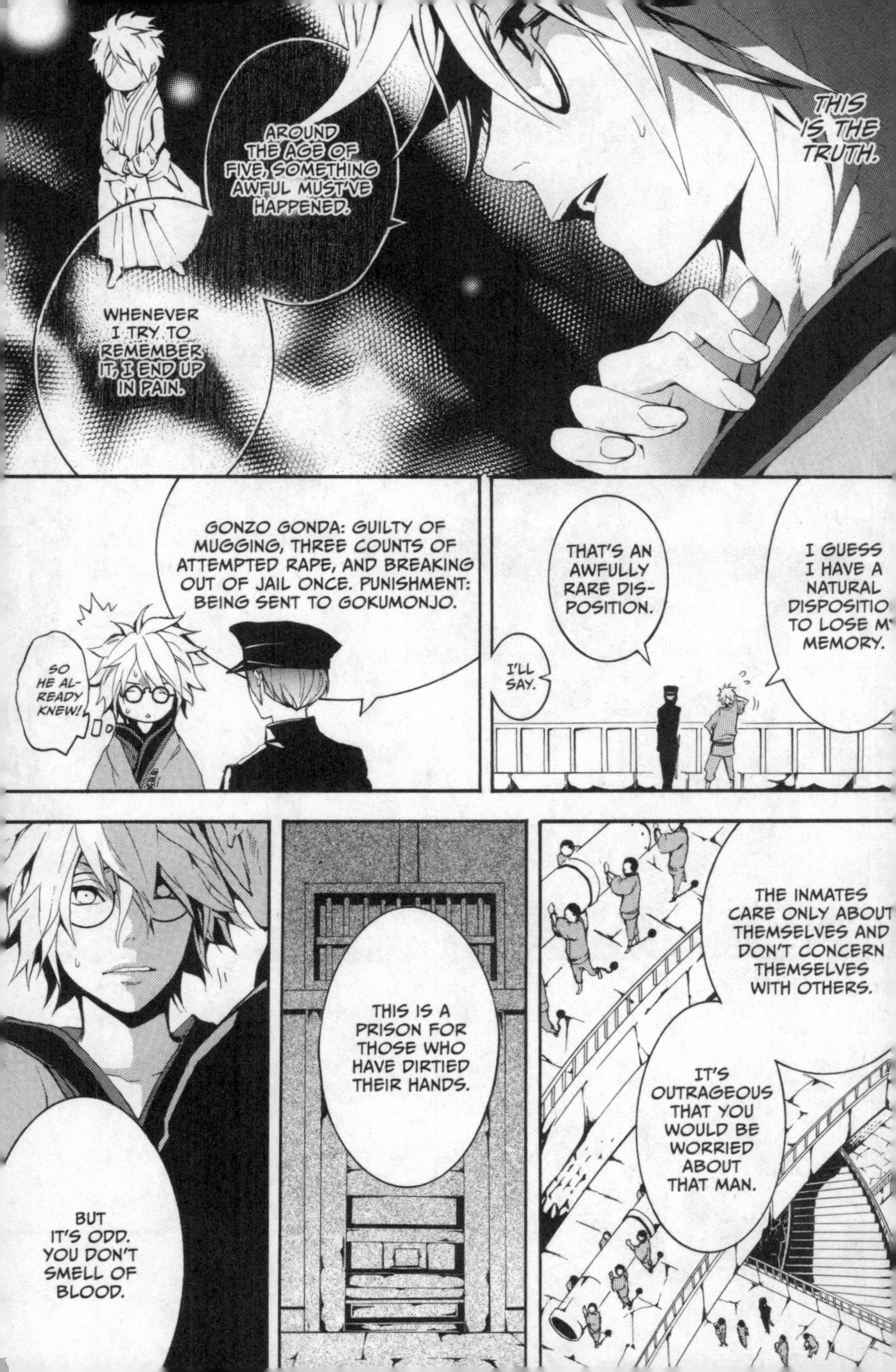
THIS IS THE TRUTH.
AROUND THE AGE OF FIVE, SOMETHING AWFUL MUST'VE HAPPENED.
WHENEVER I TRY TO REMEMBER IT, I END UP IN PAIN.
I GUESS I HAVE A NATURAL DISPOSITIO TO LOSE M MEMORY.
THAT'S AN AWFULLY RARE DIS-POSITION.
I'LL SAY.
GONZO GONDA: GUILTY OF MUGGING, THREE COUNTS OF ATTEMPTED RAPE, AND BREAKING OUT OF JAIL ONCE. PUNISHMENT: BEING SENT TO GOKUMONJO.
SO HE AL-READY KNEW!
THE INMATES CARE ONLY ABOUT THEMSELVES AND DON'T CONCERN THEMSELVES WITH OTHERS.
IT'S OUTRAGEOUS THAT YOU WOULD BE WORRIED ABOUT THAT MAN.
THIS IS A PRISON FOR THOSE WHO HAVE DIRTIED THEIR HANDS.
BUT IT'S ODD. YOU DON'T SMELL OF BLOOD.

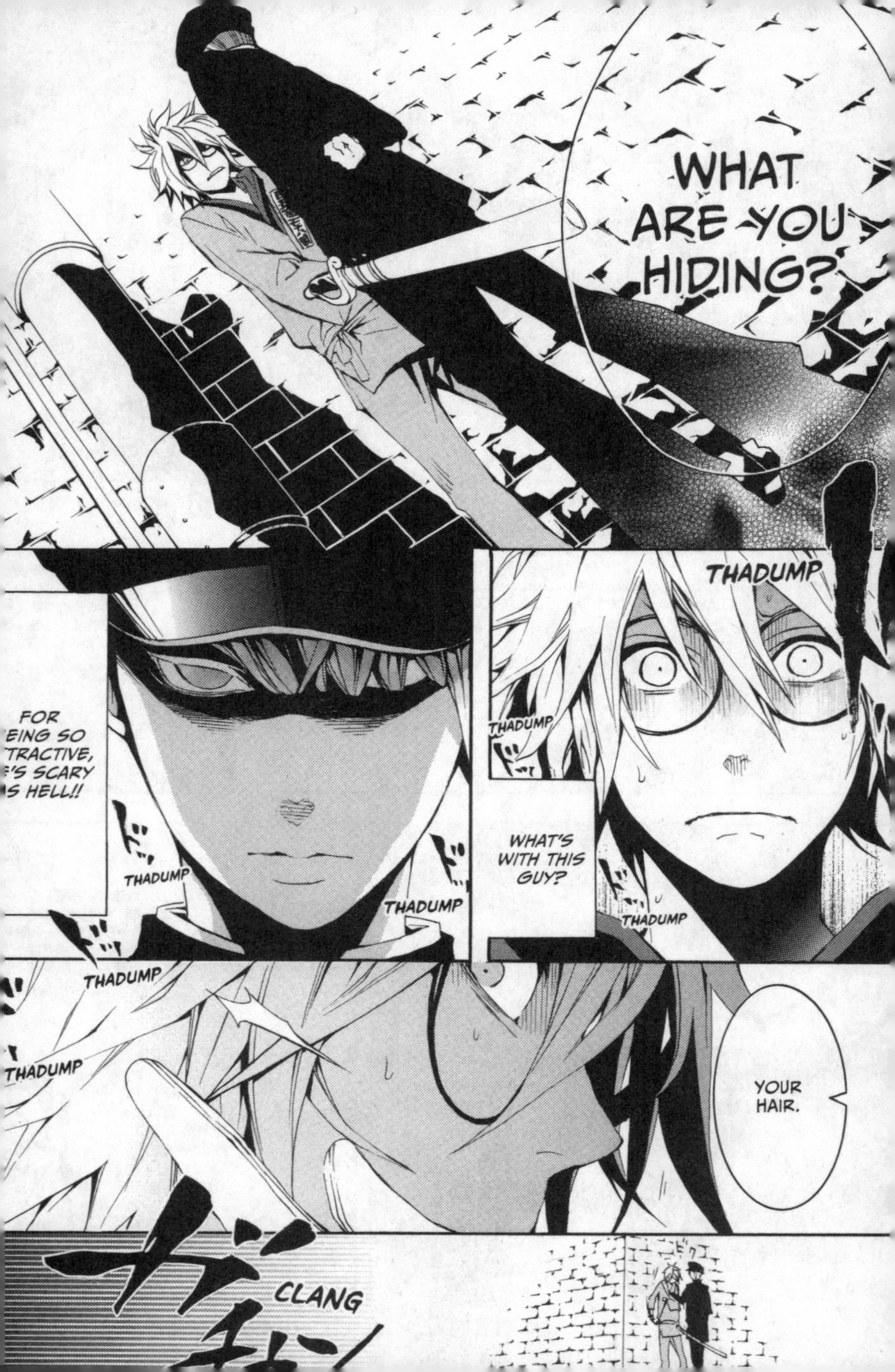
WHAT ARE YOU HIDING?
THADUMP
THADUMP
WHAT'S WITH THIS GUY?
THADUMP
FOR
EING SO
TRACTIVE,
E'S SCARY
S HELL!!
THADUMP
THADUMP
YOUR HAIR.
THADUMP
THADUMP
CLANG

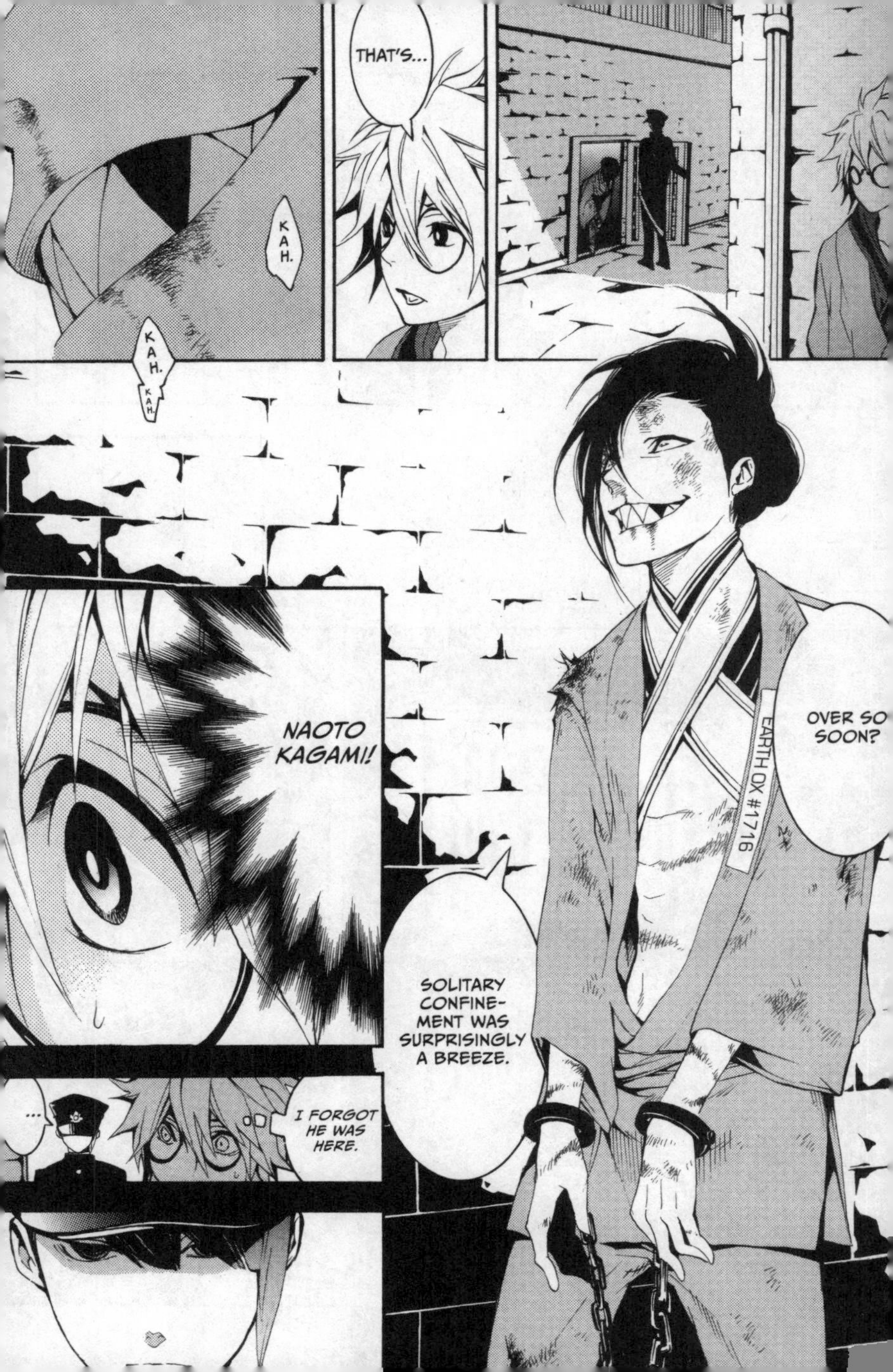

THAT'S...
KAH.
KAH.
KAH.
EARTH OX #1716
OVER SO SOON?
SOLITARY CONFINE-MENT WAS SURPRISINGLY A BREEZE.
NAOTO KAGAMI!
I FORGOT HE WAS HERE.
...

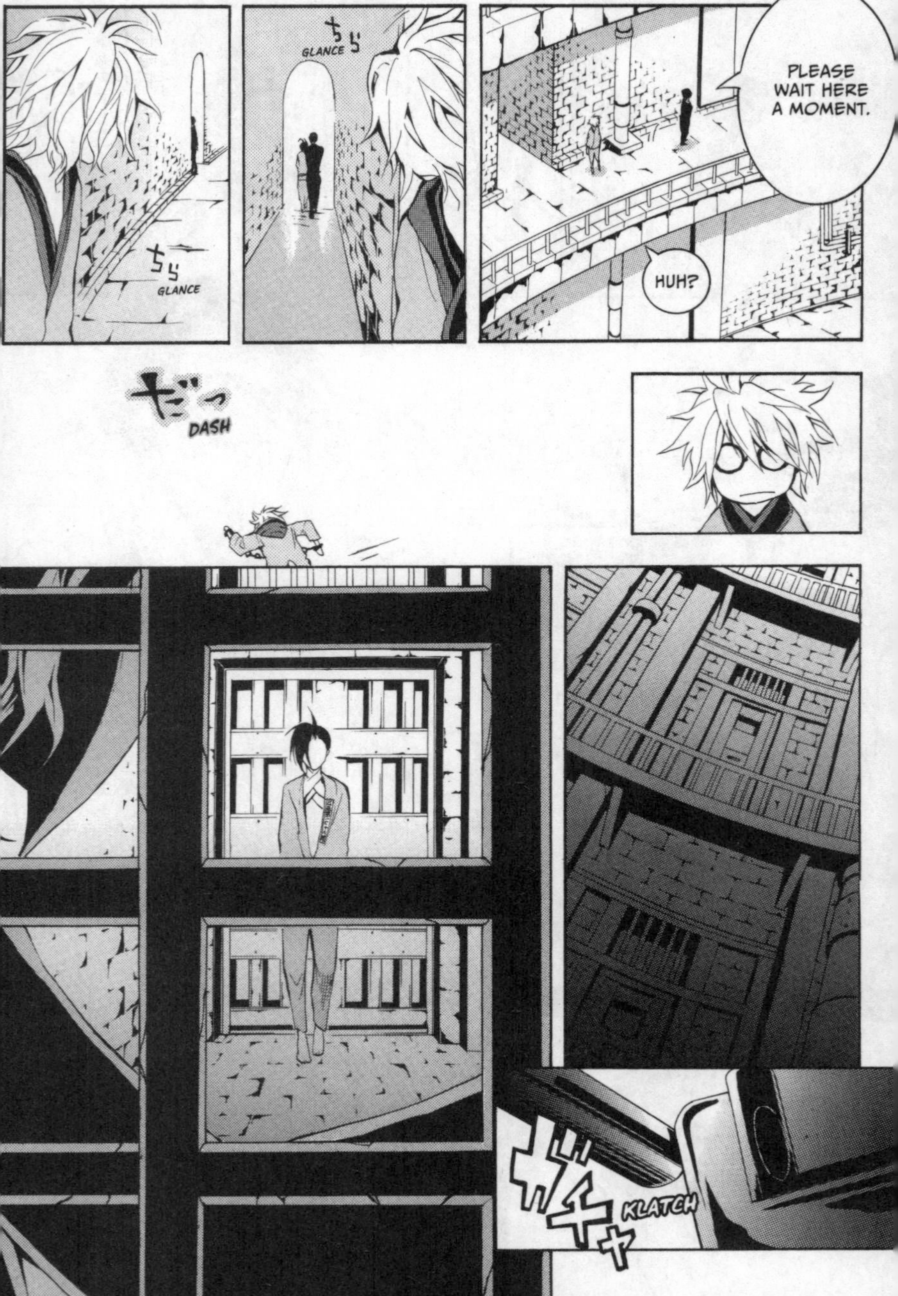
PLEASE WAIT HERE A MOMENT.
HUH?
GLANCE
GLANCE
DASH
KLATCH

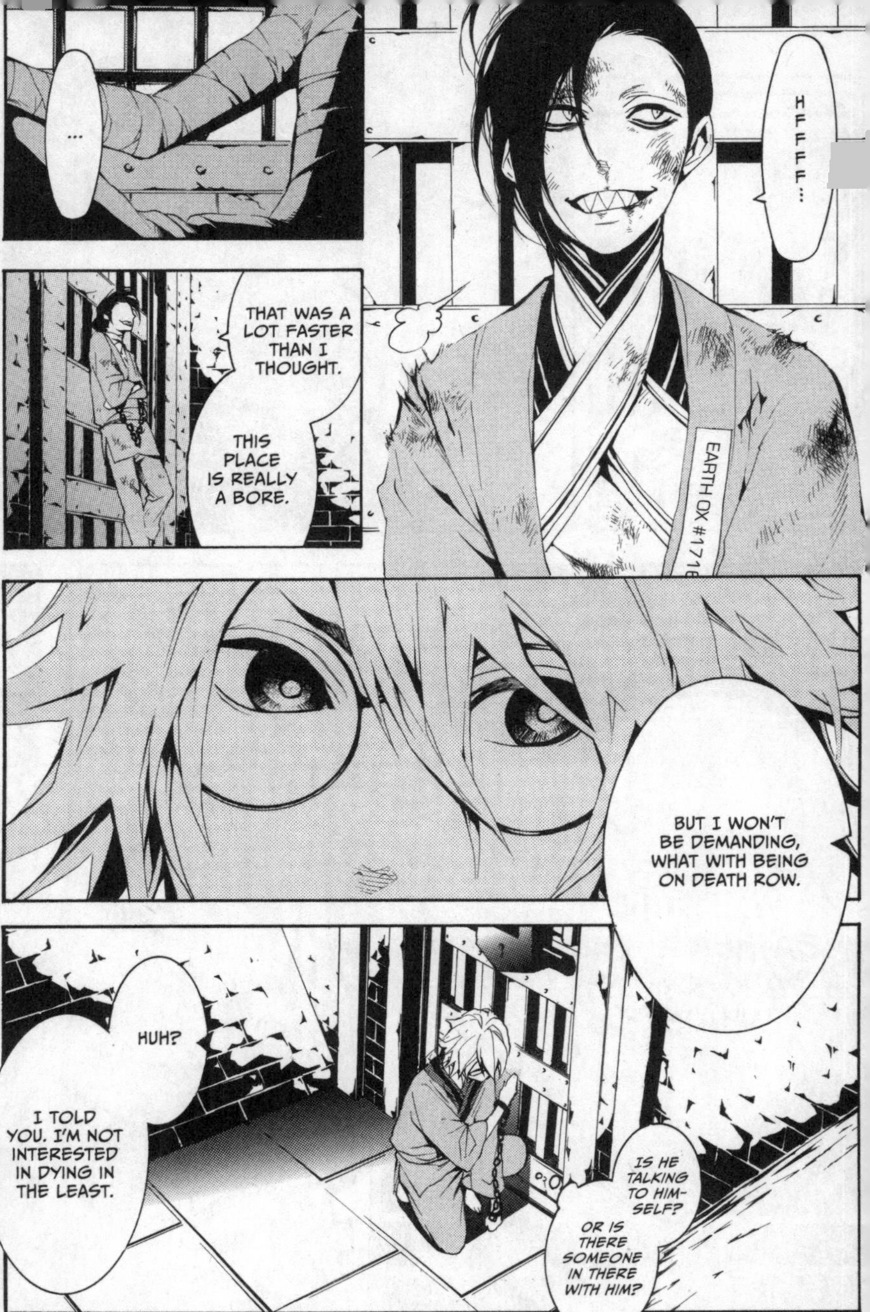
HFFF...
EARTH OX #171
...
THAT WAS A LOT FASTER THAN I THOUGHT.
THIS PLACE IS REALLY A BORE.
BUT I WON'T BE DEMANDING, WHAT WITH BEING ON DEATH ROW.
HUH?
I TOLD YOU. I'M NOT INTERESTED IN DYING IN THE LEAST.
IS HE TALKING TO HIM-SELF?
OR IS THERE SOMEONE IN THERE WITH HIM?

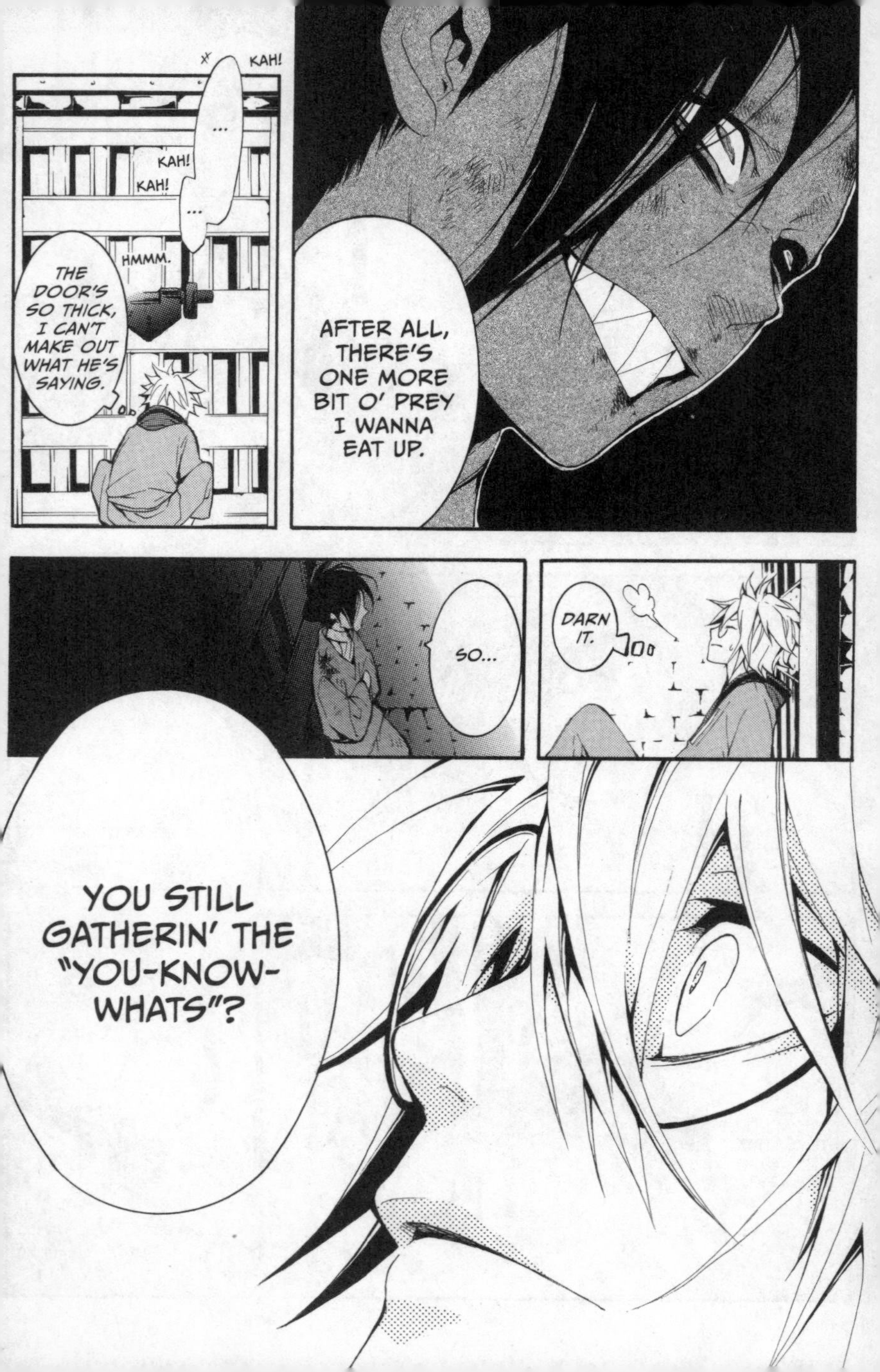
AFTER ALL, THERE'S ONE MORE BIT O' PREY I WANNA EAT UP.
KAH!
...
KAH!
KAH!
...
HMMM.
THE DOOR'S SO THICK, I CAN'T MAKE OUT WHAT HE'S SAYING.
DARN IT.
SO...
YOU STILL GATHERIN' THE "YOU-KNOW-WHATS"?

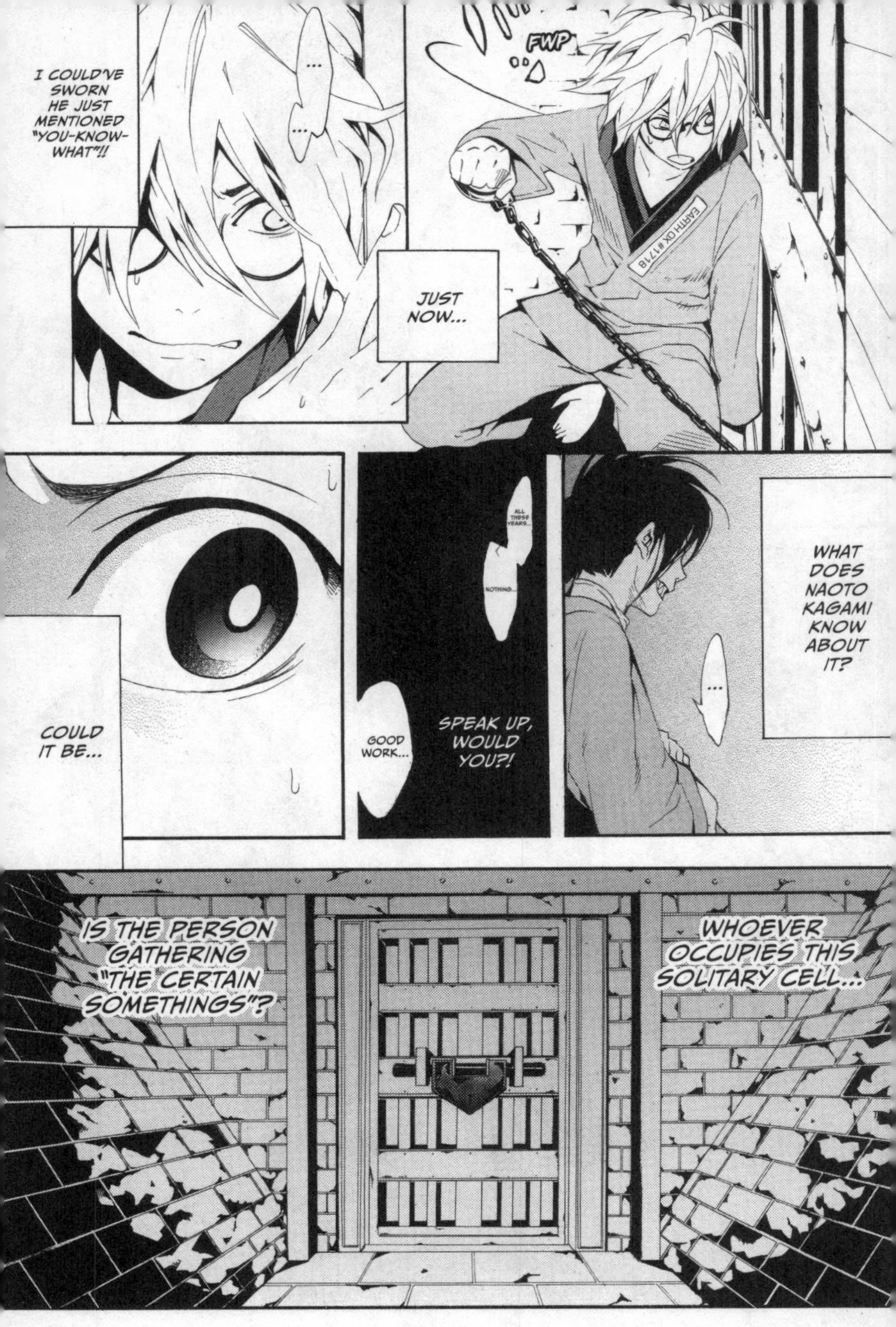
FWP
EARTH OX #1718
JUST NOW...
...
...
I COULD'VE SWORN HE JUST MENTIONED "YOU-KNOW-WHAT"!!
WHAT DOES NAOTO KAGAMI KNOW ABOUT IT?
...
ALL THESE YEARS...
NOTHING...
SPEAK UP, WOULD YOU?!
GOOD WORK...
COULD IT BE...
WHOEVER OCCUPIES THIS SOLITARY CELL...
IS THE PERSON GATHERING "THE CERTAIN SOMETHINGS"?

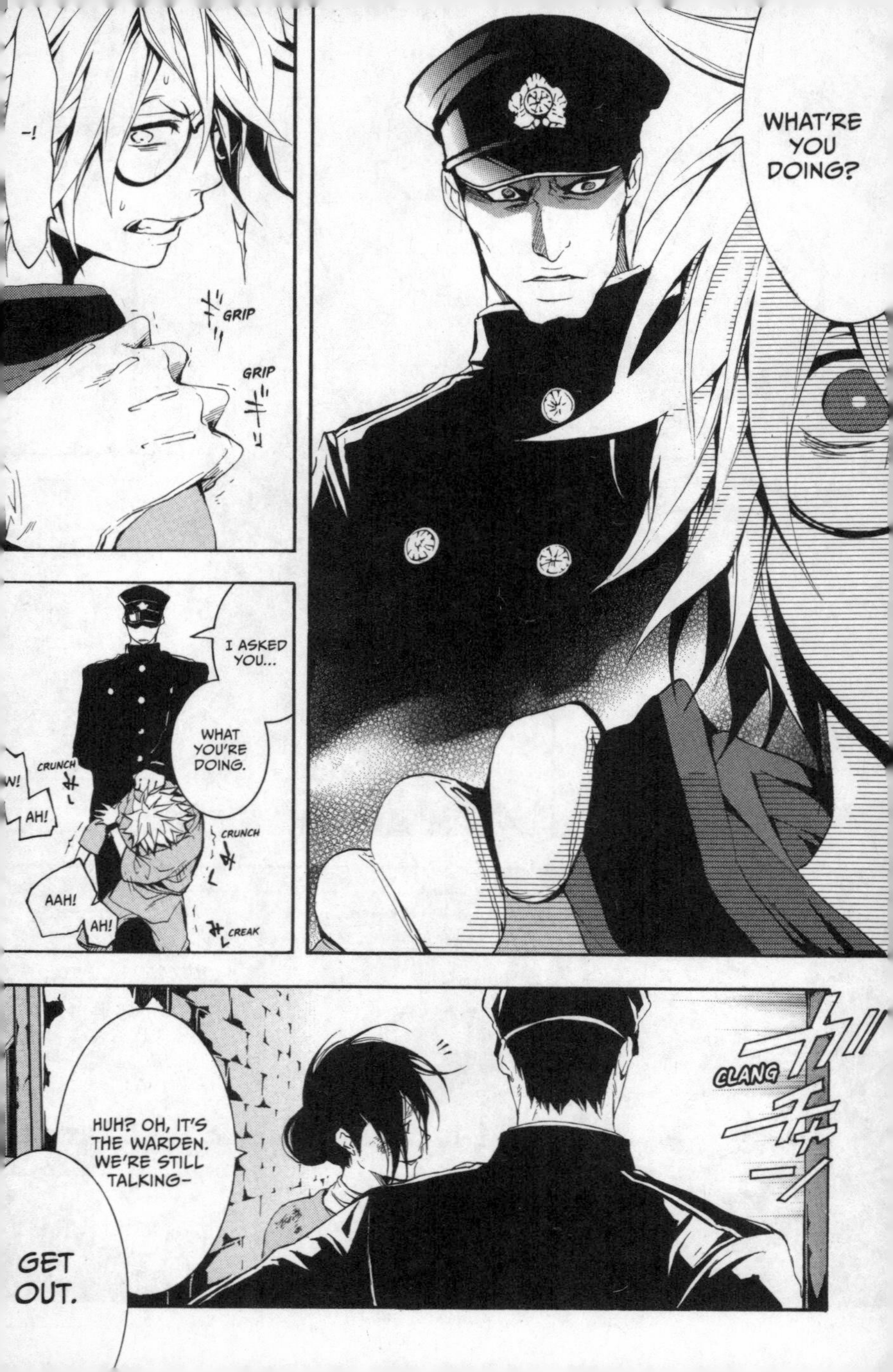
WHAT'RE YOU DOING?
–!
GRIP
GRIP
I ASKED YOU...
WHAT YOU'RE DOING.
CRUNCH
W!
AH!
CRUNCH
AAH!
AH!
CREAK
CLANG
HUH? OH, IT'S THE WARDEN. WE'RE STILL TALKING–
GET OUT.

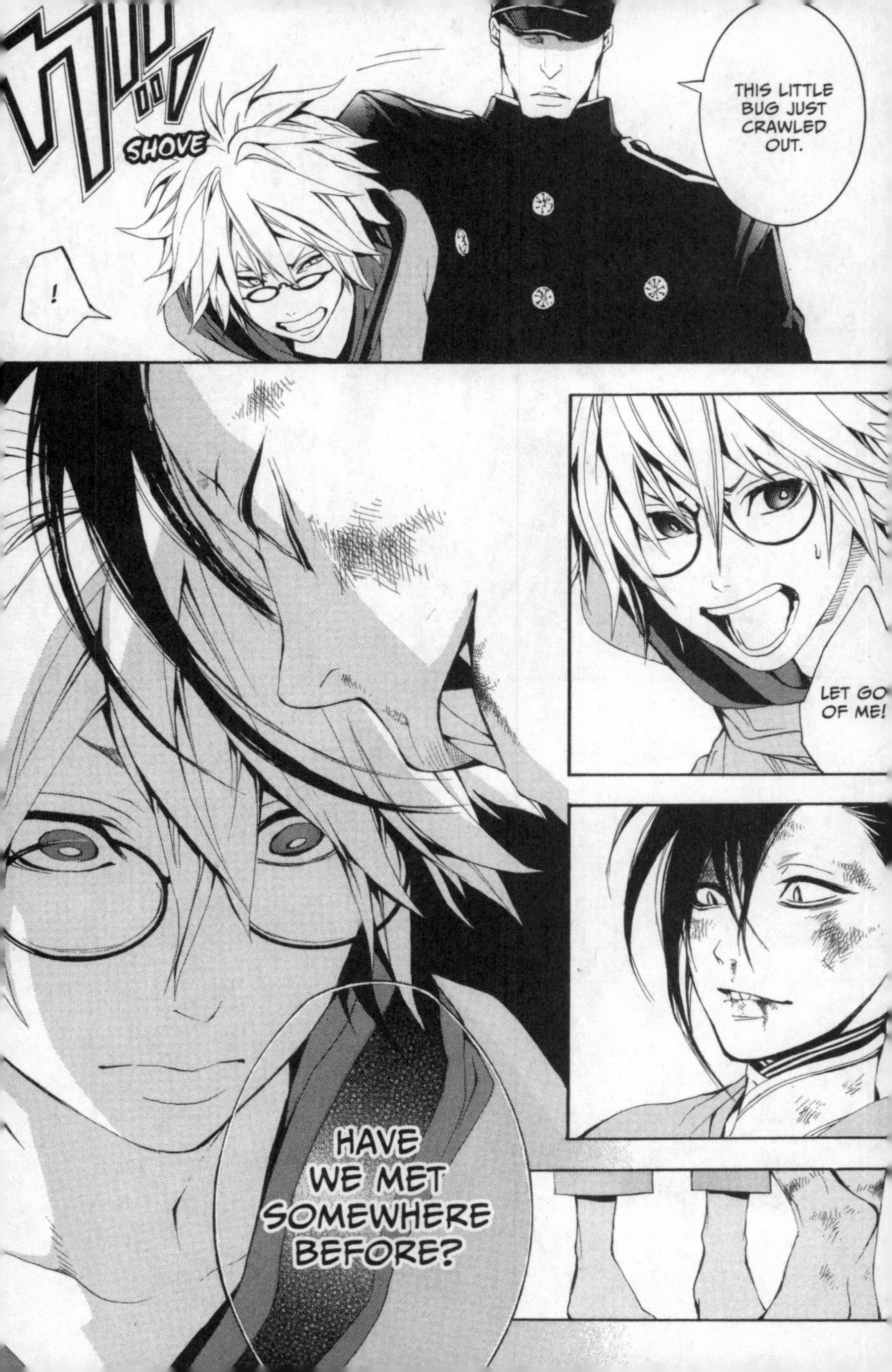
THIS LITTLE BUG JUST CRAWLED OUT.
SHOVE
!
LET GO OF ME!
HAVE WE MET SOMEWHERE BEFORE?

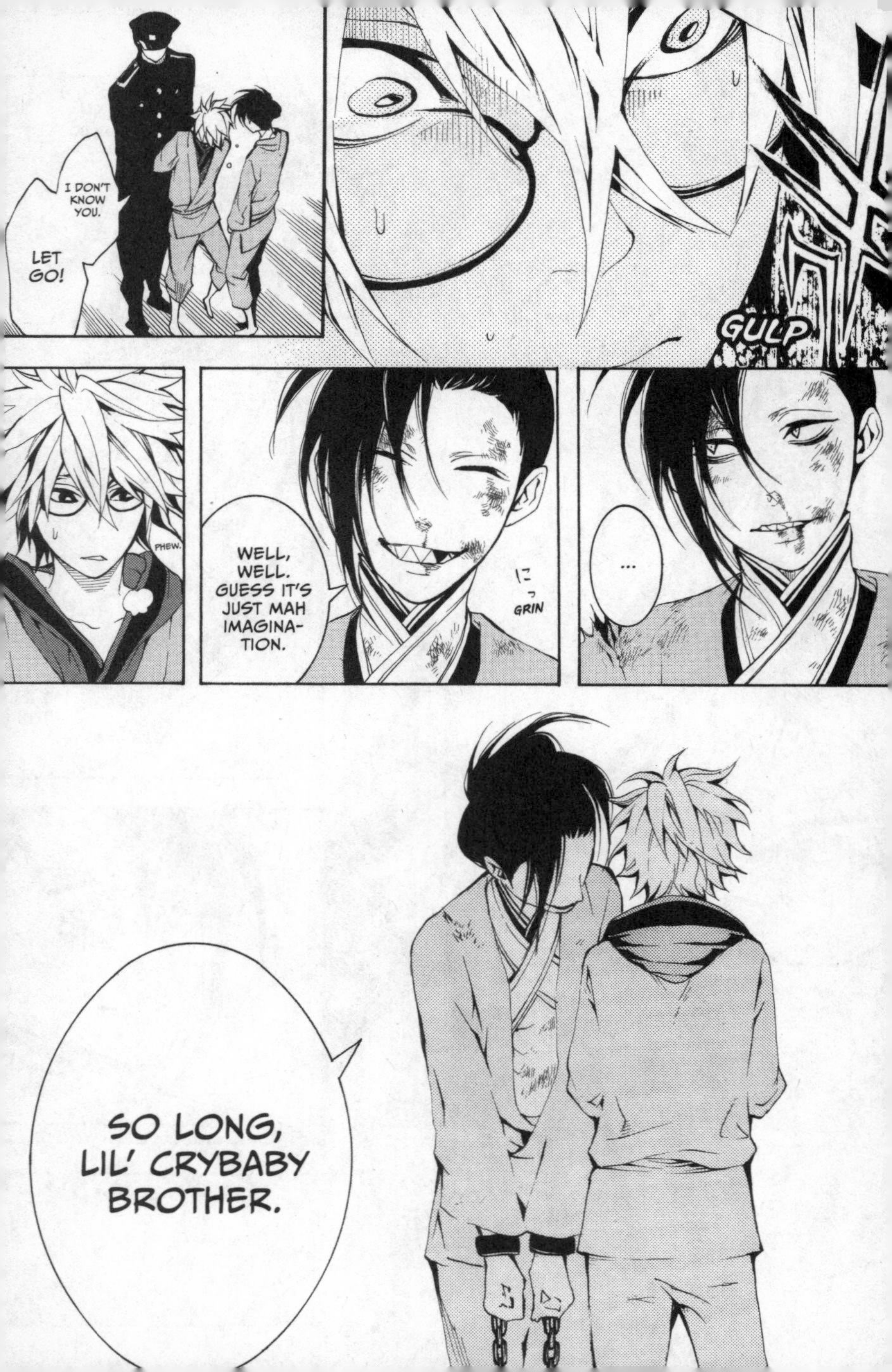
GULP
I DON'T KNOW YOU.
LET GO!
...
WELL, WELL. GUESS IT'S JUST MAH IMAGINA-TION.
にっ
GRIN
PHEW.
SO LONG, LIL' CRYBABY BROTHER.

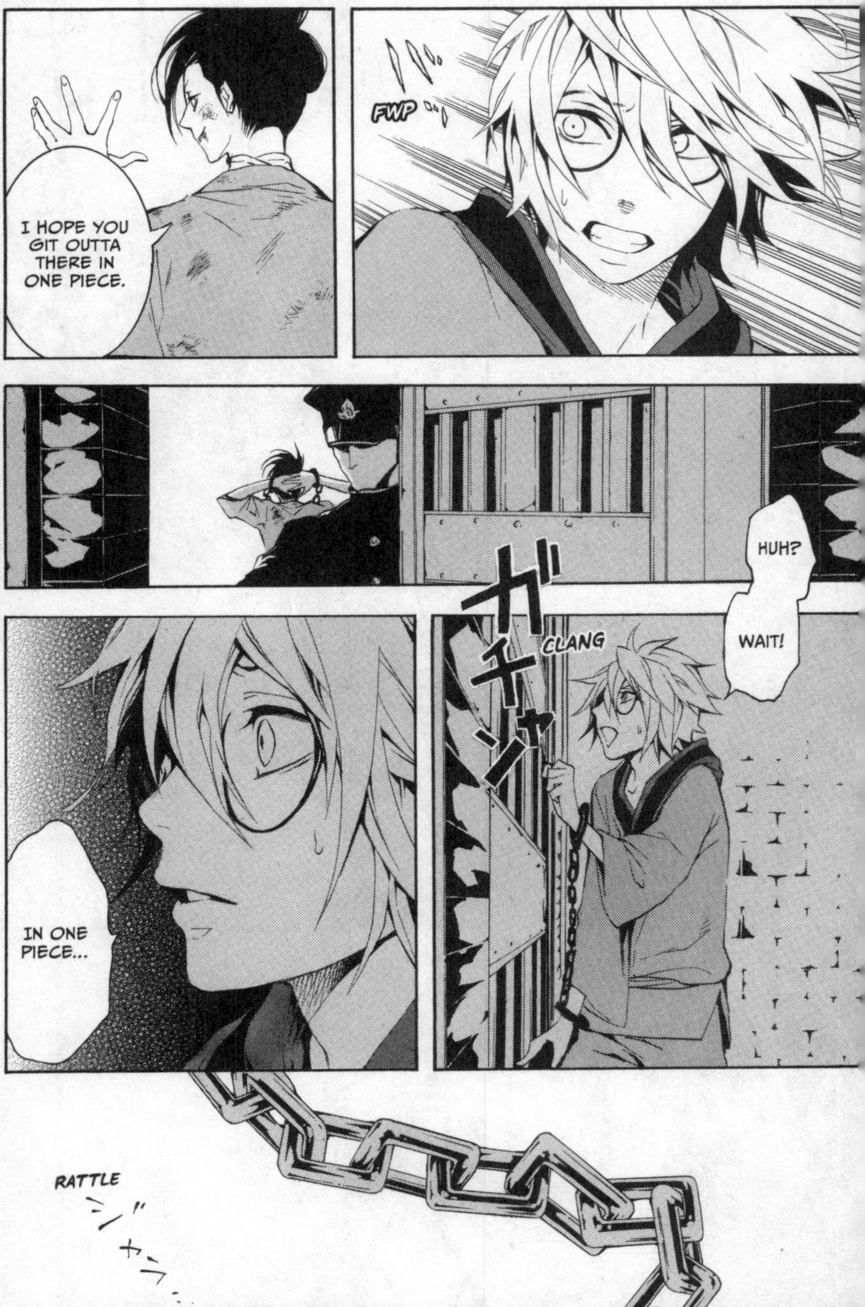
FWP
I HOPE YOU GIT OUTTA THERE IN ONE PIECE.
HUH?
CLANG
WAIT!
IN ONE PIECE...
RATTLE

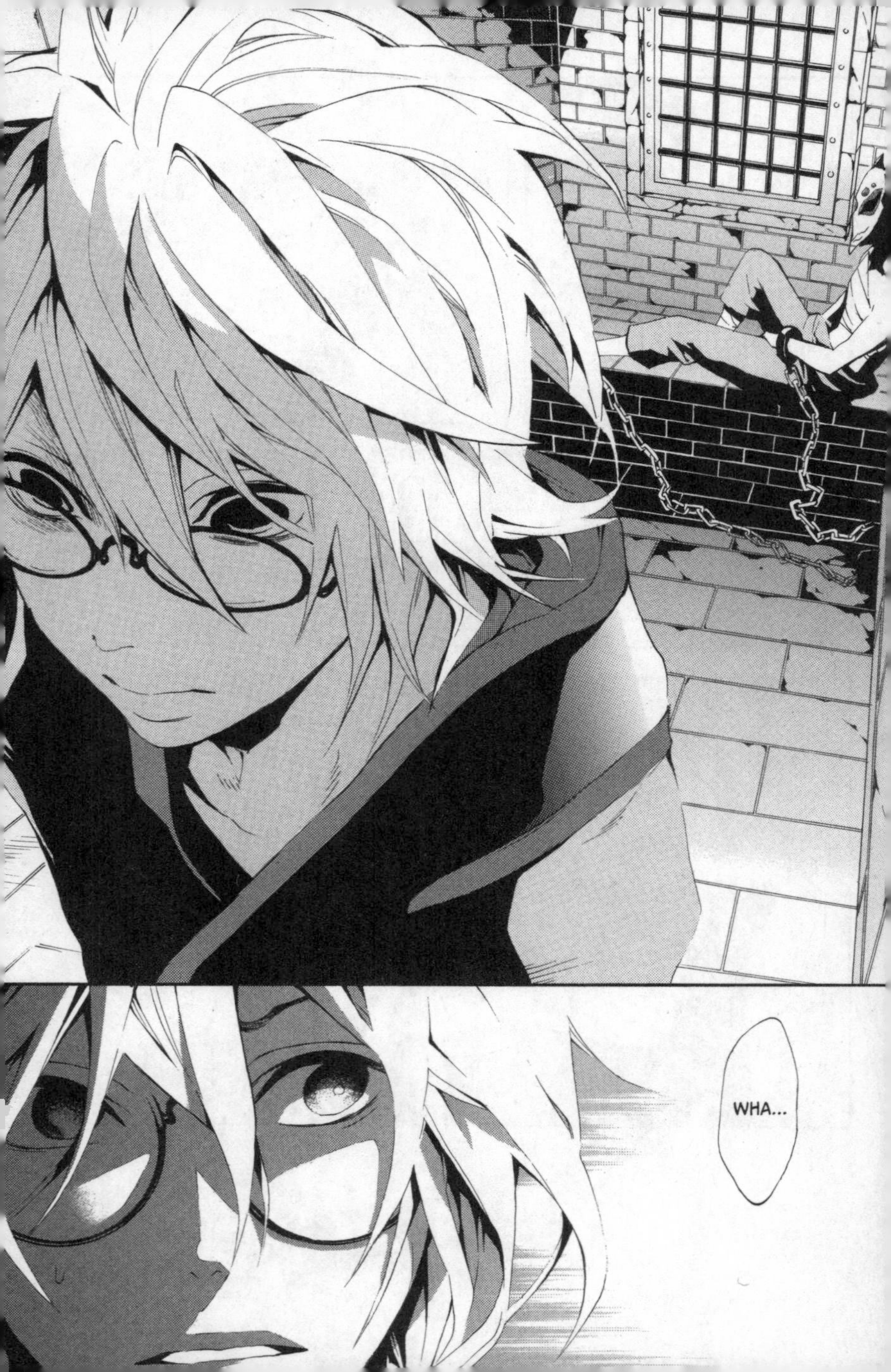
WHA...

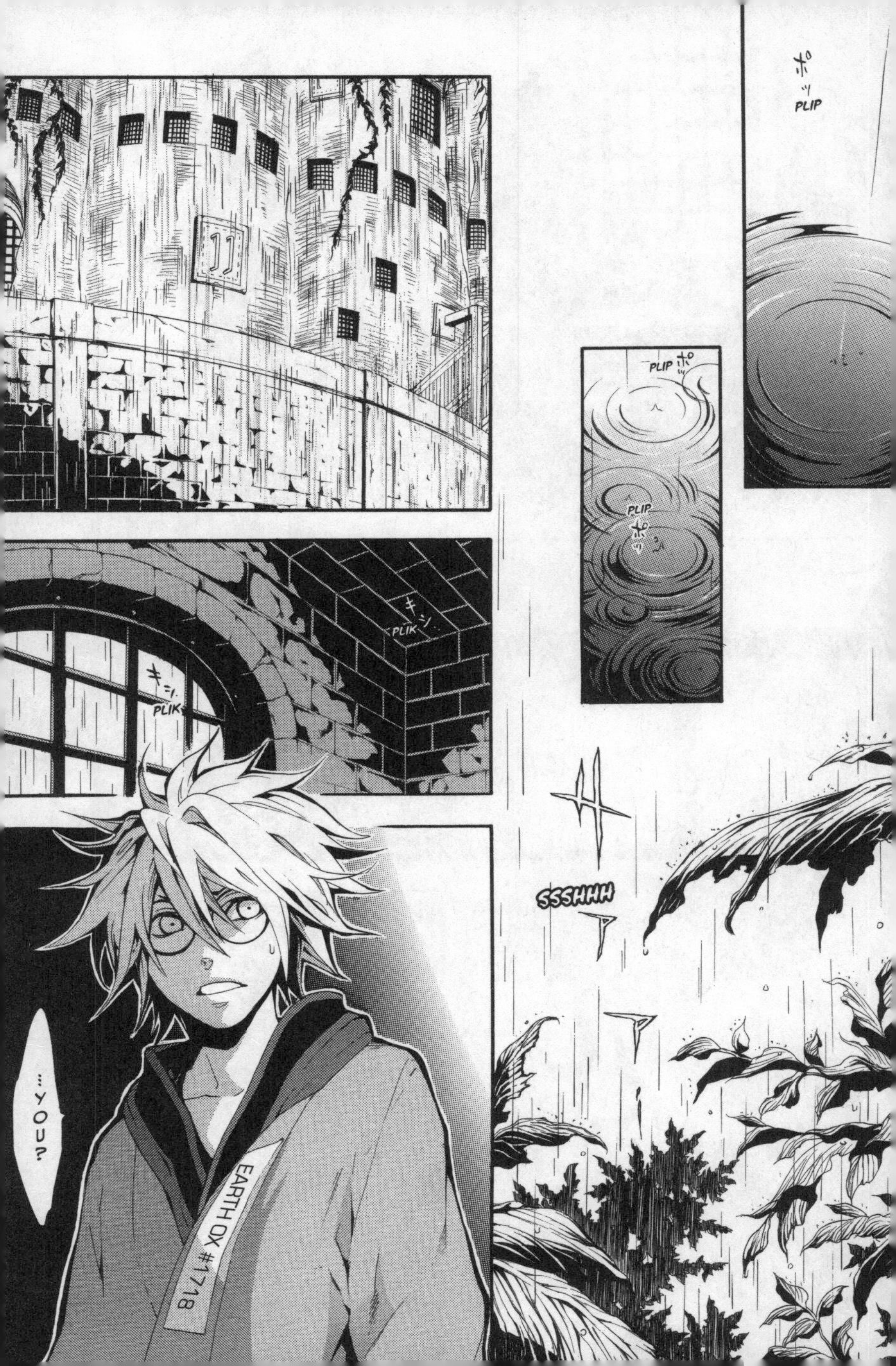
PLIP
PLIP
PLIP
PLIK
PLIK
SSSHHH
...YOU?
EARTH OX #1718

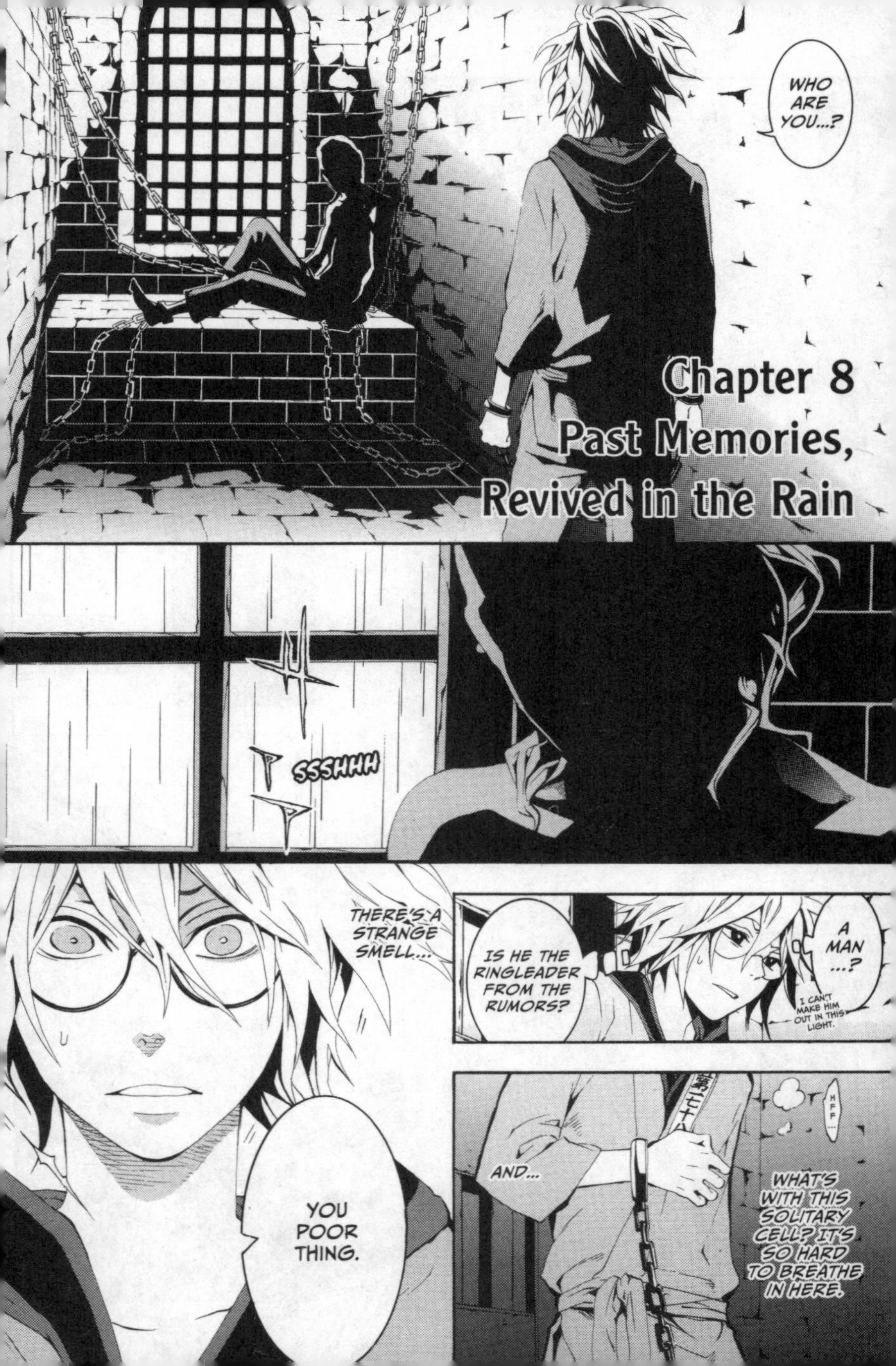
WHO ARE YOU...?
Chapter 8
Past Memories, Revived in the Rain
SSSHHH
A MAN ...?
I CAN'T MAKE HIM OUT IN THIS LIGHT.
IS HE THE RINGLEADER FROM THE RUMORS?
HFF...
WHAT'S WITH THIS SOLITARY CELL? IT'S SO HARD TO BREATHE IN HERE.
AND...
THERE'S A STRANGE SMELL...
YOU POOR THING.

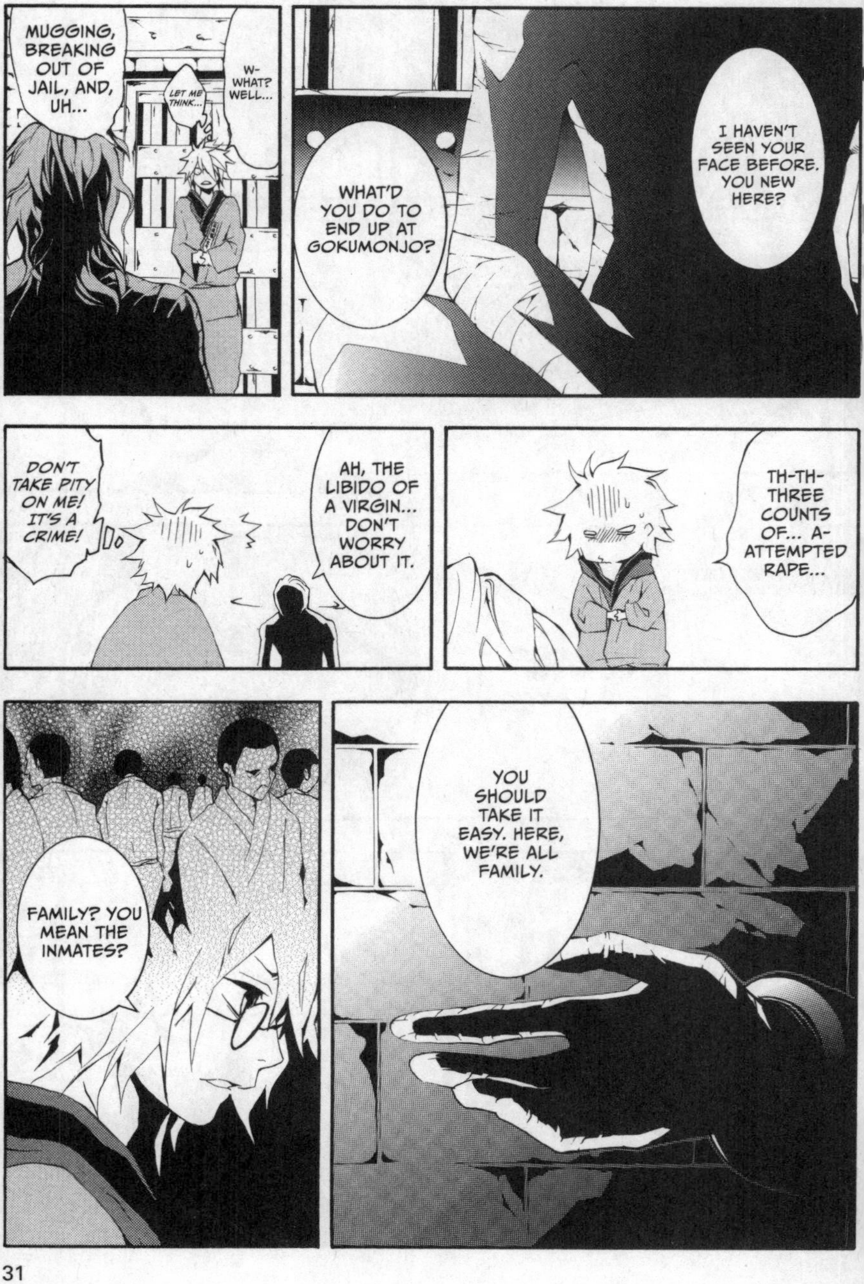
I HAVEN'T SEEN YOUR FACE BEFORE. YOU NEW HERE?
WHAT'D YOU DO TO END UP AT GOKUMONJO?
W-WHAT? WELL...
LET ME THINK...
MUGGING, BREAKING OUT OF JAIL, AND, UH...
TH-TH-THREE COUNTS OF... A-ATTEMPTED RAPE...
AH, THE LIBIDO OF A VIRGIN... DON'T WORRY ABOUT IT.
DON'T TAKE PITY ON ME! IT'S A CRIME!
YOU SHOULD TAKE IT EASY. HERE, WE'RE ALL FAMILY.
FAMILY? YOU MEAN THE INMATES?

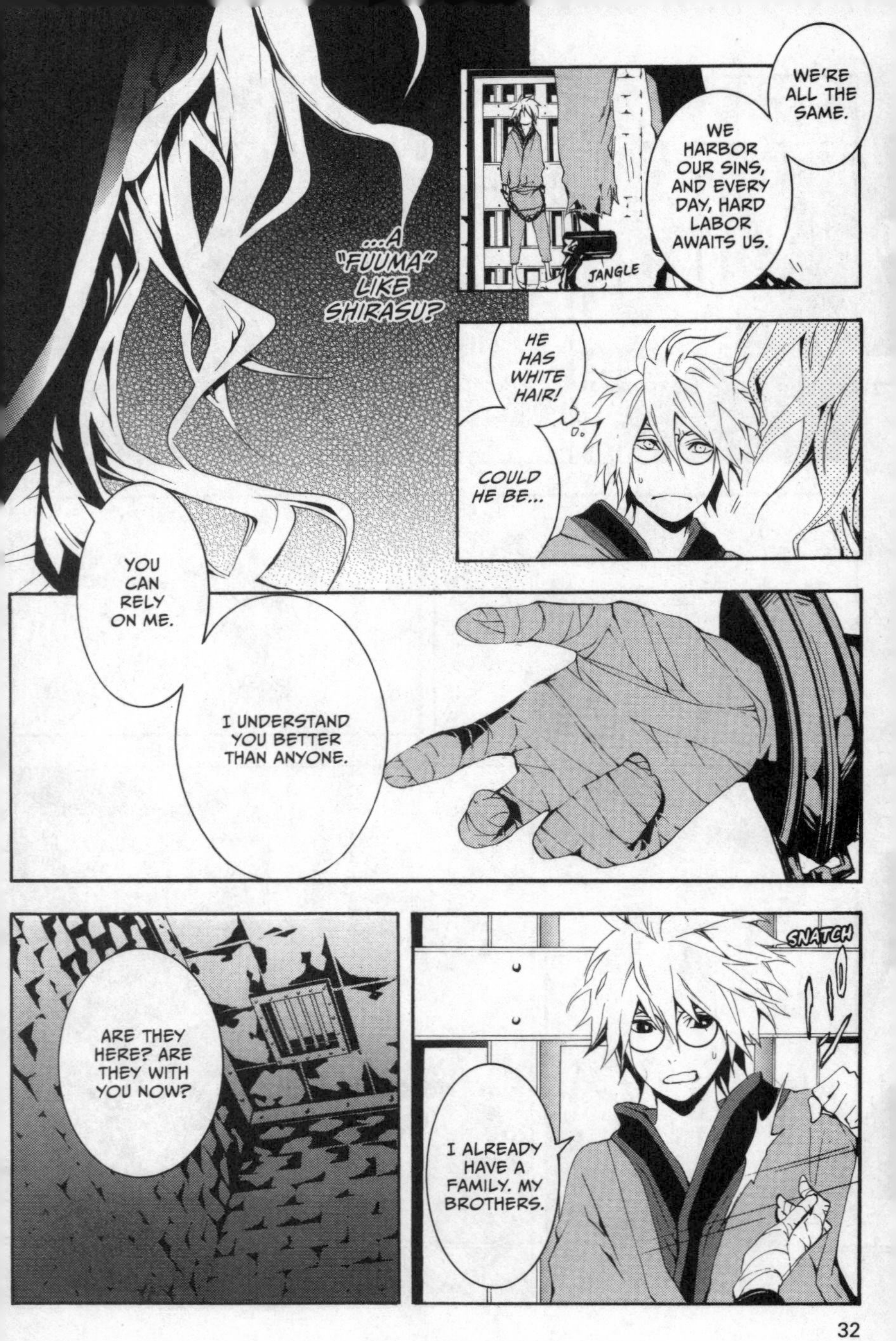
WE'RE ALL THE SAME.
WE HARBOR OUR SINS, AND EVERY DAY, HARD LABOR AWAITS US.
JANGLE
HE HAS WHITE HAIR!
COULD HE BE...
...A "FUUMA" LIKE SHIRASU?
YOU CAN RELY ON ME.
I UNDERSTAND YOU BETTER THAN ANYONE.
SNATCH
I ALREADY HAVE A FAMILY. MY BROTHERS.
ARE THEY HERE? ARE THEY WITH YOU NOW?

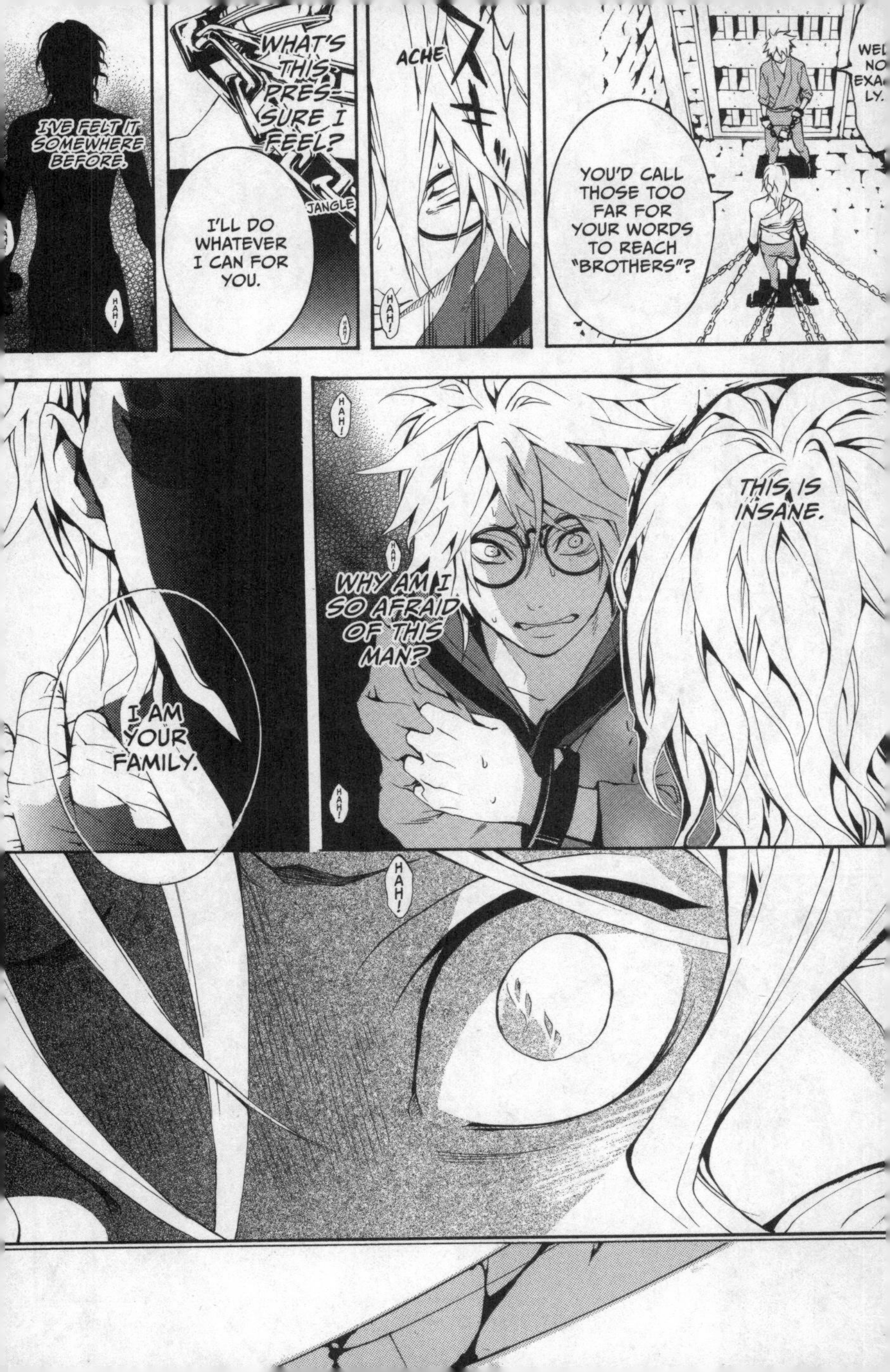
WEL
NO
EXA
LY.
YOU'D CALL THOSE TOO FAR FOR YOUR WORDS TO REACH "BROTHERS"?
ACHE
HAH!
HAH!
WHAT'S THIS PRES-SURE I FEEL?
JANGLE
I'LL DO WHATEVER I CAN FOR YOU.
I'VE FELT IT SOMEWHERE BEFORE.
HAH!
THIS IS INSANE.
HAH!
HAH!
WHY AM I SO AFRAID OF THIS MAN?
HAH!
I AM YOUR FAMILY.
HAH!

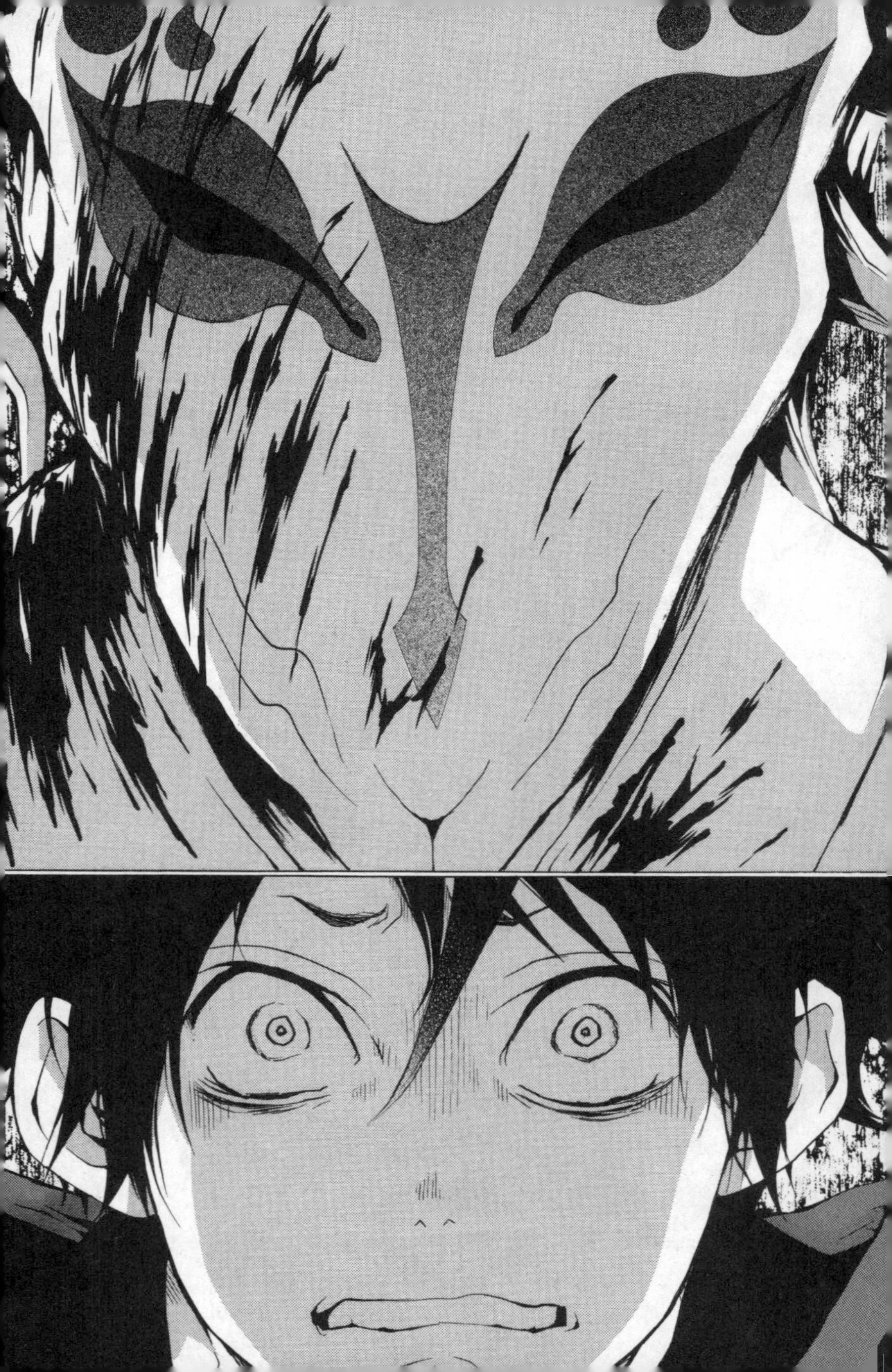

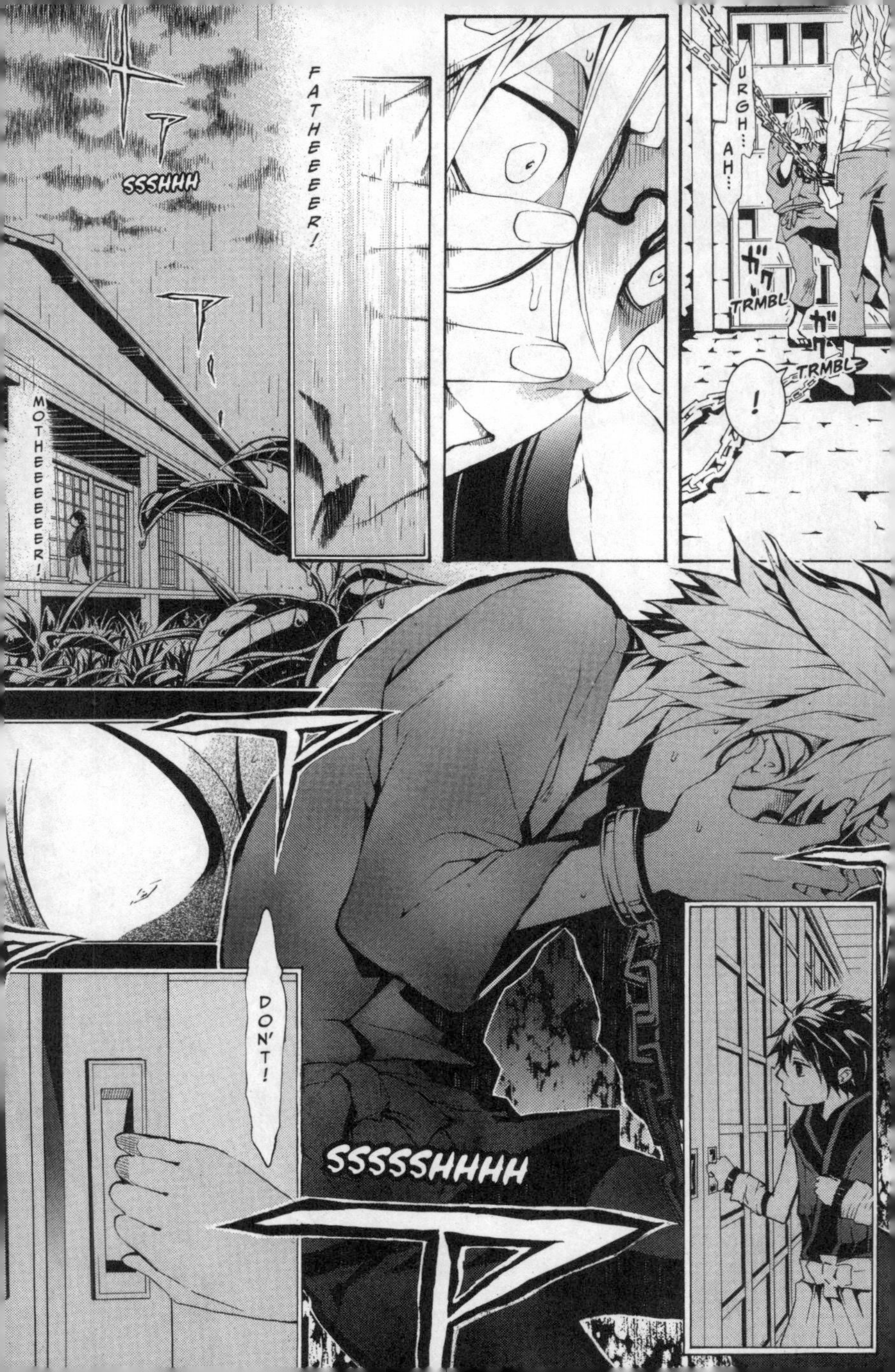
URGH... AH...
TRMBL
TRMBL
!
FATHEEEEER!
SSSHHH
MOTHEEEEEEER!
SSSSSHHHH
DON'T!

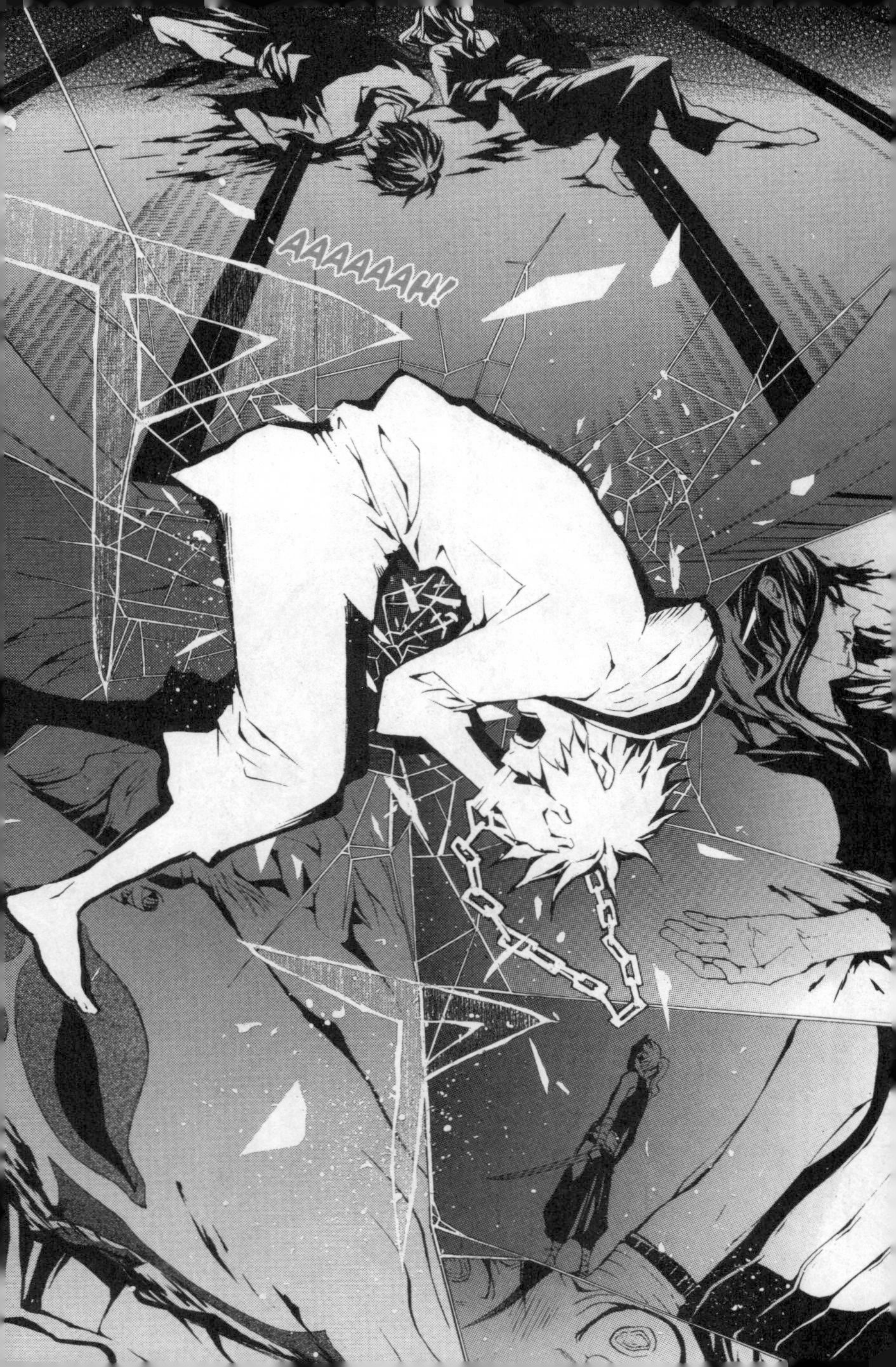
AAAAAAAH!

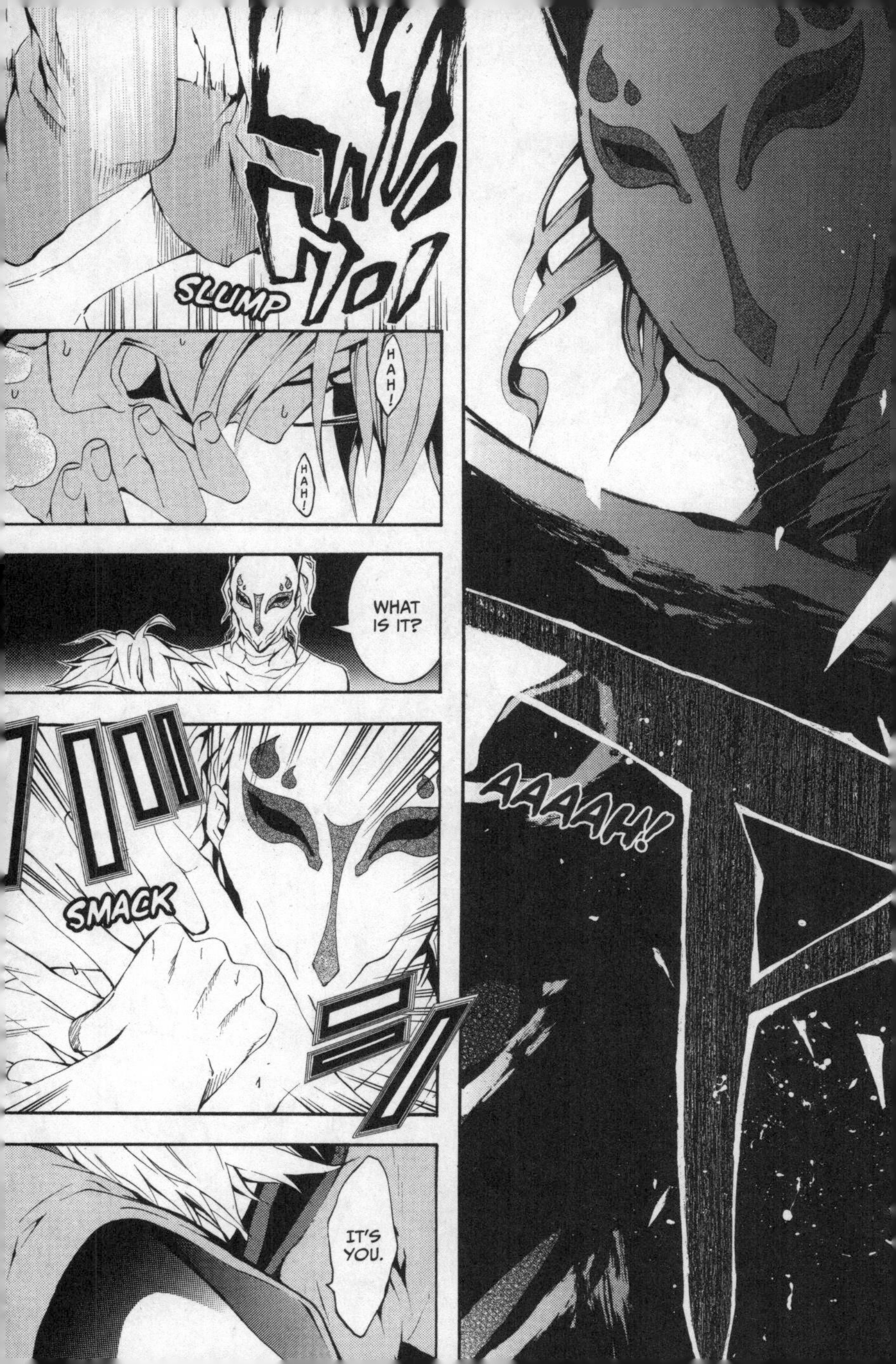
AAAAAH!
SLUMP
HAH!
HAH!
WHAT IS IT?
SMACK
IT'S YOU.

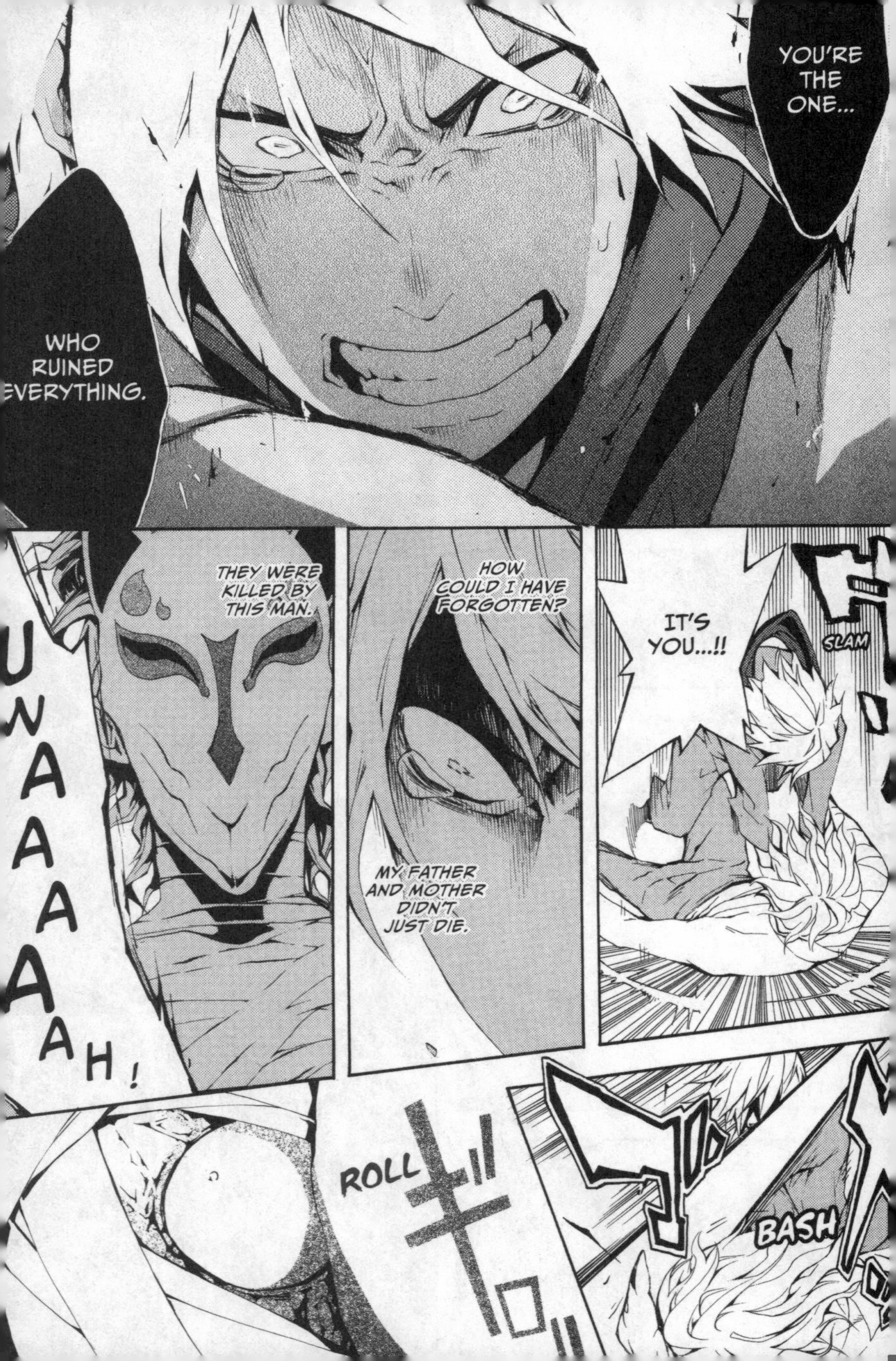
YOU'RE THE ONE...
WHO RUINED EVERYTHING.
IT'S YOU...!!
SLAM
HOW COULD I HAVE FORGOTTEN?
MY FATHER AND MOTHER DIDN'T JUST DIE.
THEY WERE KILLED BY THIS MAN.
UWAAAAAAH!
BASH
ROLL

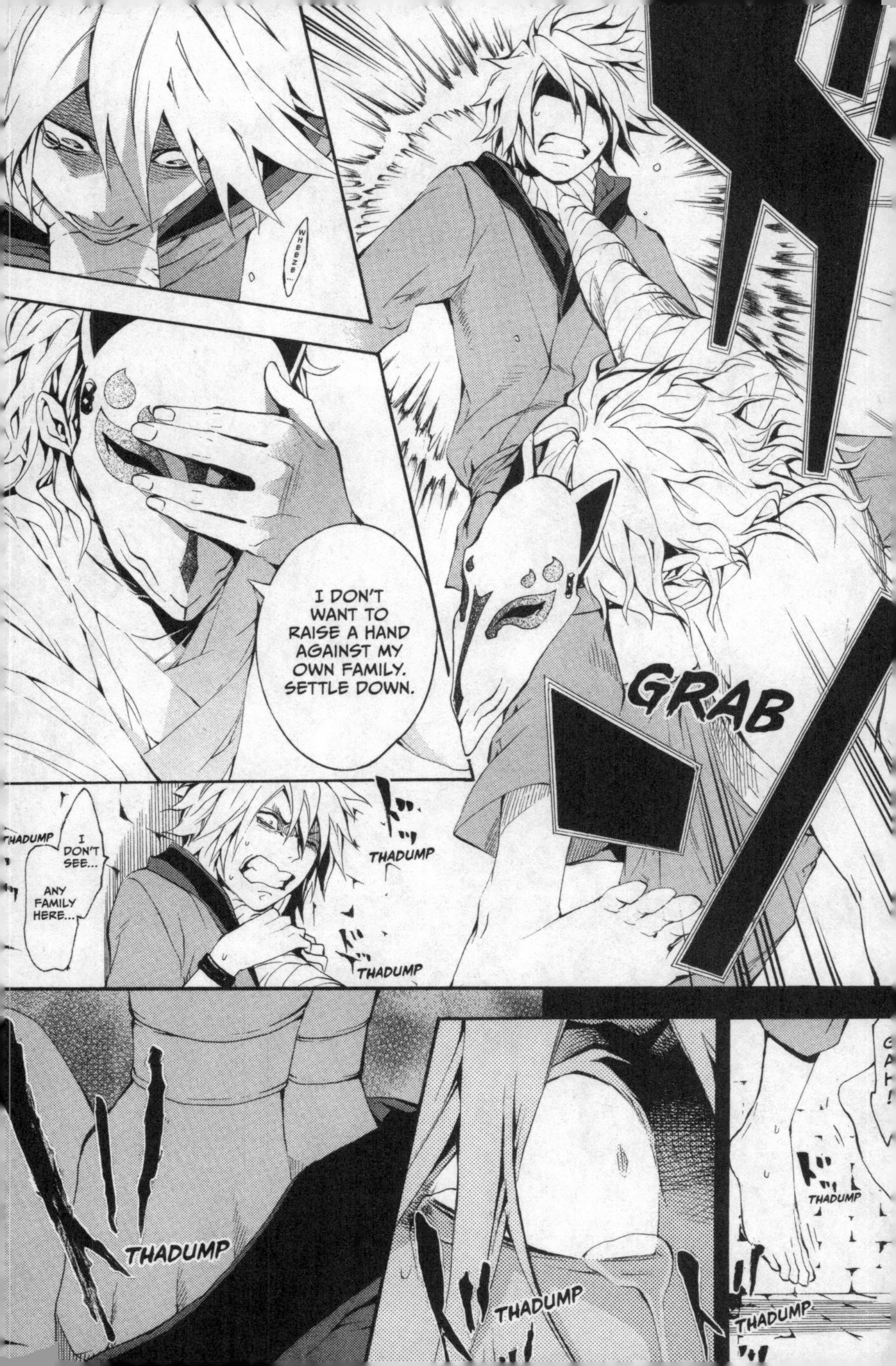
GRAB
WHEEZE...
I DON'T WANT TO RAISE A HAND AGAINST MY OWN FAMILY. SETTLE DOWN.
THADUMP
THADUMP
I DON'T SEE...
ANY FAMILY HERE...
THADUMP
GAH!
THADUMP
THADUMP
THADUMP
THADUMP

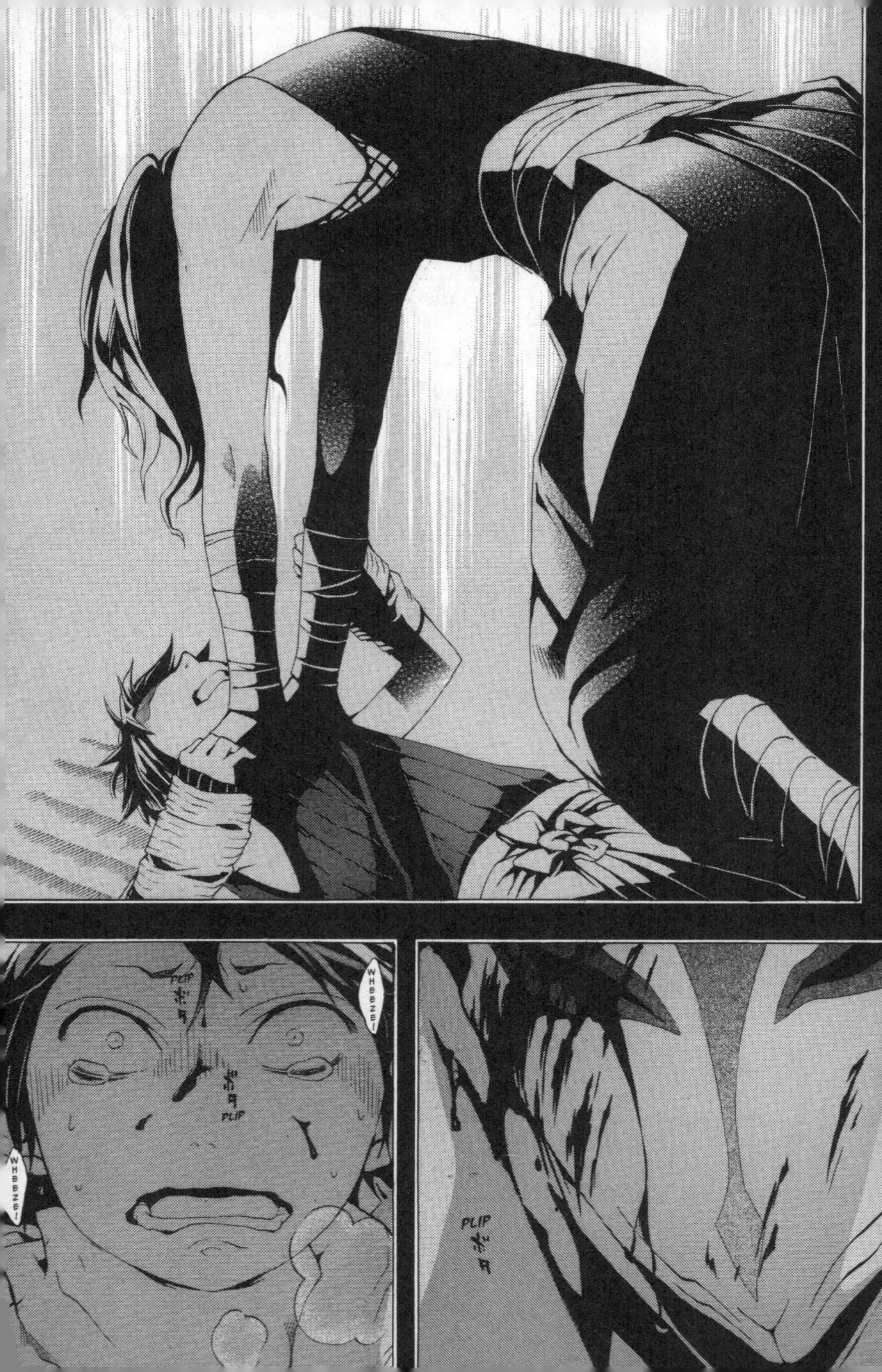
PLIP
WHEEZE!
PLIP
PLIP
WHEEZE!

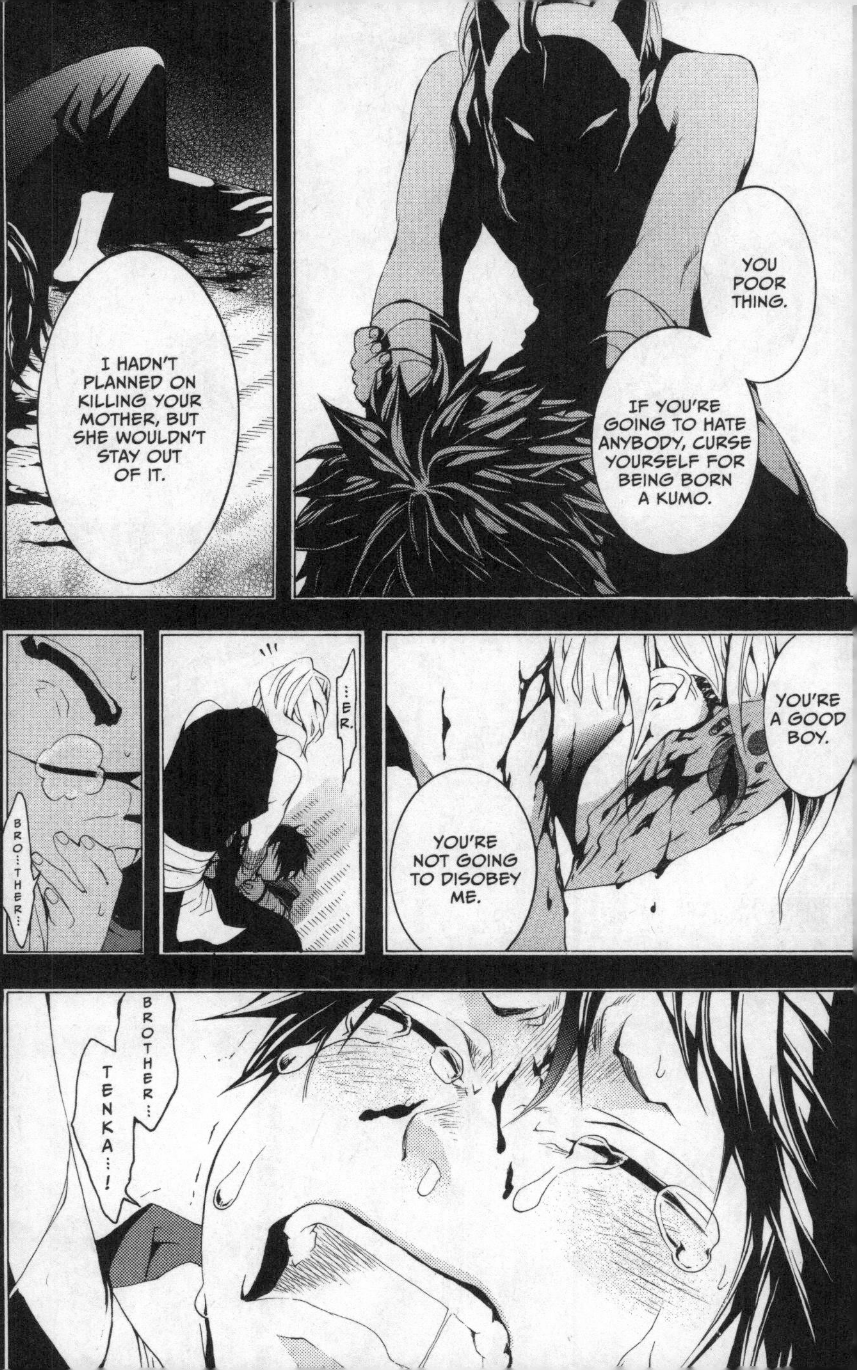
YOU POOR THING.
IF YOU'RE GOING TO HATE ANYBODY, CURSE YOURSELF FOR BEING BORN A KUMO.
I HADN'T PLANNED ON KILLING YOUR MOTHER, BUT SHE WOULDN'T STAY OUT OF IT.
YOU'RE A GOOD BOY.
YOU'RE NOT GOING TO DISOBEY ME.
...ER.
BRO...THER...
BROTHER...
TENKA...!

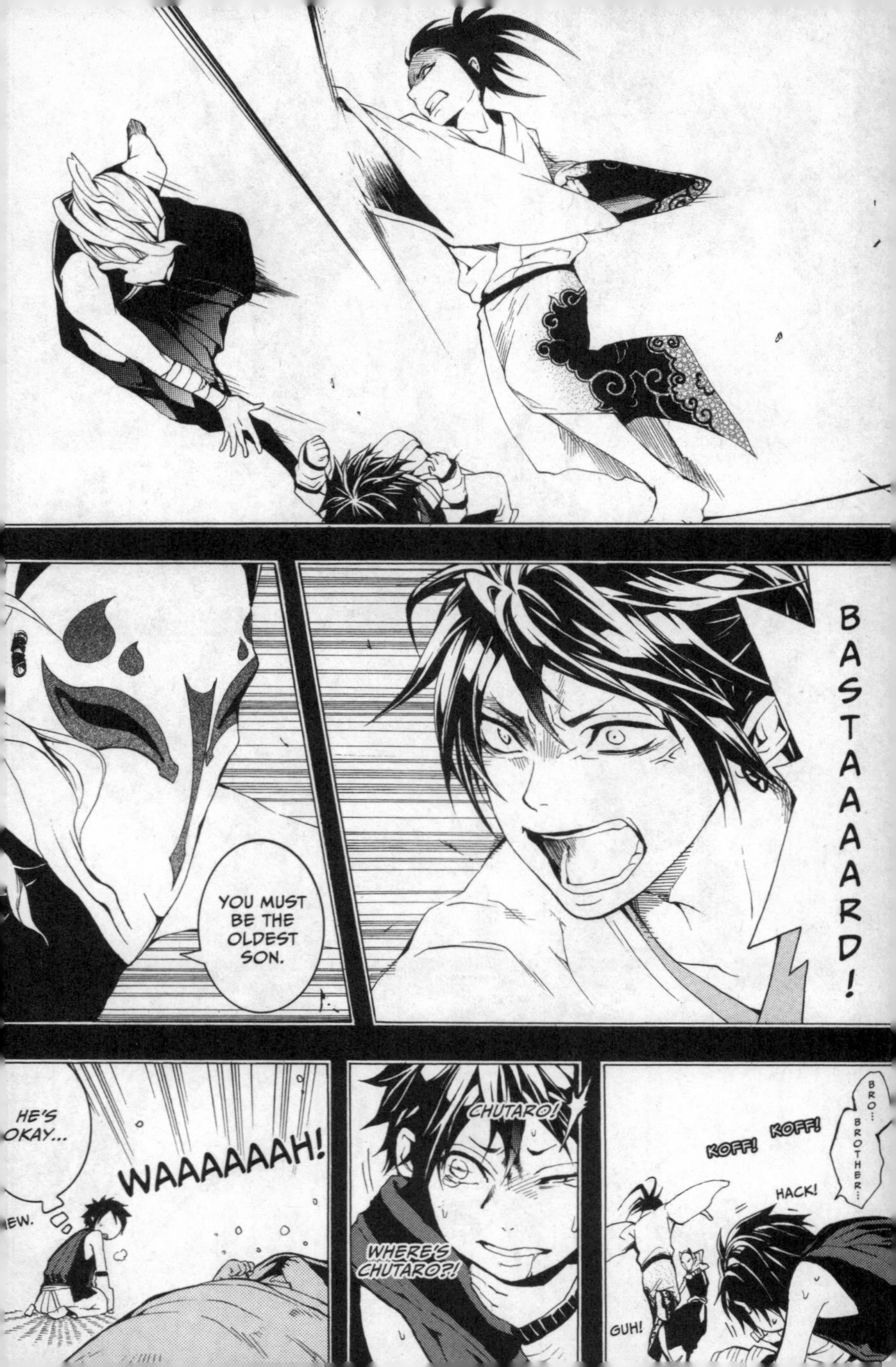
BASTAAAAAARD!
YOU MUST BE THE OLDEST SON.
BRO... BROTHER...
KOFF! KOFF!
HACK!
GUH!
CHUTARO!
WHERE'S CHUTARO?!
HE'S OKAY...
WAAAAAAH!

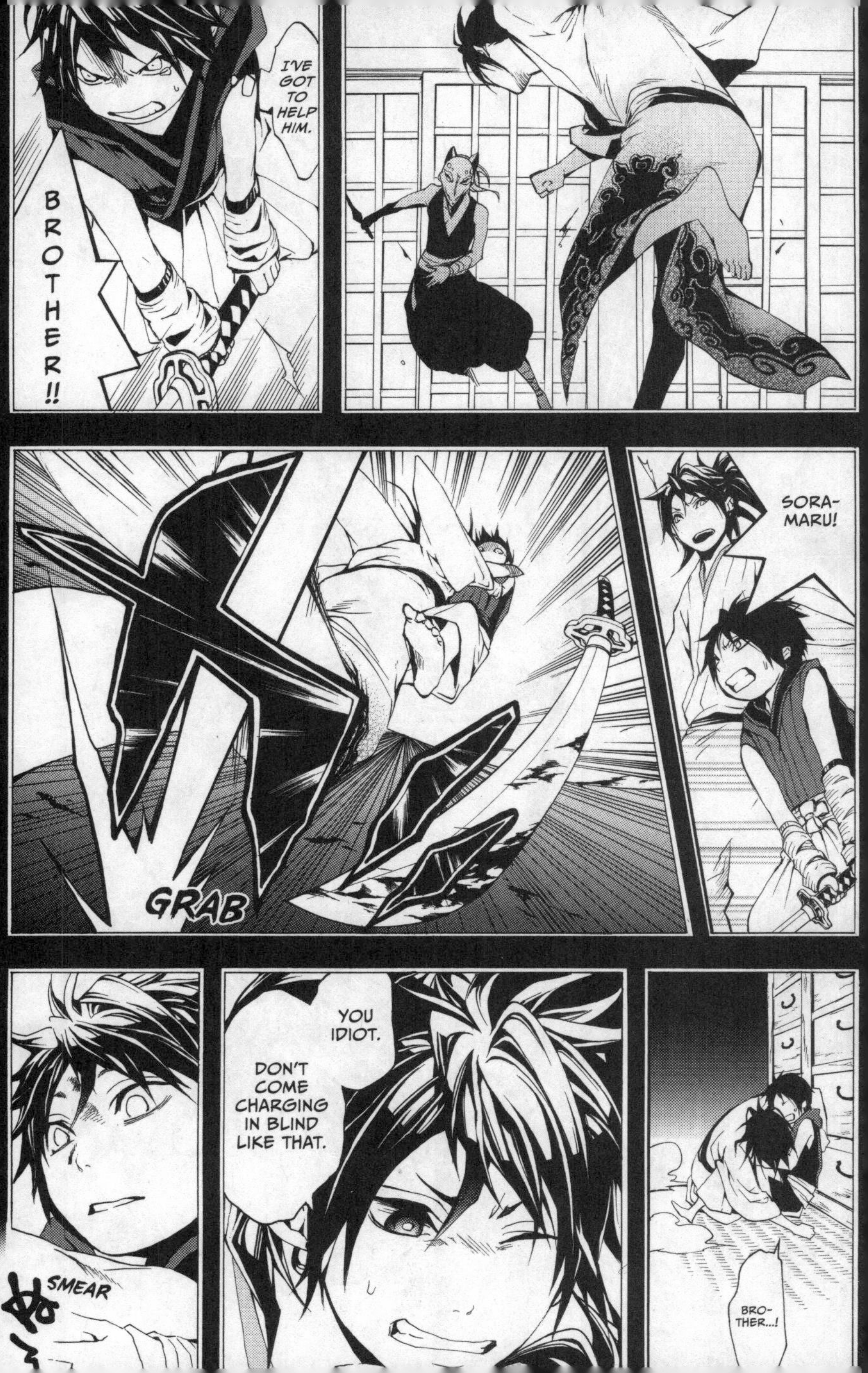
I'VE GOT TO HELP HIM.
BROTHER!!
SORA-MARU!
GRAB
BRO-THER...!
YOU IDIOT.
DON'T COME CHARGING IN BLIND LIKE THAT.
SMEAR

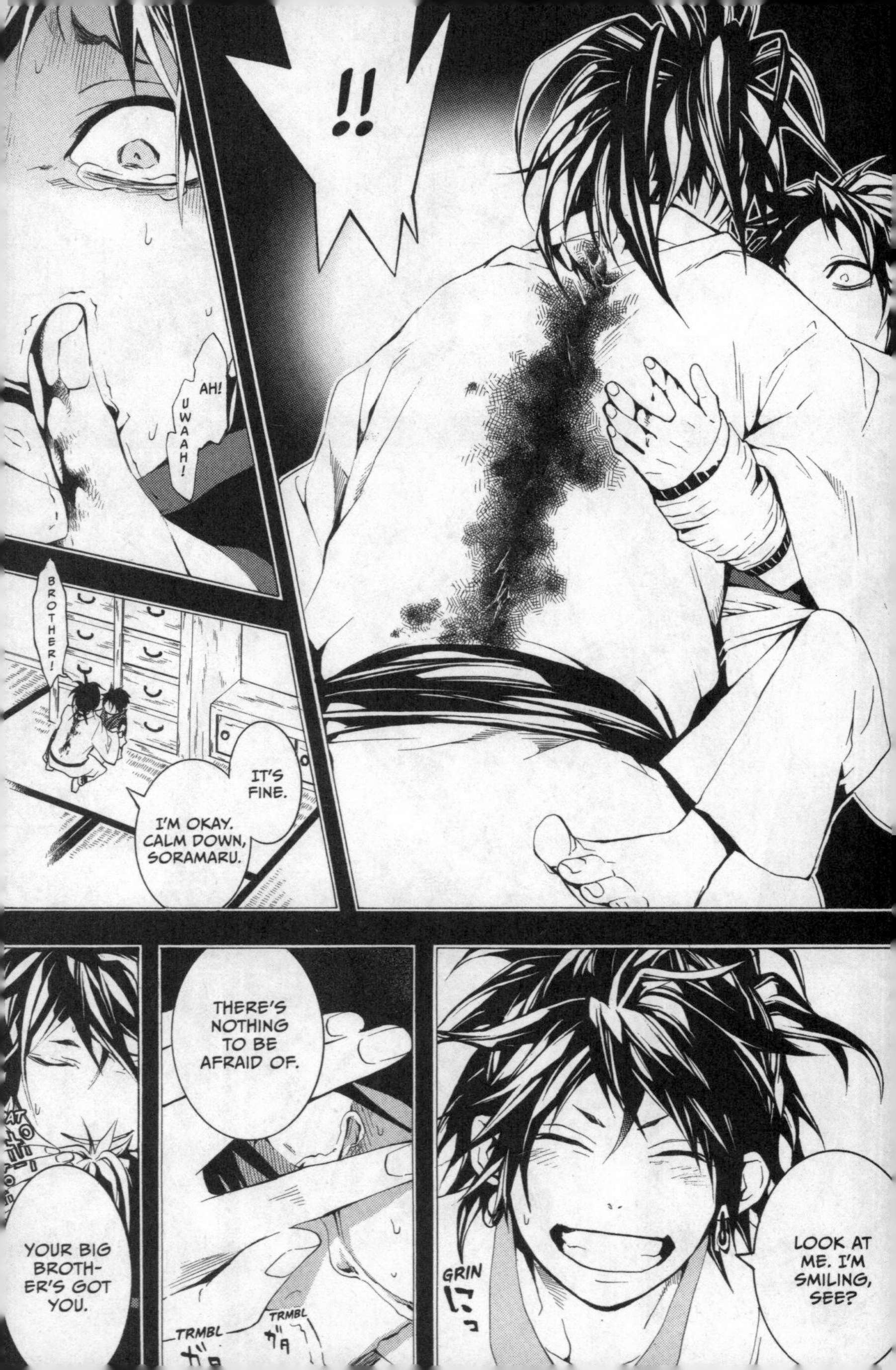

!!
AH!
UWAAH!
BROTHER!
IT'S FINE.
I'M OKAY. CALM DOWN, SORAMARU.
LOOK AT ME. I'M SMILING, SEE?
GRIN
THERE'S NOTHING TO BE AFRAID OF.
TRMBL
TRMBL
YOUR BIG BROTHER'S GOT YOU.

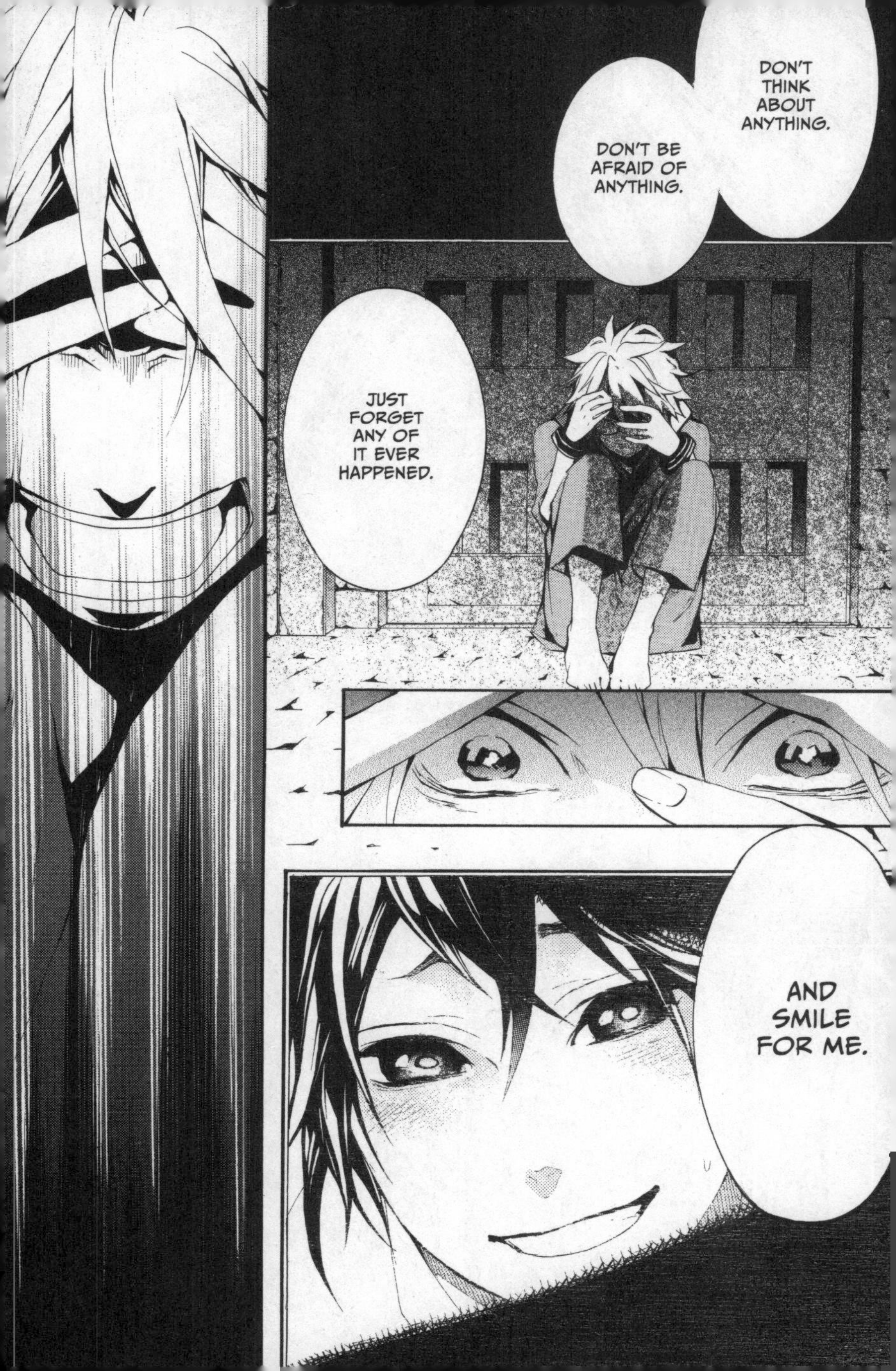
DON'T THINK ABOUT ANYTHING.
DON'T BE AFRAID OF ANYTHING.
JUST FORGET ANY OF IT EVER HAPPENED.
AND SMILE FOR ME.

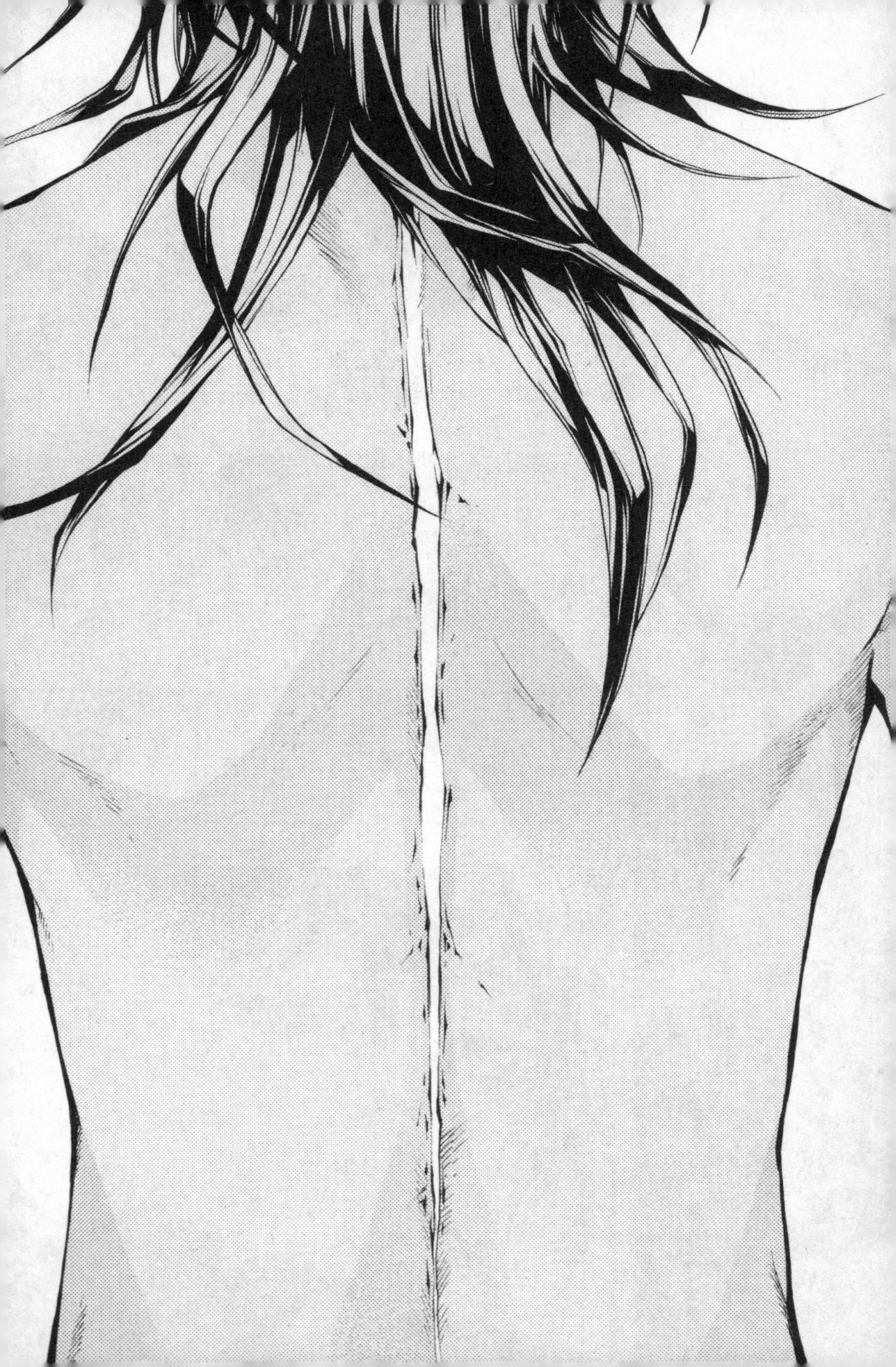

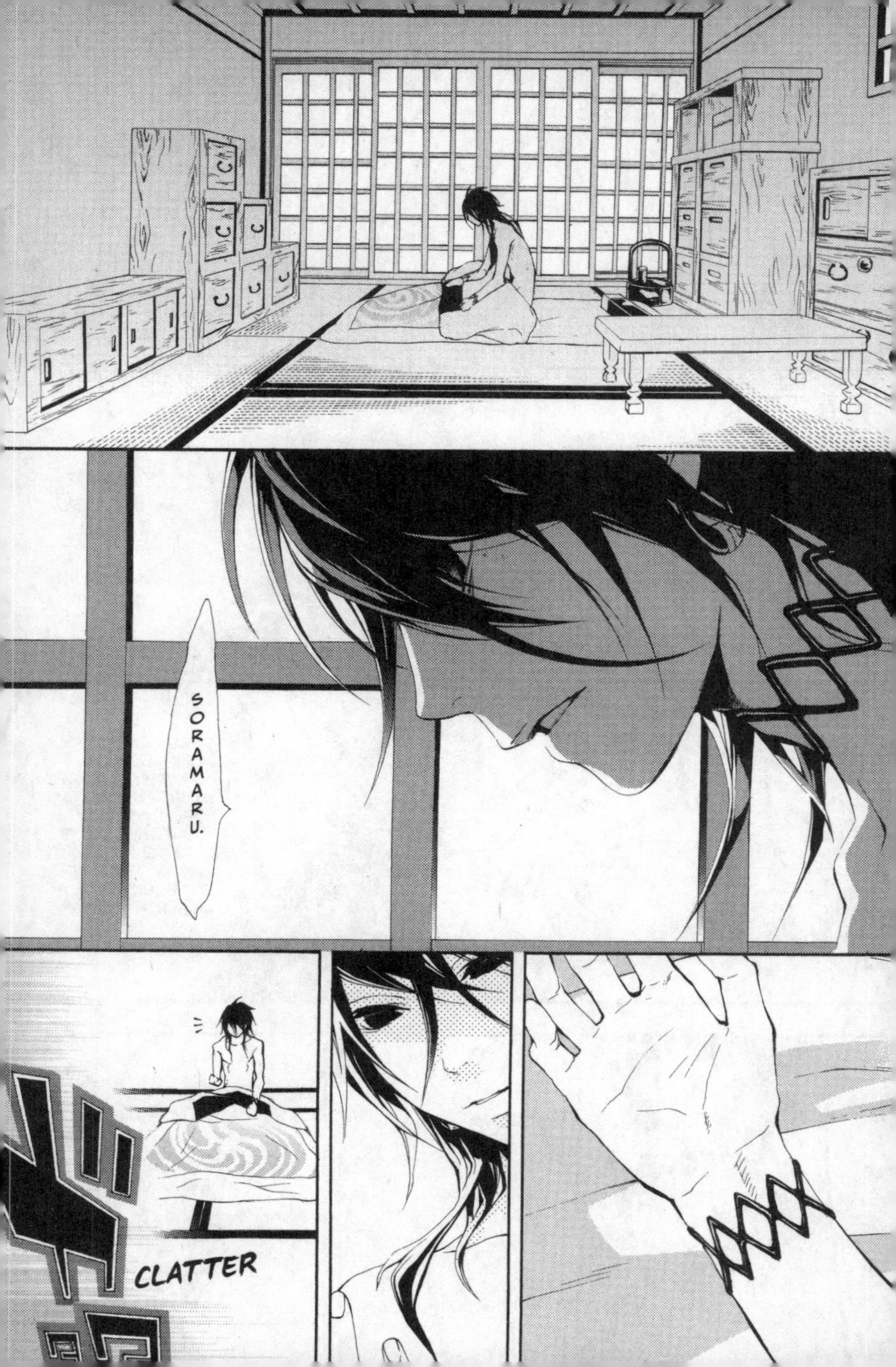
SORAMARU.
CLATTER

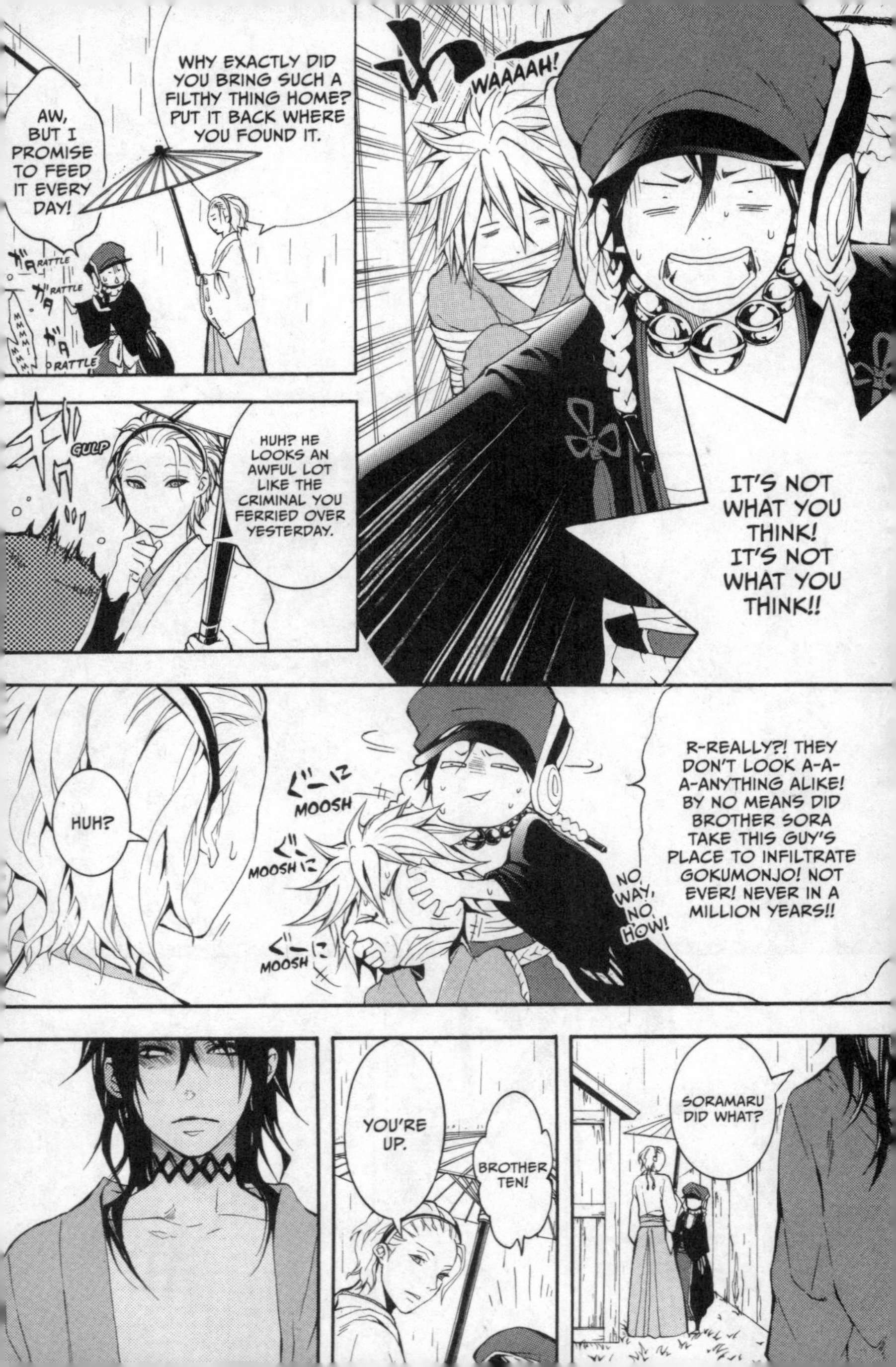
WAAAAH!
IT'S NOT WHAT YOU THINK! IT'S NOT WHAT YOU THINK!!
WHY EXACTLY DID YOU BRING SUCH A FILTHY THING HOME? PUT IT BACK WHERE YOU FOUND IT.
AW, BUT I PROMISE TO FEED IT EVERY DAY!
RATTLE
RATTLE
RATTLE
MMMM!
HUH? HE LOOKS AN AWFUL LOT LIKE THE CRIMINAL YOU FERRIED OVER YESTERDAY.
GULP
R-REALLY?! THEY DON'T LOOK A-A-A-ANYTHING ALIKE! BY NO MEANS DID BROTHER SORA TAKE THIS GUY'S PLACE TO INFILTRATE GOKUMONJO! NOT EVER! NEVER IN A MILLION YEARS!!
NO WAY, NO HOW!
MOOSH
MOOSH
MOOSH
HUH?
SORAMARU DID WHAT?
BROTHER TEN!
YOU'RE UP.

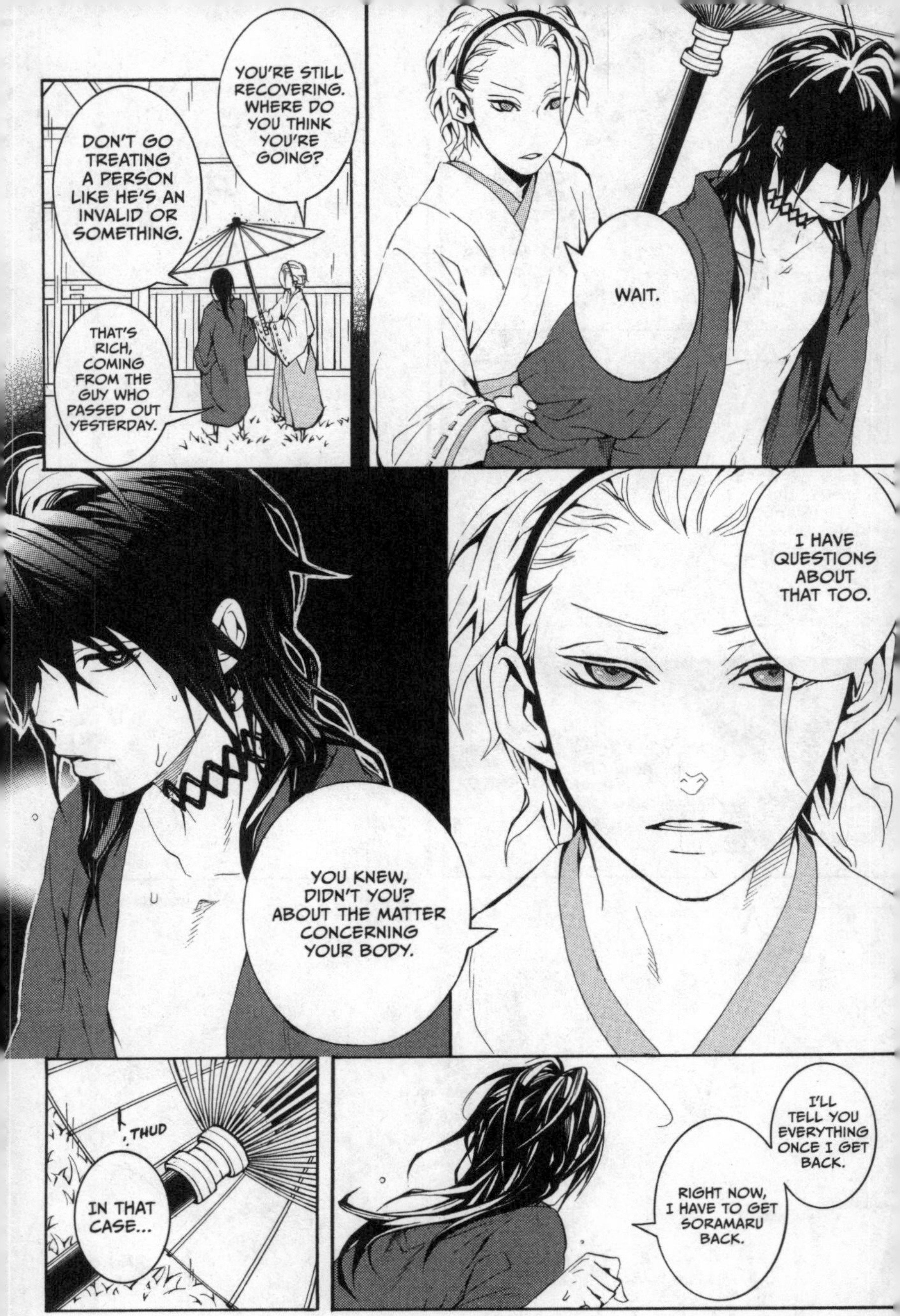
WAIT.
YOU'RE STILL RECOVERING. WHERE DO YOU THINK YOU'RE GOING?
DON'T GO TREATING A PERSON LIKE HE'S AN INVALID OR SOMETHING.
THAT'S RICH, COMING FROM THE GUY WHO PASSED OUT YESTERDAY.
I HAVE QUESTIONS ABOUT THAT TOO.
YOU KNEW, DIDN'T YOU? ABOUT THE MATTER CONCERNING YOUR BODY.
I'LL TELL YOU EVERYTHING ONCE I GET BACK.
RIGHT NOW, I HAVE TO GET SORAMARU BACK.
THUD
IN THAT CASE...

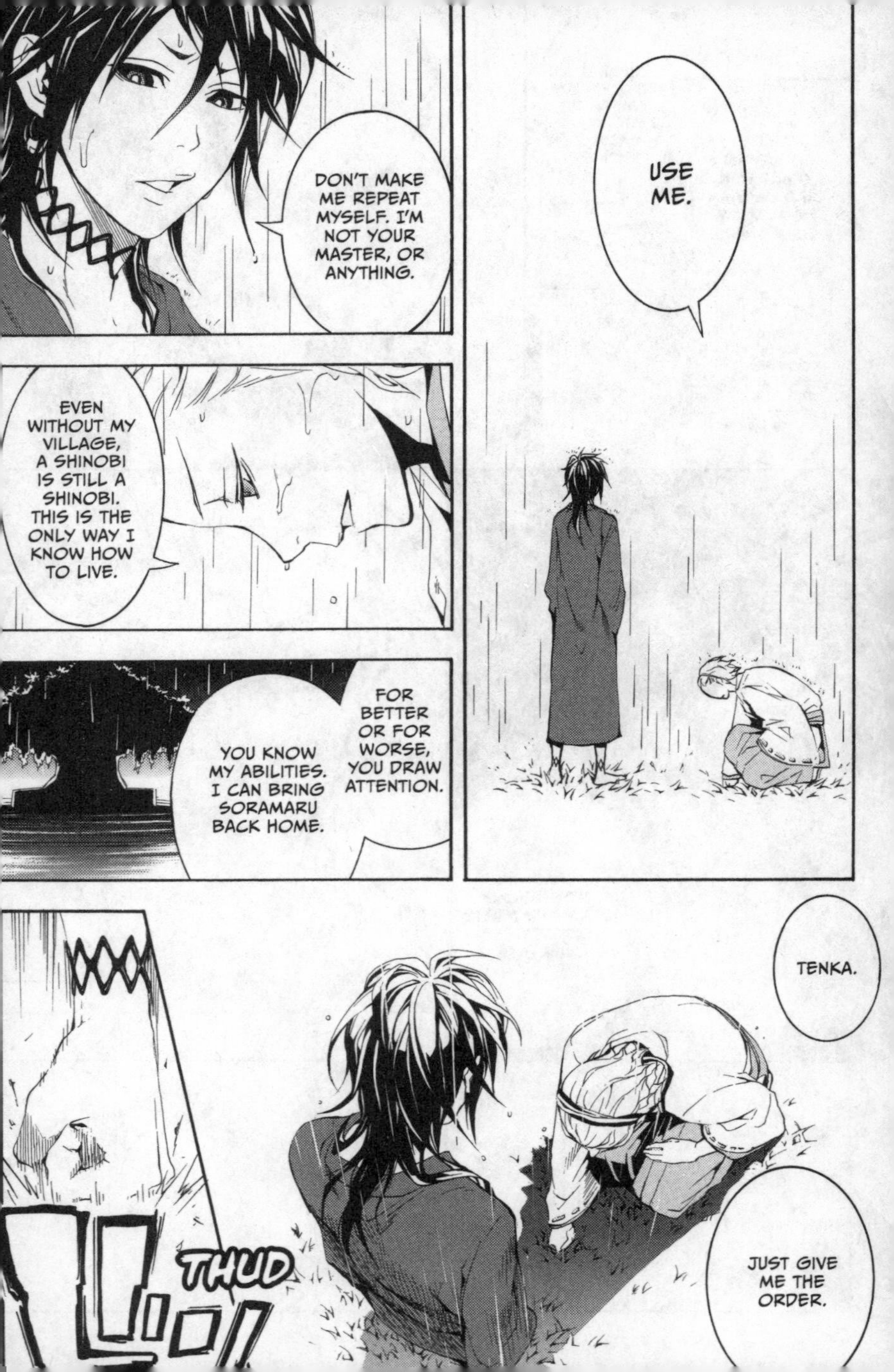
USE ME.
DON'T MAKE ME REPEAT MYSELF. I'M NOT YOUR MASTER, OR ANYTHING.
EVEN WITHOUT MY VILLAGE, A SHINOBI IS STILL A SHINOBI. THIS IS THE ONLY WAY I KNOW HOW TO LIVE.
FOR BETTER OR FOR WORSE, YOU DRAW ATTENTION.
YOU KNOW MY ABILITIES. I CAN BRING SORAMARU BACK HOME.
TENKA.
JUST GIVE ME THE ORDER.
THUD

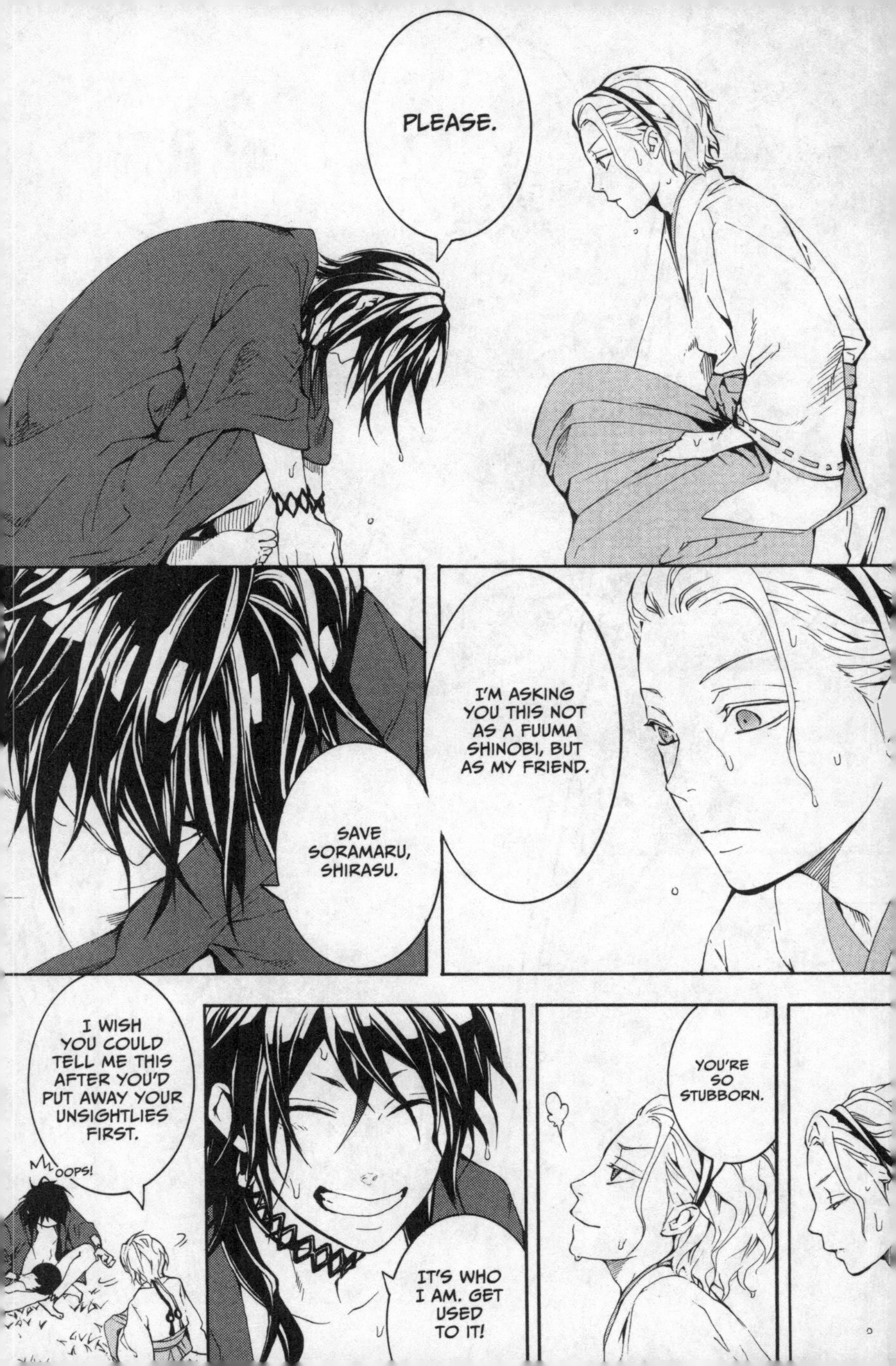
PLEASE.
I'M ASKING YOU THIS NOT AS A FUUMA SHINOBI, BUT AS MY FRIEND.
SAVE SORAMARU, SHIRASU.
YOU'RE SO STUBBORN.
IT'S WHO I AM. GET USED TO IT!
I WISH YOU COULD TELL ME THIS AFTER YOU'D PUT AWAY YOUR UNSIGHTLIES FIRST.
OOPS!

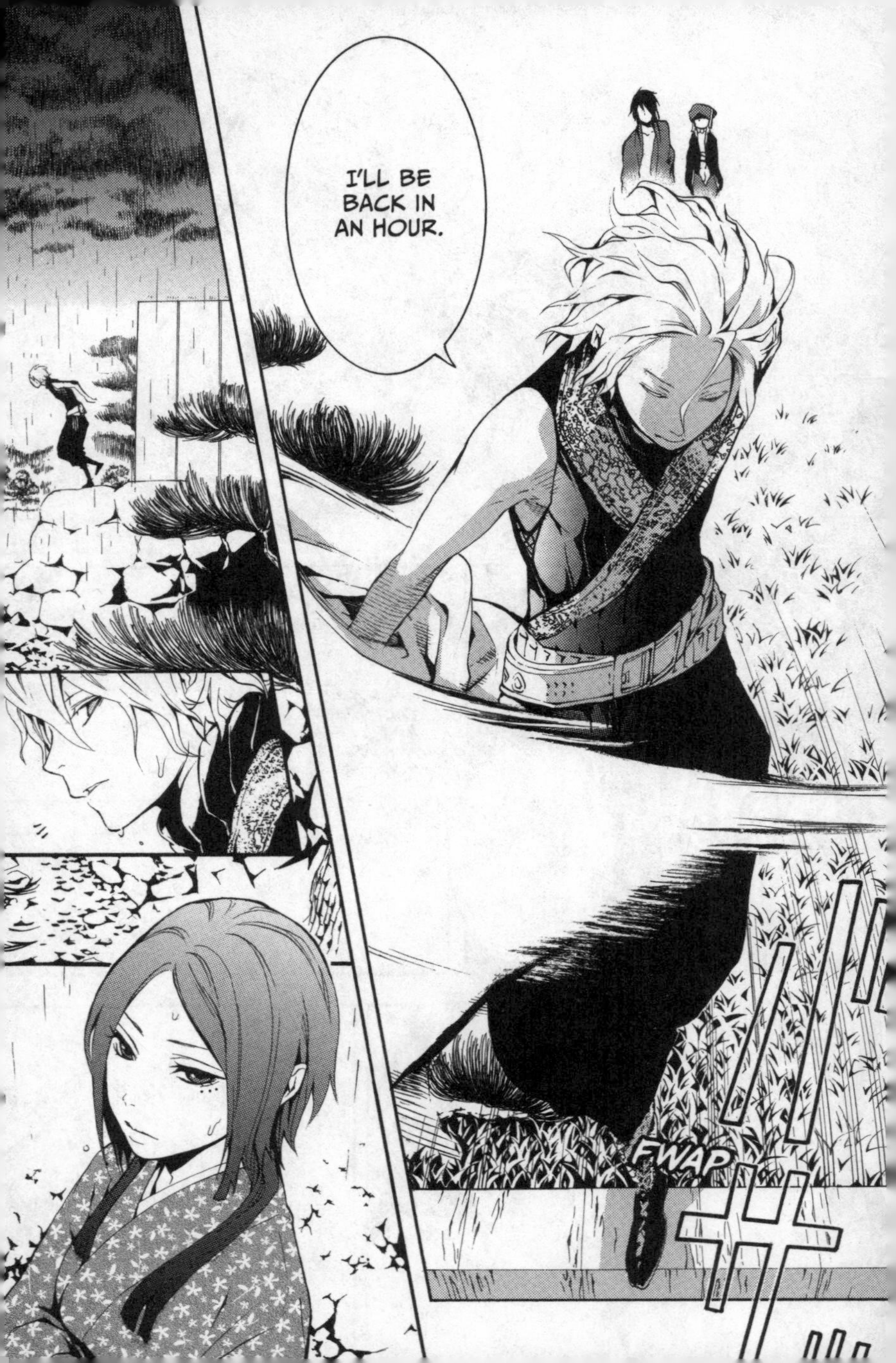
I'LL BE BACK IN AN HOUR.
FWAP

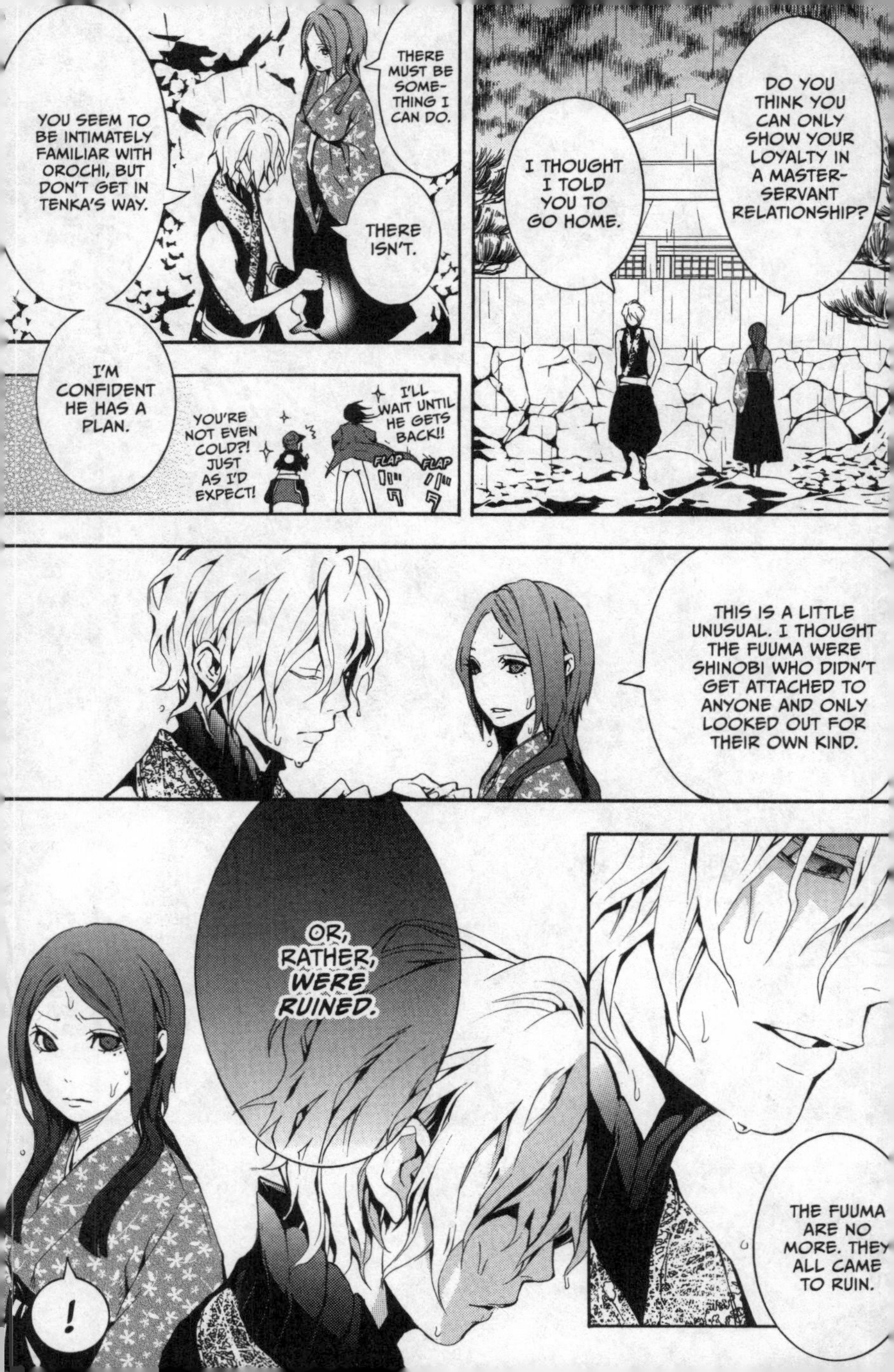
I THOUGHT I TOLD YOU TO GO HOME.
DO YOU THINK YOU CAN ONLY SHOW YOUR LOYALTY IN A MASTER-SERVANT RELATIONSHIP?
THERE MUST BE SOME-THING I CAN DO.
THERE ISN'T.
YOU SEEM TO BE INTIMATELY FAMILIAR WITH OROCHI, BUT DON'T GET IN TENKA'S WAY.
I'M CONFIDENT HE HAS A PLAN.
I'LL WAIT UNTIL HE GETS BACK!!
FLAP
FLAP
YOU'RE NOT EVEN COLD?! JUST AS I'D EXPECT!
THIS IS A LITTLE UNUSUAL. I THOUGHT THE FUUMA WERE SHINOBI WHO DIDN'T GET ATTACHED TO ANYONE AND ONLY LOOKED OUT FOR THEIR OWN KIND.
THE FUUMA ARE NO MORE. THEY ALL CAME TO RUIN.
OR, RATHER, WERE RUINED.
!

AT THE HANDS OF A SINGLE CHILD.

CAN YOU BELIEVE IT? THEY'D ALREADY BEEN A CLAN ON THE DECLINE, BUT EVEN IN THEIR WEAKENED STATE, THEY WERE STILL A UNITED NINJA CLAN.

AND THEY WERE ALL LOST IN ONE NIGHT.

AND THE "FUUMA" NAME WAS COMPLETELY ERASED FROM THIS ERA.

THE SURVIVING MEMBERS DISPERSED.

THEIR VILLAGE, REPUTATION, PARENTS, AND SIBLINGS.

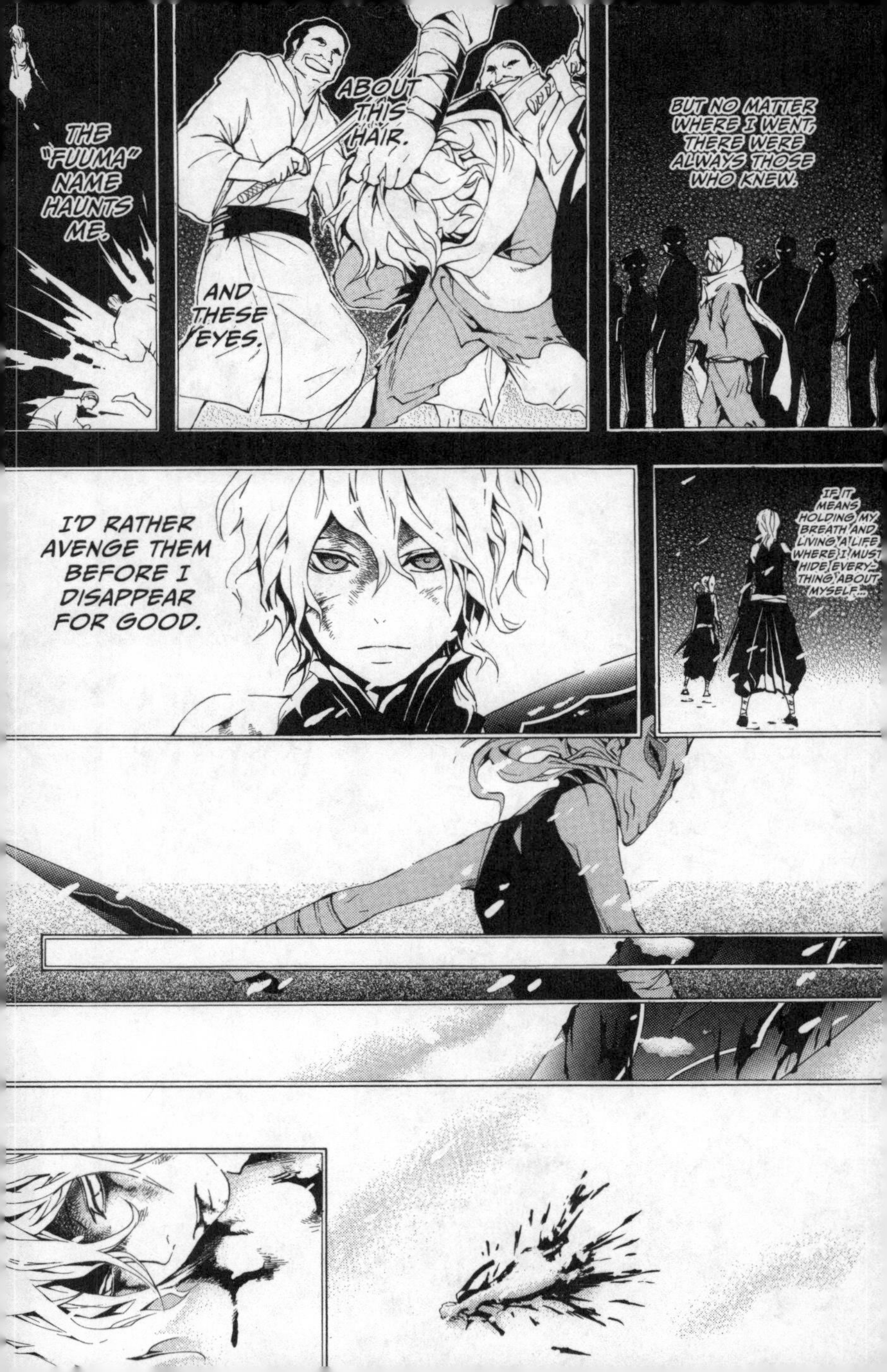
BUT NO MATTER WHERE I WENT, THERE WERE ALWAYS THOSE WHO KNEW.
ABOUT THIS HAIR.
AND THESE EYES.
THE "FUUMA" NAME HAUNTS ME.
IF IT MEANS HOLDING MY BREATH AND LIVING A LIFE WHERE I MUST HIDE EVERY-THING ABOUT MYSELF...
I'D RATHER AVENGE THEM BEFORE I DISAPPEAR FOR GOOD.

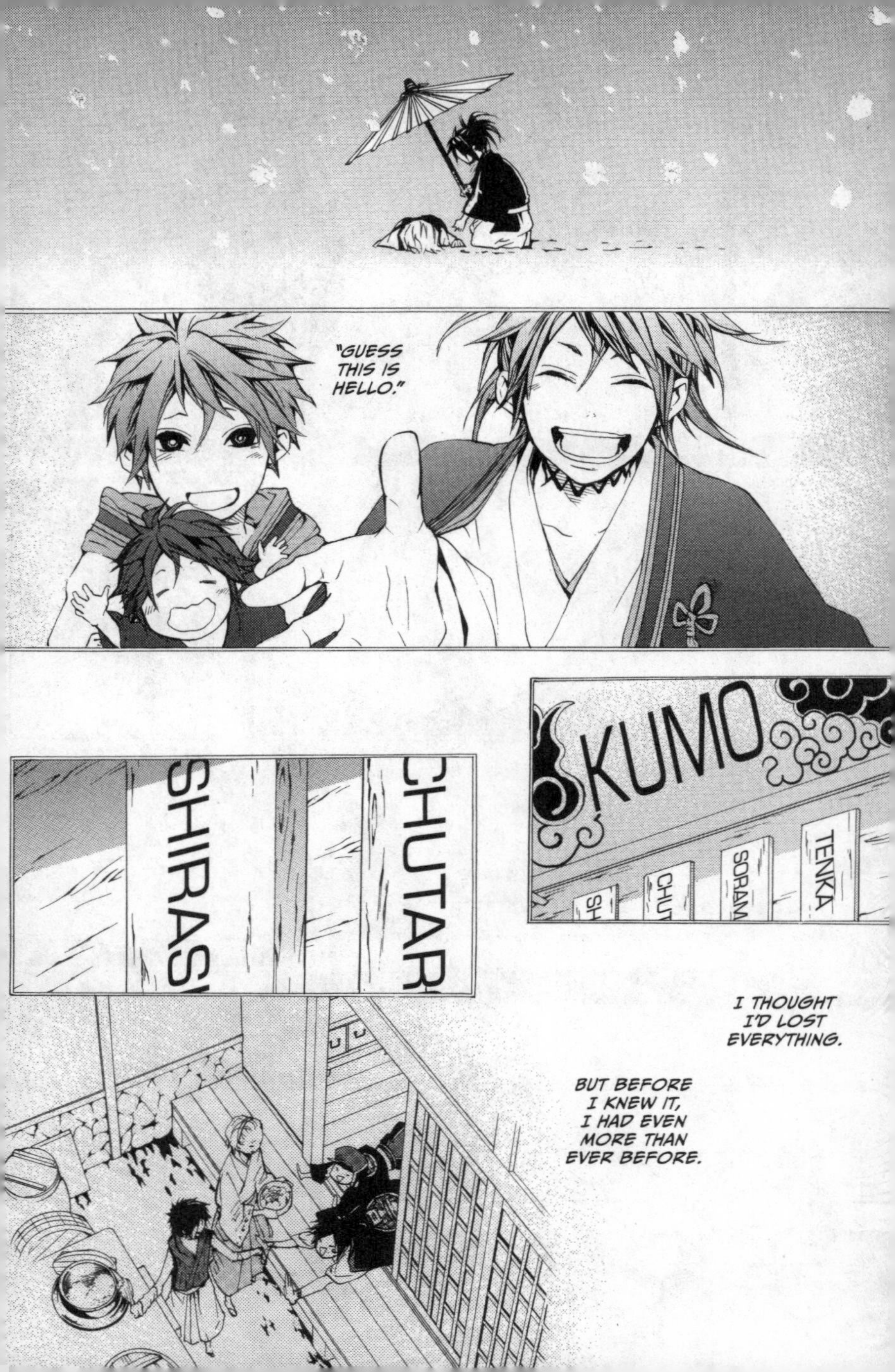

"GUESS THIS IS HELLO."
KUMO
TENKA
I THOUGHT I'D LOST EVERYTHING.
BUT BEFORE I KNEW IT, I HAD EVEN MORE THAN EVER BEFORE.

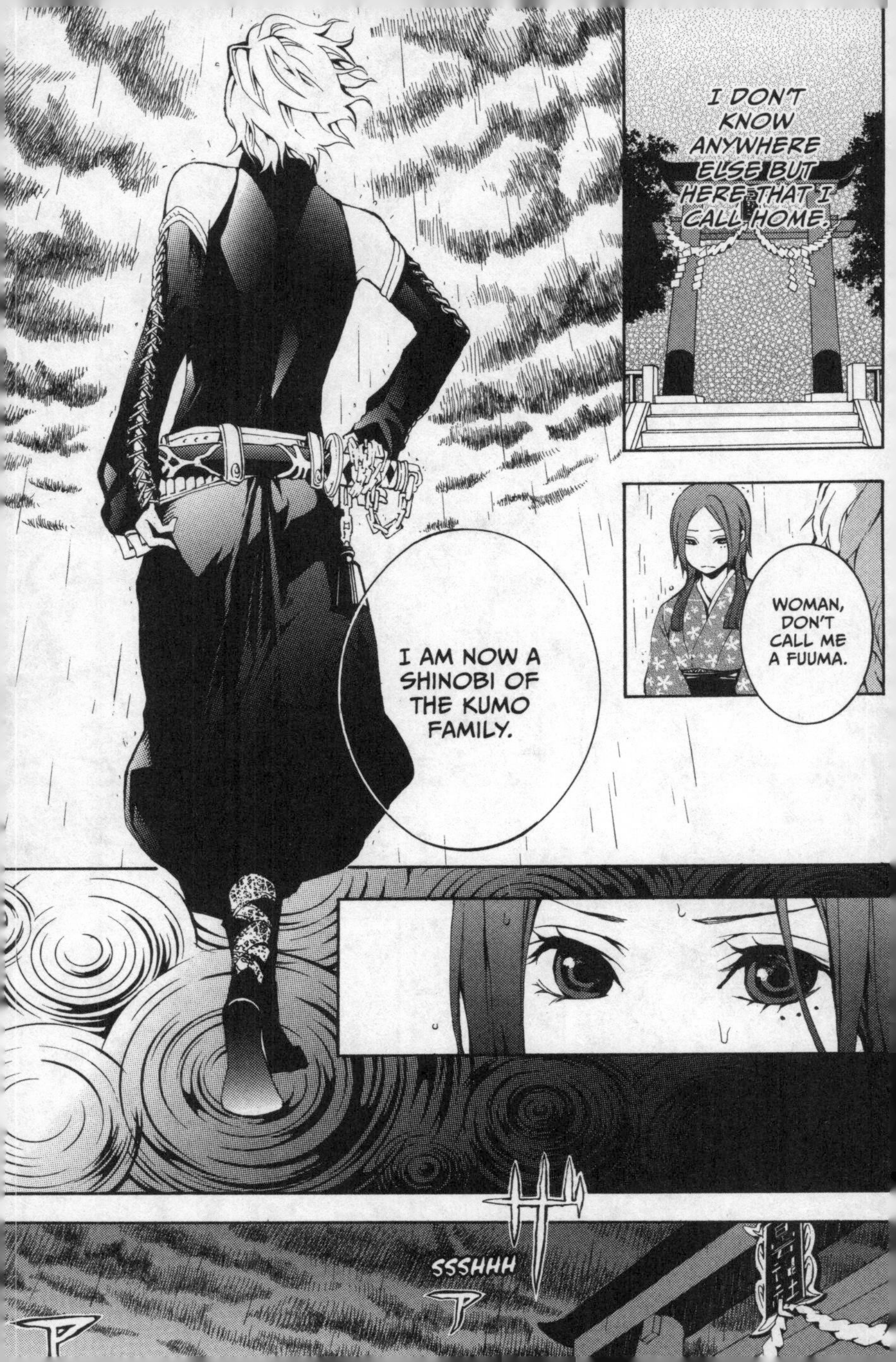
I DON'T KNOW ANYWHERE ELSE BUT HERE THAT I CALL HOME.
WOMAN, DON'T CALL ME A FUUMA.
I AM NOW A SHINOBI OF THE KUMO FAMILY.
SSSHHH

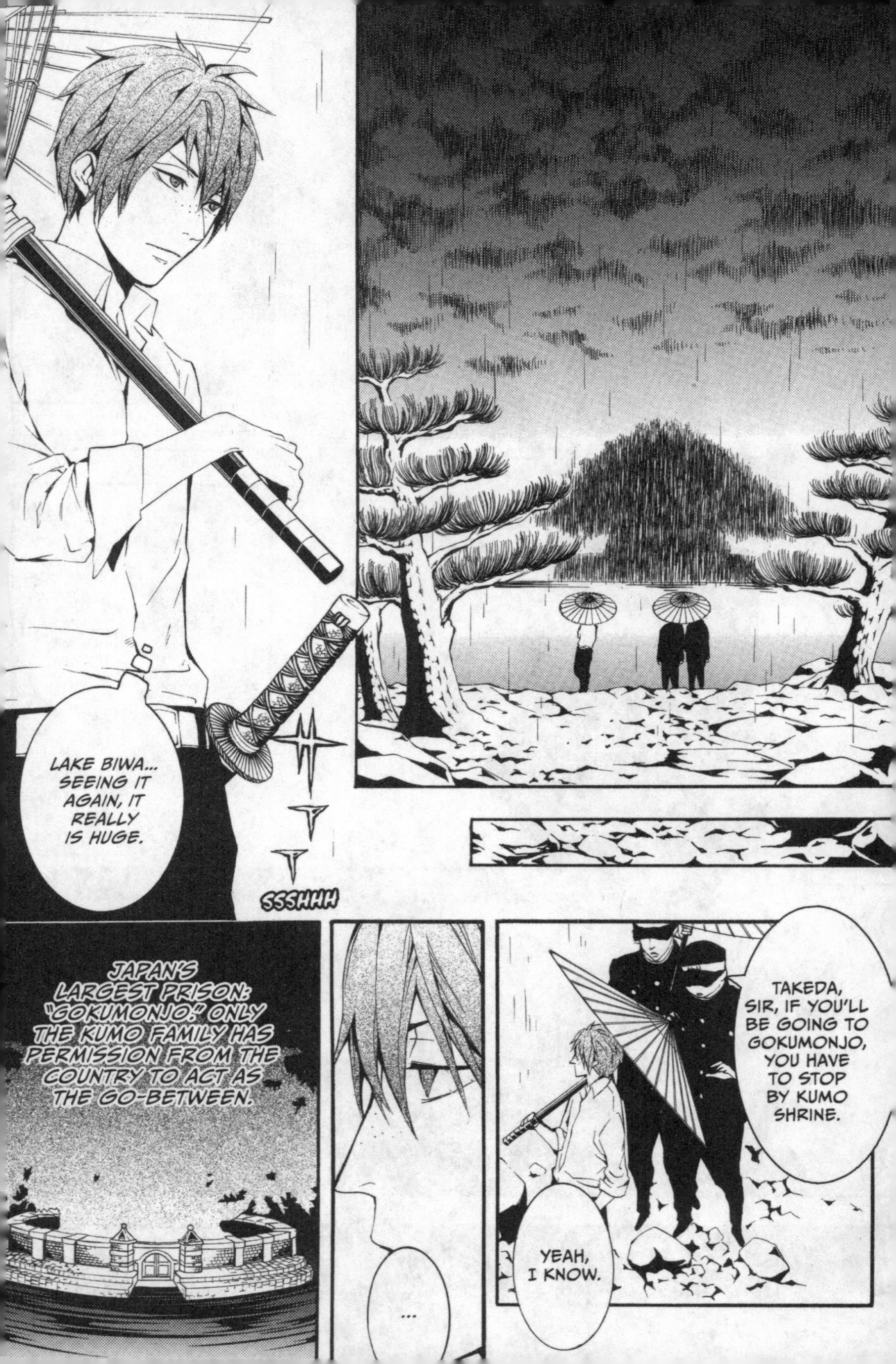
LAKE BIWA... SEEING IT AGAIN, IT REALLY IS HUGE.
SSSHHH
TAKEDA, SIR, IF YOU'LL BE GOING TO GOKUMONJO, YOU HAVE TO STOP BY KUMO SHRINE.
YEAH, I KNOW.
...
JAPAN'S LARGEST PRISON: "GOKUMONJO." ONLY THE KUMO FAMILY HAS PERMISSION FROM THE COUNTRY TO ACT AS THE GO-BETWEEN.

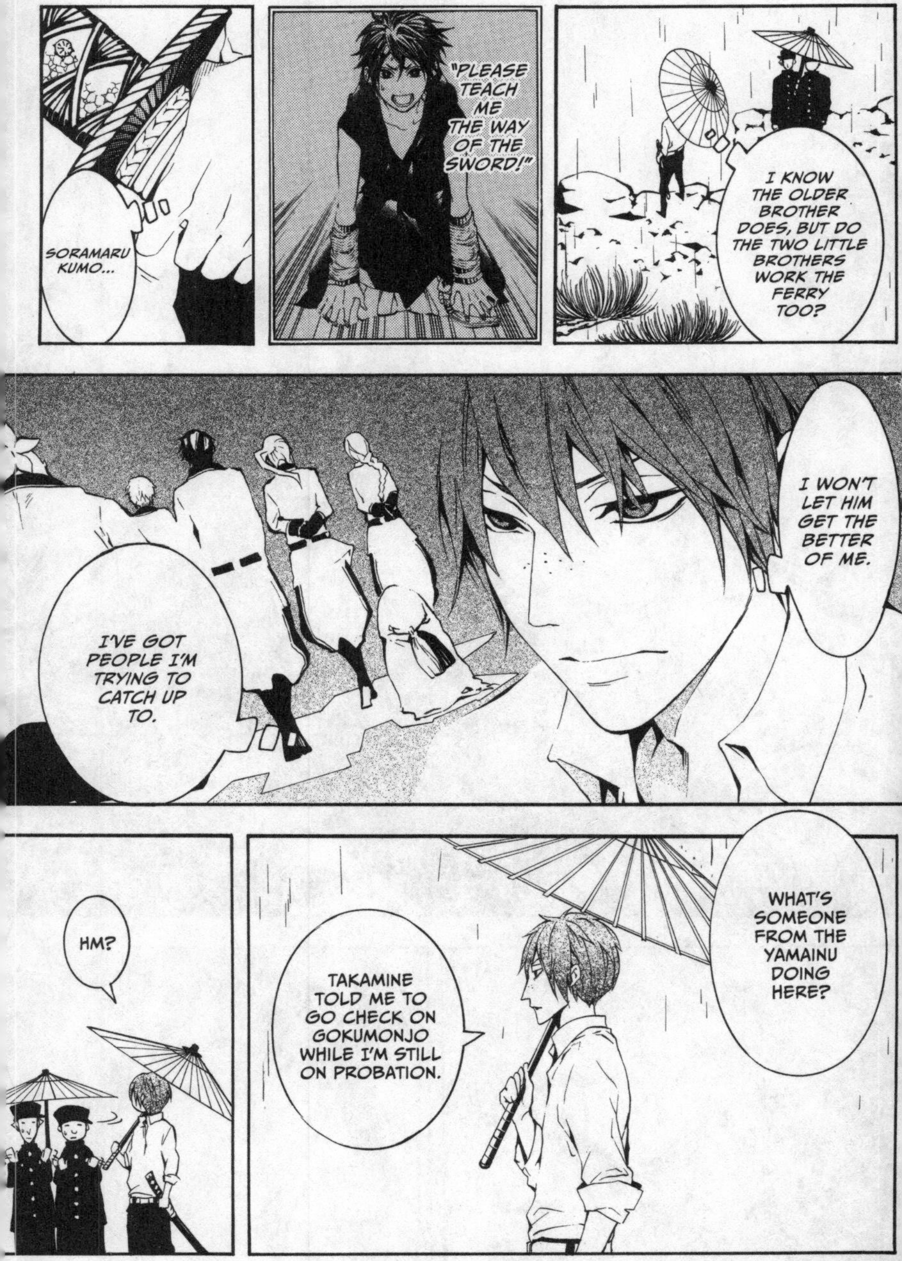
I KNOW THE OLDER BROTHER DOES, BUT DO THE TWO LITTLE BROTHERS WORK THE FERRY TOO?
"PLEASE TEACH ME THE WAY OF THE SWORD!"
SORAMARU KUMO...
I WON'T LET HIM GET THE BETTER OF ME.
I'VE GOT PEOPLE I'M TRYING TO CATCH UP TO.
WHAT'S SOMEONE FROM THE YAMAINU DOING HERE?
TAKAMINE TOLD ME TO GO CHECK ON GOKUMONJO WHILE I'M STILL ON PROBATION.
HM?

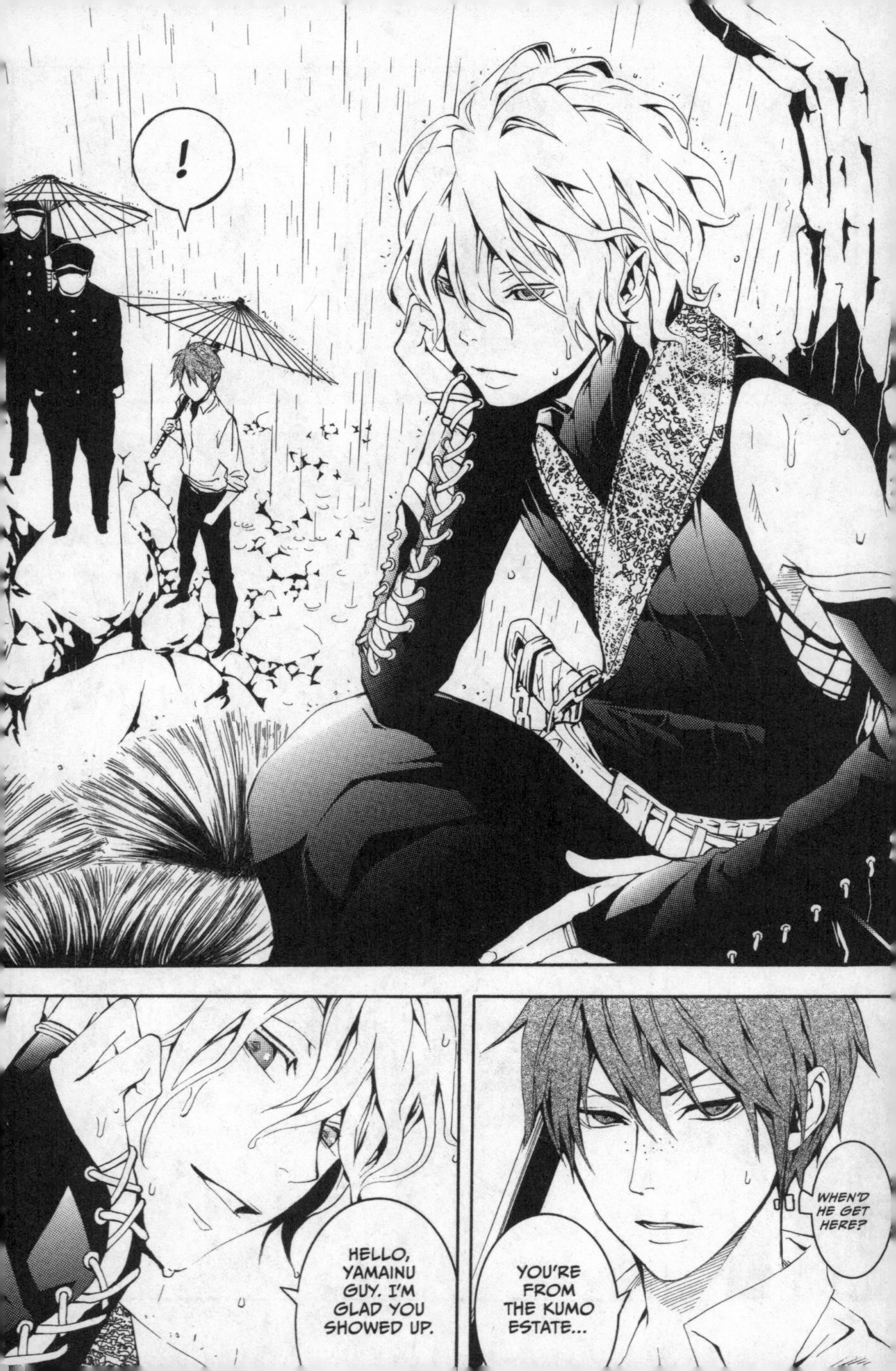
!
WHEN'D HE GET HERE?
YOU'RE FROM THE KUMO ESTATE...
HELLO, YAMAINU GUY. I'M GLAD YOU SHOWED UP.

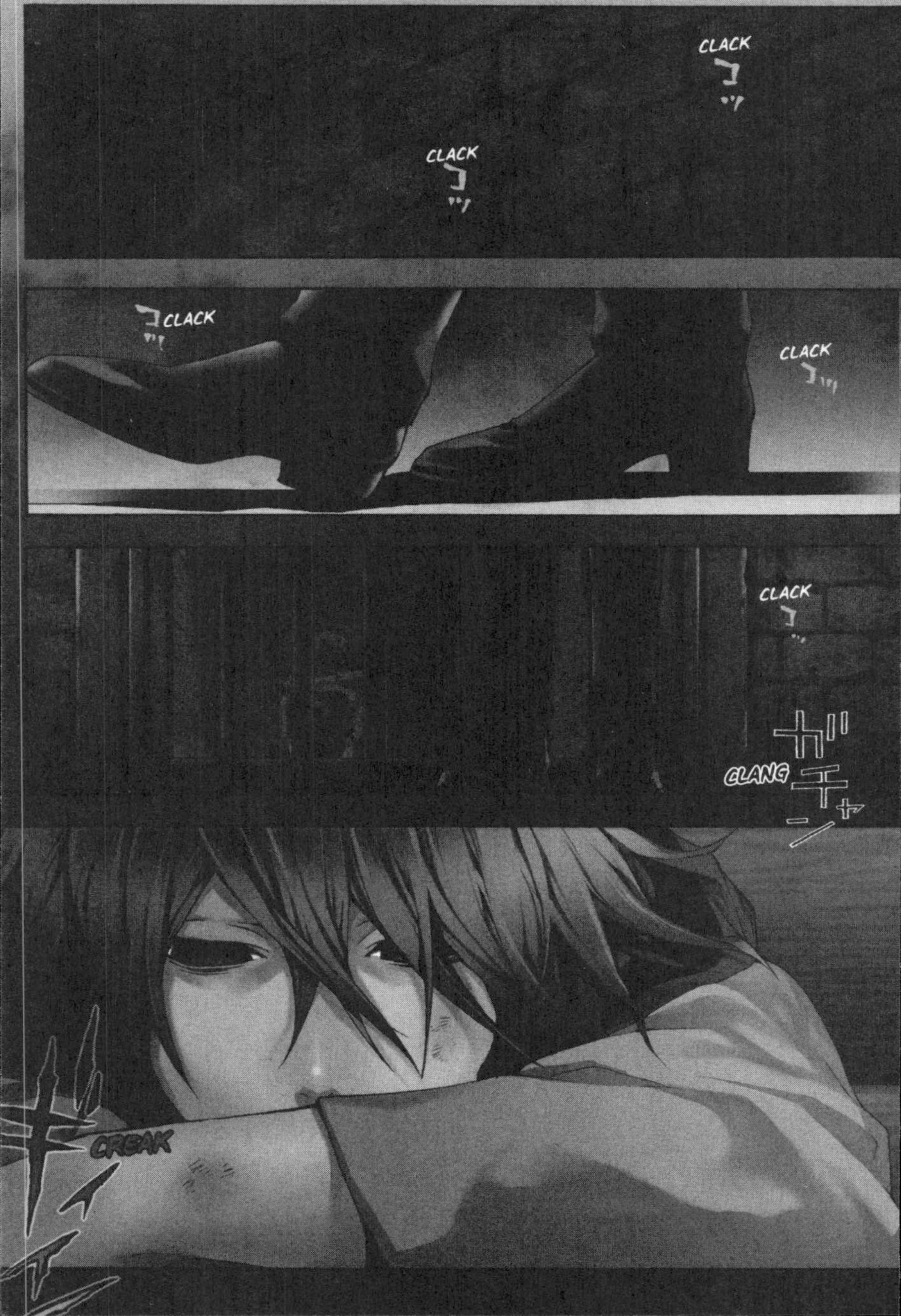
CLACK
CLACK
CLACK
CLACK
CLACK
CLANG
CREAK

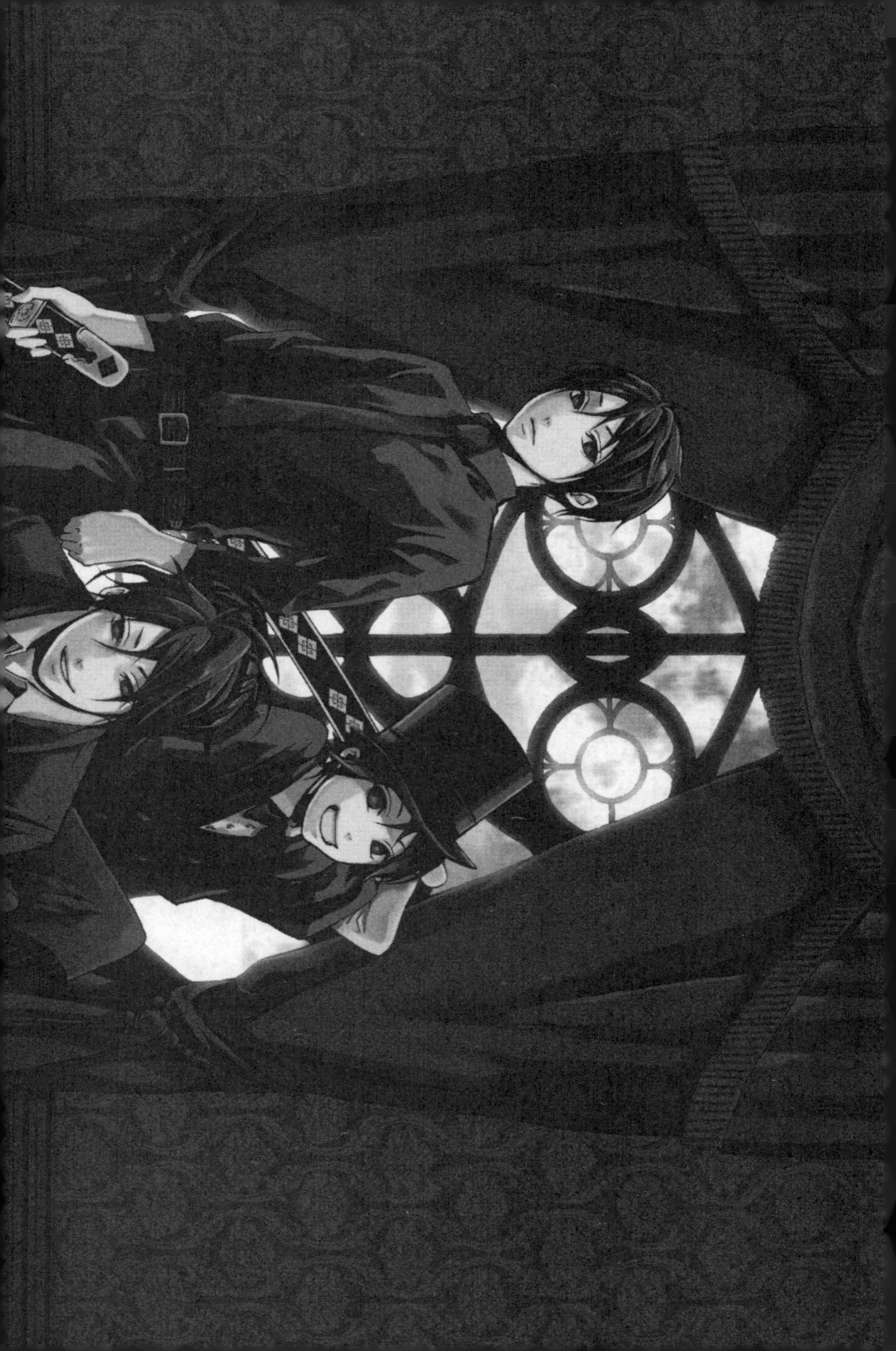

Chapter 9
A Fuuma, Hiding in Gokumonjo

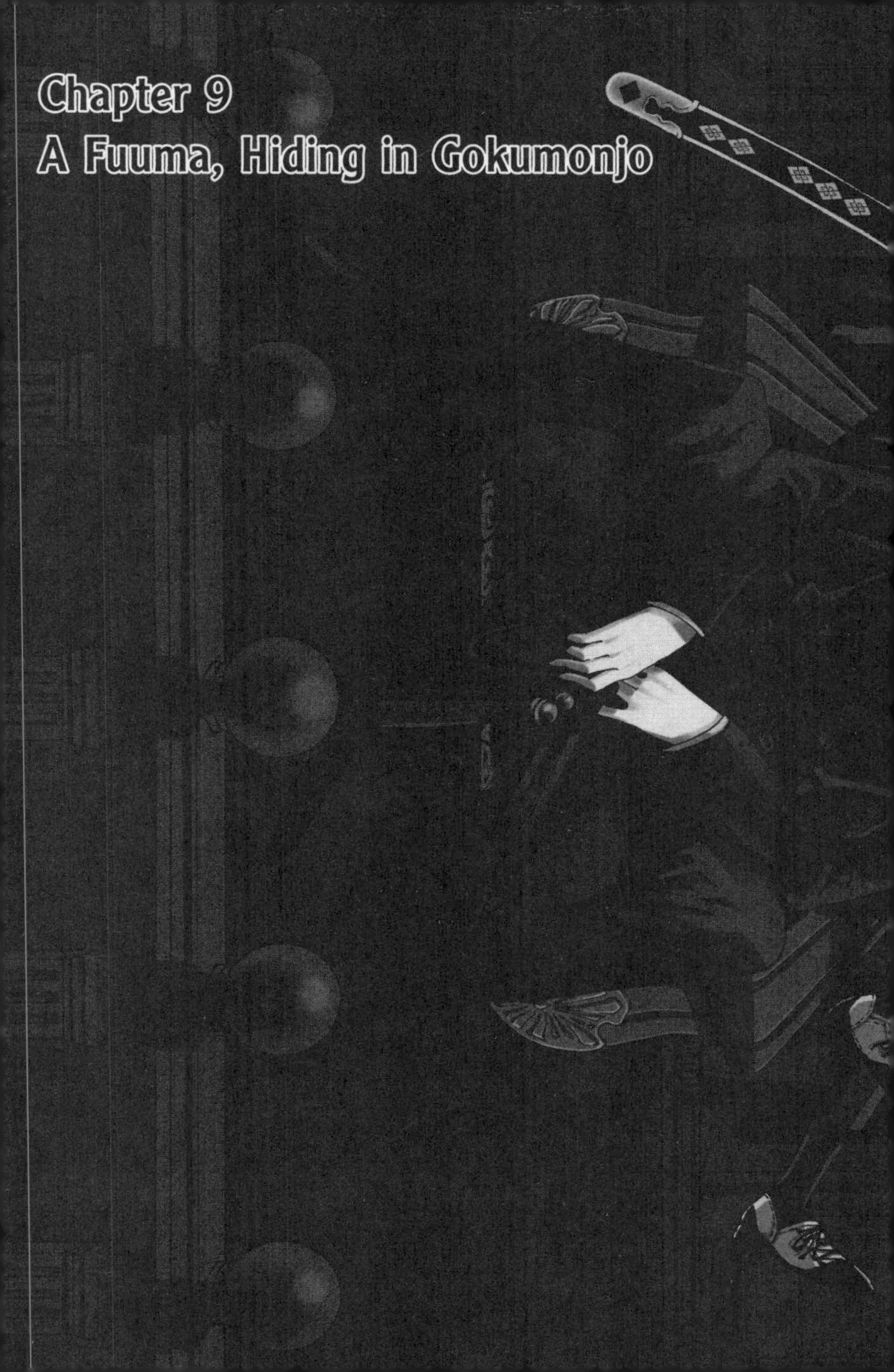

LAUGHING *UNDER* *THE* CLOUDS

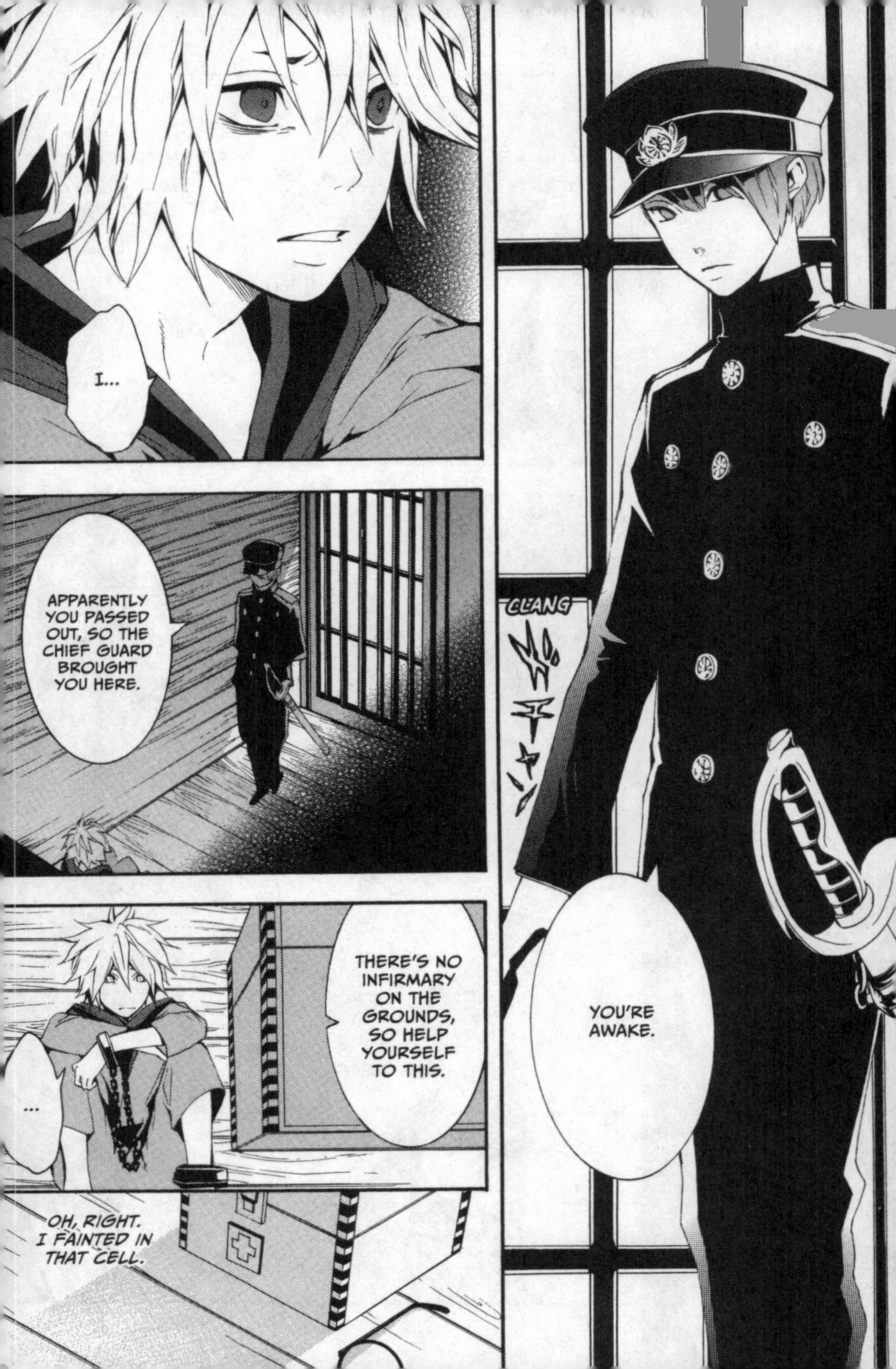
CLANG
YOU'RE AWAKE.
I...
APPARENTLY YOU PASSED OUT, SO THE CHIEF GUARD BROUGHT YOU HERE.
THERE'S NO INFIRMARY ON THE GROUNDS, SO HELP YOURSELF TO THIS.
...
OH, RIGHT. I FAINTED IN THAT CELL.

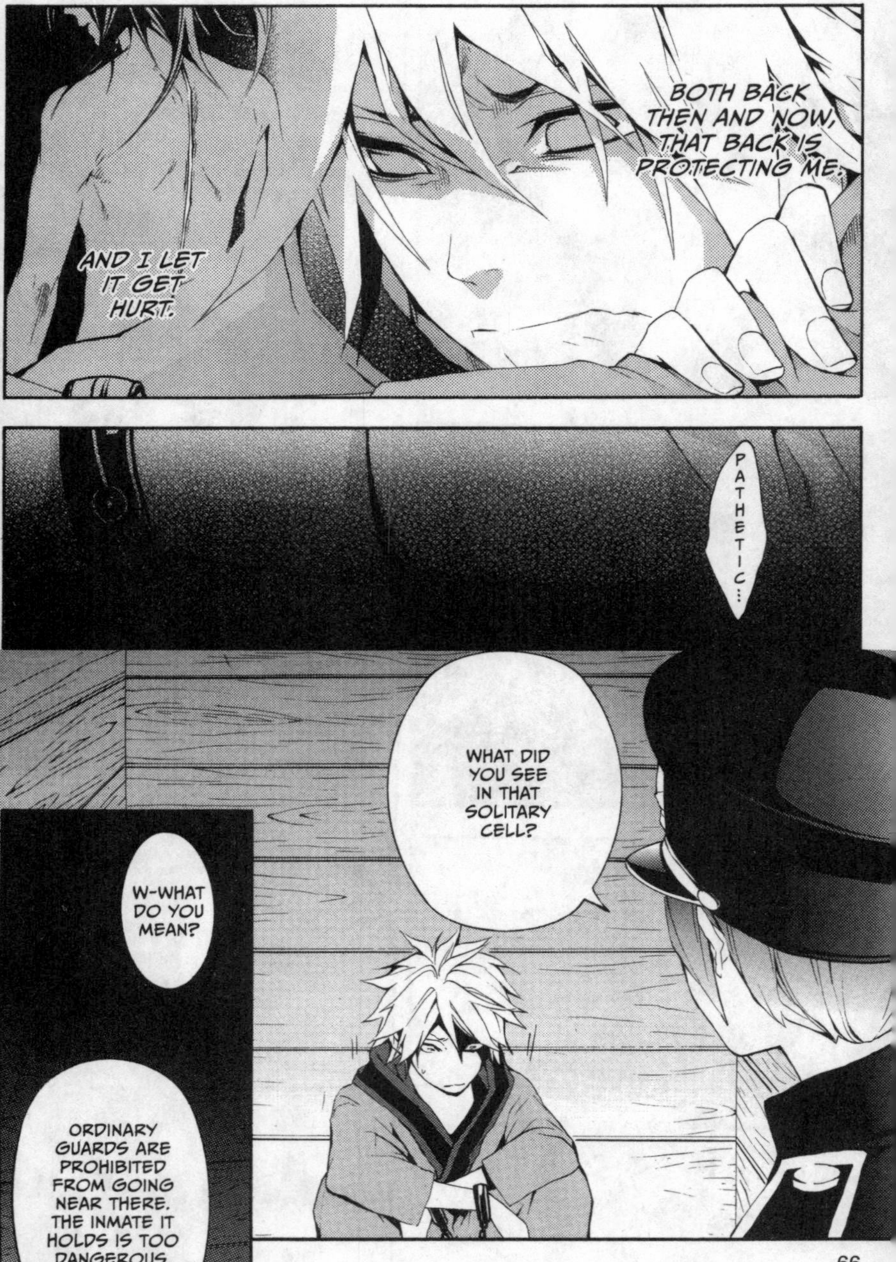
BOTH BACK THEN AND NOW, THAT BACK IS PROTECTING ME.
AND I LET IT GET HURT.
PATHETIC...
WHAT DID YOU SEE IN THAT SOLITARY CELL?
W-WHAT DO YOU MEAN?
ORDINARY GUARDS ARE PROHIBITED FROM GOING NEAR THERE. THE INMATE IT HOLDS IS TOO DANGEROUS.

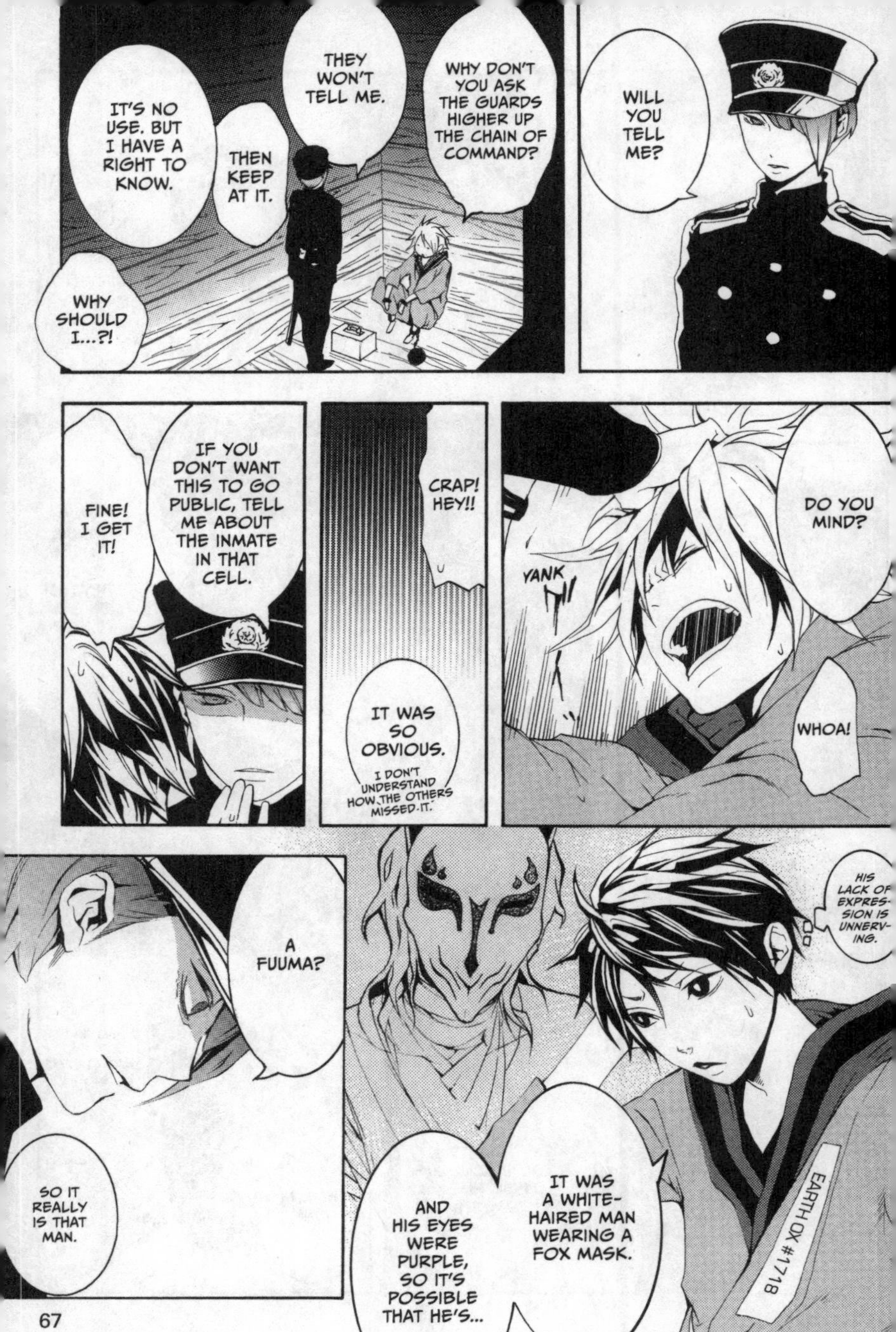
WILL YOU TELL ME?
WHY DON'T YOU ASK THE GUARDS HIGHER UP THE CHAIN OF COMMAND?
THEY WON'T TELL ME.
THEN KEEP AT IT.
IT'S NO USE. BUT I HAVE A RIGHT TO KNOW.
WHY SHOULD I...?!
DO YOU MIND?
YANK
WHOA!
CRAP! HEY!!
IT WAS SO OBVIOUS.
I DON'T UNDERSTAND HOW THE OTHERS MISSED IT.
IF YOU DON'T WANT THIS TO GO PUBLIC, TELL ME ABOUT THE INMATE IN THAT CELL.
FINE! I GET IT!
HIS LACK OF EXPRESSION IS UNNERVING.
EARTH OX #1718
IT WAS A WHITE-HAIRED MAN WEARING A FOX MASK.
AND HIS EYES WERE PURPLE, SO IT'S POSSIBLE THAT HE'S...
A FUUMA?
SO IT REALLY IS THAT MAN.

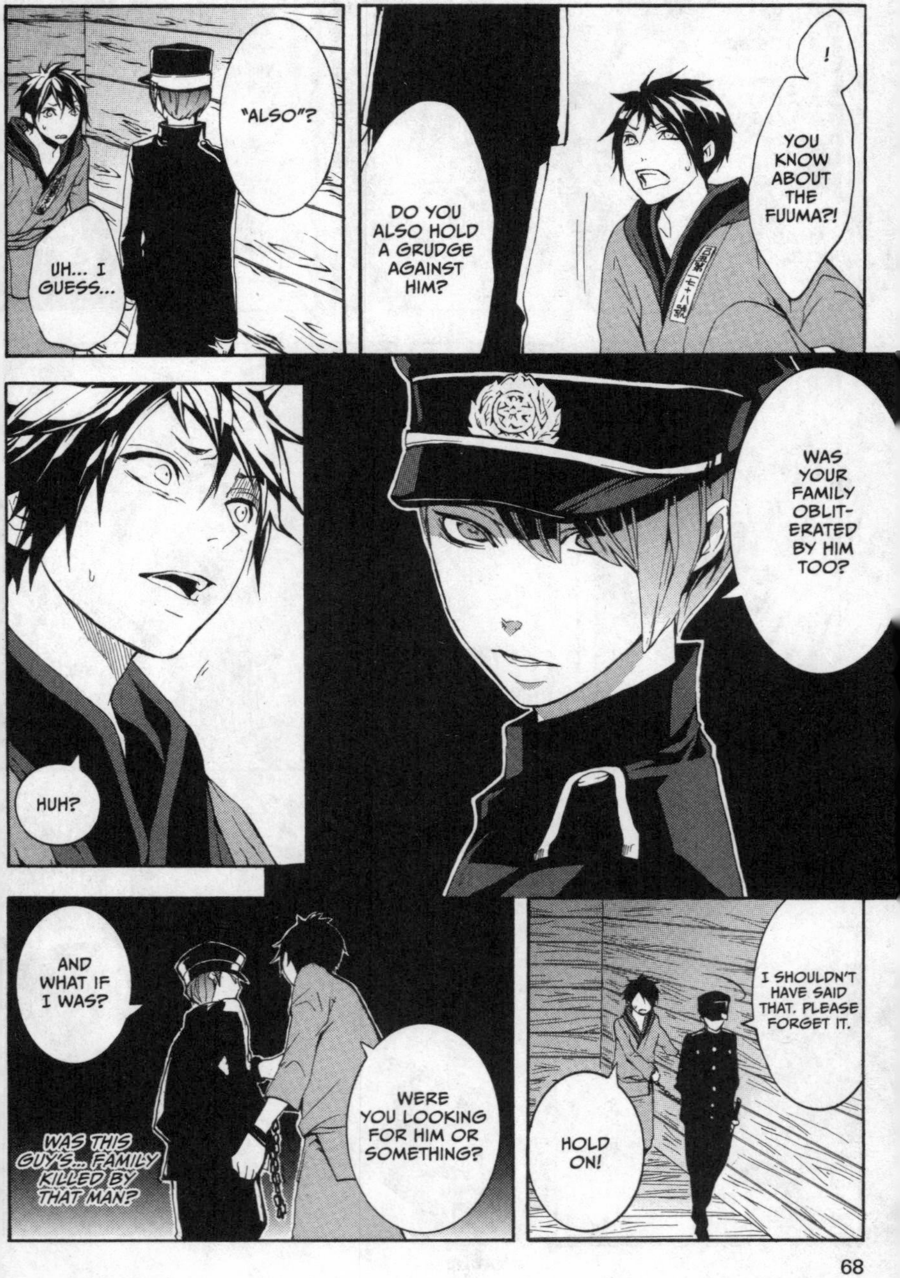
!
YOU KNOW ABOUT THE FUUMA?!
DO YOU ALSO HOLD A GRUDGE AGAINST HIM?
"ALSO"?
UH... I GUESS...
WAS YOUR FAMILY OBLIT-ERATED BY HIM TOO?
HUH?
I SHOULDN'T HAVE SAID THAT. PLEASE FORGET IT.
HOLD ON!
AND WHAT IF I WAS?
WERE YOU LOOKING FOR HIM OR SOMETHING?
WAS THIS GUY'S... FAMILY KILLED BY THAT MAN?

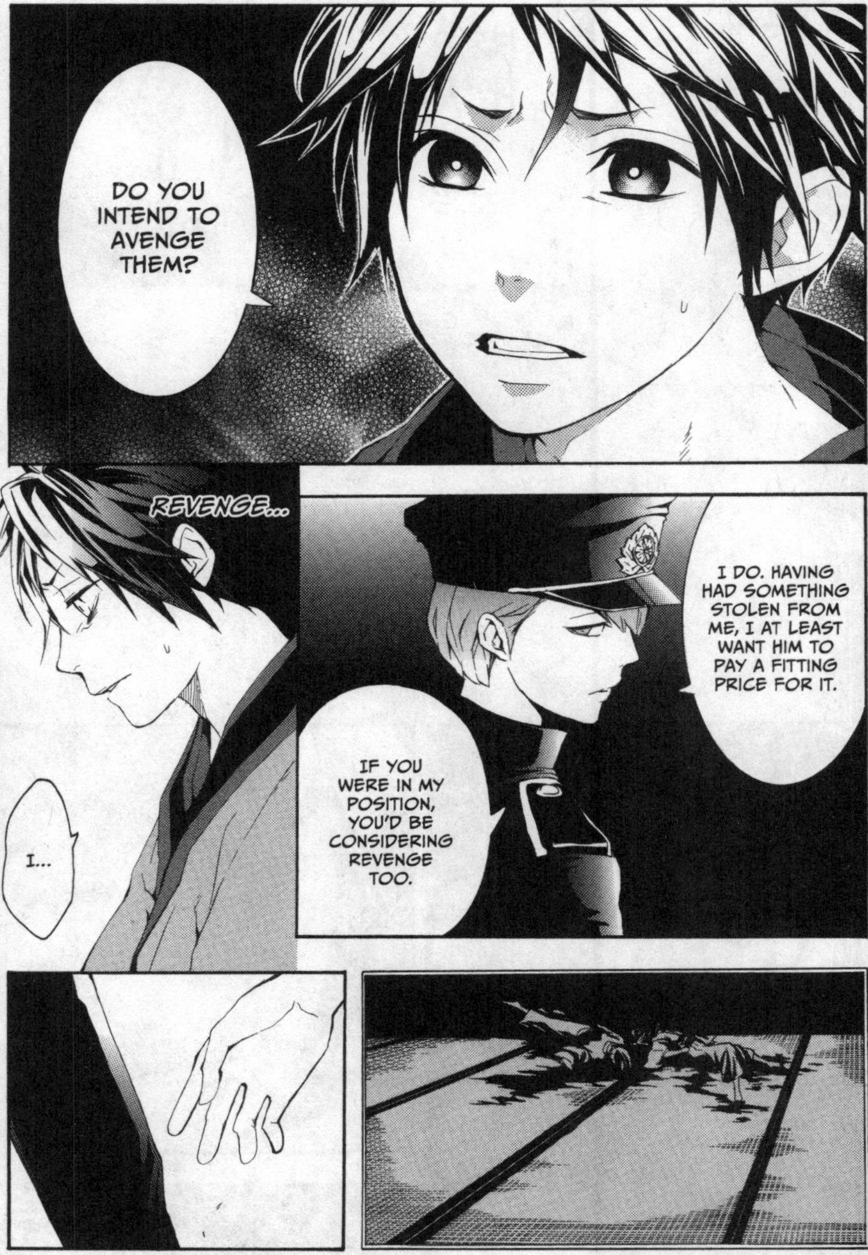
DO YOU INTEND TO AVENGE THEM?
I DO. HAVING HAD SOMETHING STOLEN FROM ME, I AT LEAST WANT HIM TO PAY A FITTING PRICE FOR IT.
IF YOU WERE IN MY POSITION, YOU'D BE CONSIDERING REVENGE TOO.
REVENGE...
I...

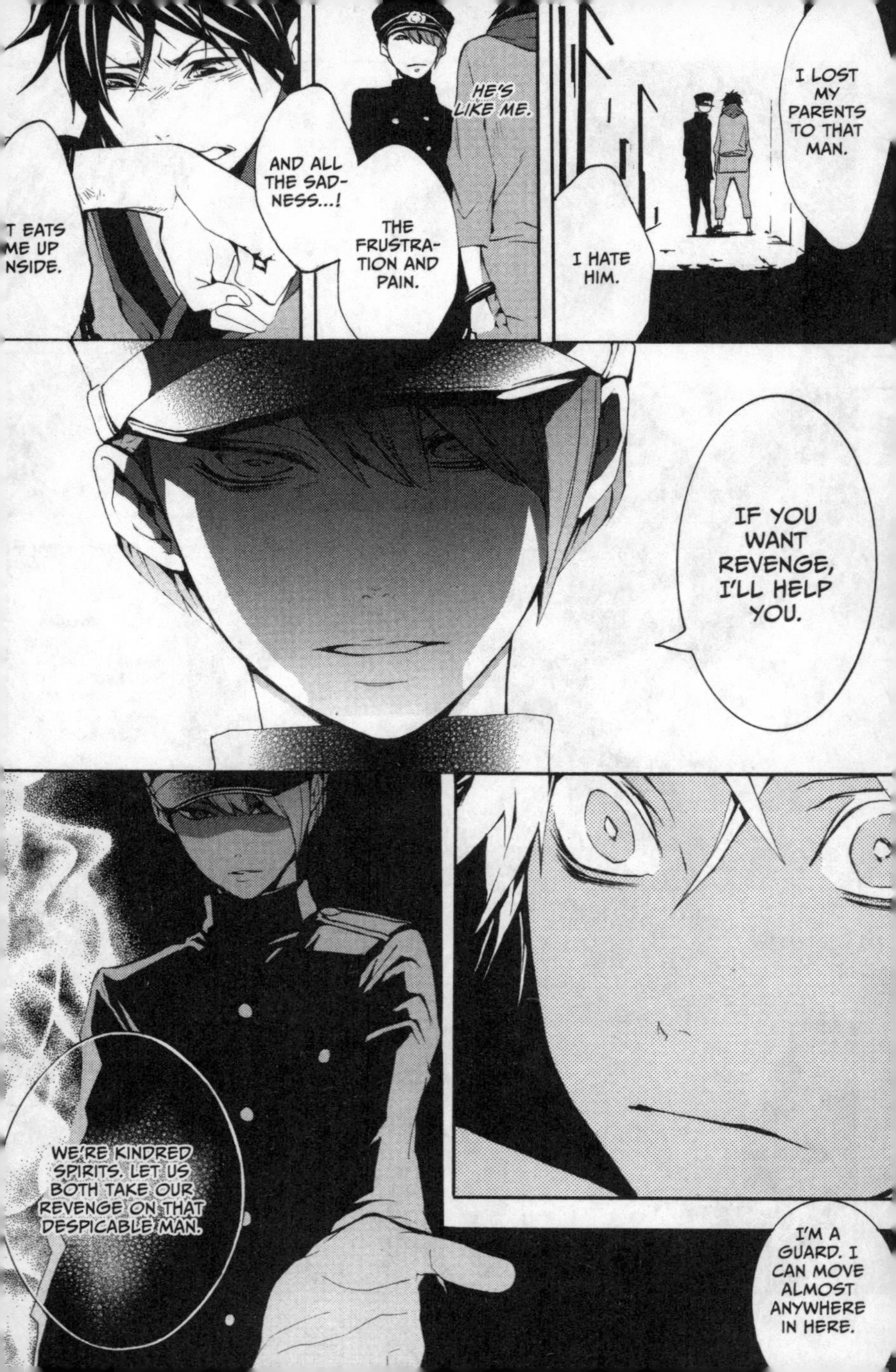
I LOST MY PARENTS TO THAT MAN.
I HATE HIM.
HE'S LIKE ME.
THE FRUSTRATION AND PAIN.
AND ALL THE SADNESS...!
T EATS ME UP NSIDE.
IF YOU WANT REVENGE, I'LL HELP YOU.
I'M A GUARD. I CAN MOVE ALMOST ANYWHERE IN HERE.
WE'RE KINDRED SPIRITS. LET US BOTH TAKE OUR REVENGE ON THAT DESPICABLE MAN.

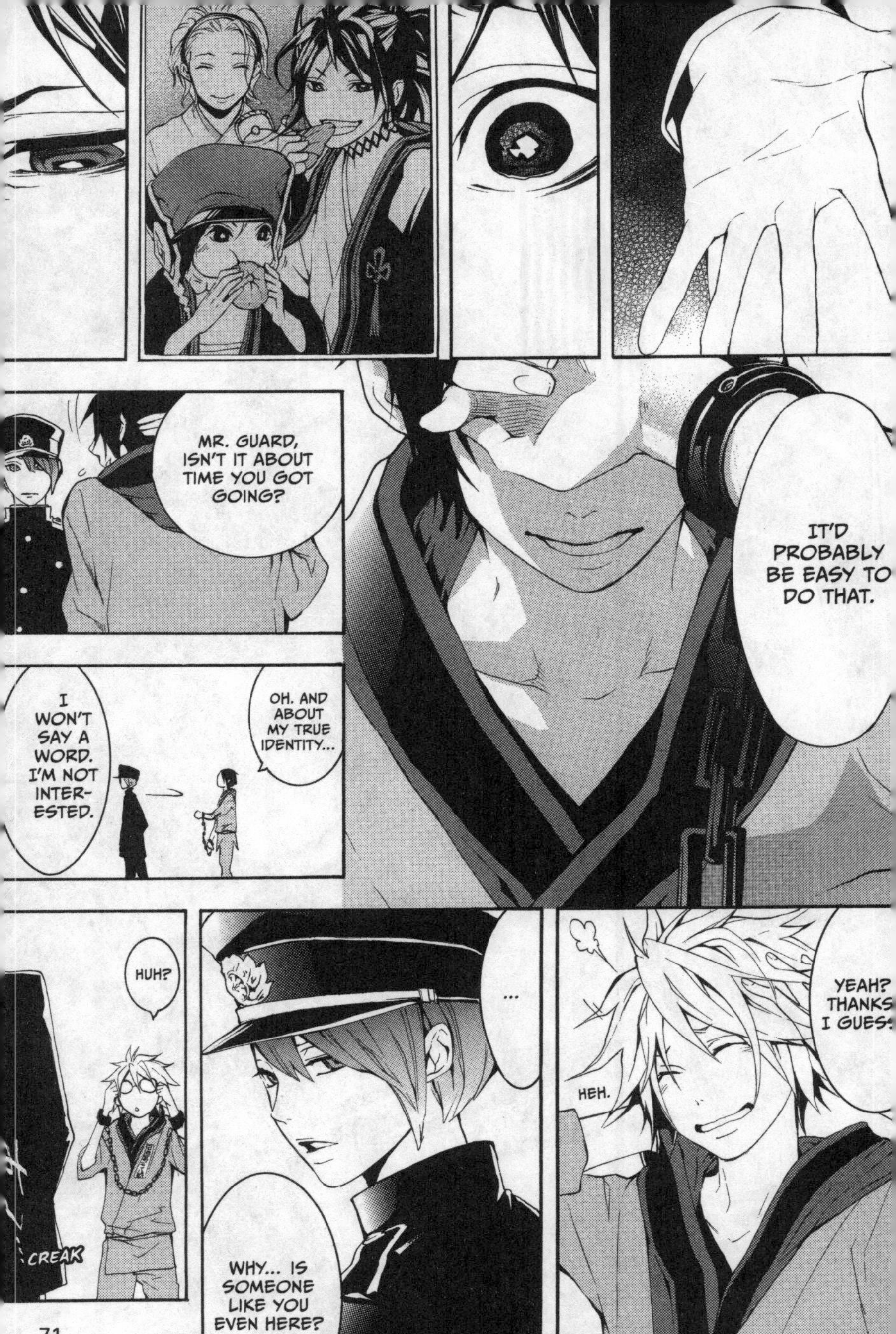
IT'D PROBABLY BE EASY TO DO THAT.
MR. GUARD, ISN'T IT ABOUT TIME YOU GOT GOING?
OH. AND ABOUT MY TRUE IDENTITY...
I WON'T SAY A WORD. I'M NOT INTER- ESTED.
YEAH? THANKS I GUES
HEH.
...
WHY... IS SOMEONE LIKE YOU EVEN HERE?
HUH?
CREAK

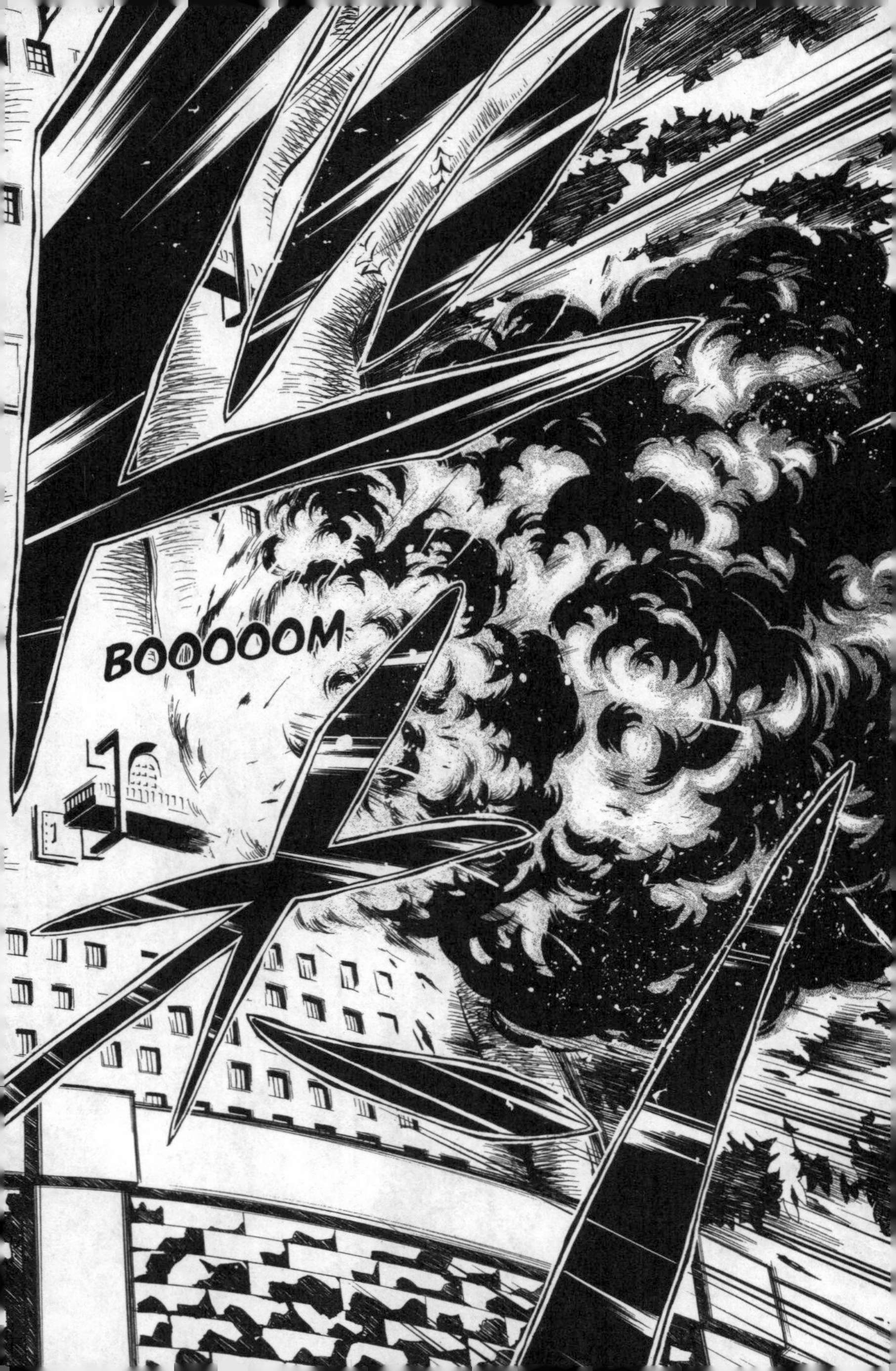
BOOOOOM

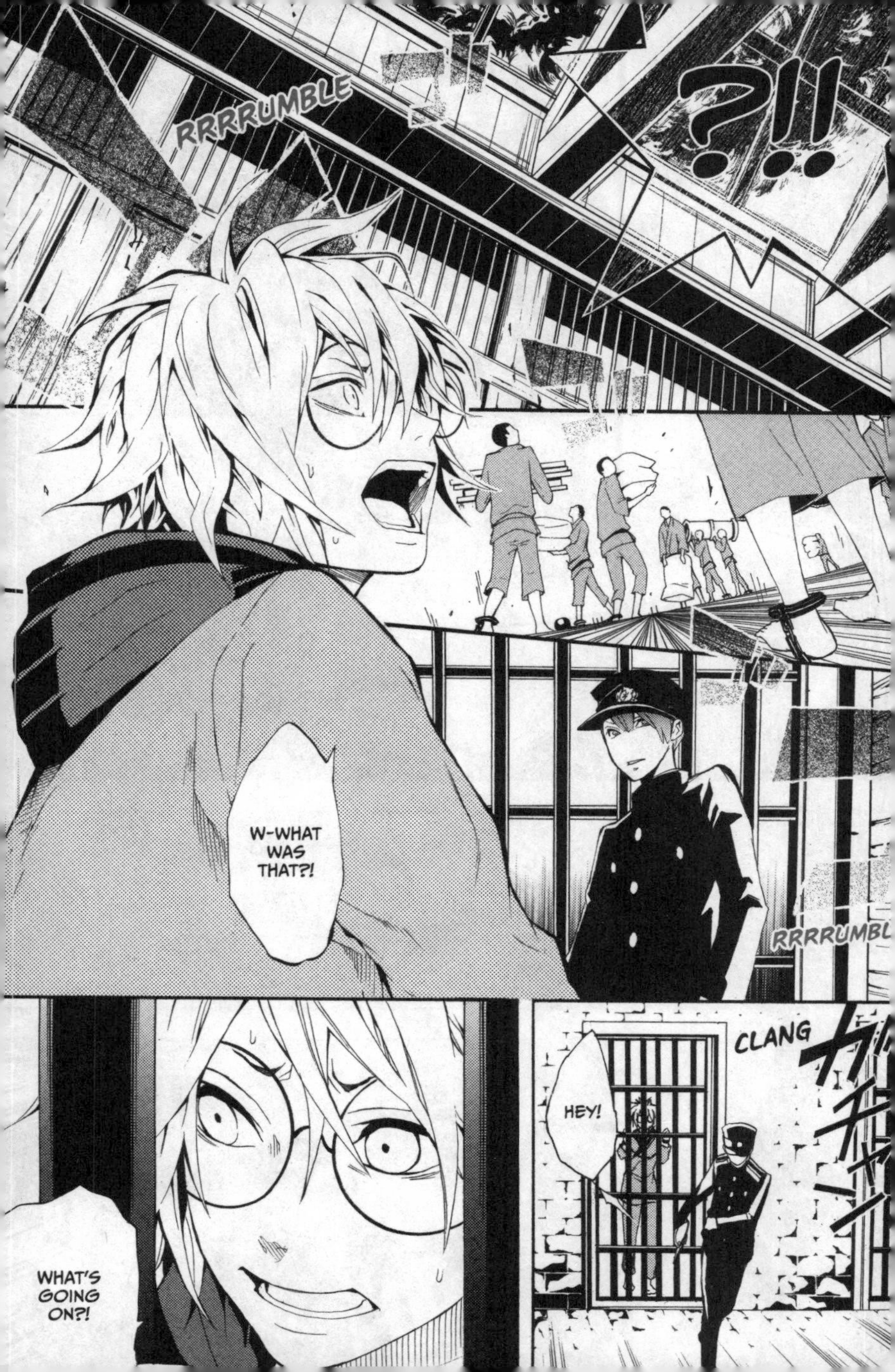
RRRRUMBLE
?!!
W-WHAT WAS THAT?!
RRRRUMBL
CLANG
HEY!
WHAT'S GOING ON?!

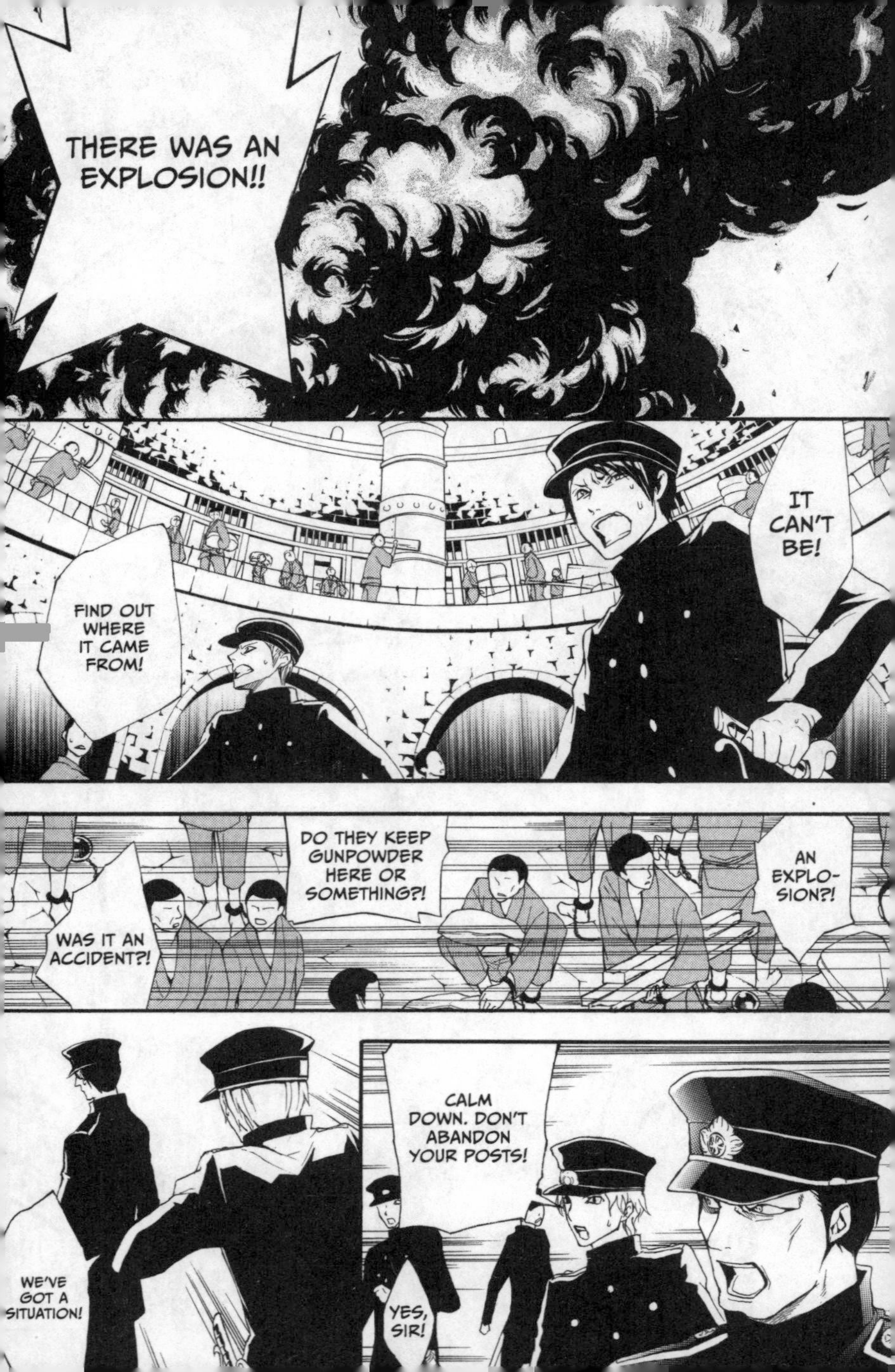
THERE WAS AN EXPLOSION!!
IT CAN'T BE!
FIND OUT WHERE IT CAME FROM!
AN EXPLO-SION?!
DO THEY KEEP GUNPOWDER HERE OR SOMETHING?!
WAS IT AN ACCIDENT?!
CALM DOWN. DON'T ABANDON YOUR POSTS!
YES, SIR!
WE'VE GOT A SITUATION!

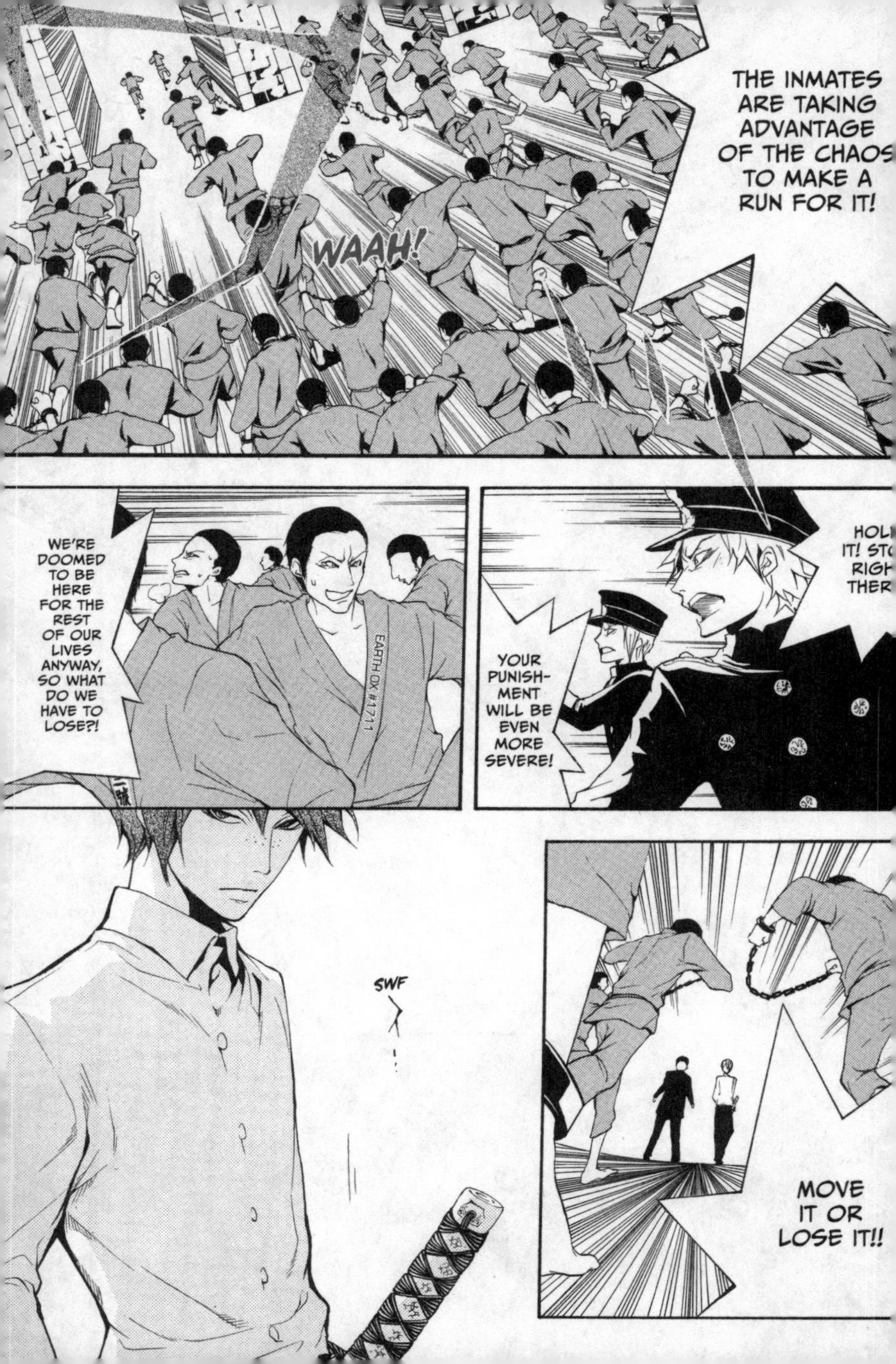
THE INMATES ARE TAKING ADVANTAGE OF THE CHAOS TO MAKE A RUN FOR IT!
WAAH!
HOL IT! STO RIGH THER
YOUR PUNISH-MENT WILL BE EVEN MORE SEVERE!
WE'RE DOOMED TO BE HERE FOR THE REST OF OUR LIVES ANYWAY, SO WHAT DO WE HAVE TO LOSE?!
EARTH OX #1711
MOVE IT OR LOSE IT!!
SWF

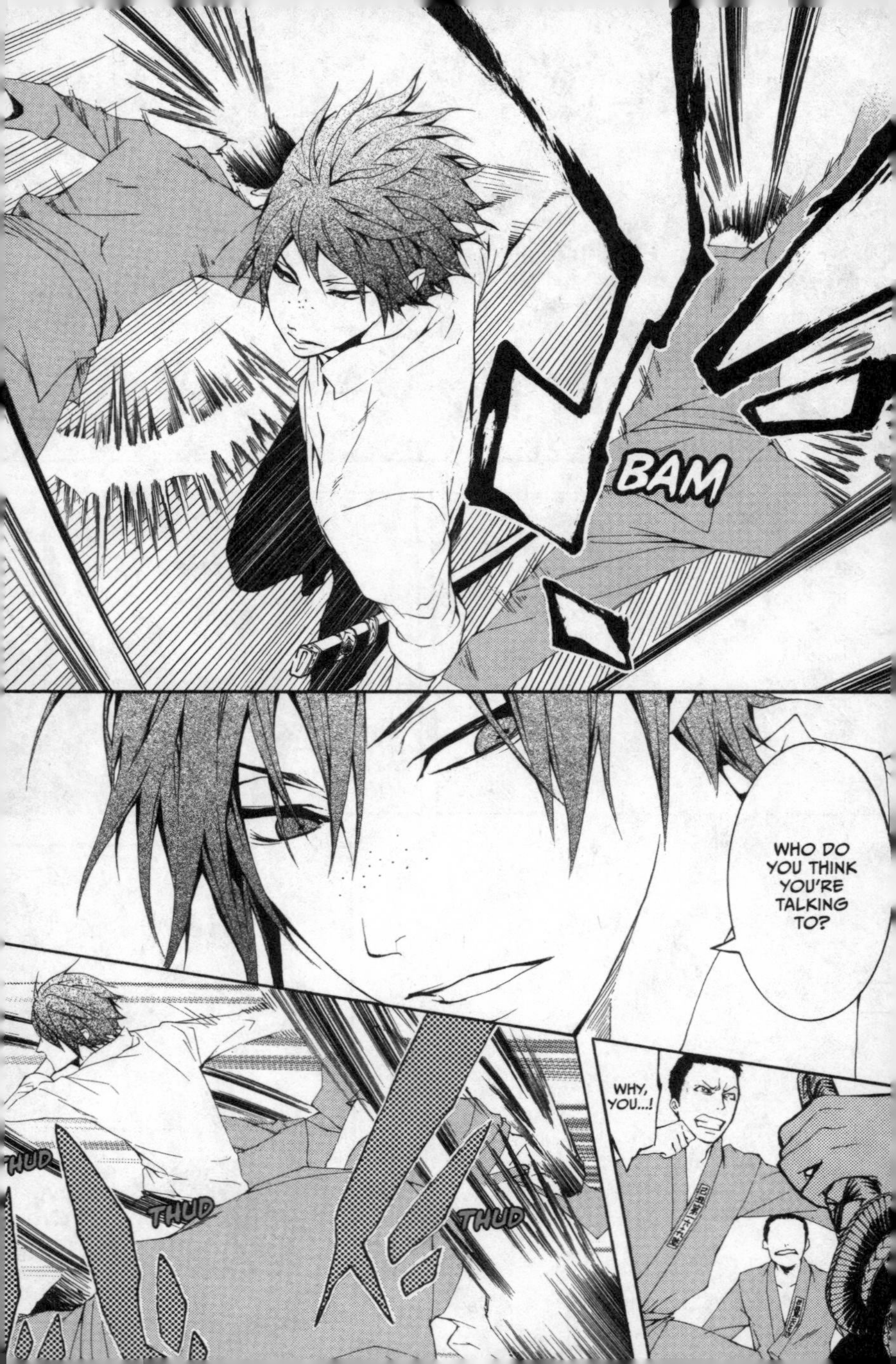
BAM
WHO DO YOU THINK YOU'RE TALKING TO?
WHY, YOU...!
THUD
THUD
THUD

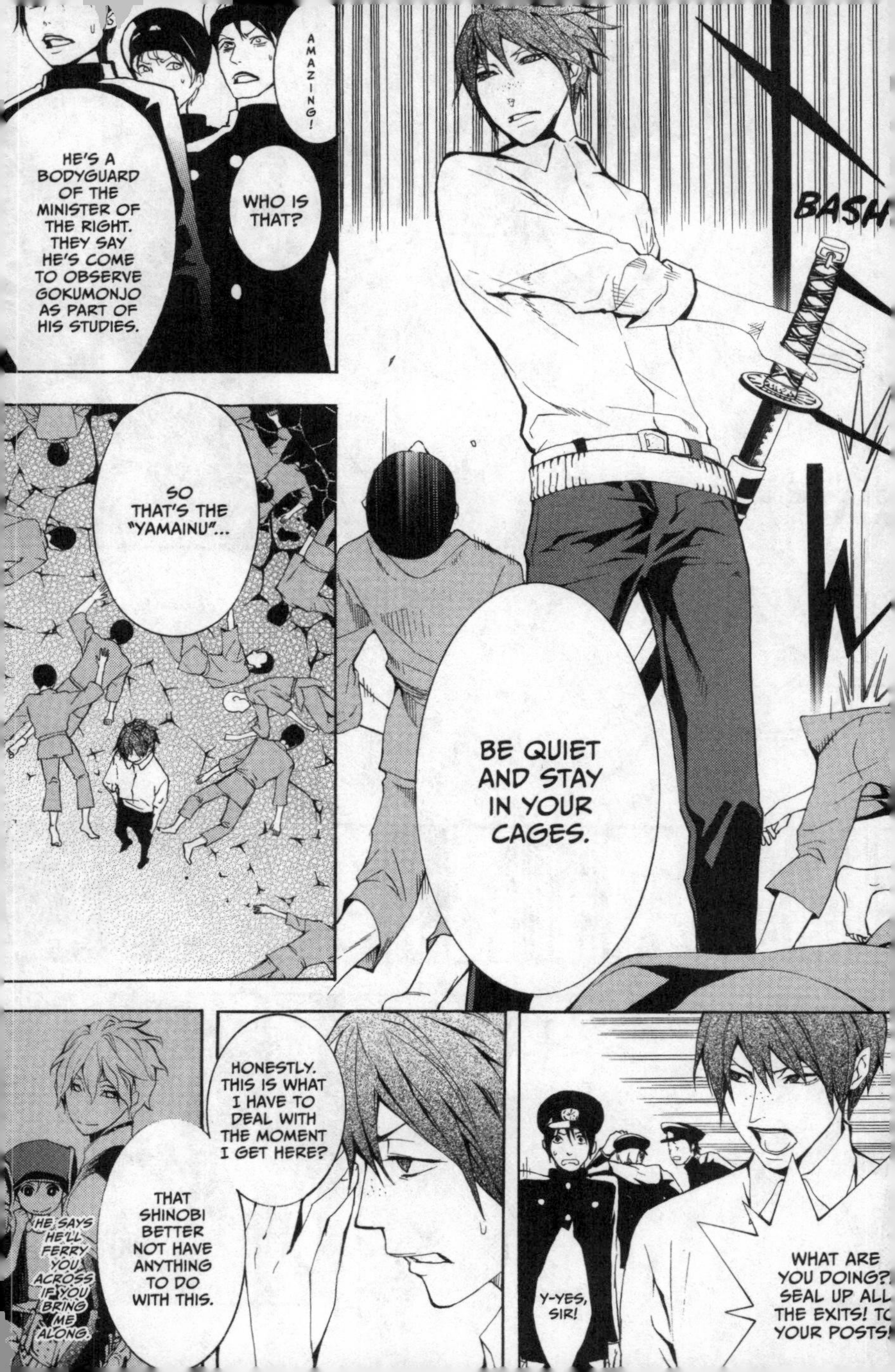
BASH
BE QUIET AND STAY IN YOUR CAGES.
AMAZING!
WHO IS THAT?
HE'S A BODYGUARD OF THE MINISTER OF THE RIGHT. THEY SAY HE'S COME TO OBSERVE GOKUMONJO AS PART OF HIS STUDIES.
SO THAT'S THE "YAMAINU"...
WHAT ARE YOU DOING?! SEAL UP ALL THE EXITS! TO YOUR POSTS!
Y-YES, SIR!
HONESTLY. THIS IS WHAT I HAVE TO DEAL WITH THE MOMENT I GET HERE?
THAT SHINOBI BETTER NOT HAVE ANYTHING TO DO WITH THIS.
HE SAYS HE'LL FERRY YOU ACROSS IF YOU BRING ME ALONG.

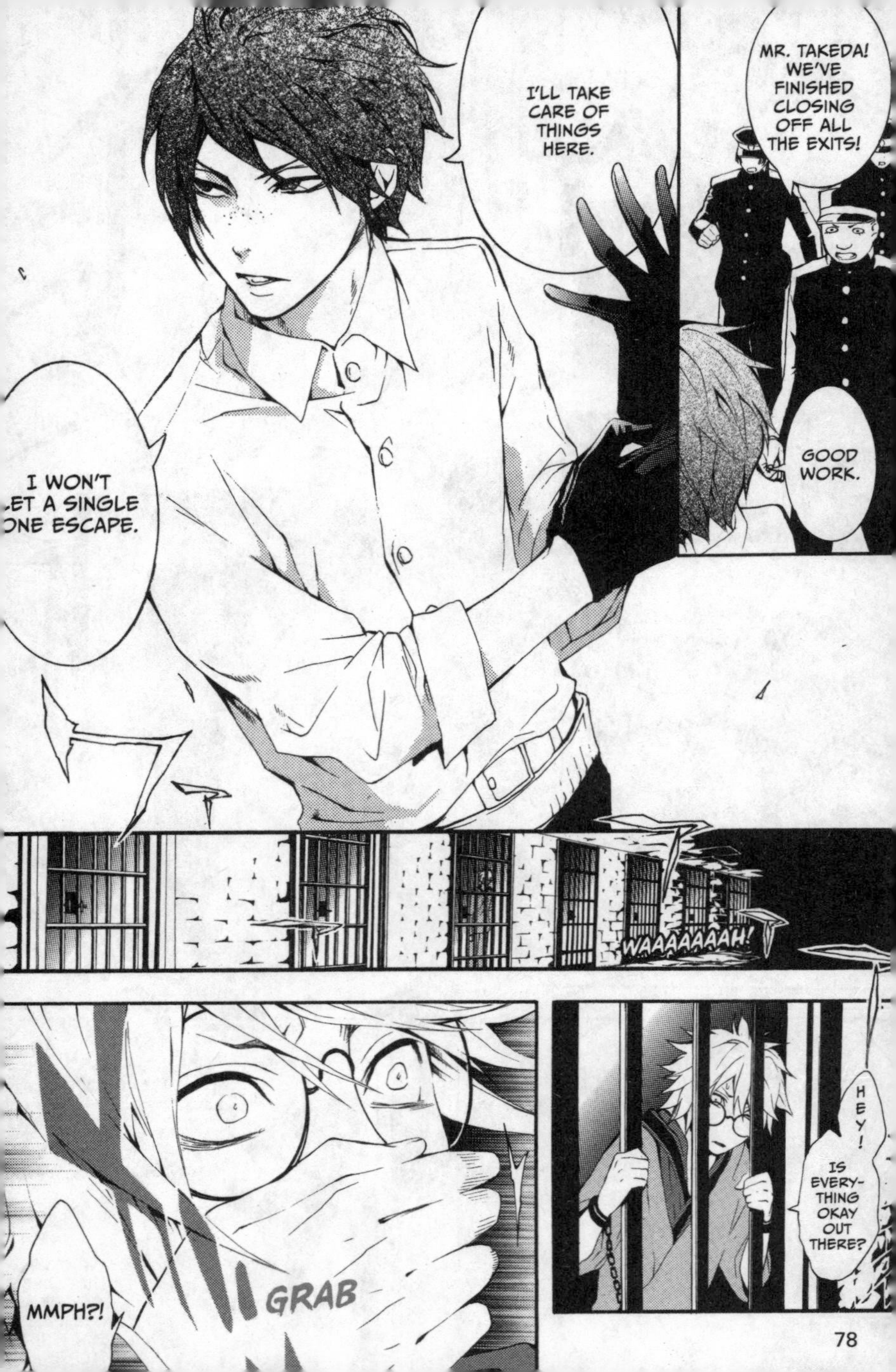
MR. TAKEDA! WE'VE FINISHED CLOSING OFF ALL THE EXITS!
GOOD WORK.
I'LL TAKE CARE OF THINGS HERE.
I WON'T ET A SINGLE ONE ESCAPE.
WAAAAAAAH!
HEY! IS EVERYTHING OKAY OUT THERE?
GRAB
MMPH?!

!

UP YOU GO.

HUH?!

THIS GUY'S...

ME...?

PEOPLE ARE SO HEAVY WHEN THEY'RE UNCONSCIOUS.

SORRY I'M LATE. I'VE COME TO BRING YOU HOME.

SHIRASU!

WHAT ARE YOU DOING HERE?!

HUH?

IT'S A DRUG TO MUDDLE HIS MEMORIES.

WHAT'RE YOU...?

HE WAS DISGUISED AS YOU ON THE WAY OVER, SO IT'S FINE.

...

HERE. GET CHANGED.

DID HE SAY ANYTHING?

YOU KNOW CHUTARO CAN'T TELL A LIE.

MY OLDER BROTHER KNOWS ABOUT THIS, DOESN'T HE?

TELL ME ALL ABOUT IT ONCE WE GET BACK, OKAY?

I DON'T KNOW WHY YOU DID THIS, BUT YOU MUST'VE HAD YOUR REASONS, SORAMARU.

HE RAN OUT OF THE HOUSE INTO THE RAIN HALF NAKED.

CLINK

YIKES...

DAMN IT.

HE'S TREATING ME LIKE A CHILD.

PAT

I'M SORRY...!

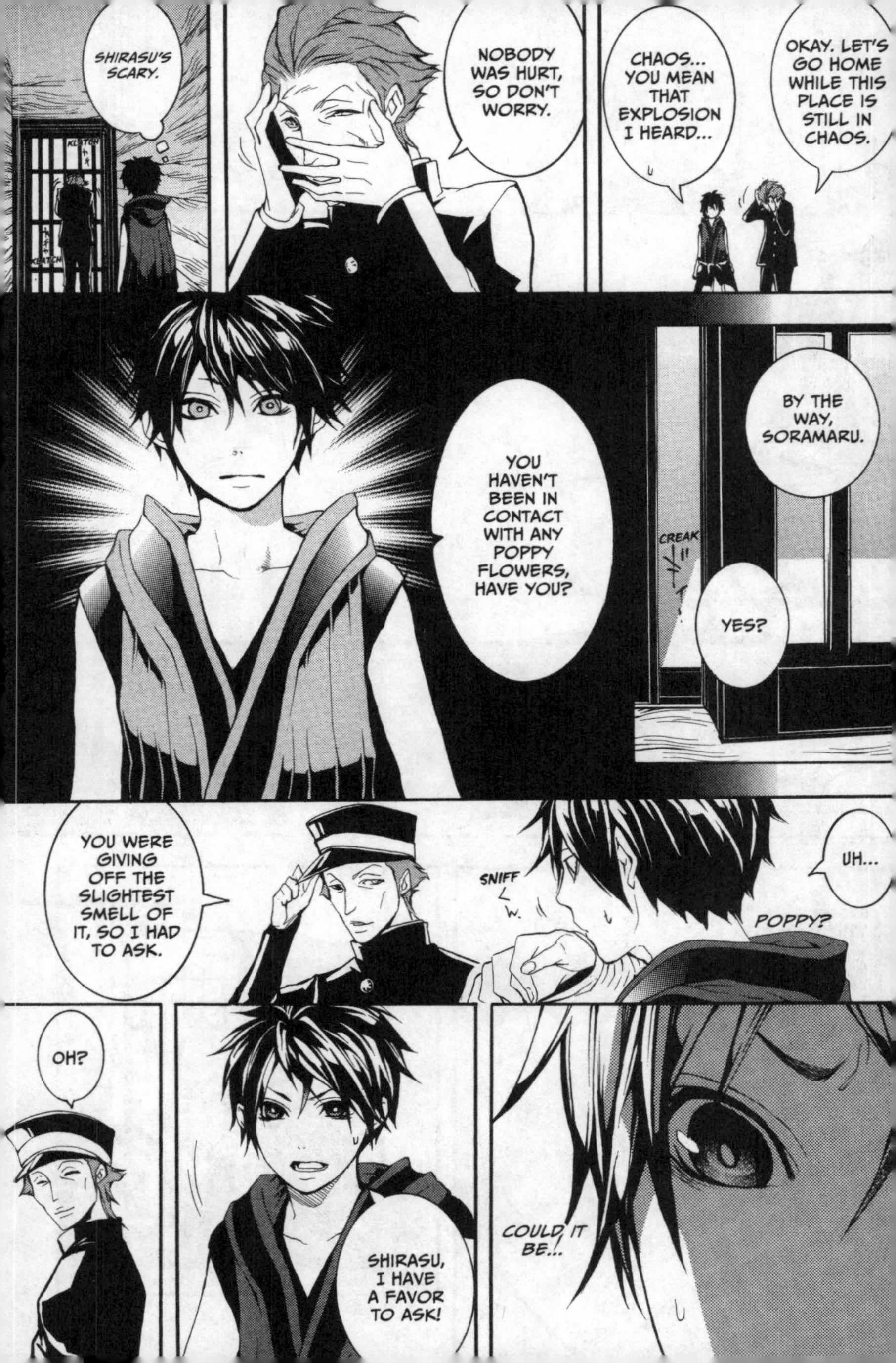
OKAY. LET'S GO HOME WHILE THIS PLACE IS STILL IN CHAOS.
CHAOS... YOU MEAN THAT EXPLOSION I HEARD...
NOBODY WAS HURT, SO DON'T WORRY.
SHIRASU'S SCARY.
BY THE WAY, SORAMARU.
CREAK
YES?
YOU HAVEN'T BEEN IN CONTACT WITH ANY POPPY FLOWERS, HAVE YOU?
UH...
POPPY?
SNIFF
YOU WERE GIVING OFF THE SLIGHTEST SMELL OF IT, SO I HAD TO ASK.
COULD IT BE...!
SHIRASU, I HAVE A FAVOR TO ASK!
OH?

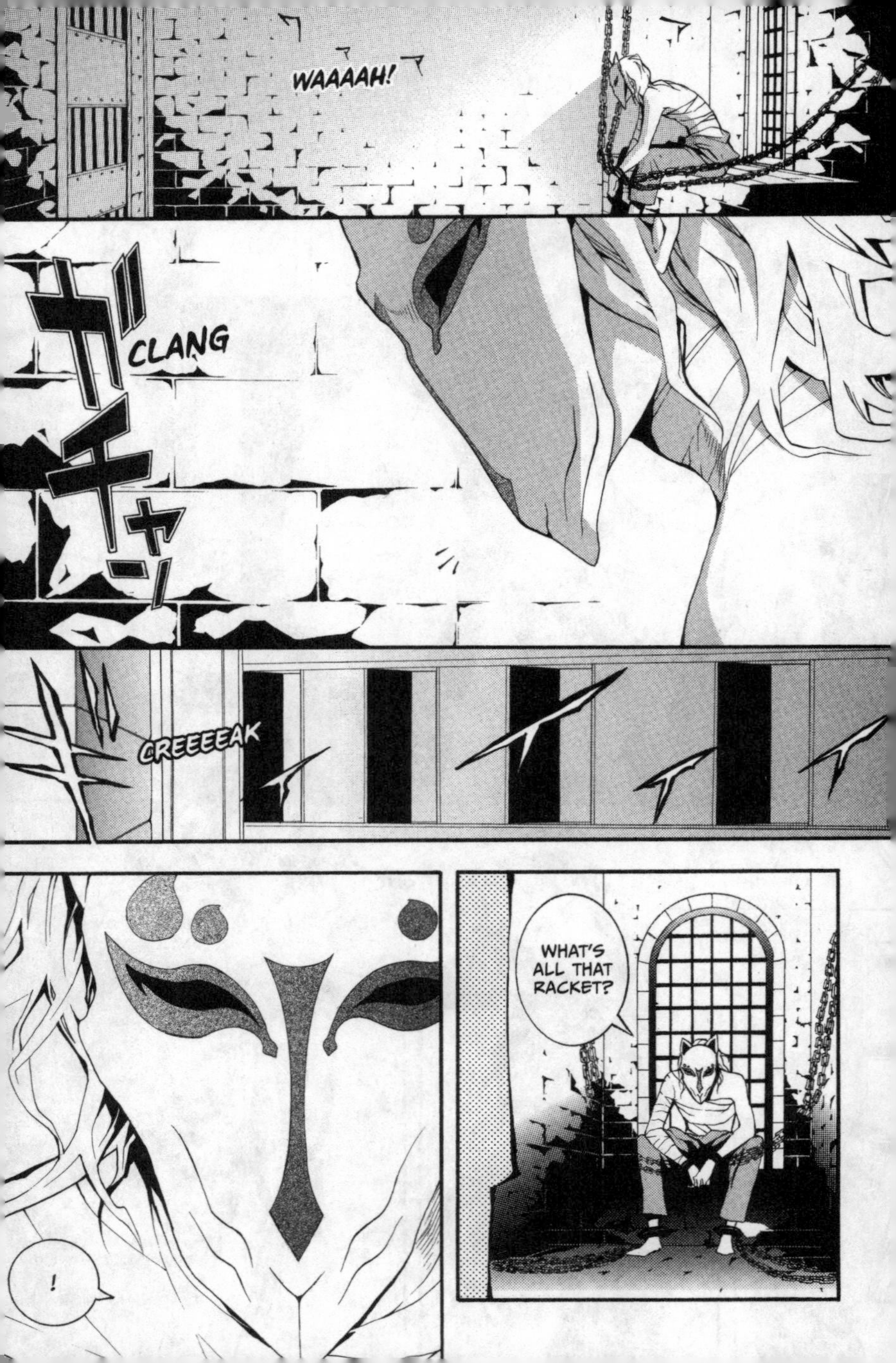
WAAAAH!
ガチャーン
CLANG
CREEEEAK
WHAT'S ALL THAT RACKET?
!

DO YOU REMEMBER WHAT HAPPENED 11 YEARS AGO?

...

THAT DESCRIBES SO MANY SCENARIOS, I CAN'T POSSIBLY REMEMBER WHICH ONE THAT WAS.

I WAS ONLY FIVE WHEN YOU KILLED MY PARENTS.

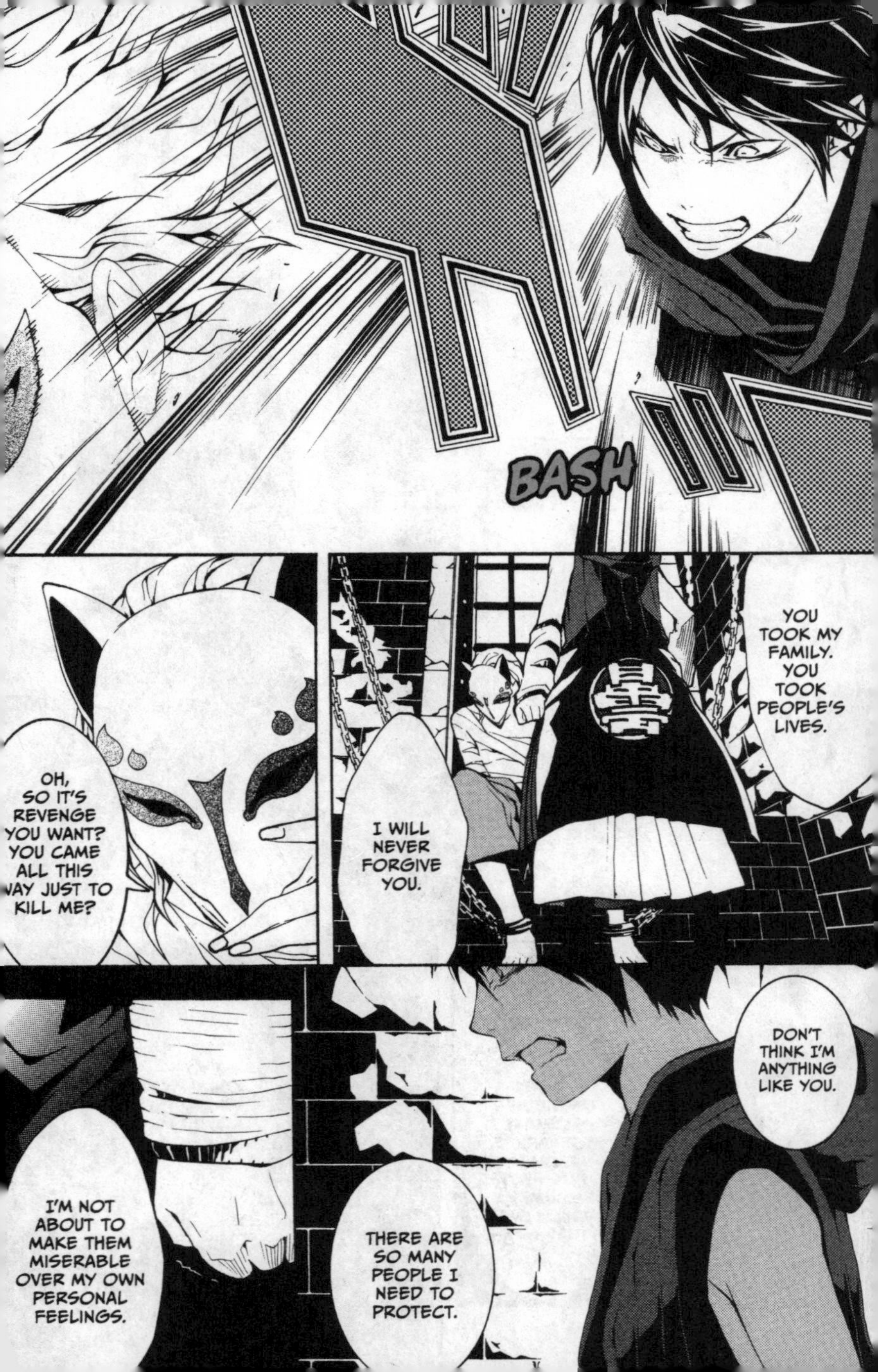
BASH
YOU TOOK MY FAMILY. YOU TOOK PEOPLE'S LIVES.
I WILL NEVER FORGIVE YOU.
OH, SO IT'S REVENGE YOU WANT? YOU CAME ALL THIS WAY JUST TO KILL ME?
DON'T THINK I'M ANYTHING LIKE YOU.
THERE ARE SO MANY PEOPLE I NEED TO PROTECT.
I'M NOT ABOUT TO MAKE THEM MISERABLE OVER MY OWN PERSONAL FEELINGS.

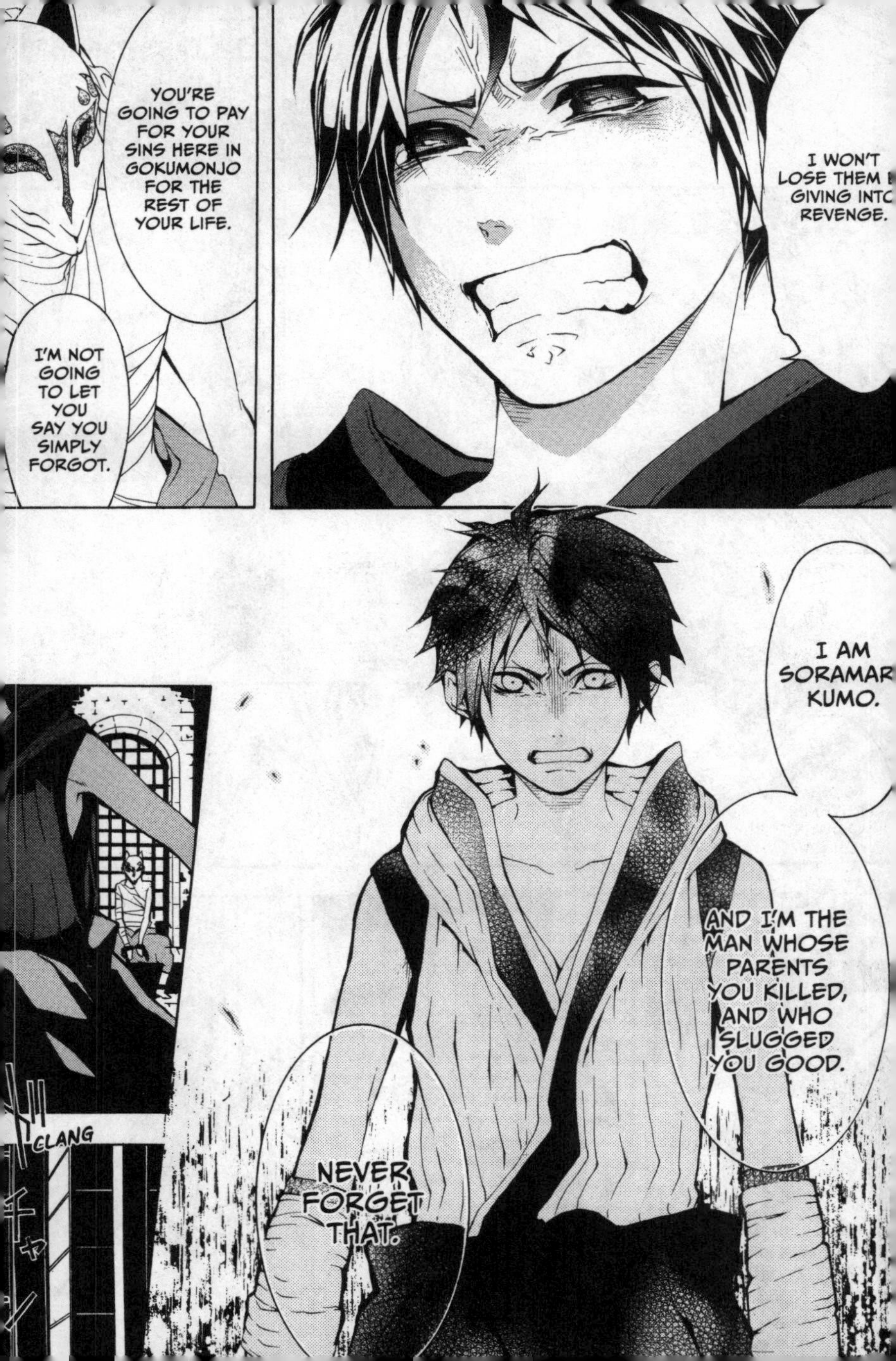
I WON'T LOSE THEM GIVING INTO REVENGE.
YOU'RE GOING TO PAY FOR YOUR SINS HERE IN GOKUMONJO FOR THE REST OF YOUR LIFE.
I'M NOT GOING TO LET YOU SAY YOU SIMPLY FORGOT.
I AM SORAMAR KUMO.
AND I'M THE MAN WHOSE PARENTS YOU KILLED, AND WHO SLUGGED YOU GOOD.
CLANG
NEVER FORGET THAT.

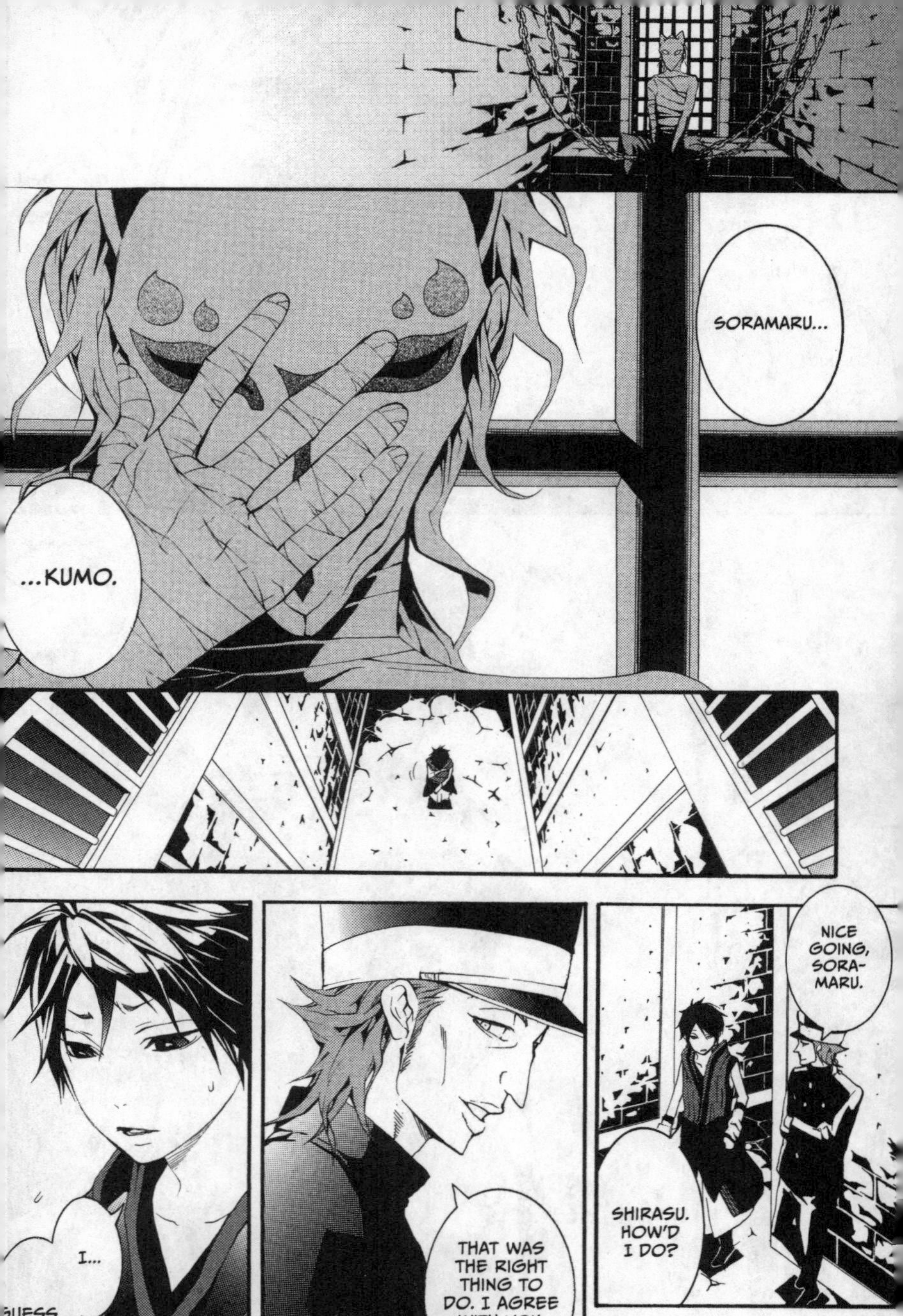
SORAMARU...
...KUMO.
NICE GOING, SORA-MARU.
SHIRASU. HOW'D I DO?
THAT WAS THE RIGHT THING TO DO. I AGREE WITH YOU.
I...
GUESS...

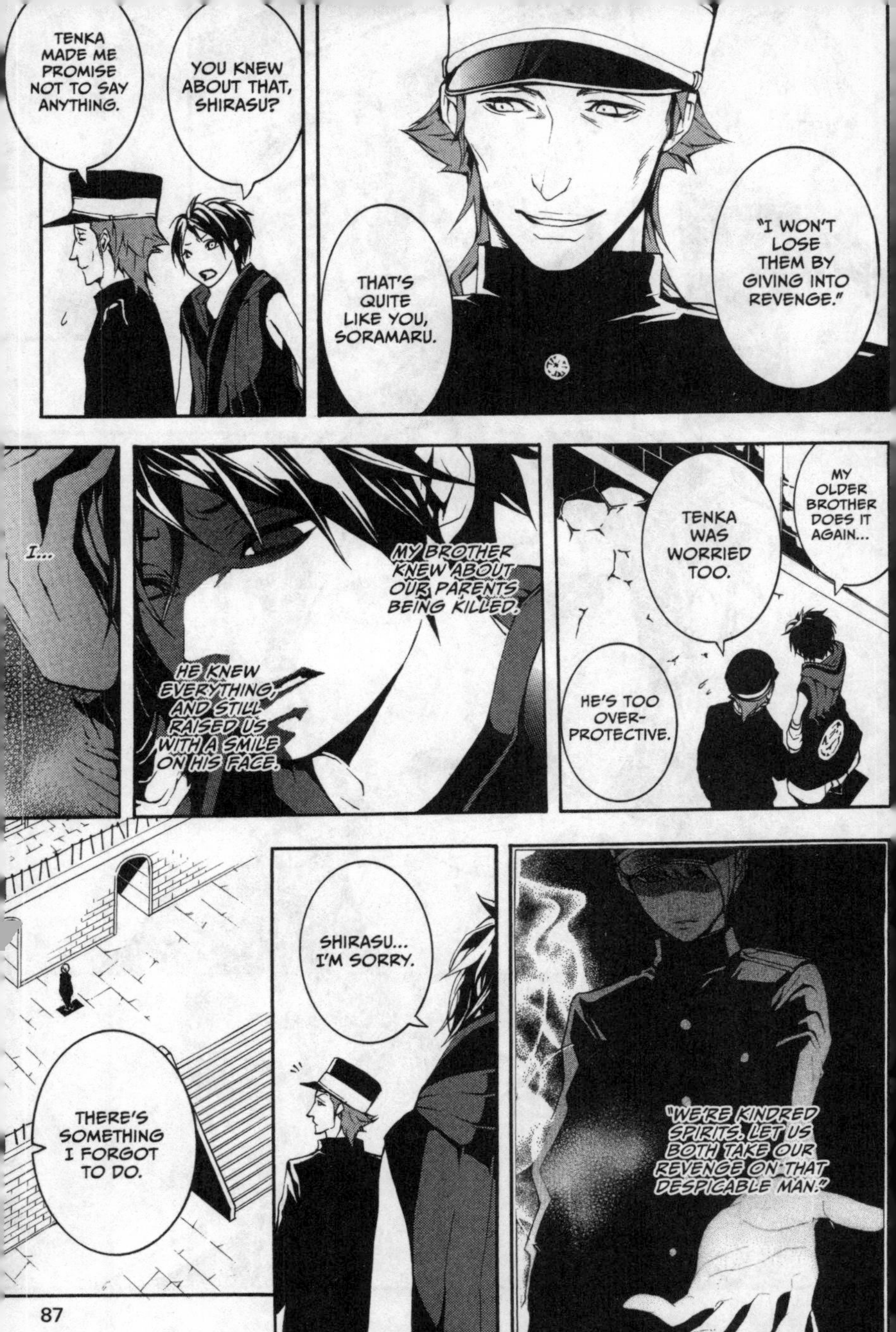
"I WON'T LOSE THEM BY GIVING INTO REVENGE."
THAT'S QUITE LIKE YOU, SORAMARU.
YOU KNEW ABOUT THAT, SHIRASU?
TENKA MADE ME PROMISE NOT TO SAY ANYTHING.
MY OLDER BROTHER DOES IT AGAIN...
TENKA WAS WORRIED TOO.
HE'S TOO OVER-PROTECTIVE.
MY BROTHER KNEW ABOUT OUR PARENTS BEING KILLED.
HE KNEW EVERYTHING, AND STILL RAISED US WITH A SMILE ON HIS FACE.
I...
"WE'RE KINDRED SPIRITS. LET US BOTH TAKE OUR REVENGE ON THAT DESPICABLE MAN."
SHIRASU... I'M SORRY.
THERE'S SOMETHING I FORGOT TO DO.

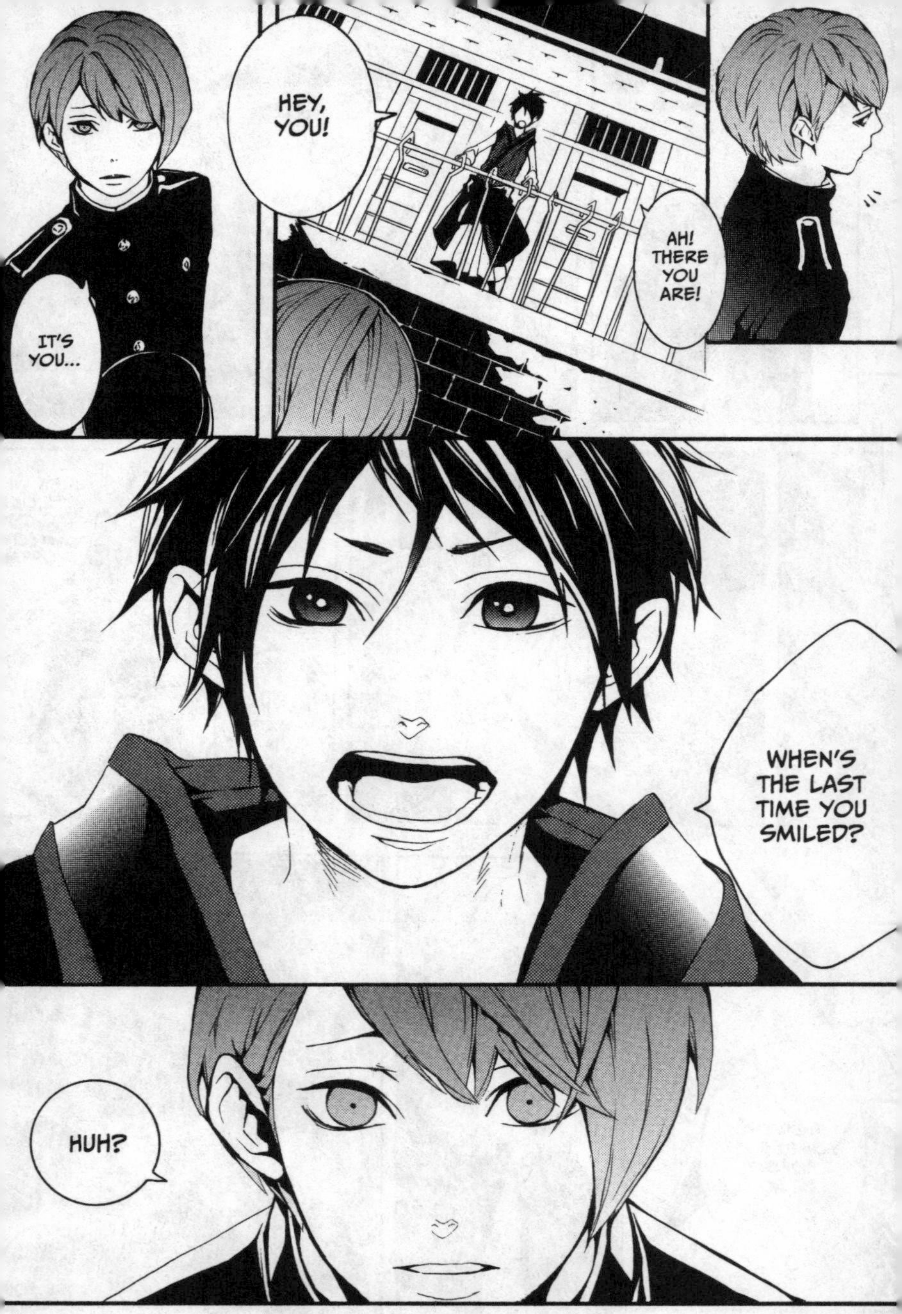
HEY, YOU!
AH! THERE YOU ARE!
IT'S YOU...
WHEN'S THE LAST TIME YOU SMILED?
HUH?

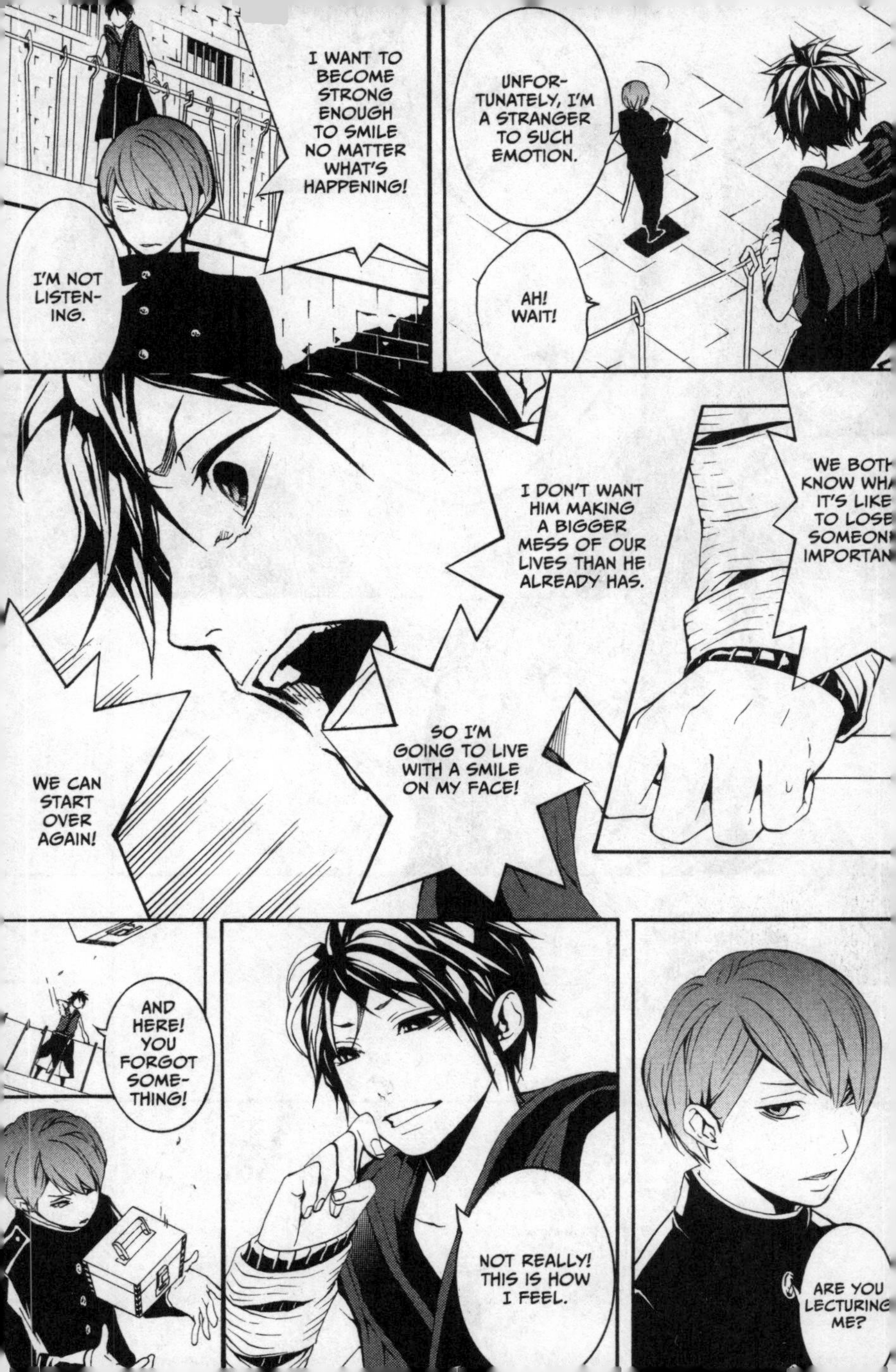
UNFORTUNATELY, I'M A STRANGER TO SUCH EMOTION.
AH! WAIT!
I WANT TO BECOME STRONG ENOUGH TO SMILE NO MATTER WHAT'S HAPPENING!
I'M NOT LISTENING.
WE BOTH KNOW WHA IT'S LIKE TO LOSE SOMEON IMPORTAN
I DON'T WANT HIM MAKING A BIGGER MESS OF OUR LIVES THAN HE ALREADY HAS.
SO I'M GOING TO LIVE WITH A SMILE ON MY FACE!
WE CAN START OVER AGAIN!
ARE YOU LECTURING ME?
NOT REALLY! THIS IS HOW I FEEL.
AND HERE! YOU FORGOT SOMETHING!

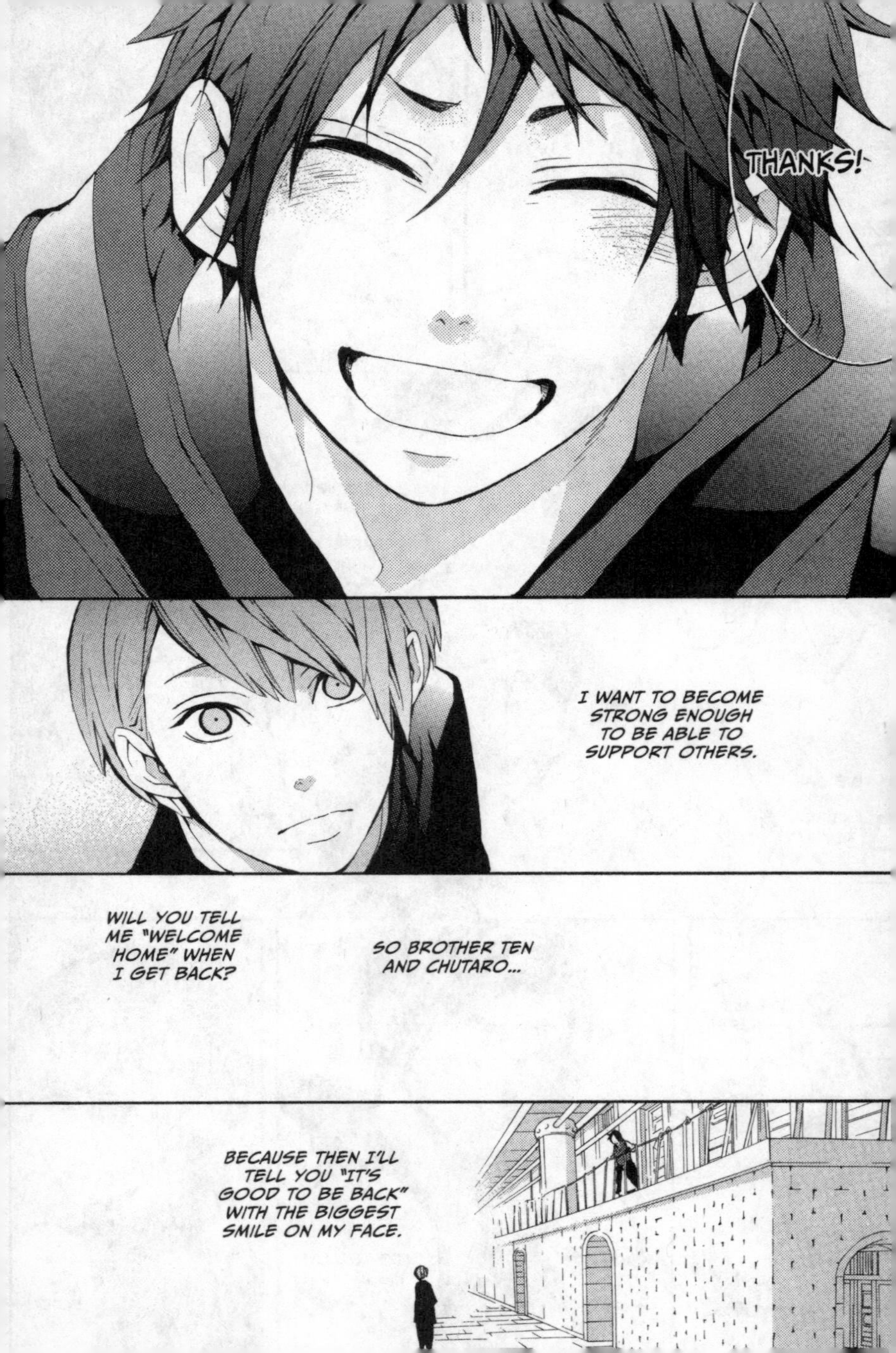
THANKS!
I WANT TO BECOME STRONG ENOUGH TO BE ABLE TO SUPPORT OTHERS.
SO BROTHER TEN AND CHUTARO...
WILL YOU TELL ME "WELCOME HOME" WHEN I GET BACK?
BECAUSE THEN I'LL TELL YOU "IT'S GOOD TO BE BACK" WITH THE BIGGEST SMILE ON MY FACE.

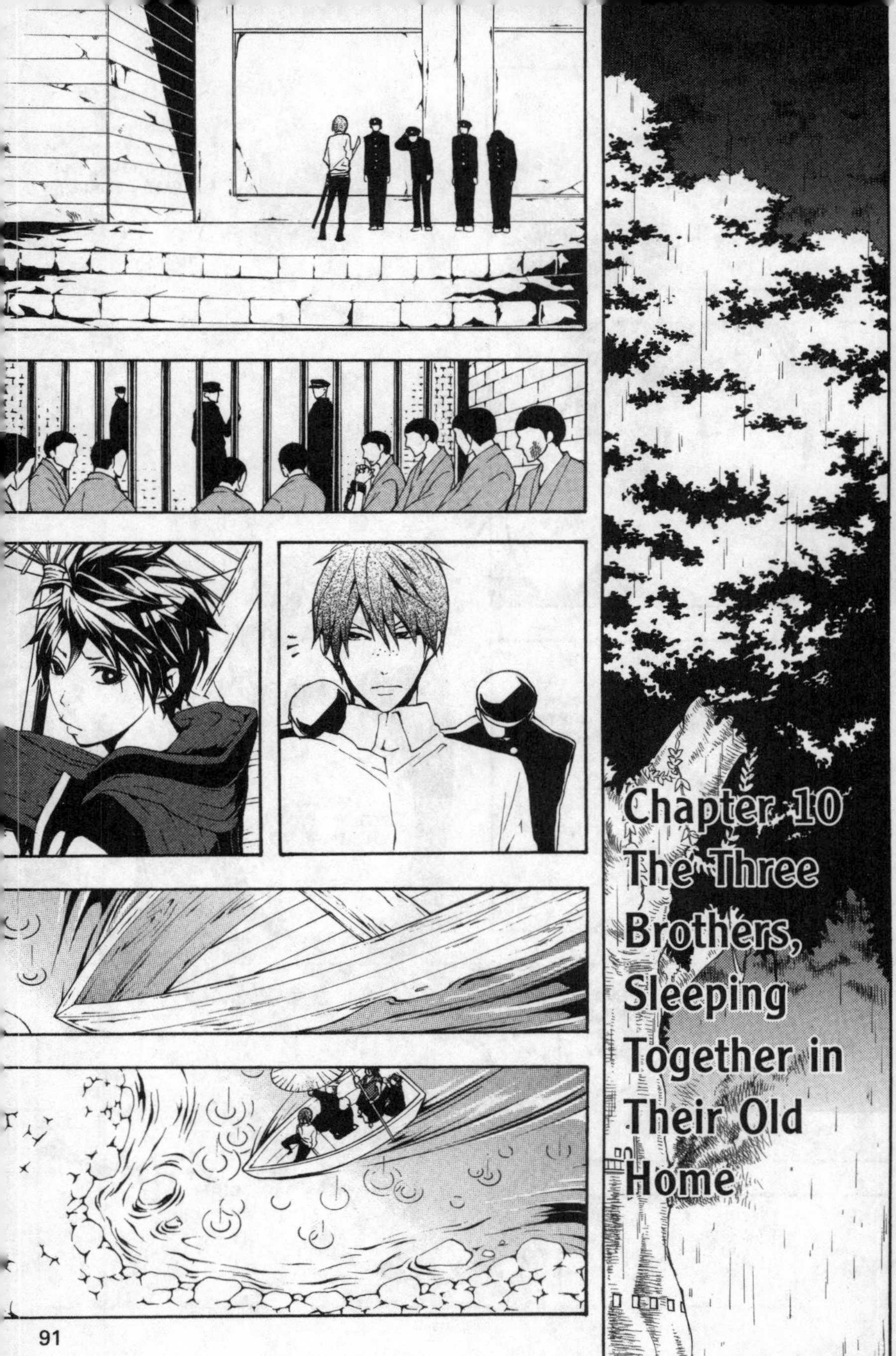
Chapter 10
The Three Brothers, Sleeping Together in Their Old Home

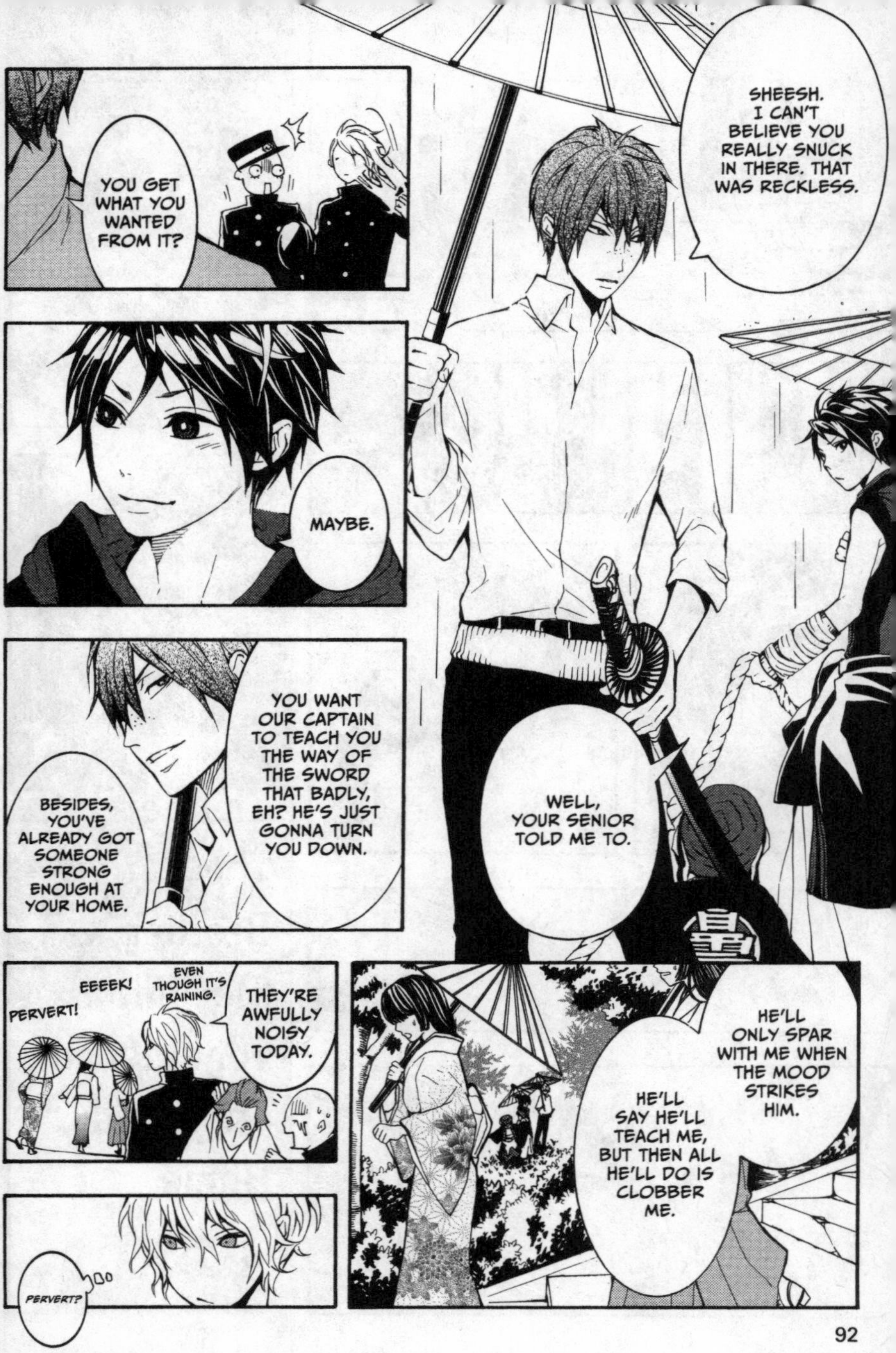

SHEESH. I CAN'T BELIEVE YOU REALLY SNUCK IN THERE. THAT WAS RECKLESS.
WELL, YOUR SENIOR TOLD ME TO.
YOU GET WHAT YOU WANTED FROM IT?
MAYBE.
YOU WANT OUR CAPTAIN TO TEACH YOU THE WAY OF THE SWORD THAT BADLY, EH? HE'S JUST GONNA TURN YOU DOWN.
BESIDES, YOU'VE ALREADY GOT SOMEONE STRONG ENOUGH AT YOUR HOME.
HE'LL ONLY SPAR WITH ME WHEN THE MOOD STRIKES HIM.
HE'LL SAY HE'LL TEACH ME, BUT THEN ALL HE'LL DO IS CLOBBER ME.
THEY'RE AWFULLY NOISY TODAY.
EVEN THOUGH IT'S RAINING.
EEEEK!
PERVERT!
PERVERT?

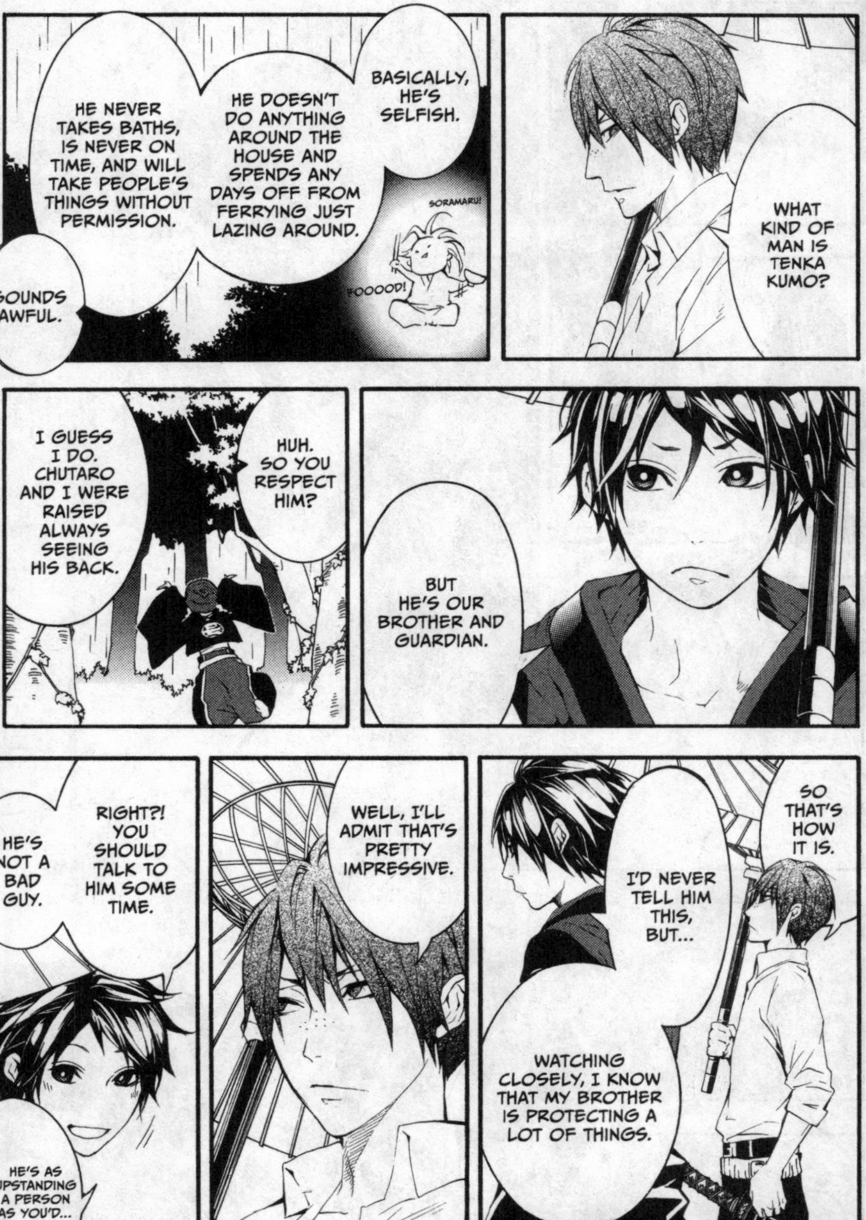
WHAT KIND OF MAN IS TENKA KUMO?
BASICALLY, HE'S SELFISH.
HE DOESN'T DO ANYTHING AROUND THE HOUSE AND SPENDS ANY DAYS OFF FROM FERRYING JUST LAZING AROUND.
HE NEVER TAKES BATHS, IS NEVER ON TIME, AND WILL TAKE PEOPLE'S THINGS WITHOUT PERMISSION.
SORAMARU!
FOOOOD!
SOUNDS AWFUL.
BUT HE'S OUR BROTHER AND GUARDIAN.
HUH. SO YOU RESPECT HIM?
I GUESS I DO. CHUTARO AND I WERE RAISED ALWAYS SEEING HIS BACK.
SO THAT'S HOW IT IS.
I'D NEVER TELL HIM THIS, BUT...
WATCHING CLOSELY, I KNOW THAT MY BROTHER IS PROTECTING A LOT OF THINGS.
WELL, I'LL ADMIT THAT'S PRETTY IMPRESSIVE.
RIGHT?! YOU SHOULD TALK TO HIM SOME TIME.
HE'S NOT A BAD GUY.
HE'S AS UPSTANDING A PERSON AS YOU'D...

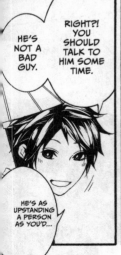

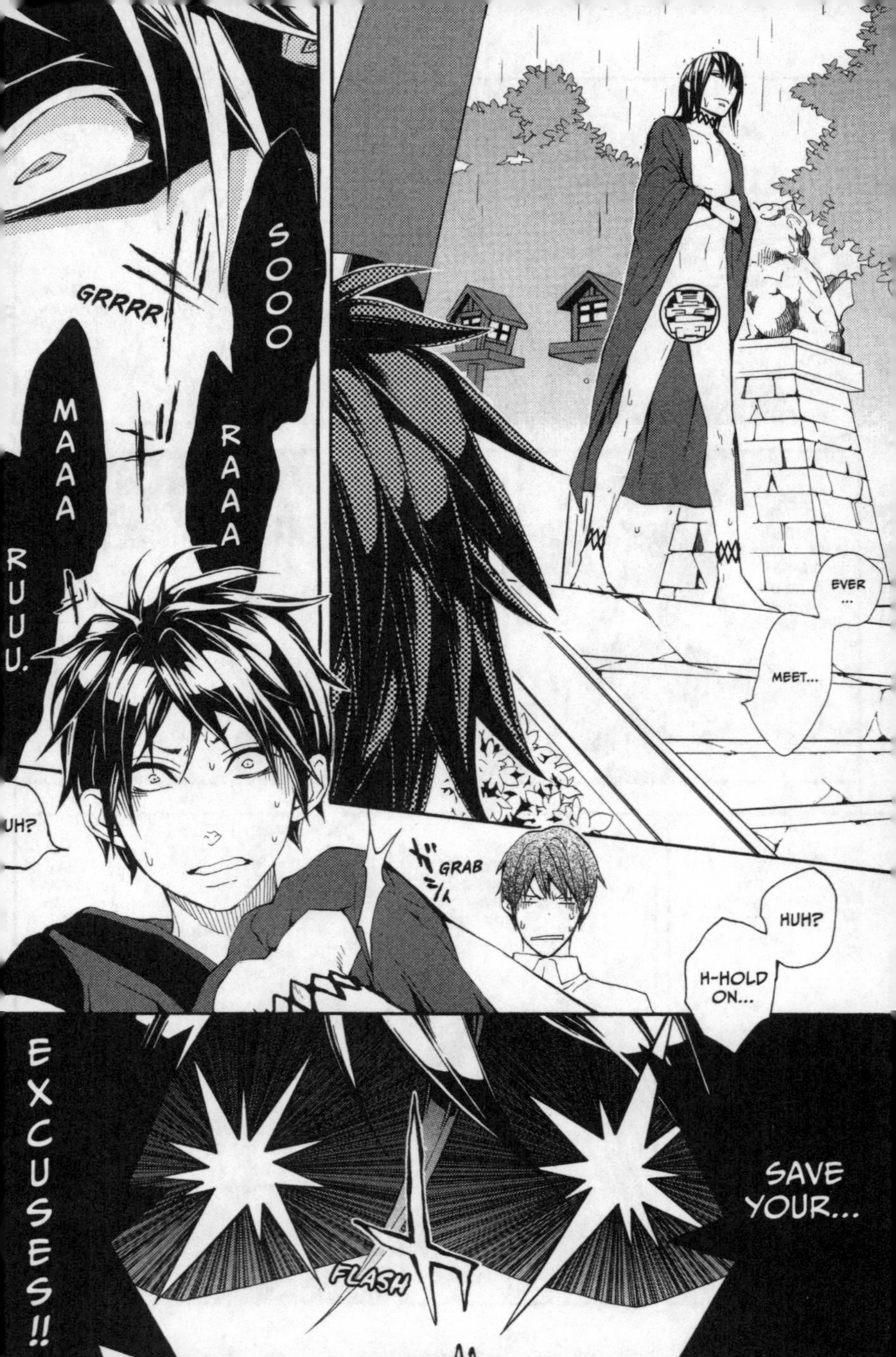
EVER...
MEET...
GRRRR
SOOO RAAAA
MAAA RUUU.
HUH?
H-HOLD ON...
GRAB
UH?
SAVE YOUR...
FLASH
EXCUSES!!

RRRUMBLE

MURMUR

MURMUR

MURMUR

ONLY IF SORAMARU NEVER LEAVES HOME LIKE THAT AGAIN.

PLEASE DON'T DO THAT ANYMORE.

I'M REALLY VERY SORRY!!

IT'S SORAMARU'S FAULT.

I'M SORRY. I'M SO SORRY.

I WAS TOLD THERE WAS A CREEP ABOUT, BUT IT WAS JUST TENKA. THAT WAS QUITE THE SHOCK.

BROTHER! HOW COULD YOU TROUBLE EVERYBODY LIKE THAT?!

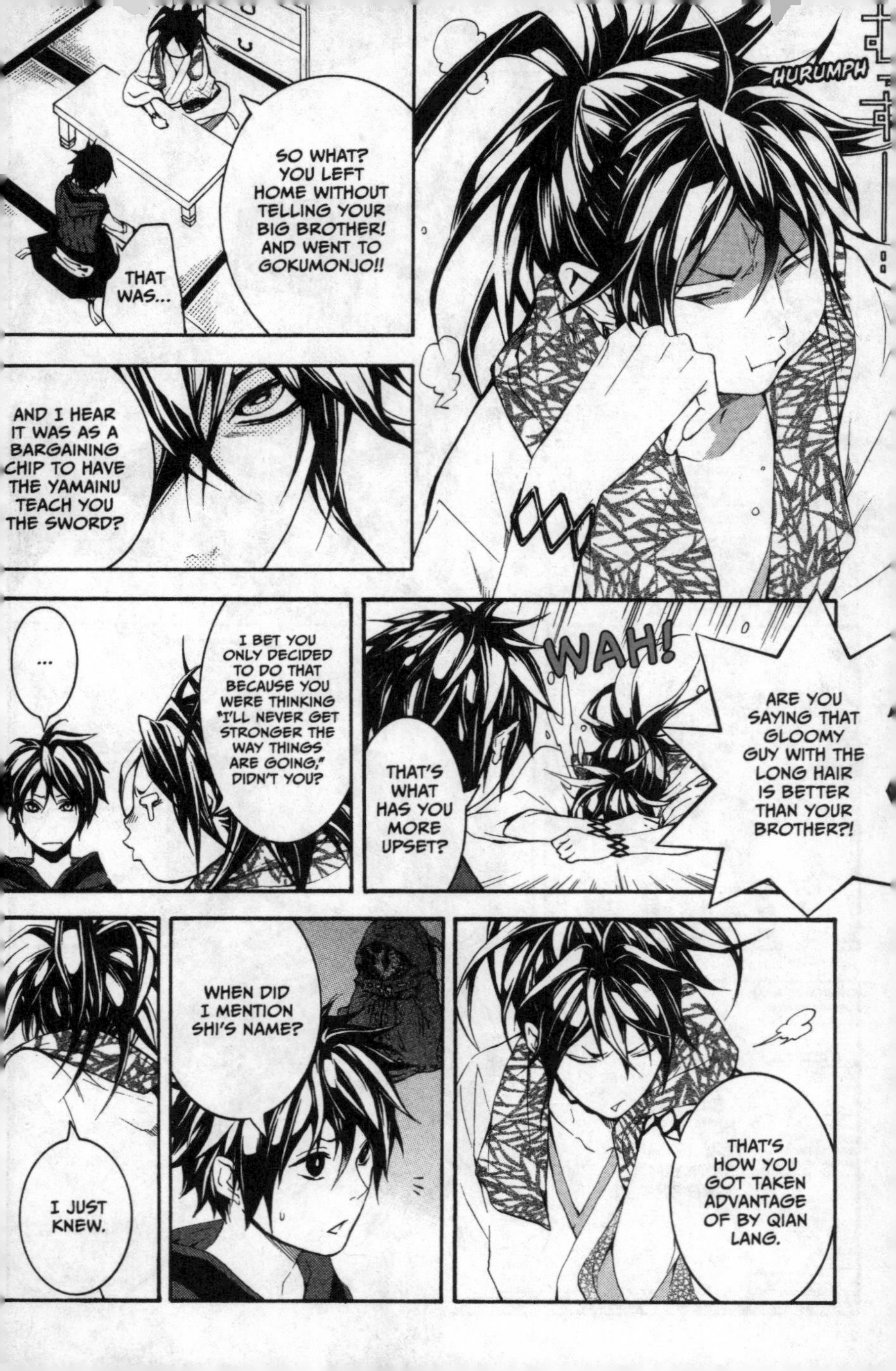
HURUMPH
SO WHAT? YOU LEFT HOME WITHOUT TELLING YOUR BIG BROTHER! AND WENT TO GOKUMONJO!!
THAT WAS...
AND I HEAR IT WAS AS A BARGAINING CHIP TO HAVE THE YAMAINU TEACH YOU THE SWORD?
WAH!
ARE YOU SAYING THAT GLOOMY GUY WITH THE LONG HAIR IS BETTER THAN YOUR BROTHER?!
THAT'S WHAT HAS YOU MORE UPSET?
I BET YOU ONLY DECIDED TO DO THAT BECAUSE YOU WERE THINKING "I'LL NEVER GET STRONGER THE WAY THINGS ARE GOING," DIDN'T YOU?
...
THAT'S HOW YOU GOT TAKEN ADVANTAGE OF BY QIAN LANG.
WHEN DID I MENTION SHI'S NAME?
I JUST KNEW.

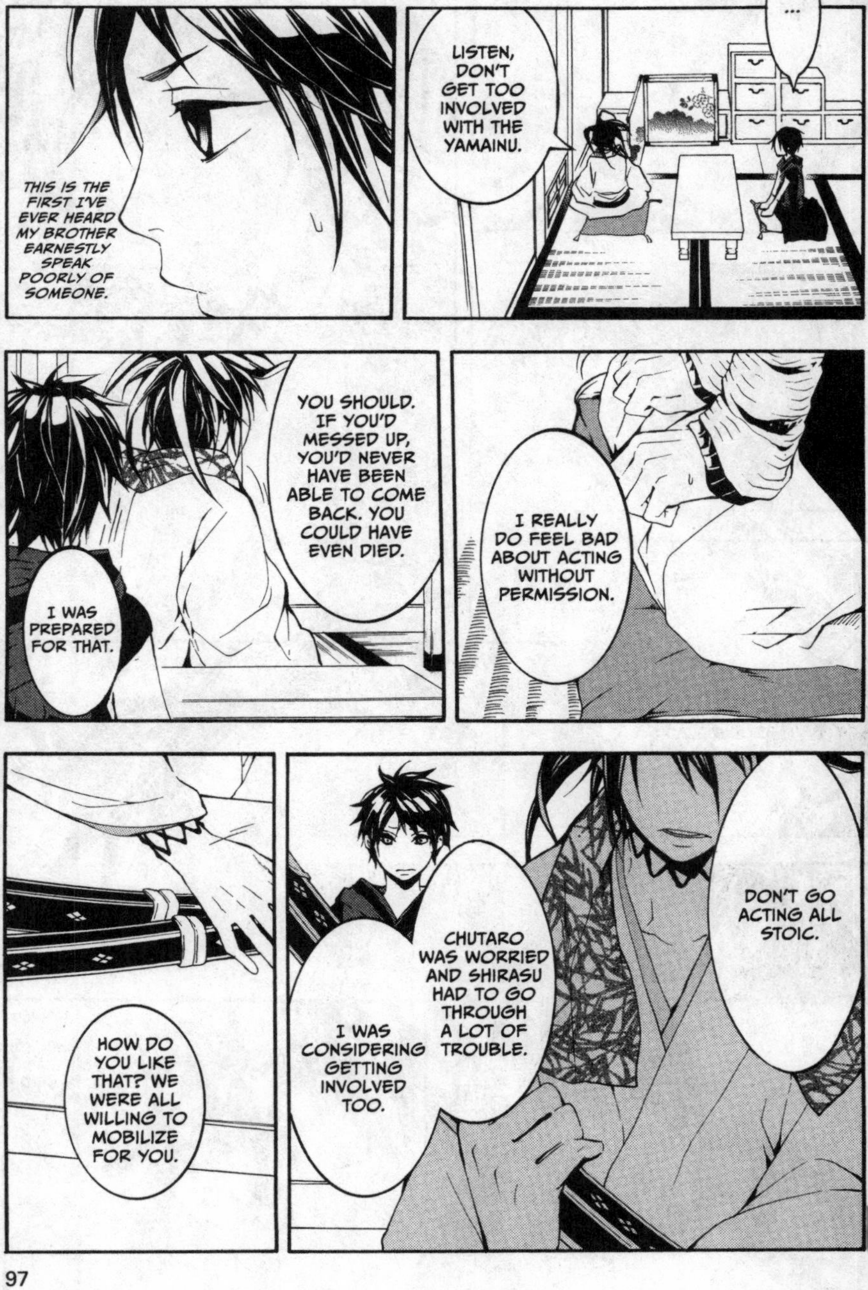
...
LISTEN, DON'T GET TOO INVOLVED WITH THE YAMAINU.
THIS IS THE FIRST I'VE EVER HEARD MY BROTHER EARNESTLY SPEAK POORLY OF SOMEONE.
I REALLY DO FEEL BAD ABOUT ACTING WITHOUT PERMISSION.
YOU SHOULD. IF YOU'D MESSED UP, YOU'D NEVER HAVE BEEN ABLE TO COME BACK. YOU COULD HAVE EVEN DIED.
I WAS PREPARED FOR THAT.
DON'T GO ACTING ALL STOIC.
CHUTARO WAS WORRIED AND SHIRASU HAD TO GO THROUGH A LOT OF TROUBLE.
I WAS CONSIDERING GETTING INVOLVED TOO.
HOW DO YOU LIKE THAT? WE WERE ALL WILLING TO MOBILIZE FOR YOU.

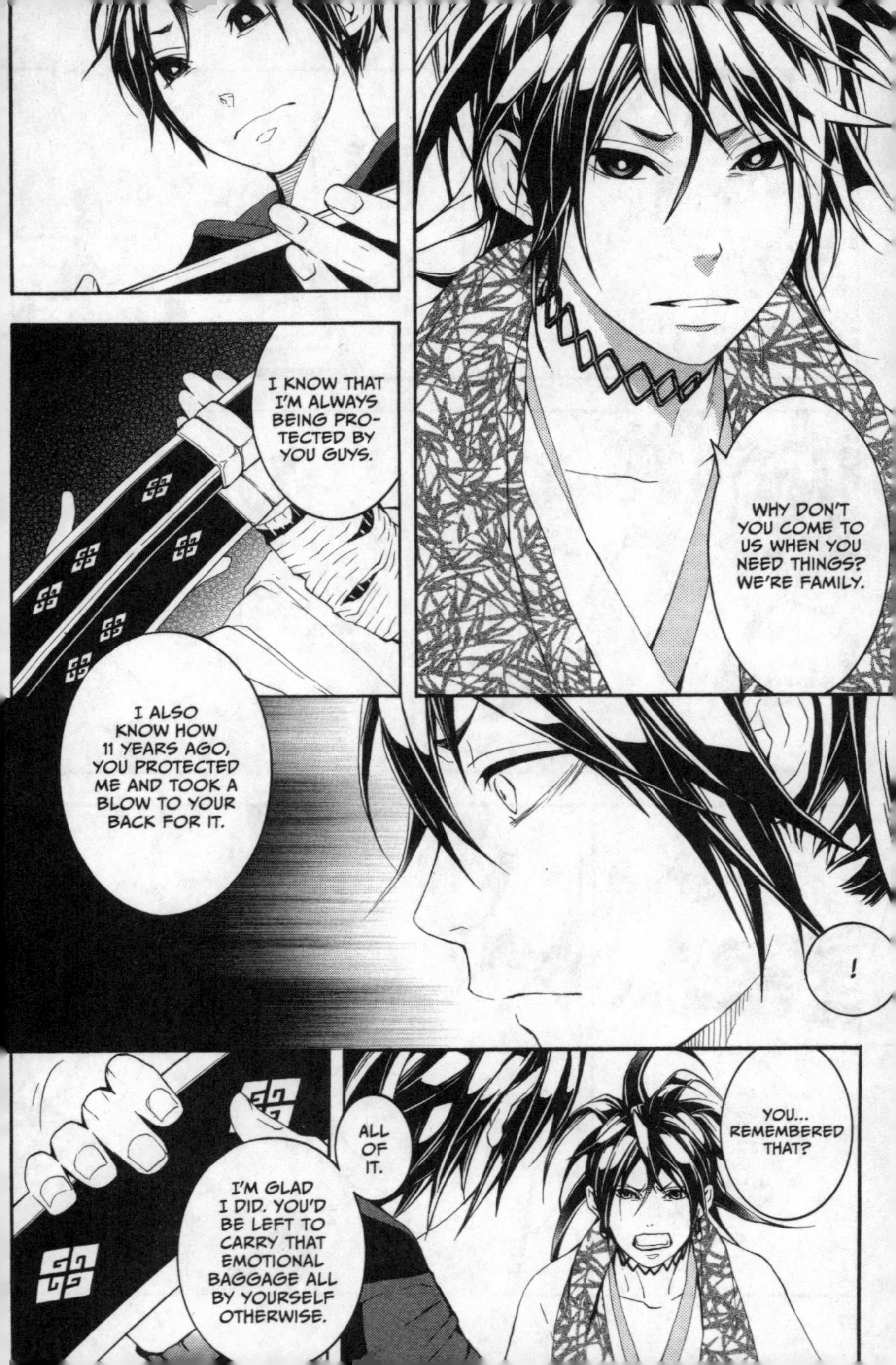
WHY DON'T YOU COME TO US WHEN YOU NEED THINGS? WE'RE FAMILY.
I KNOW THAT I'M ALWAYS BEING PRO-TECTED BY YOU GUYS.
I ALSO KNOW HOW 11 YEARS AGO, YOU PROTECTED ME AND TOOK A BLOW TO YOUR BACK FOR IT.
!
YOU... REMEMBERED THAT?
ALL OF IT.
I'M GLAD I DID. YOU'D BE LEFT TO CARRY THAT EMOTIONAL BAGGAGE ALL BY YOURSELF OTHERWISE.

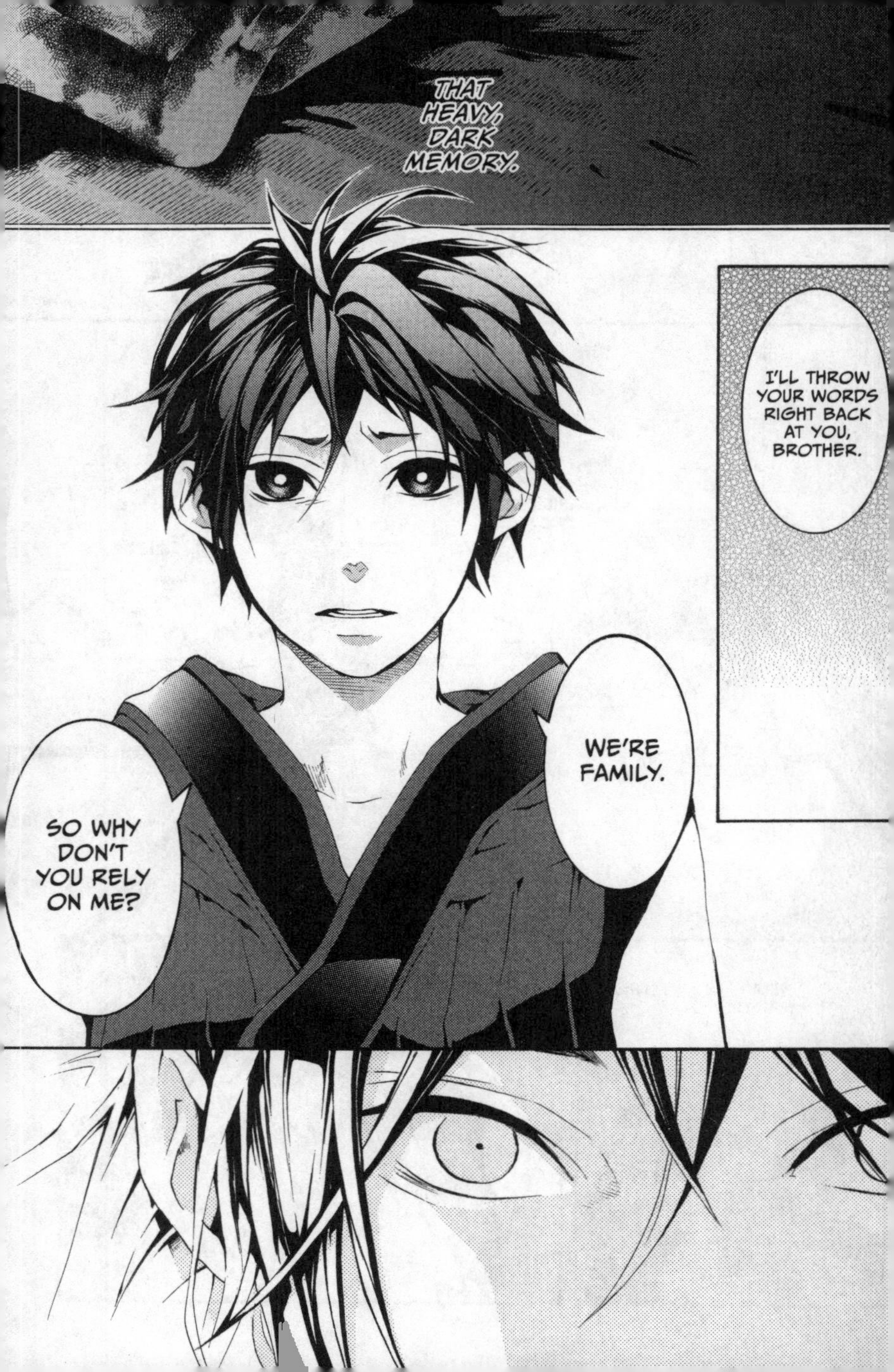
THAT HEAVY, DARK MEMORY.
I'LL THROW YOUR WORDS RIGHT BACK AT YOU, BROTHER.
WE'RE FAMILY.
SO WHY DON'T YOU RELY ON ME?

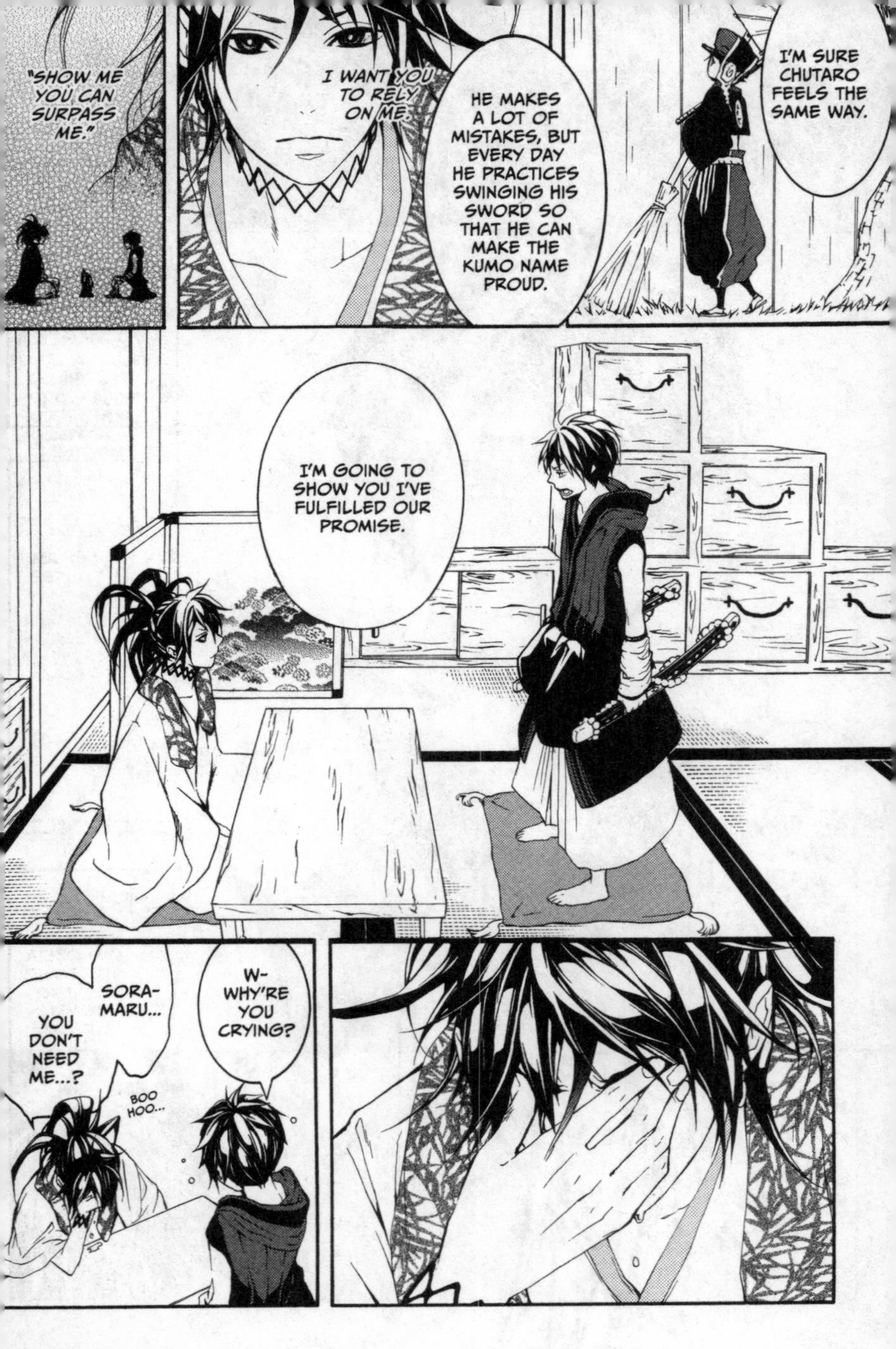
I'M SURE CHUTARO FEELS THE SAME WAY.
HE MAKES A LOT OF MISTAKES, BUT EVERY DAY HE PRACTICES SWINGING HIS SWORD SO THAT HE CAN MAKE THE KUMO NAME PROUD.
I WANT YOU TO RELY ON ME.
"SHOW ME YOU CAN SURPASS ME."
I'M GOING TO SHOW YOU I'VE FULFILLED OUR PROMISE.
W-WHY'RE YOU CRYING?
SORA-MARU...
YOU DON'T NEED ME...?
BOO HOO...

...

PARDON THE RACKET.

SHUT UP, YOU BIG LOSER!

CALL ME BIG BROTHER THE WAY YOU DID WHEN YOU WERE LITTLE!

THAT'S NOT VERY NICE!

SORAMARU'S LEAVING THE NEST!

I NEVER SAID THAT!

WAAAAH!

FINE!

PSSHT

CIRCUM-STANCE?

WHY AM I HERE?

SORRY FOR WORRYING YOU!

I'M OUTTA HERE. AND YOU'RE COMING WITH ME!

WAIT... ME?

TAKE CARE.

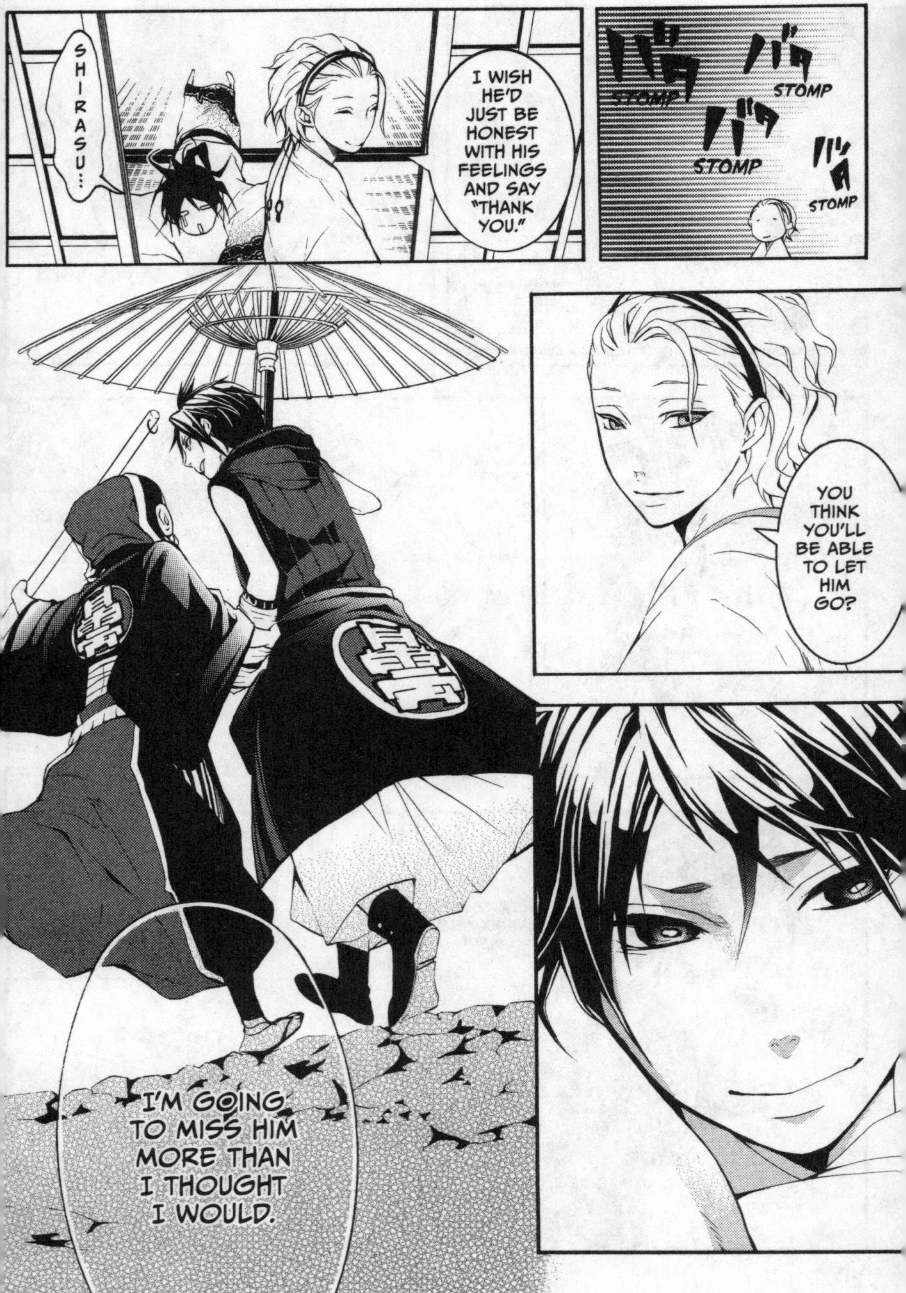
バタ
STOMP
バタ
STOMP
バタ
STOMP
バタ
STOMP
I WISH HE'D JUST BE HONEST WITH HIS FEELINGS AND SAY "THANK YOU."
SHIRASU...
YOU THINK YOU'LL BE ABLE TO LET HIM GO?
I'M GOING TO MISS HIM MORE THAN I THOUGHT I WOULD.

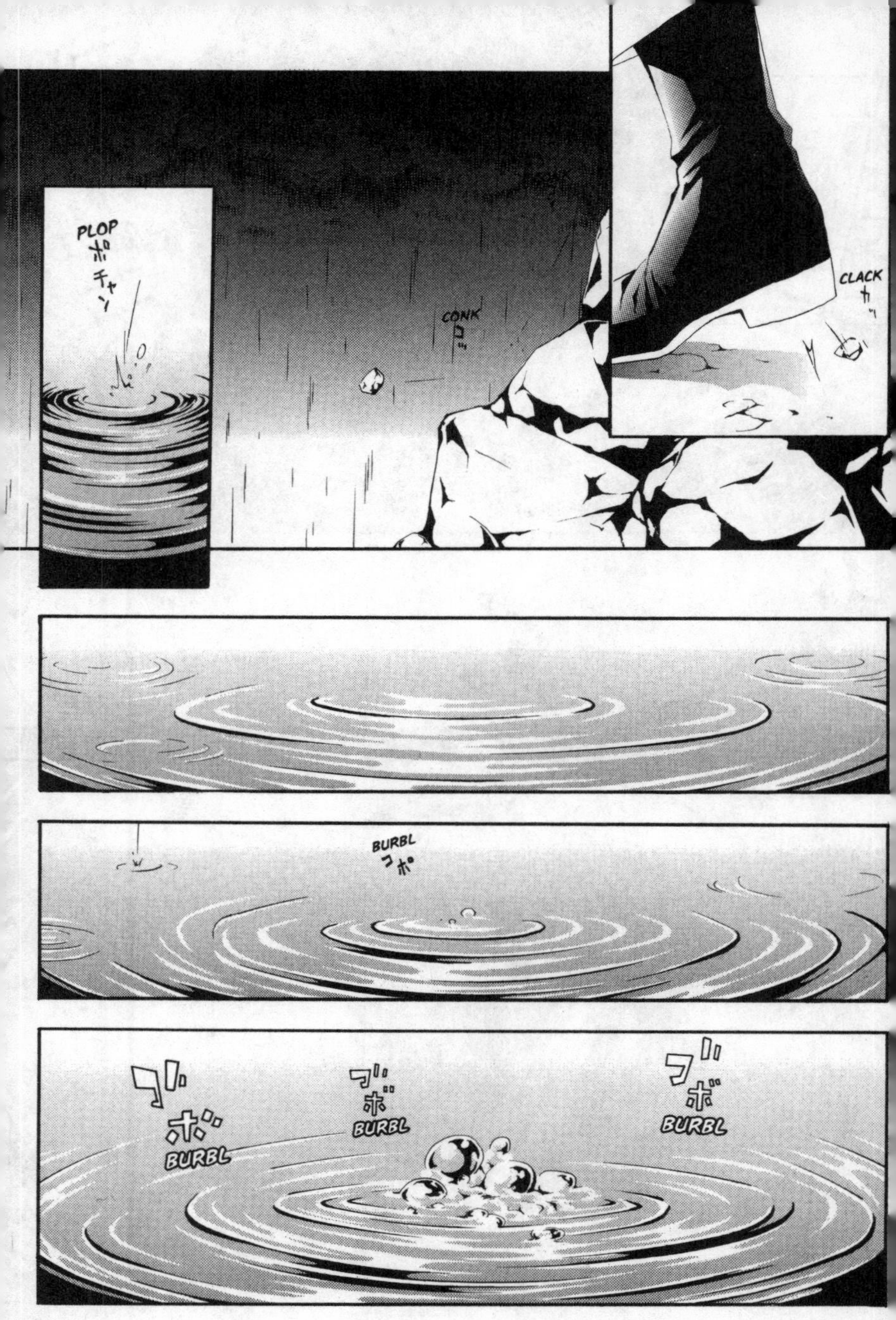
CLACK
カッ
CONK
ゴッ
PLOP
ポチャン
BURBL
コポ
ゴボ
BURBL
ゴボ
BURBL
ゴボ
BURBL

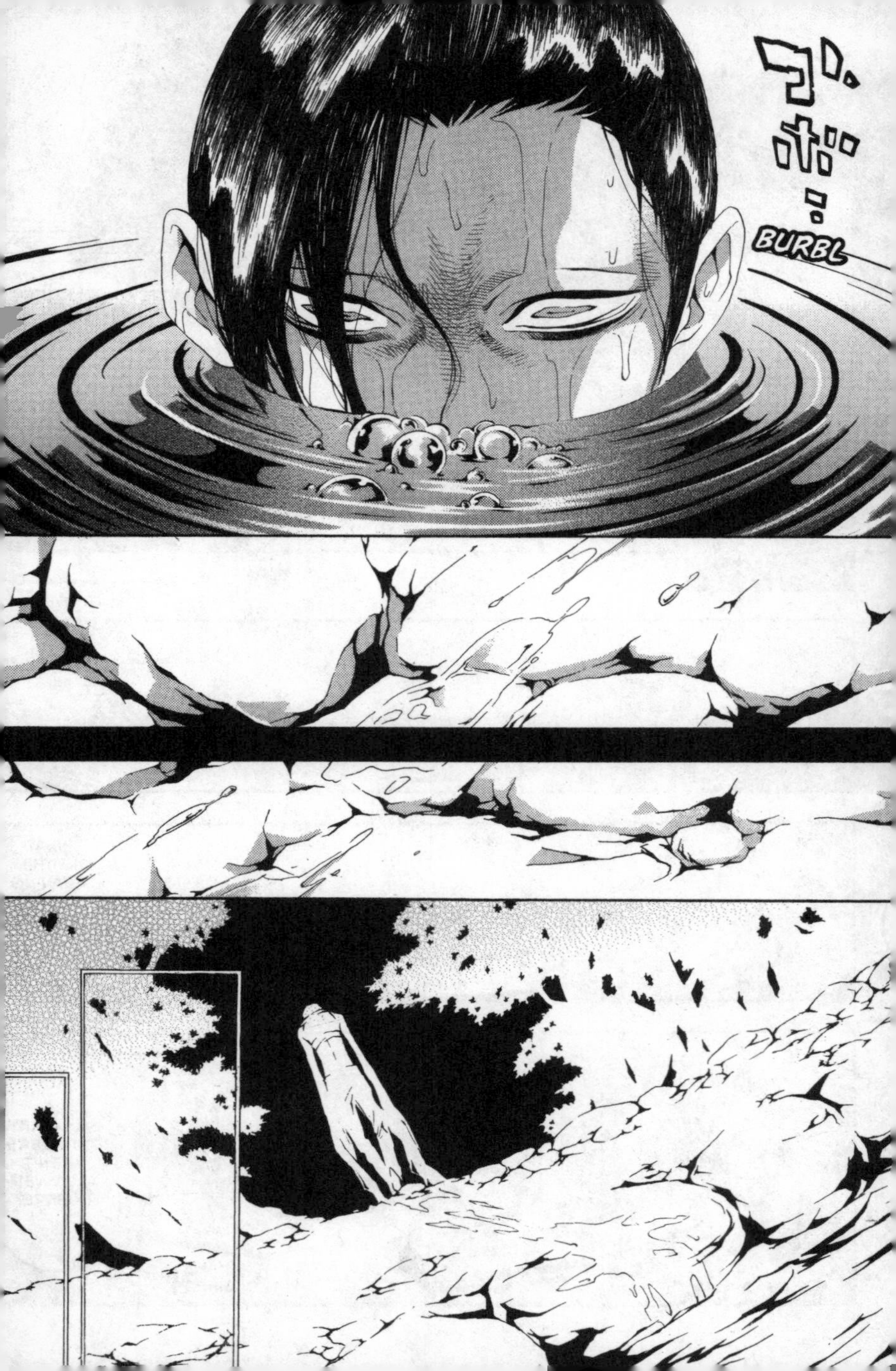
BURBL

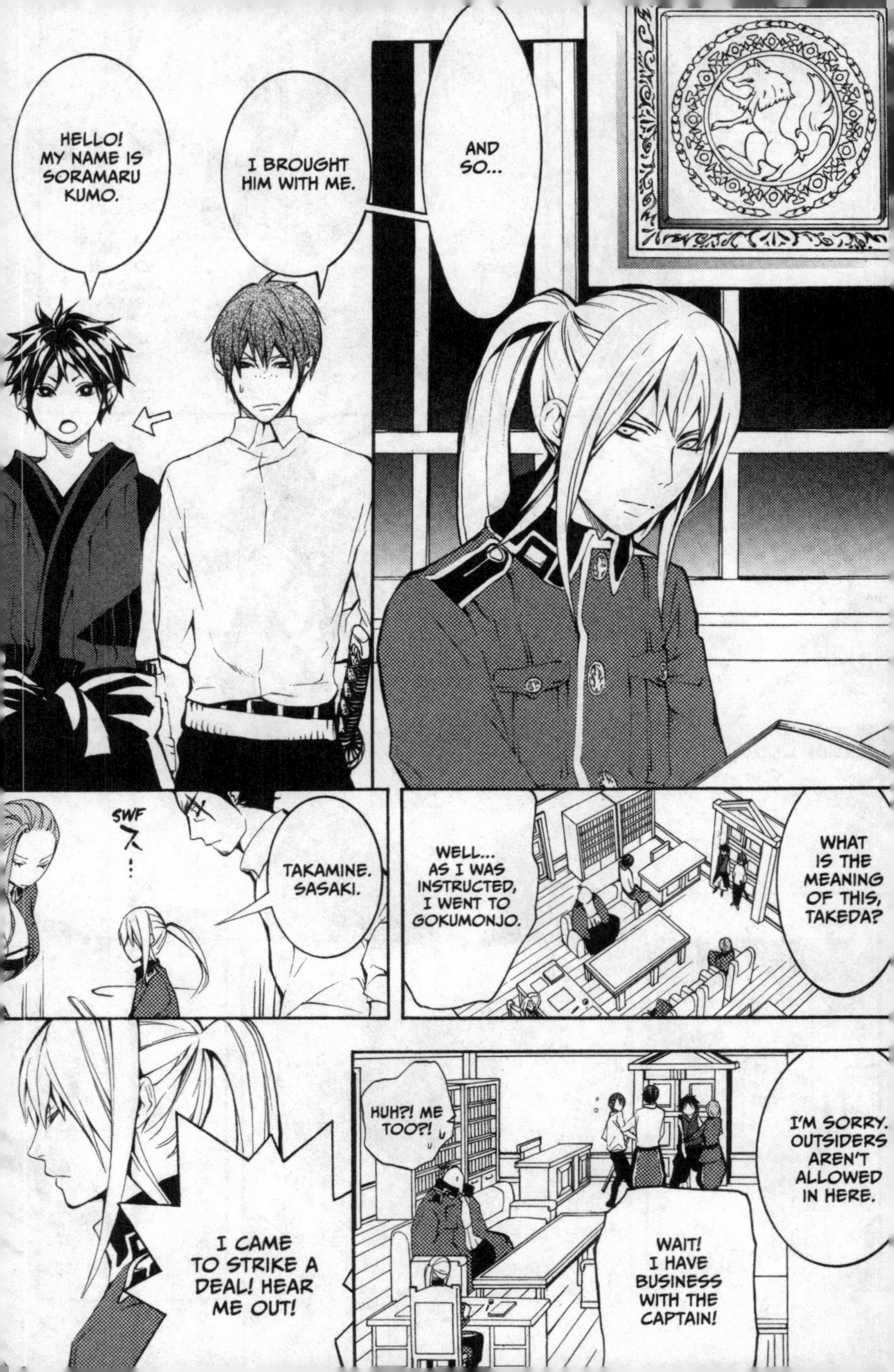
AND SO...
I BROUGHT HIM WITH ME.
HELLO! MY NAME IS SORAMARU KUMO.
WHAT IS THE MEANING OF THIS, TAKEDA?
WELL... AS I WAS INSTRUCTED, I WENT TO GOKUMONJO.
TAKAMINE. SASAKI.
SWF
I'M SORRY. OUTSIDERS AREN'T ALLOWED IN HERE.
HUH?! ME TOO?!
WAIT! I HAVE BUSINESS WITH THE CAPTAIN!
I CAME TO STRIKE A DEAL! HEAR ME OUT!

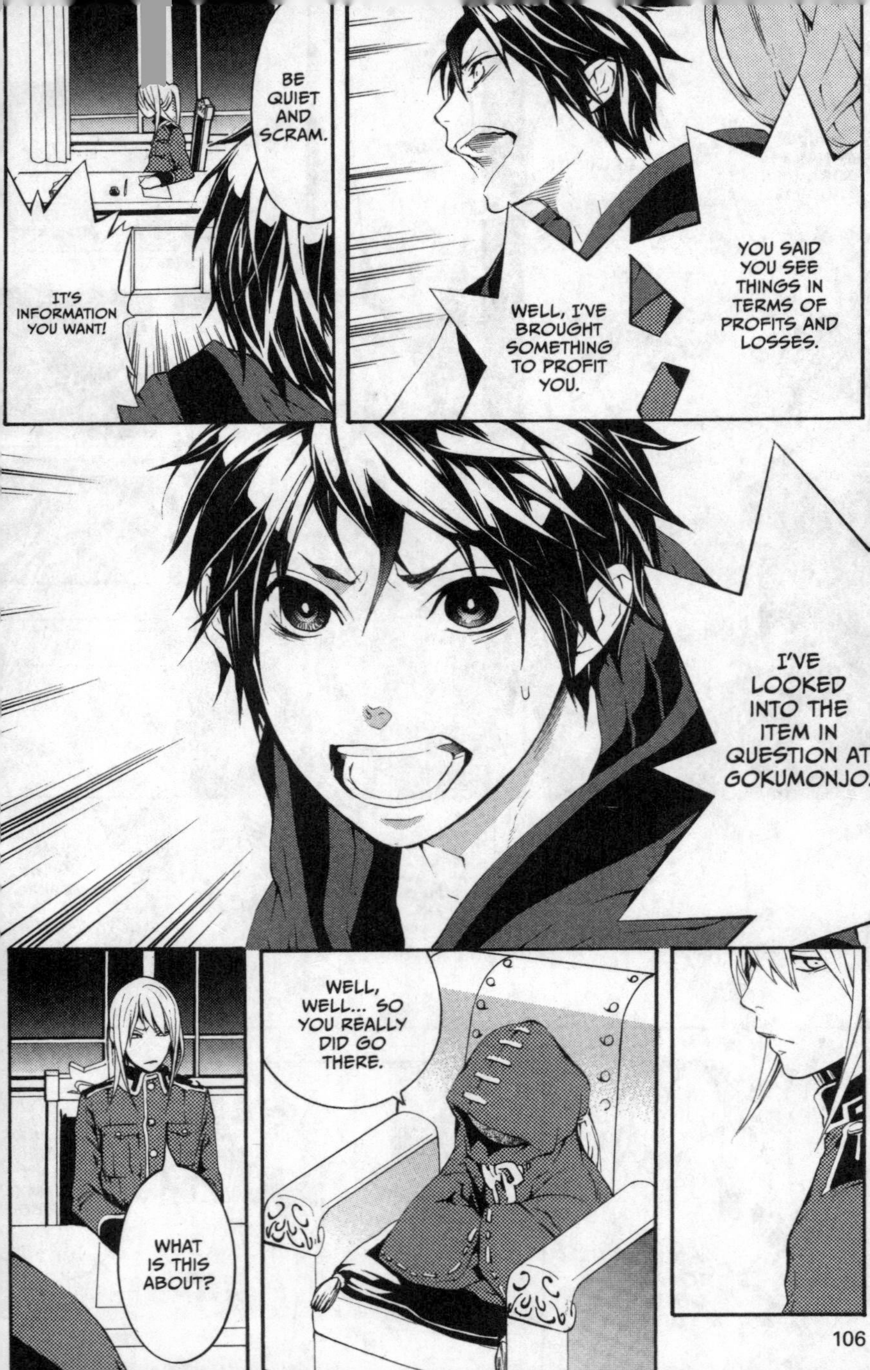
YOU SAID YOU SEE THINGS IN TERMS OF PROFITS AND LOSSES.
WELL, I'VE BROUGHT SOMETHING TO PROFIT YOU.
BE QUIET AND SCRAM.
IT'S INFORMATION YOU WANT!
I'VE LOOKED INTO THE ITEM IN QUESTION AT GOKUMONJO.
WELL, WELL... SO YOU REALLY DID GO THERE.
WHAT IS THIS ABOUT?

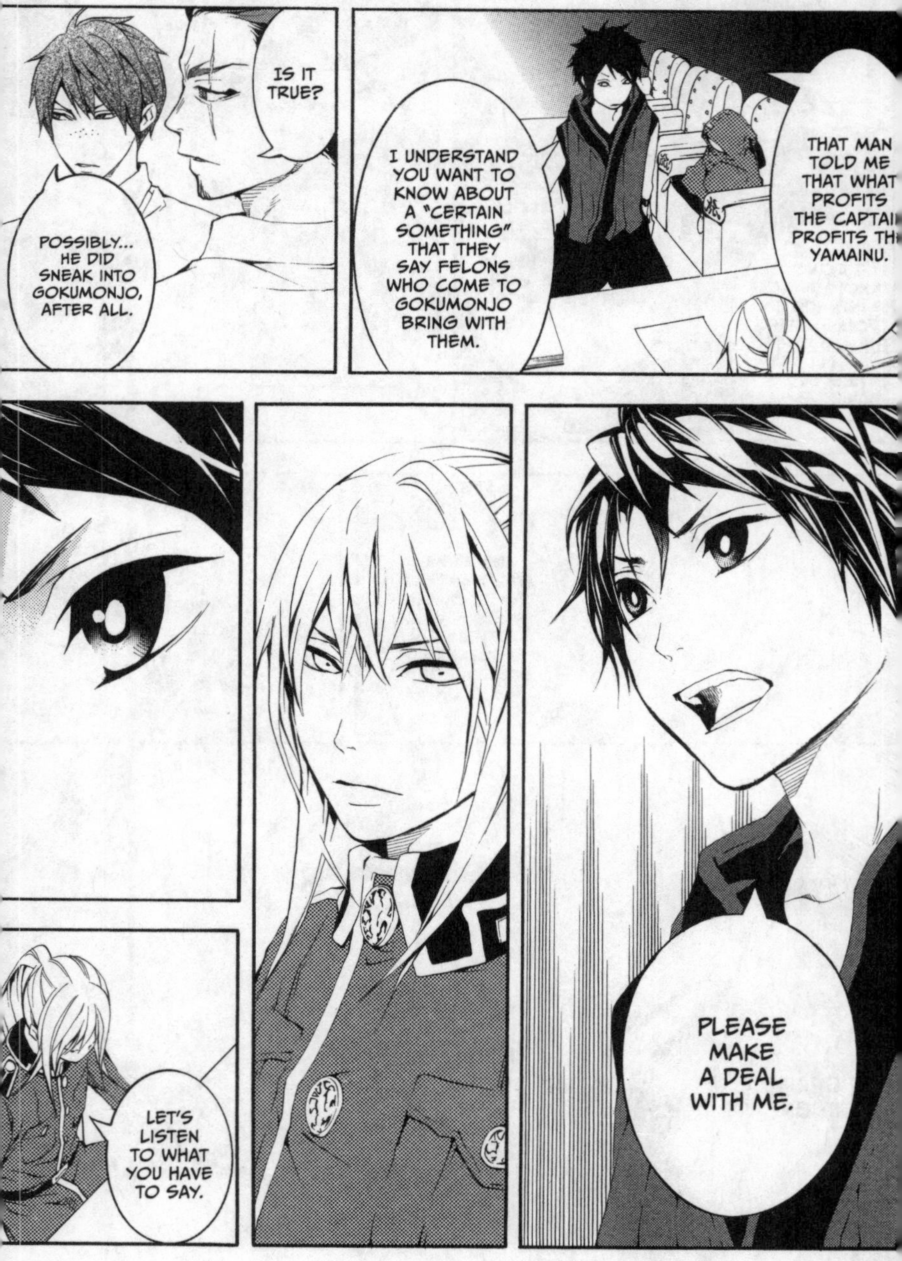
THAT MAN TOLD ME THAT WHAT PROFITS THE CAPTAI PROFITS TH YAMAINU.
I UNDERSTAND YOU WANT TO KNOW ABOUT A "CERTAIN SOMETHING" THAT THEY SAY FELONS WHO COME TO GOKUMONJO BRING WITH THEM.
IS IT TRUE?
POSSIBLY... HE DID SNEAK INTO GOKUMONJO, AFTER ALL.
PLEASE MAKE A DEAL WITH ME.
LET'S LISTEN TO WHAT YOU HAVE TO SAY.

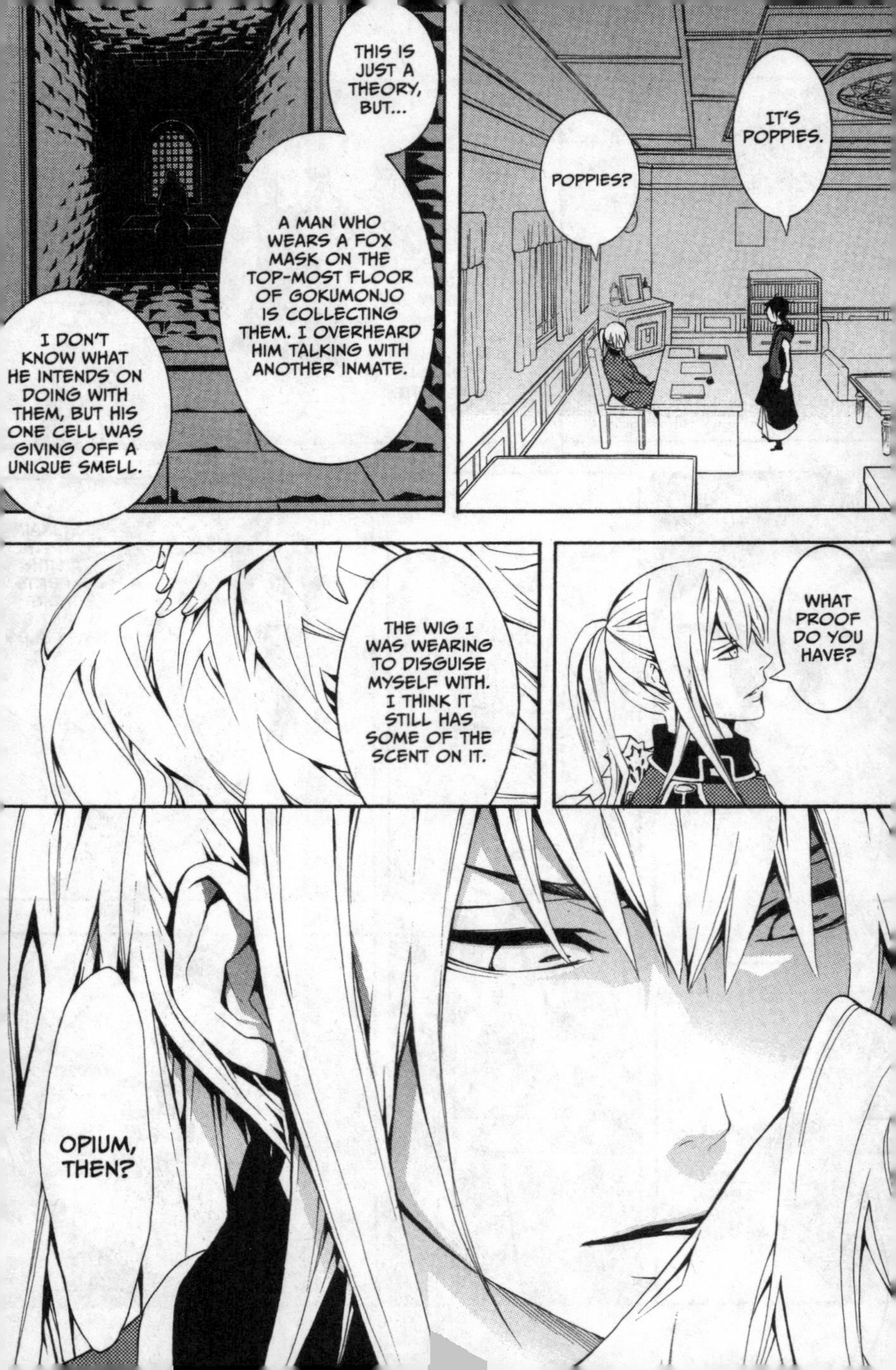

IT'S POPPIES.
POPPIES?
THIS IS JUST A THEORY, BUT...
A MAN WHO WEARS A FOX MASK ON THE TOP-MOST FLOOR OF GOKUMONJO IS COLLECTING THEM. I OVERHEARD HIM TALKING WITH ANOTHER INMATE.
I DON'T KNOW WHAT HE INTENDS ON DOING WITH THEM, BUT HIS ONE CELL WAS GIVING OFF A UNIQUE SMELL.
WHAT PROOF DO YOU HAVE?
THE WIG I WAS WEARING TO DISGUISE MYSELF WITH. I THINK IT STILL HAS SOME OF THE SCENT ON IT.
OPIUM, THEN?

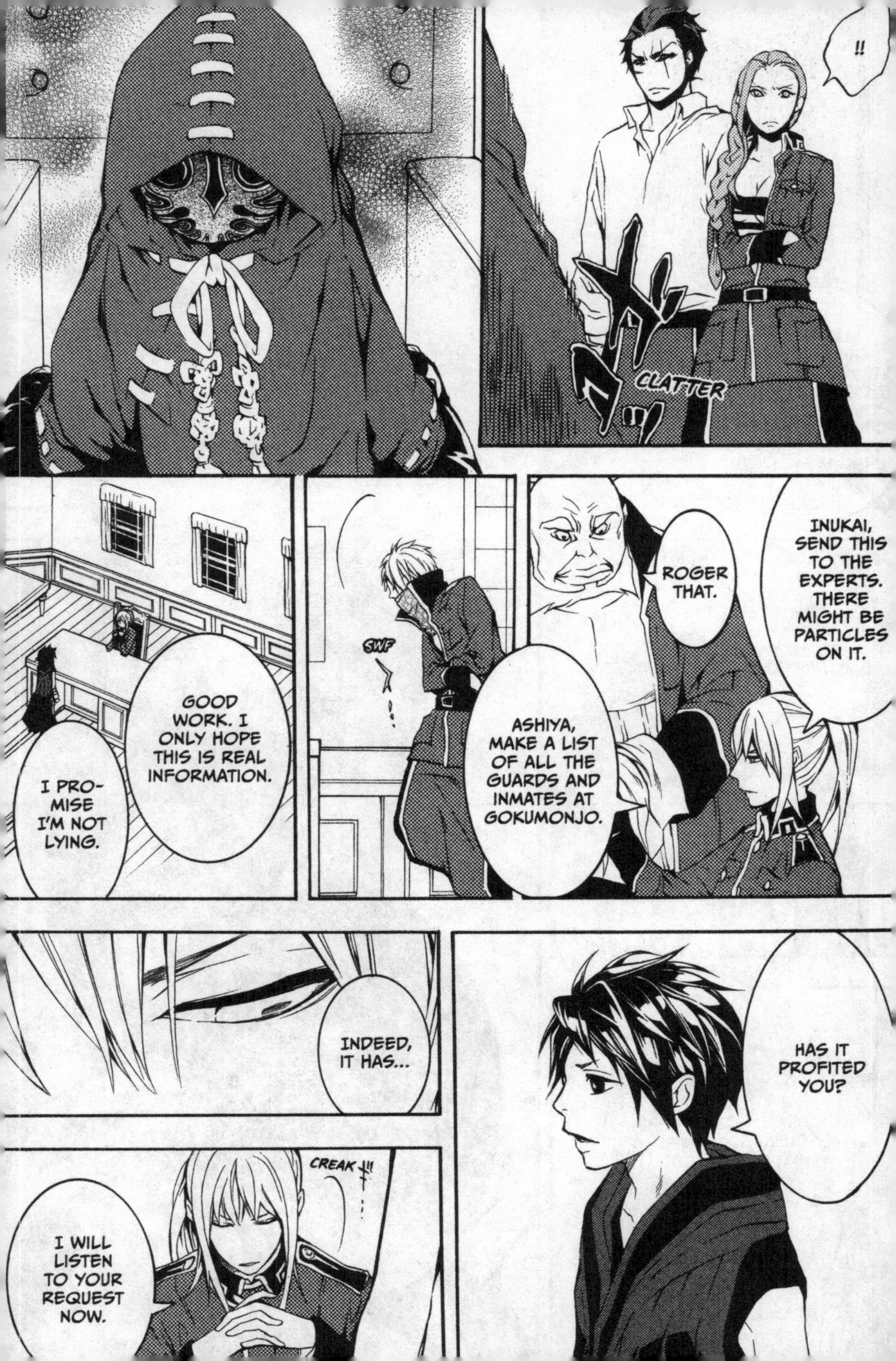
!!
CLATTER
INUKAI, SEND THIS TO THE EXPERTS. THERE MIGHT BE PARTICLES ON IT.
ROGER THAT.
ASHIYA, MAKE A LIST OF ALL THE GUARDS AND INMATES AT GOKUMONJO.
SWF
GOOD WORK. I ONLY HOPE THIS IS REAL INFORMATION.
I PRO-MISE I'M NOT LYING.
HAS IT PROFITED YOU?
INDEED, IT HAS...
CREAK
I WILL LISTEN TO YOUR REQUEST NOW.

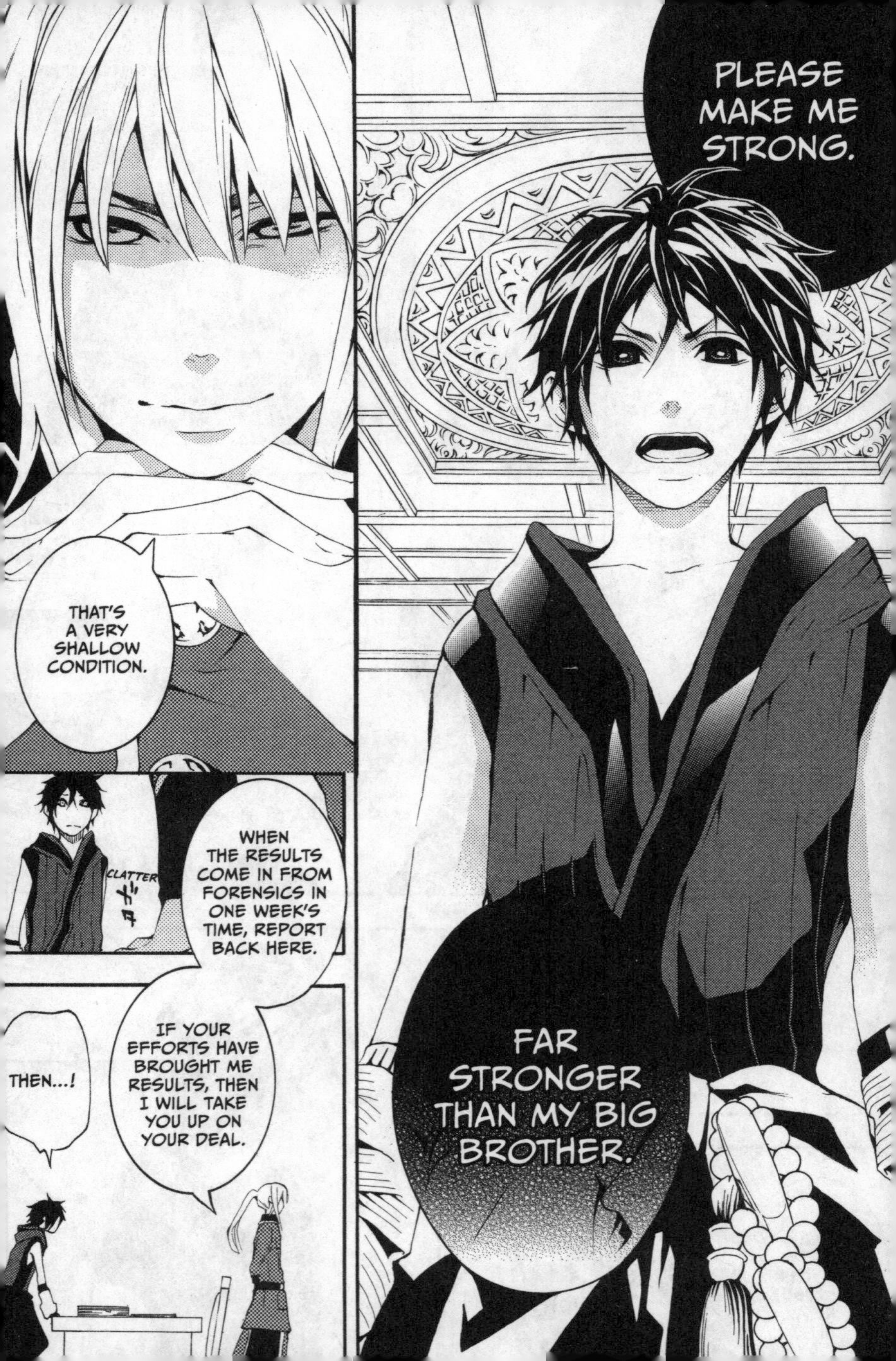
PLEASE MAKE ME STRONG.
FAR STRONGER THAN MY BIG BROTHER.
THAT'S A VERY SHALLOW CONDITION.
WHEN THE RESULTS COME IN FROM FORENSICS IN ONE WEEK'S TIME, REPORT BACK HERE.
CLATTER
ガタ
IF YOUR EFFORTS HAVE BROUGHT ME RESULTS, THEN I WILL TAKE YOU UP ON YOUR DEAL.
THEN...!

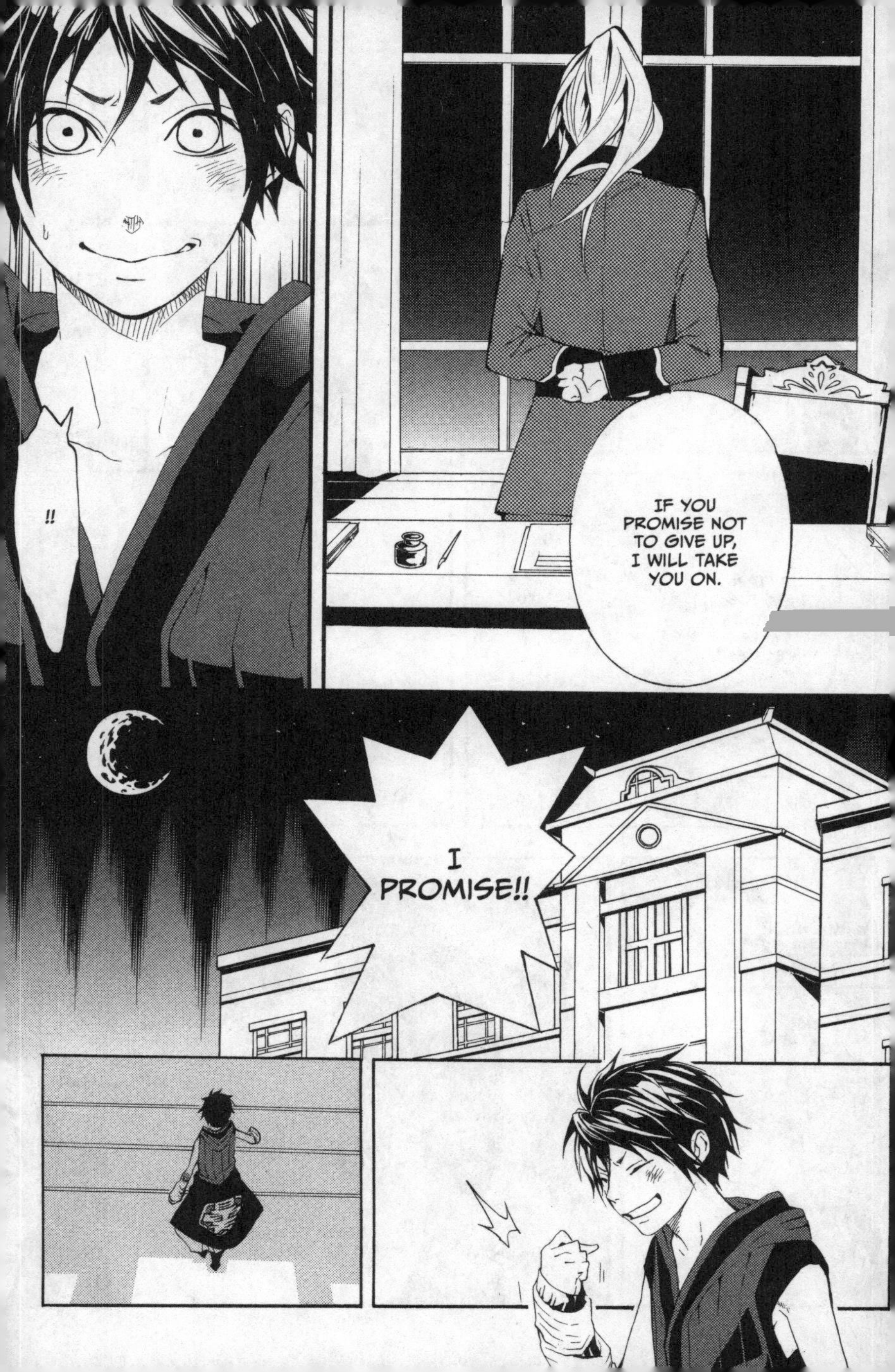
IF YOU PROMISE NOT TO GIVE UP, I WILL TAKE YOU ON.
!!
I PROMISE!!

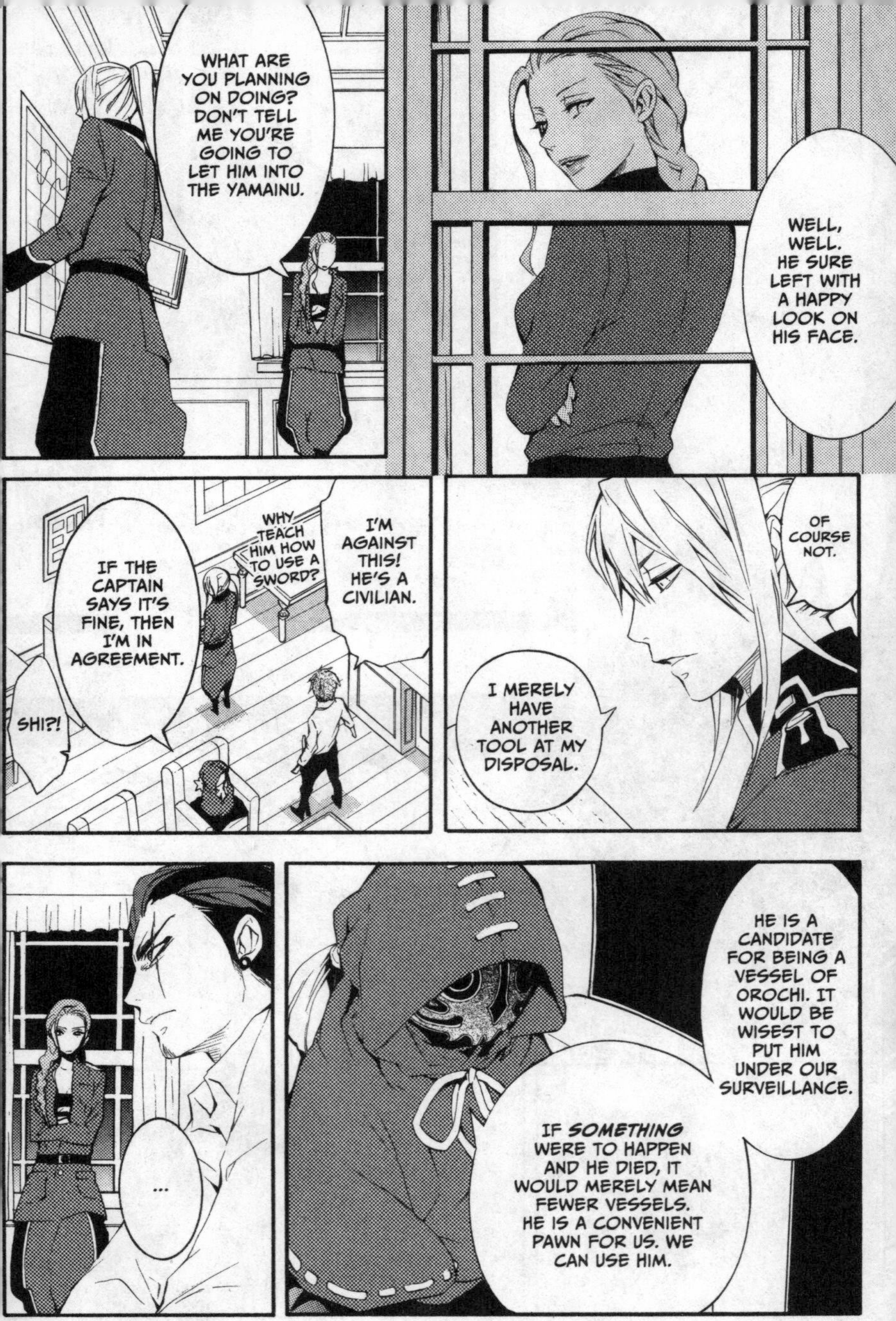
WELL, WELL. HE SURE LEFT WITH A HAPPY LOOK ON HIS FACE.
WHAT ARE YOU PLANNING ON DOING? DON'T TELL ME YOU'RE GOING TO LET HIM INTO THE YAMAINU.
OF COURSE NOT.
I MERELY HAVE ANOTHER TOOL AT MY DISPOSAL.
I'M AGAINST THIS! HE'S A CIVILIAN.
WHY TEACH HIM HOW TO USE A SWORD?
IF THE CAPTAIN SAYS IT'S FINE, THEN I'M IN AGREEMENT.
SHI?!
HE IS A CANDIDATE FOR BEING A VESSEL OF OROCHI. IT WOULD BE WISEST TO PUT HIM UNDER OUR SURVEILLANCE.
IF *SOMETHING* WERE TO HAPPEN AND HE DIED, IT WOULD MERELY MEAN FEWER VESSELS. HE IS A CONVENIENT PAWN FOR US. WE CAN USE HIM.
...

THANKS TO IT, WE GOT AHOLD OF INFORMATION WE WOULD HAVE NEVER IMAGINED, SO GREAT CONGRATULATIONS ARE IN ORDER.

BUT—

IS THAT WHY YOU SENT HIM TO GOKUMONJO?! YOU DIDN'T CARE IF HE'D DIED?!

TAKE IT OUTSIDE.

SHI. TAKEDA.

IS THAT SO? IF YOU WANTED A SWORD PARTNER, YOU SHOULD'VE SAID SO SOONER.

SO IN SHORT, TAKEDA IS JEALOUS OF THE LITTLE BROTHER?

I'M SORRY...

对不起
(SORRY...)

COME AT ME, TAKEDA.

UH.

THANKS, BUT...

LOOK, IT'S ALREADY REALLY LATE.

LOOKS LIKE I'LL BE WORKING OVERTIME TODAY.

ZOOSH

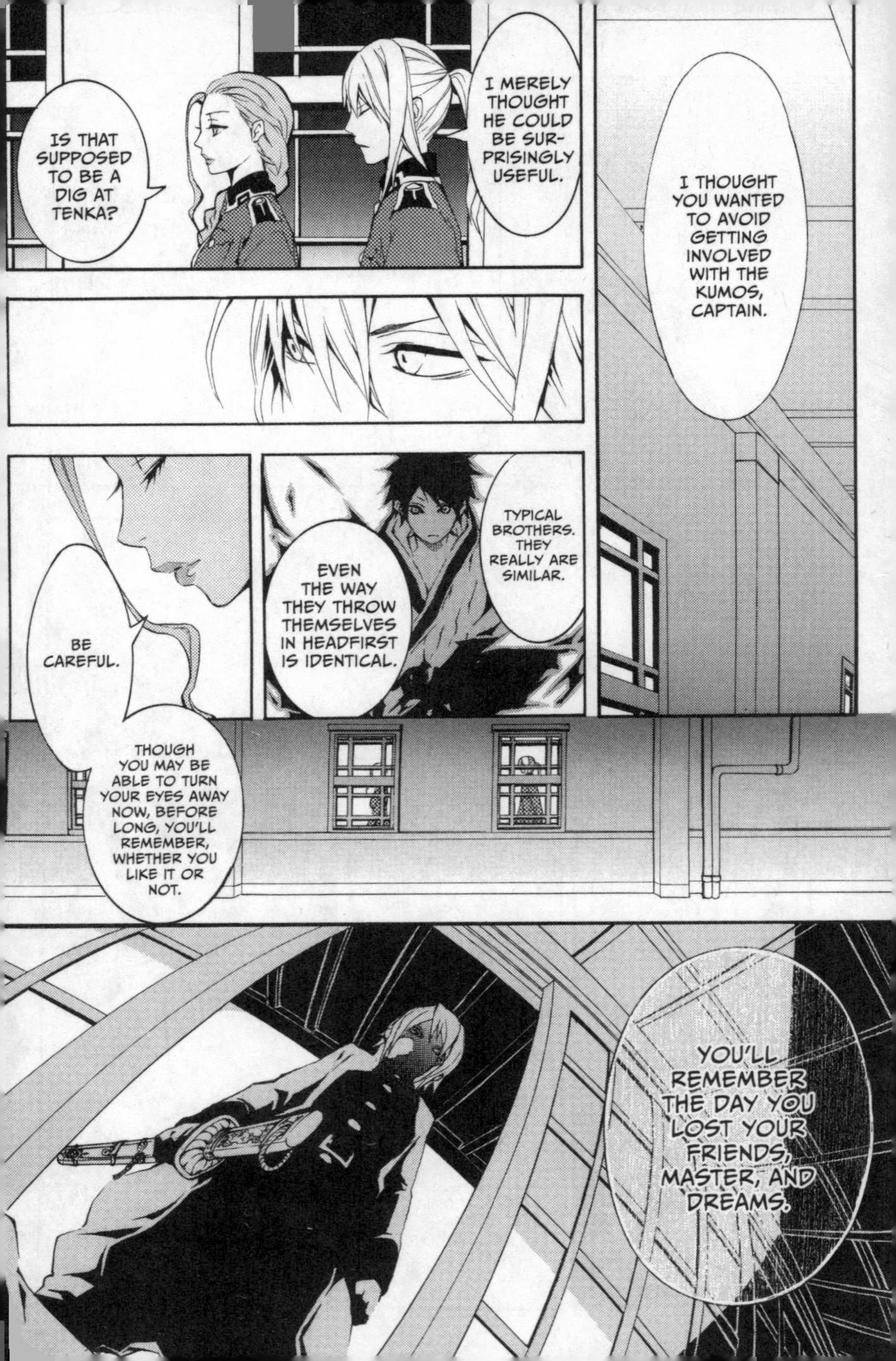
I THOUGHT YOU WANTED TO AVOID GETTING INVOLVED WITH THE KUMOS, CAPTAIN.
I MERELY THOUGHT HE COULD BE SUR-PRISINGLY USEFUL.
IS THAT SUPPOSED TO BE A DIG AT TENKA?
TYPICAL BROTHERS. THEY REALLY ARE SIMILAR.
EVEN THE WAY THEY THROW THEMSELVES IN HEADFIRST IS IDENTICAL.
BE CAREFUL.
THOUGH YOU MAY BE ABLE TO TURN YOUR EYES AWAY NOW, BEFORE LONG, YOU'LL REMEMBER, WHETHER YOU LIKE IT OR NOT.
YOU'LL REMEMBER THE DAY YOU LOST YOUR FRIENDS, MASTER, AND DREAMS.

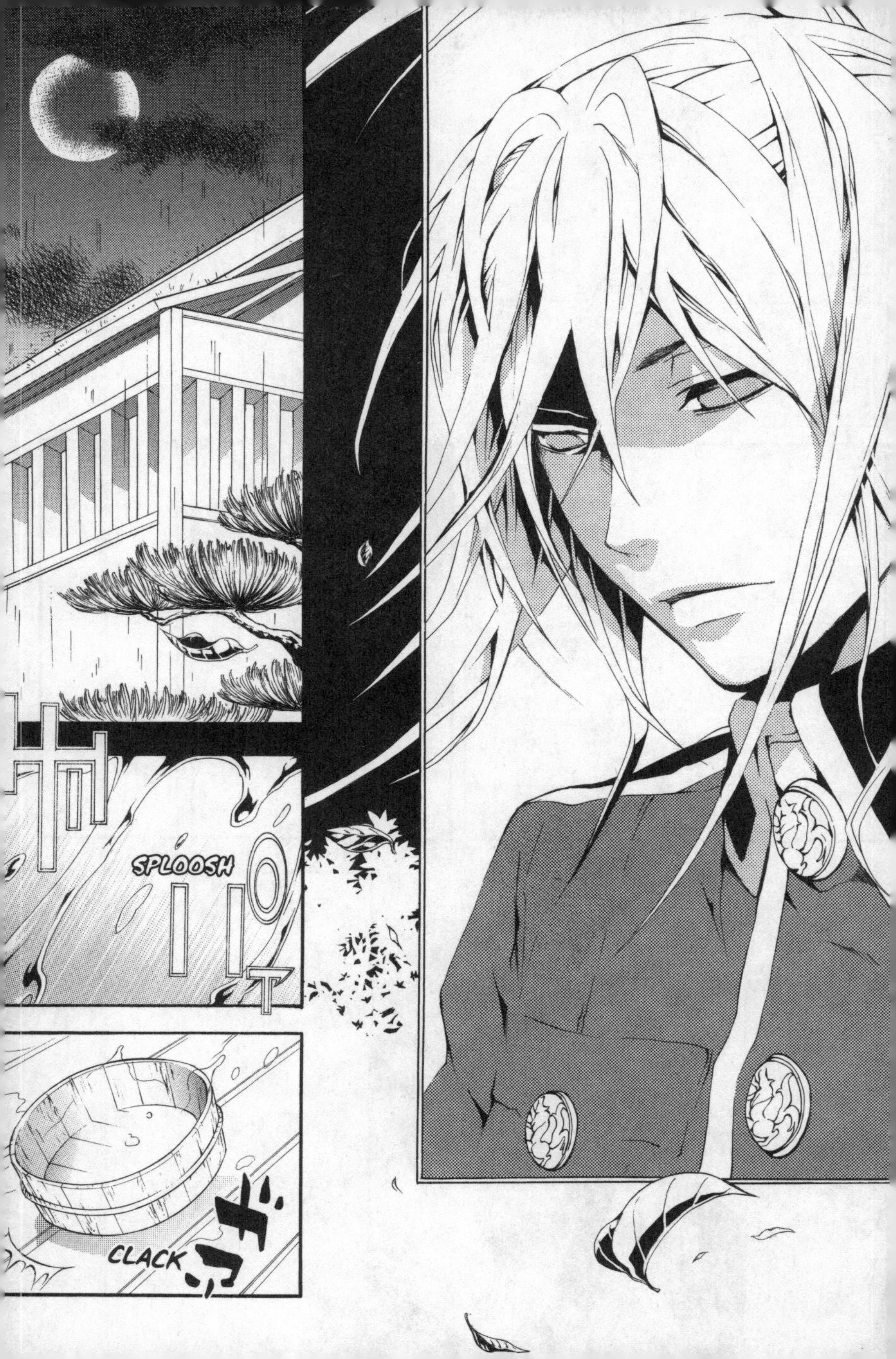
SPLOOSH
CLACK

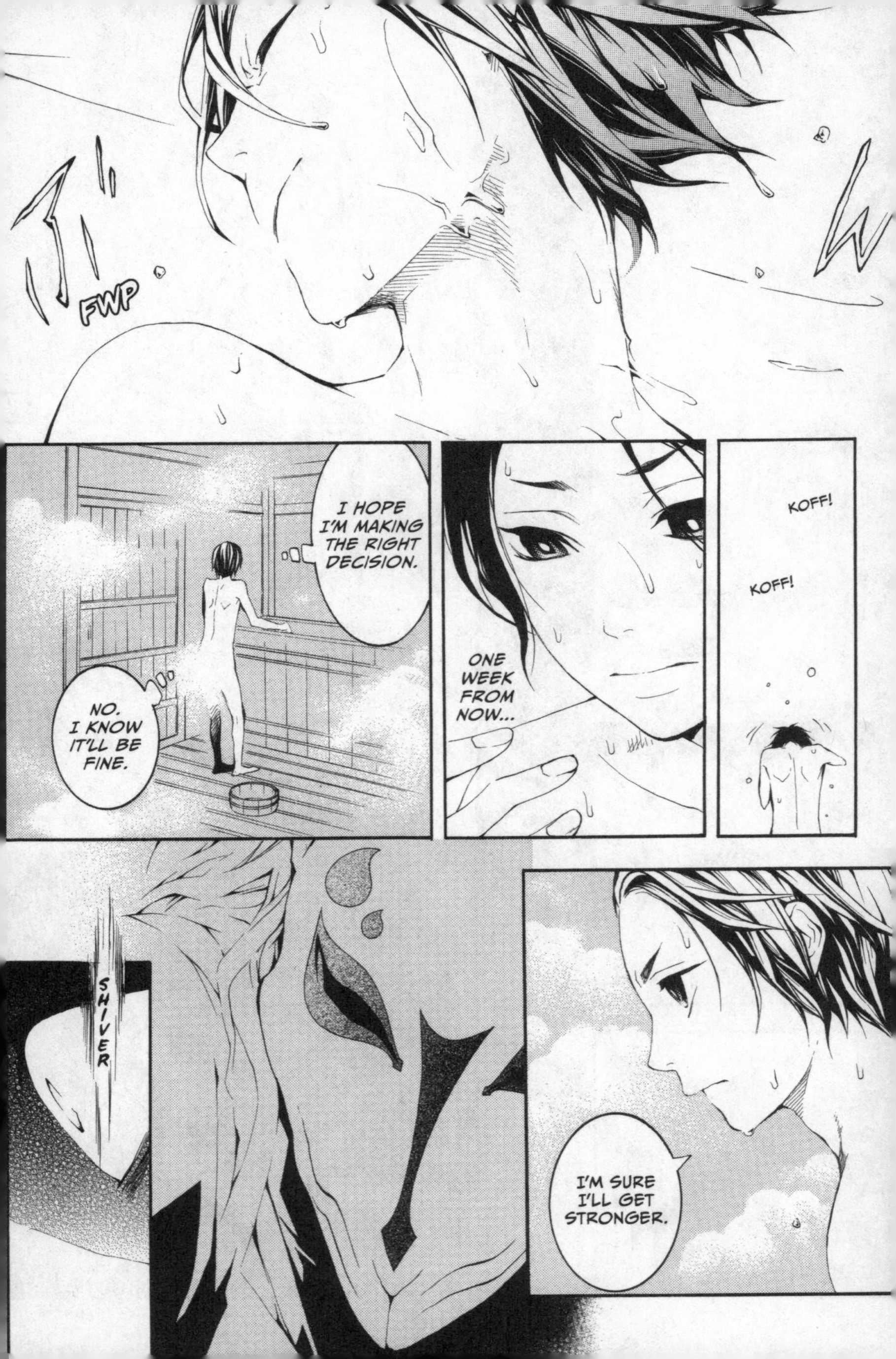
FWP
KOFF!
KOFF!
ONE WEEK FROM NOW...
I HOPE I'M MAKING THE RIGHT DECISION.
NO. I KNOW IT'LL BE FINE.
I'M SURE I'LL GET STRONGER.
SHIVER

ガクッ
THUD
!
THADUMP
WHEEZE! WHEEZE!
THADUMP
THADUMP
WHEEZE!
CALM DOWN...
IT'S OKAY.
YOU'RE OKAY NOW.
YOU'RE NOT HIM.

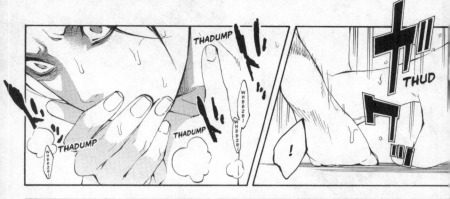

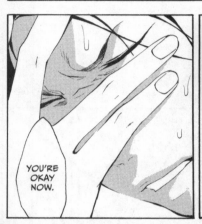

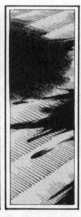

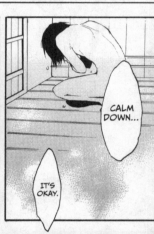

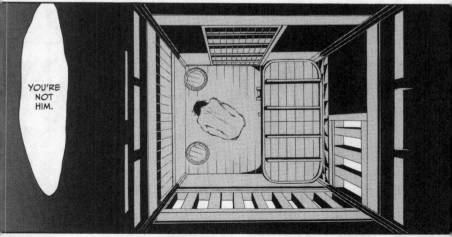

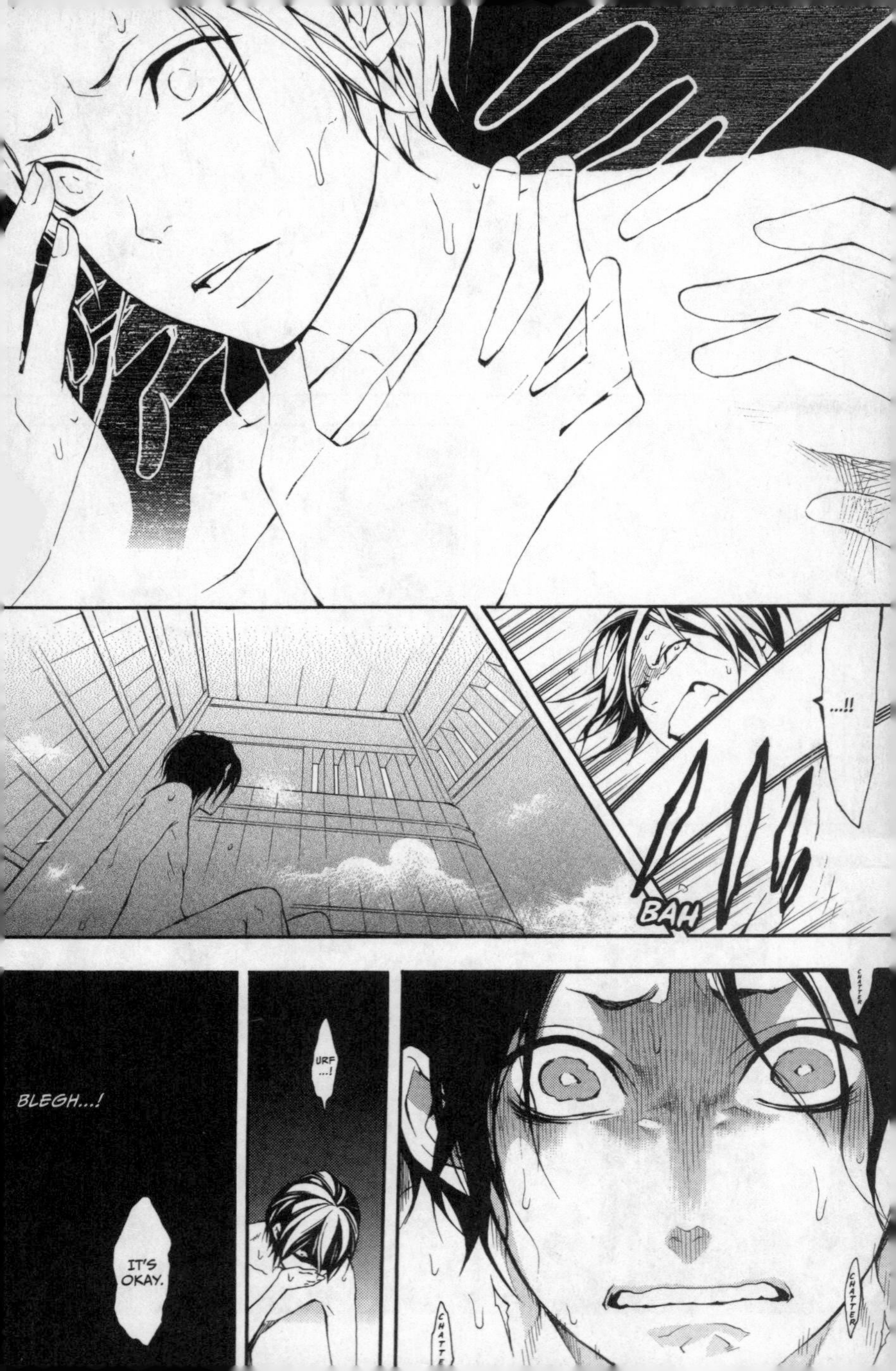

...!!
BAH
CHATTER
CHATTER
CHATTE
URF ...!
BLEGH...!
IT'S OKAY.

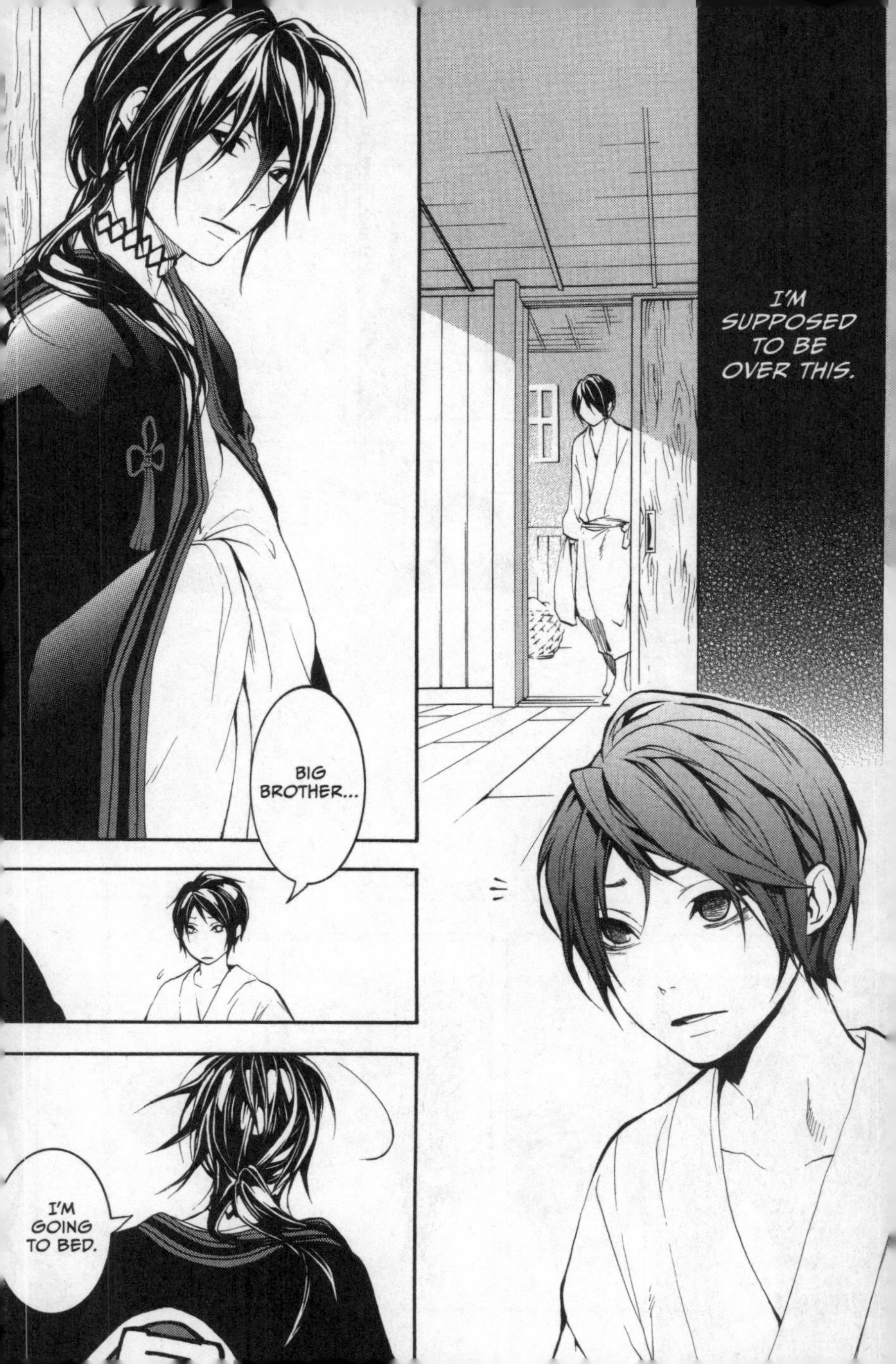
I'M SUPPOSED TO BE OVER THIS.
BIG BROTHER...
I'M GOING TO BED.

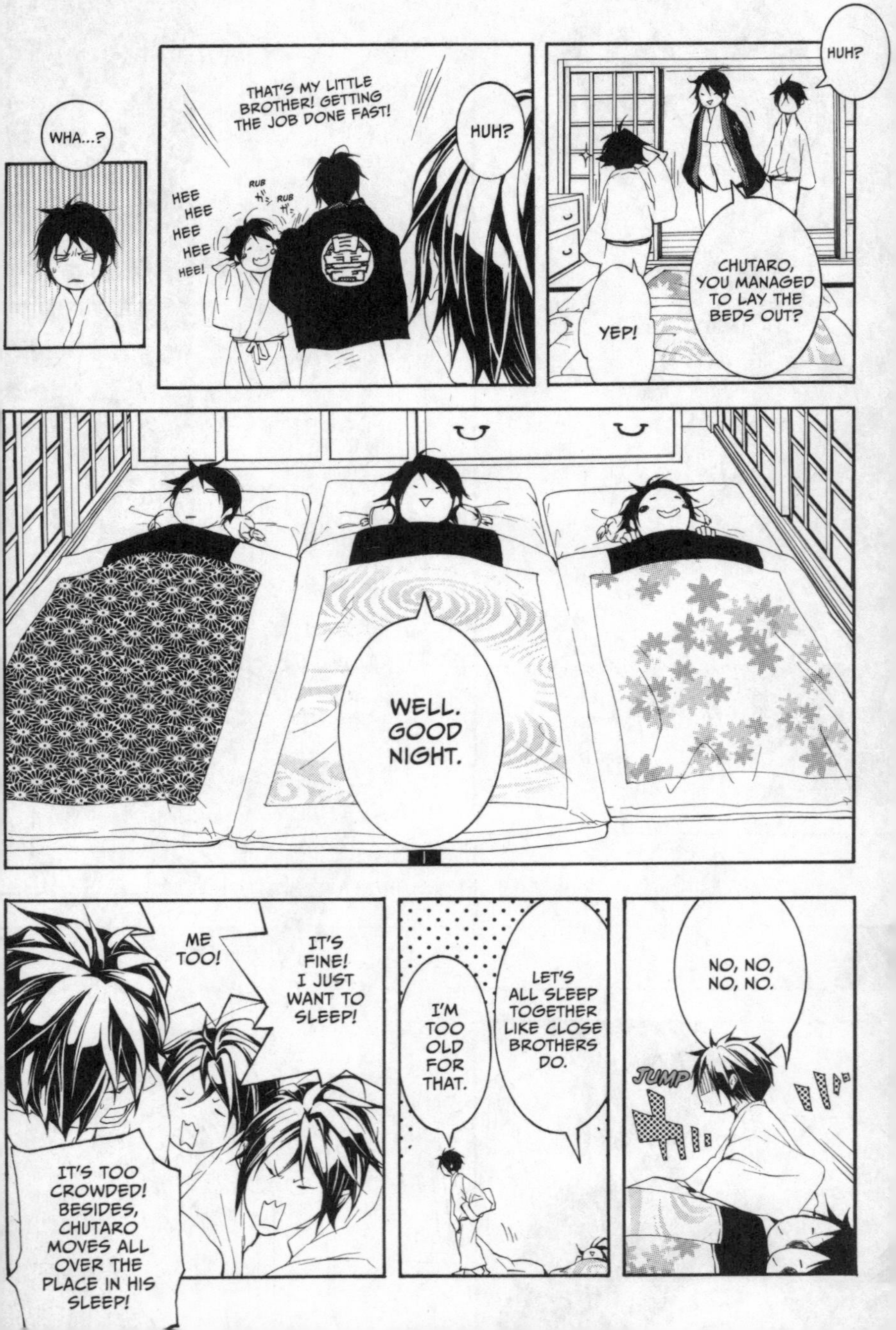
HUH?
CHUTARO, YOU MANAGED TO LAY THE BEDS OUT?
YEP!
HUH?
THAT'S MY LITTLE BROTHER! GETTING THE JOB DONE FAST!
RUB
RUB
HEE HEE HEE HEE HEE!
WHA...?
WELL. GOOD NIGHT.
NO, NO, NO, NO.
JUMP
LET'S ALL SLEEP TOGETHER LIKE CLOSE BROTHERS DO.
I'M TOO OLD FOR THAT.
IT'S FINE! I JUST WANT TO SLEEP!
ME TOO!
IT'S TOO CROWDED! BESIDES, CHUTARO MOVES ALL OVER THE PLACE IN HIS SLEEP!

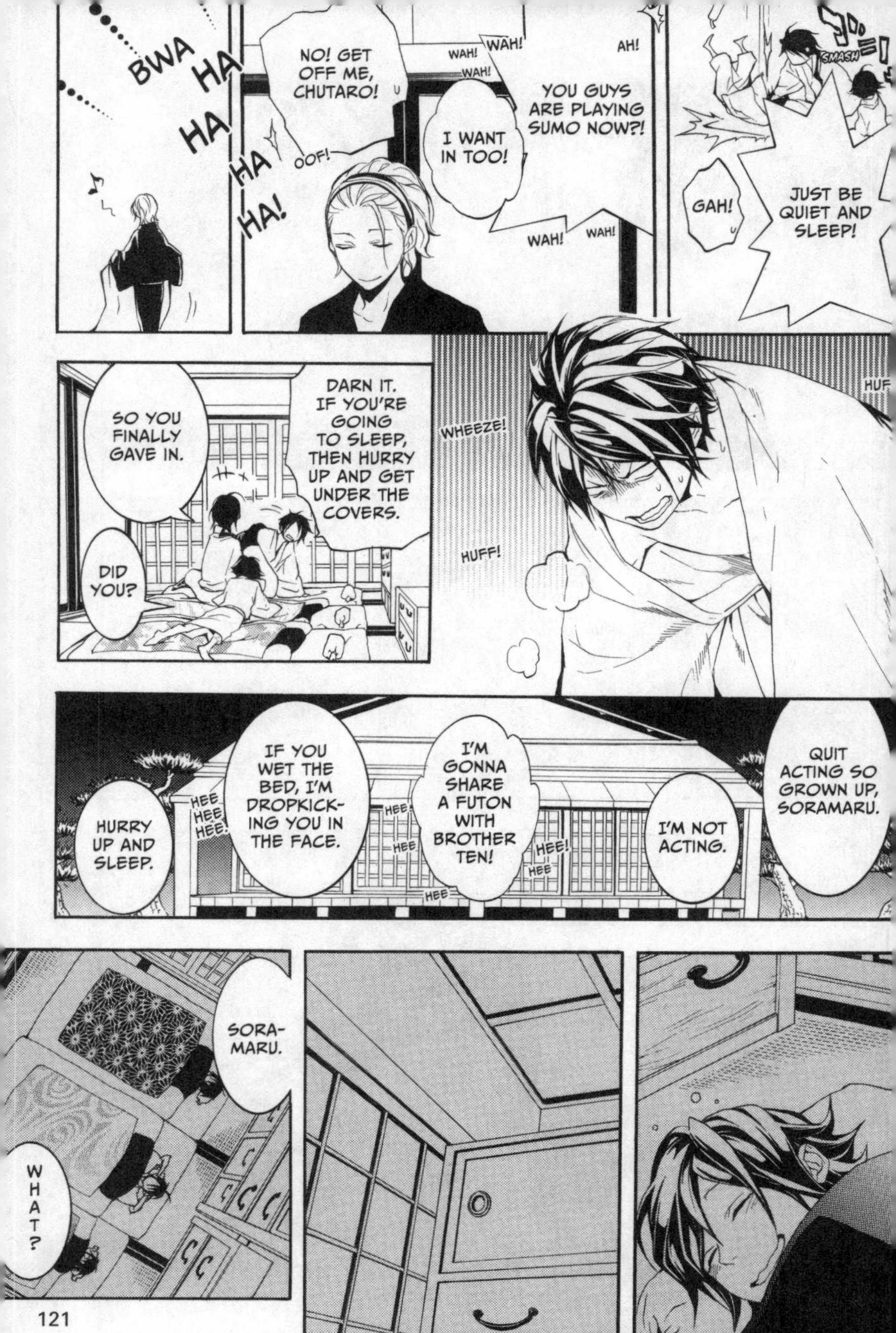
SMASH
GAH!
JUST BE QUIET AND SLEEP!
AH!
YOU GUYS ARE PLAYING SUMO NOW?!
WAH! WAH! WAH!
I WANT IN TOO!
WAH! WAH!
NO! GET OFF ME, CHUTARO!
OOF!
BWA HA HA HA HA!
HUF
WHEEZE!
HUFF!
DARN IT. IF YOU'RE GOING TO SLEEP, THEN HURRY UP AND GET UNDER THE COVERS.
SO YOU FINALLY GAVE IN.
DID YOU?
QUIT ACTING SO GROWN UP, SORAMARU.
I'M NOT ACTING.
I'M GONNA SHARE A FUTON WITH BROTHER TEN!
HEE! HEE HEE HEE HEE
IF YOU WET THE BED, I'M DROPKICKING YOU IN THE FACE.
HEE HEE HEE!
HURRY UP AND SLEEP.
SORA-MARU.
WHAT?

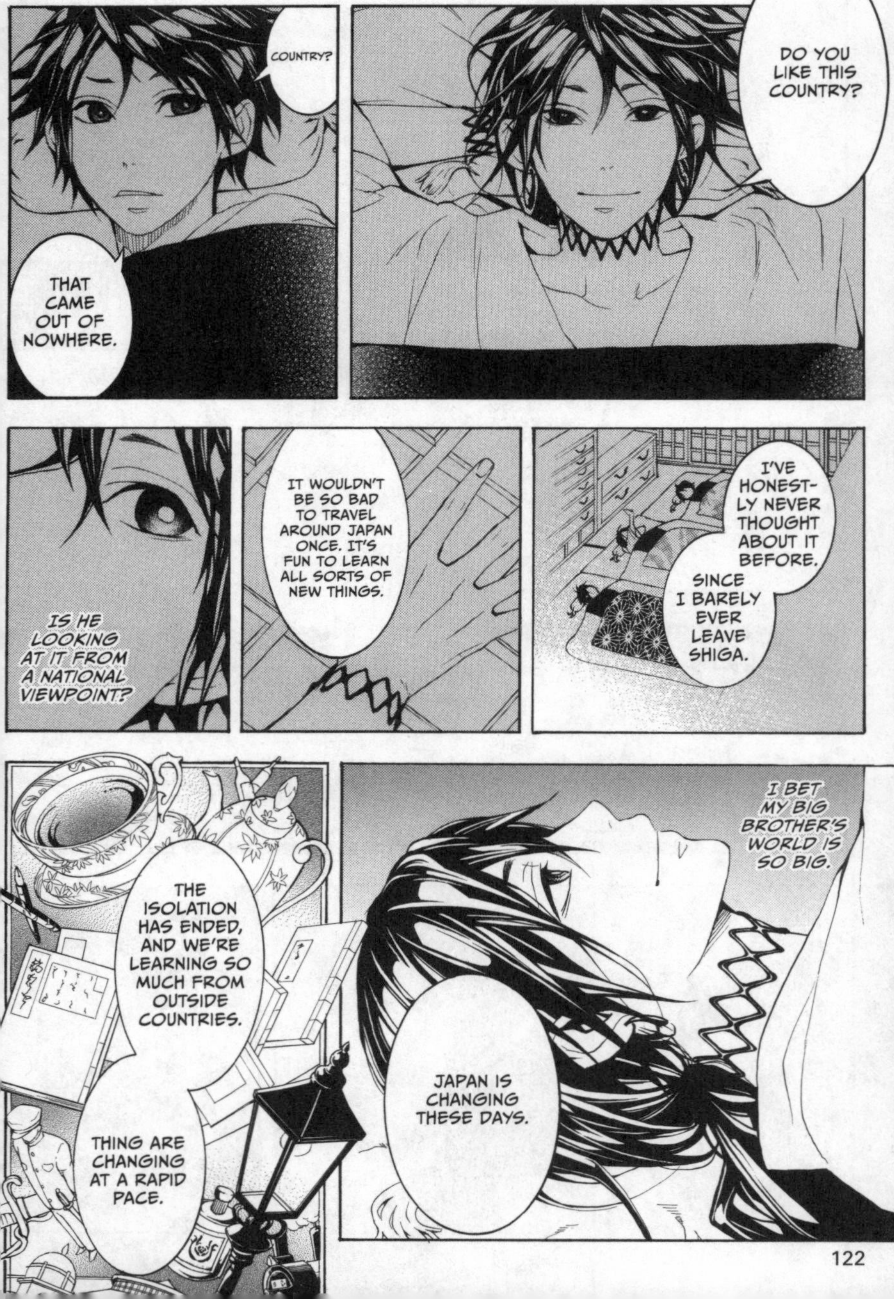
DO YOU LIKE THIS COUNTRY?
COUNTRY?
THAT CAME OUT OF NOWHERE.
I'VE HONEST-LY NEVER THOUGHT ABOUT IT BEFORE.
SINCE I BARELY EVER LEAVE SHIGA.
IT WOULDN'T BE SO BAD TO TRAVEL AROUND JAPAN ONCE. IT'S FUN TO LEARN ALL SORTS OF NEW THINGS.
IS HE LOOKING AT IT FROM A NATIONAL VIEWPOINT?
I BET MY BIG BROTHER'S WORLD IS SO BIG.
JAPAN IS CHANGING THESE DAYS.
THE ISOLATION HAS ENDED, AND WE'RE LEARNING SO MUCH FROM OUTSIDE COUNTRIES.
THING ARE CHANGING AT A RAPID PACE.

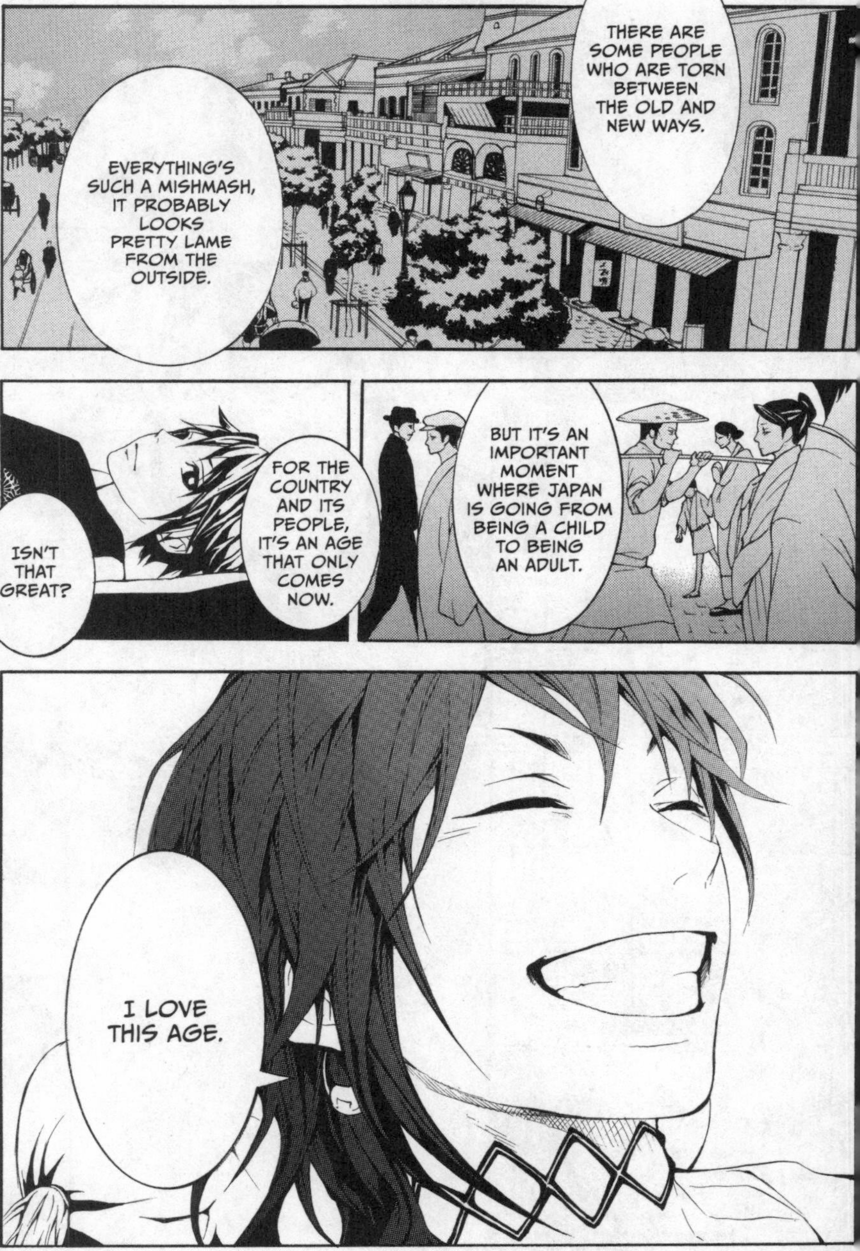
THERE ARE SOME PEOPLE WHO ARE TORN BETWEEN THE OLD AND NEW WAYS.
EVERYTHING'S SUCH A MISHMASH, IT PROBABLY LOOKS PRETTY LAME FROM THE OUTSIDE.
BUT IT'S AN IMPORTANT MOMENT WHERE JAPAN IS GOING FROM BEING A CHILD TO BEING AN ADULT.
FOR THE COUNTRY AND ITS PEOPLE, IT'S AN AGE THAT ONLY COMES NOW.
ISN'T THAT GREAT?
I LOVE THIS AGE.

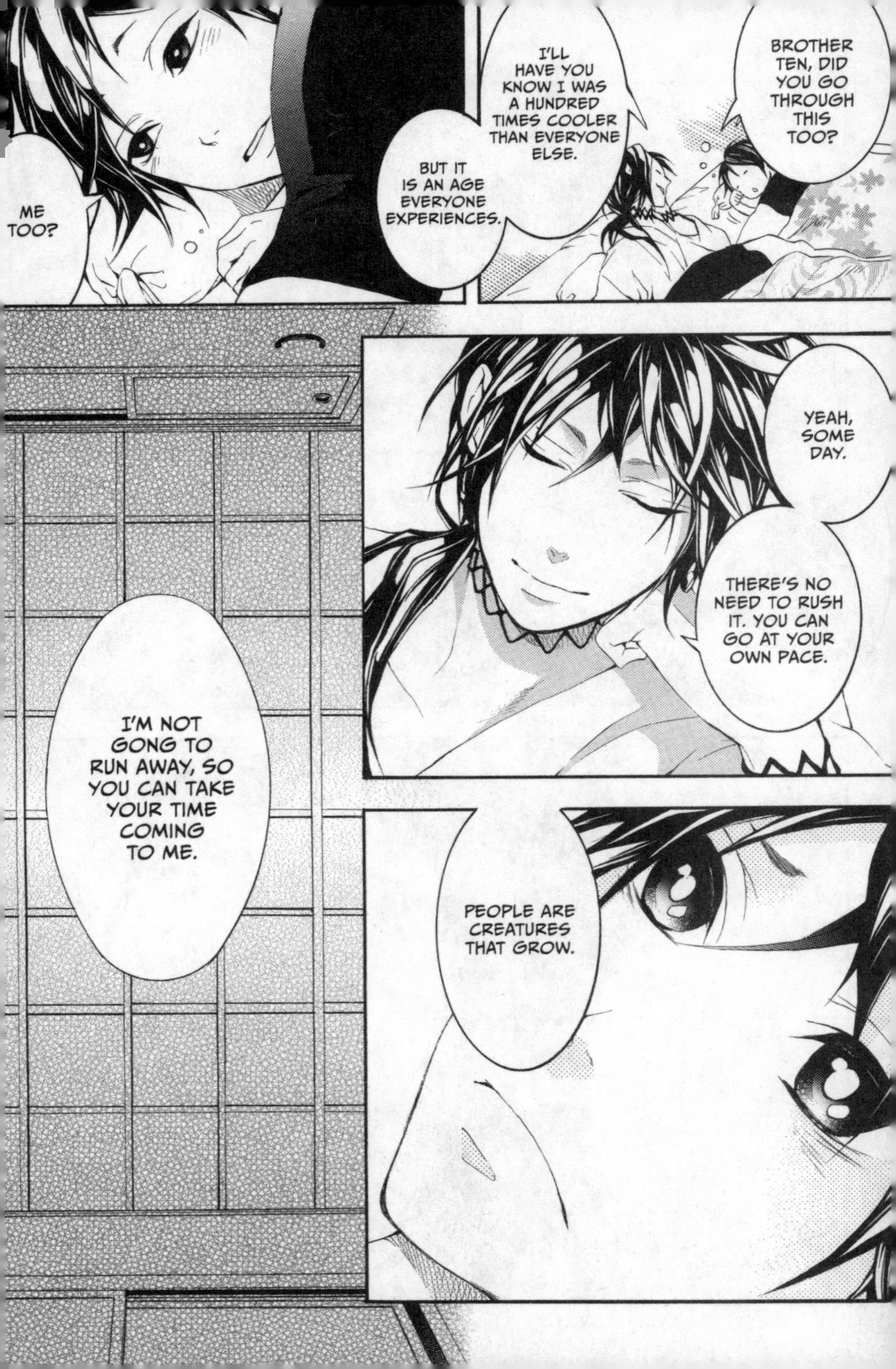
BROTHER TEN, DID YOU GO THROUGH THIS TOO?
I'LL HAVE YOU KNOW I WAS A HUNDRED TIMES COOLER THAN EVERYONE ELSE.
BUT IT IS AN AGE EVERYONE EXPERIENCES.
ME TOO?
YEAH, SOME DAY.
THERE'S NO NEED TO RUSH IT. YOU CAN GO AT YOUR OWN PACE.
PEOPLE ARE CREATURES THAT GROW.
I'M NOT GONG TO RUN AWAY, SO YOU CAN TAKE YOUR TIME COMING TO ME.

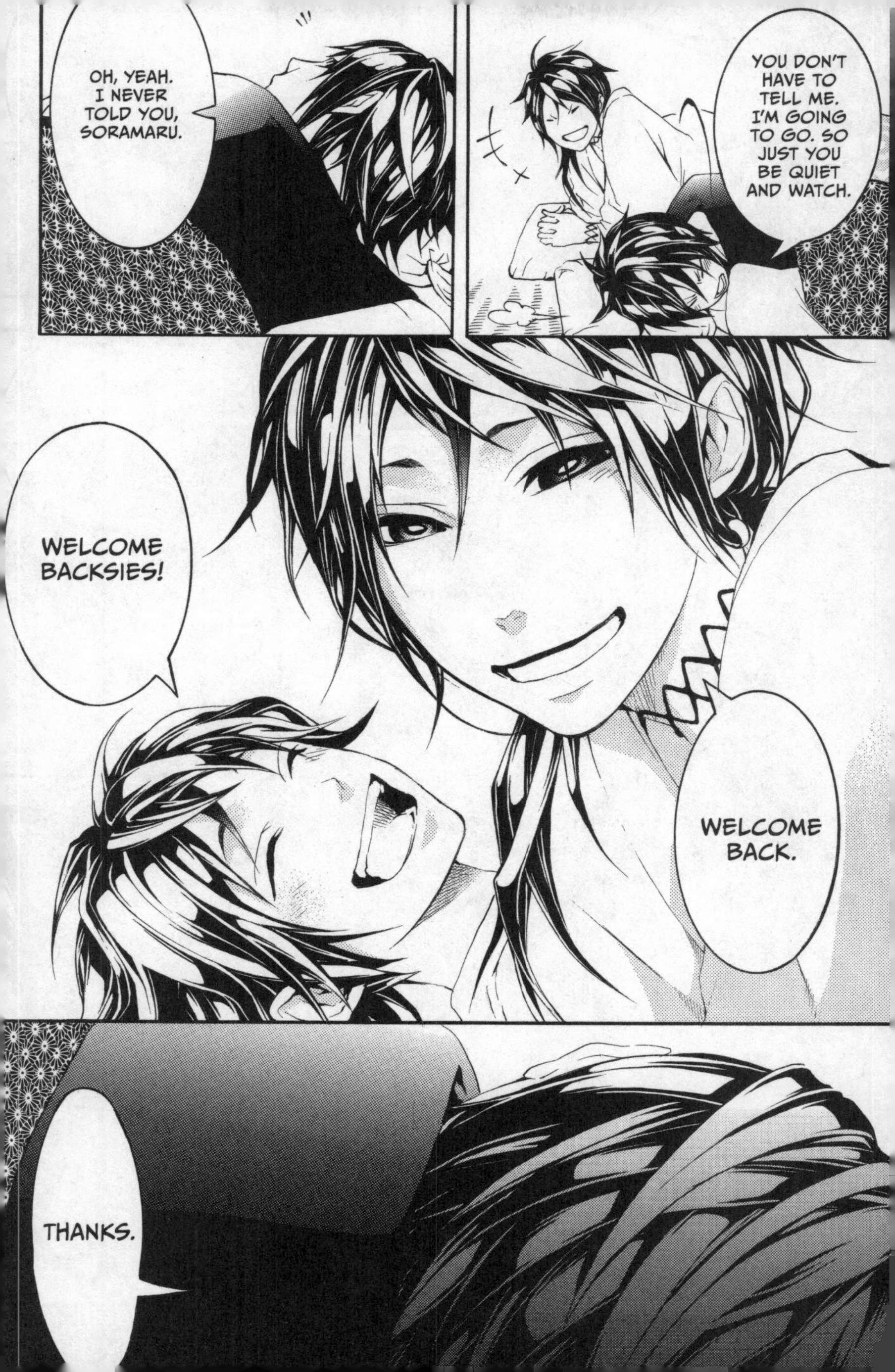
YOU DON'T HAVE TO TELL ME. I'M GOING TO GO. SO JUST YOU BE QUIET AND WATCH.
OH, YEAH. I NEVER TOLD YOU, SORAMARU.
WELCOME BACK.
WELCOME BACKSIES!
THANKS.

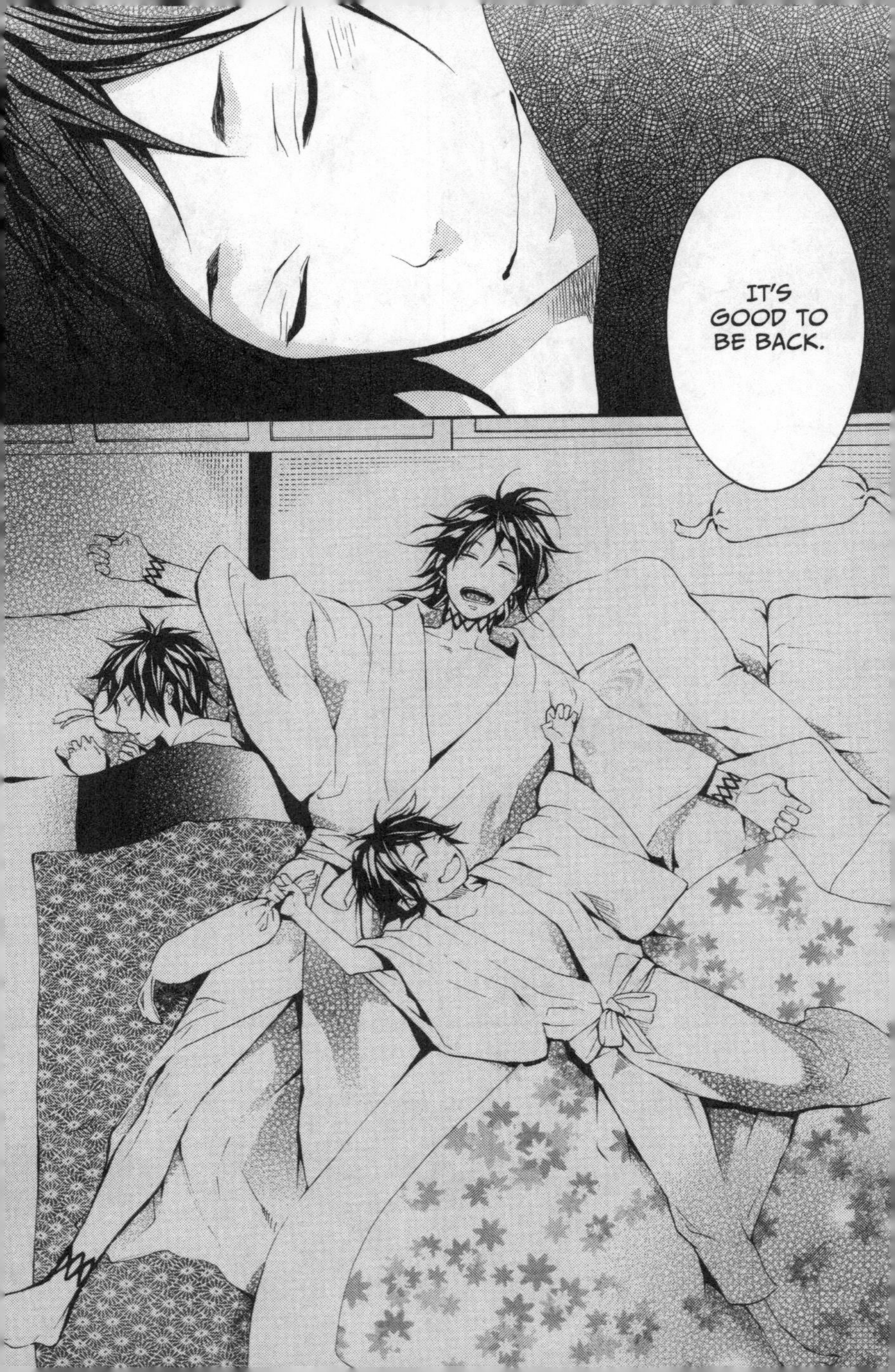
IT'S GOOD TO BE BACK.

Chapter 11
Tenka, Shaking With Worry

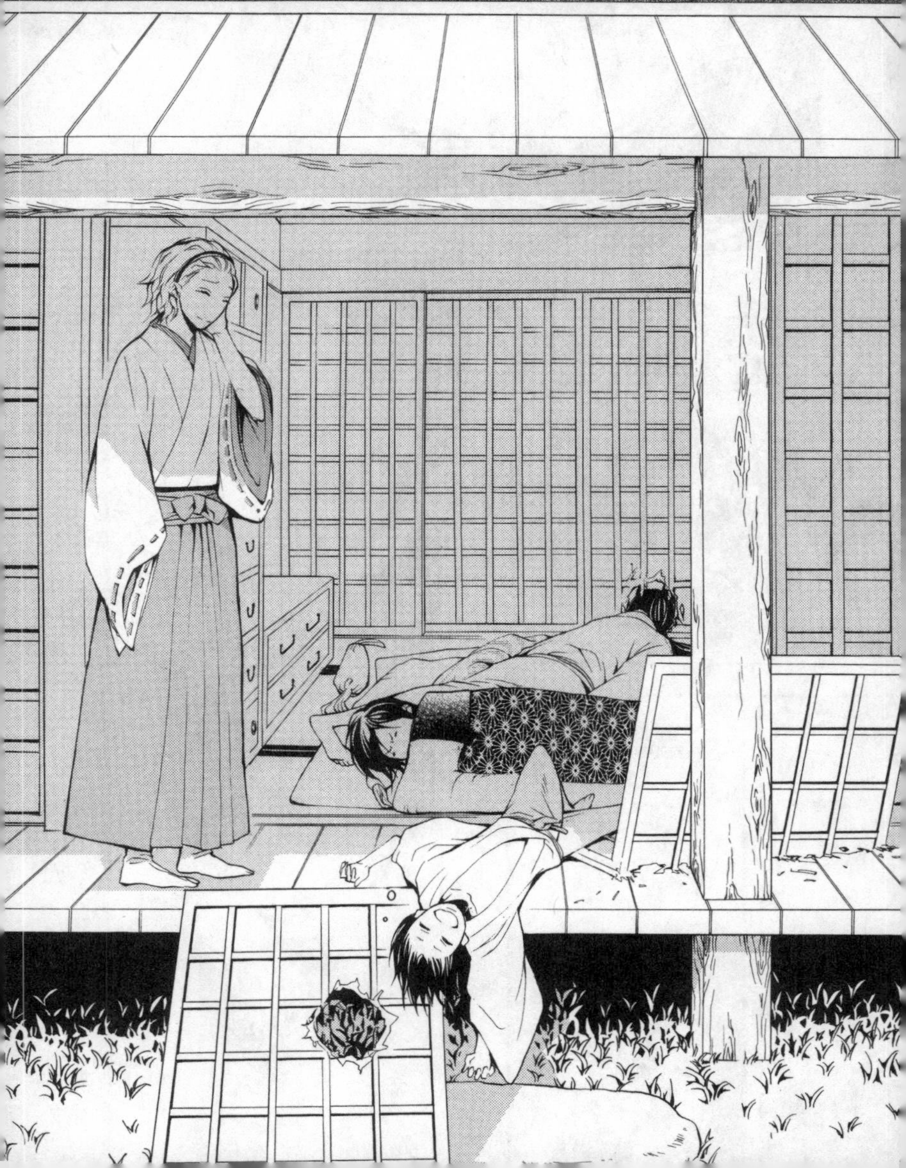

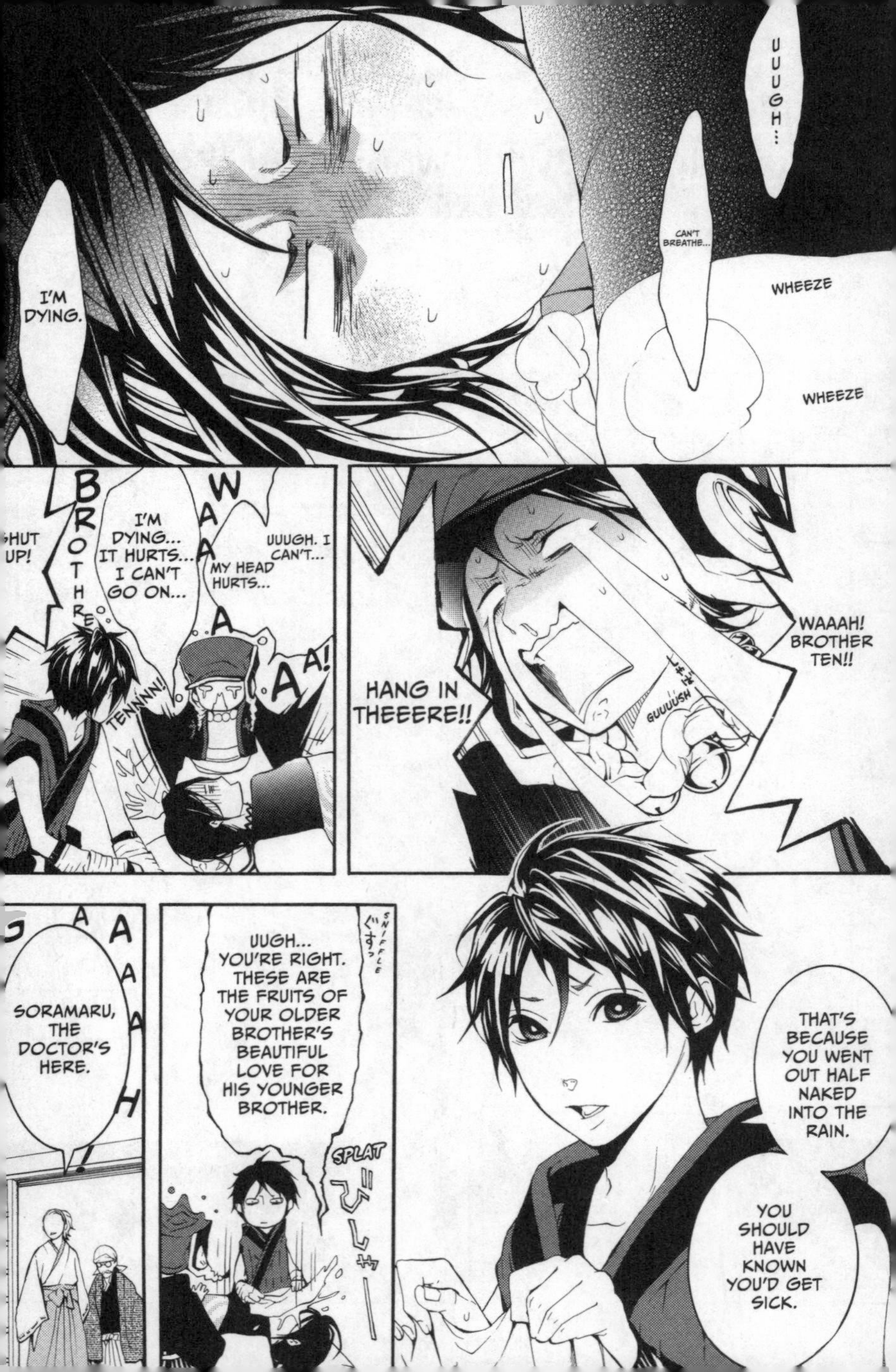

UUUGH...
CAN'T BREATHE...
WHEEZE
WHEEZE
I'M DYING.
WAAAH! BROTHER TEN!!
HANG IN THEEERE!!
GUUUUSH
UUUGH. I CAN'T... MY HEAD HURTS...
I'M DYING... IT HURTS... I CAN'T GO ON...
WAAAAAA!
BROTHER TENNNN!
SHUT UP!
THAT'S BECAUSE YOU WENT OUT HALF NAKED INTO THE RAIN.
YOU SHOULD HAVE KNOWN YOU'D GET SICK.
SNIFFLE
UUGH... YOU'RE RIGHT. THESE ARE THE FRUITS OF YOUR OLDER BROTHER'S BEAUTIFUL LOVE FOR HIS YOUNGER BROTHER.
SPLAT
GAAAAAH!
SORAMARU, THE DOCTOR'S HERE.

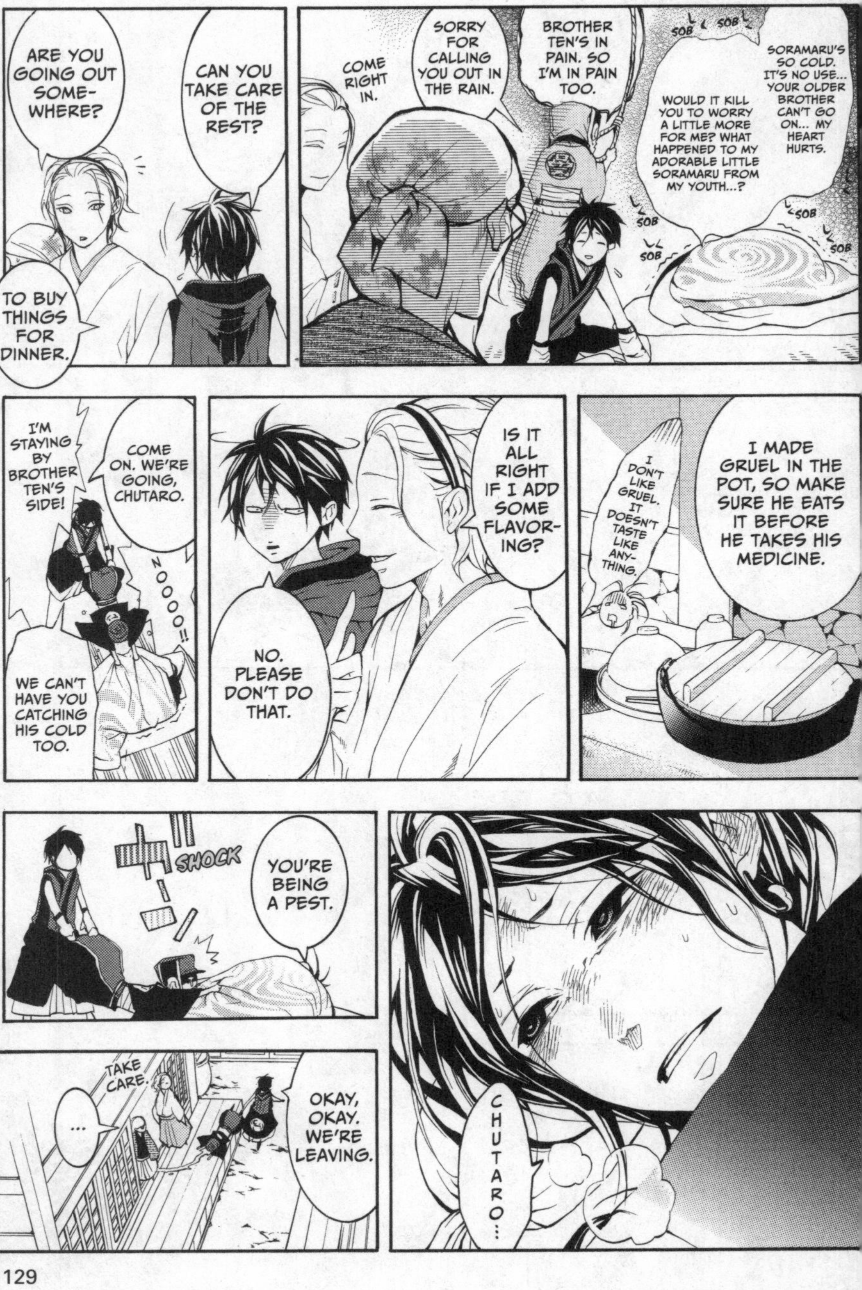
SOB SOB
SORAMARU'S SO COLD. IT'S NO USE... YOUR OLDER BROTHER CAN'T GO ON... MY HEART HURTS.
WOULD IT KILL YOU TO WORRY A LITTLE MORE FOR ME? WHAT HAPPENED TO MY ADORABLE LITTLE SORAMARU FROM MY YOUTH...?
SOB SOB
SOB SOB
BROTHER TEN'S IN PAIN. SO I'M IN PAIN TOO.
SORRY FOR CALLING YOU OUT IN THE RAIN.
COME RIGHT IN.
CAN YOU TAKE CARE OF THE REST?
ARE YOU GOING OUT SOME-WHERE?
TO BUY THINGS FOR DINNER.
I MADE GRUEL IN THE POT, SO MAKE SURE HE EATS IT BEFORE HE TAKES HIS MEDICINE.
I DON'T LIKE GRUEL. IT DOESN'T TASTE LIKE ANY-THING.
IS IT ALL RIGHT IF I ADD SOME FLAVOR-ING?
NO. PLEASE DON'T DO THAT.
COME ON. WE'RE GOING, CHUTARO.
I'M STAYING BY BROTHER TEN'S SIDE!
NOOOOO!!
WE CAN'T HAVE YOU CATCHING HIS COLD TOO.
CHUTARO...
YOU'RE BEING A PEST.
SHOCK
OKAY, OKAY. WE'RE LEAVING.
TAKE CARE.
...

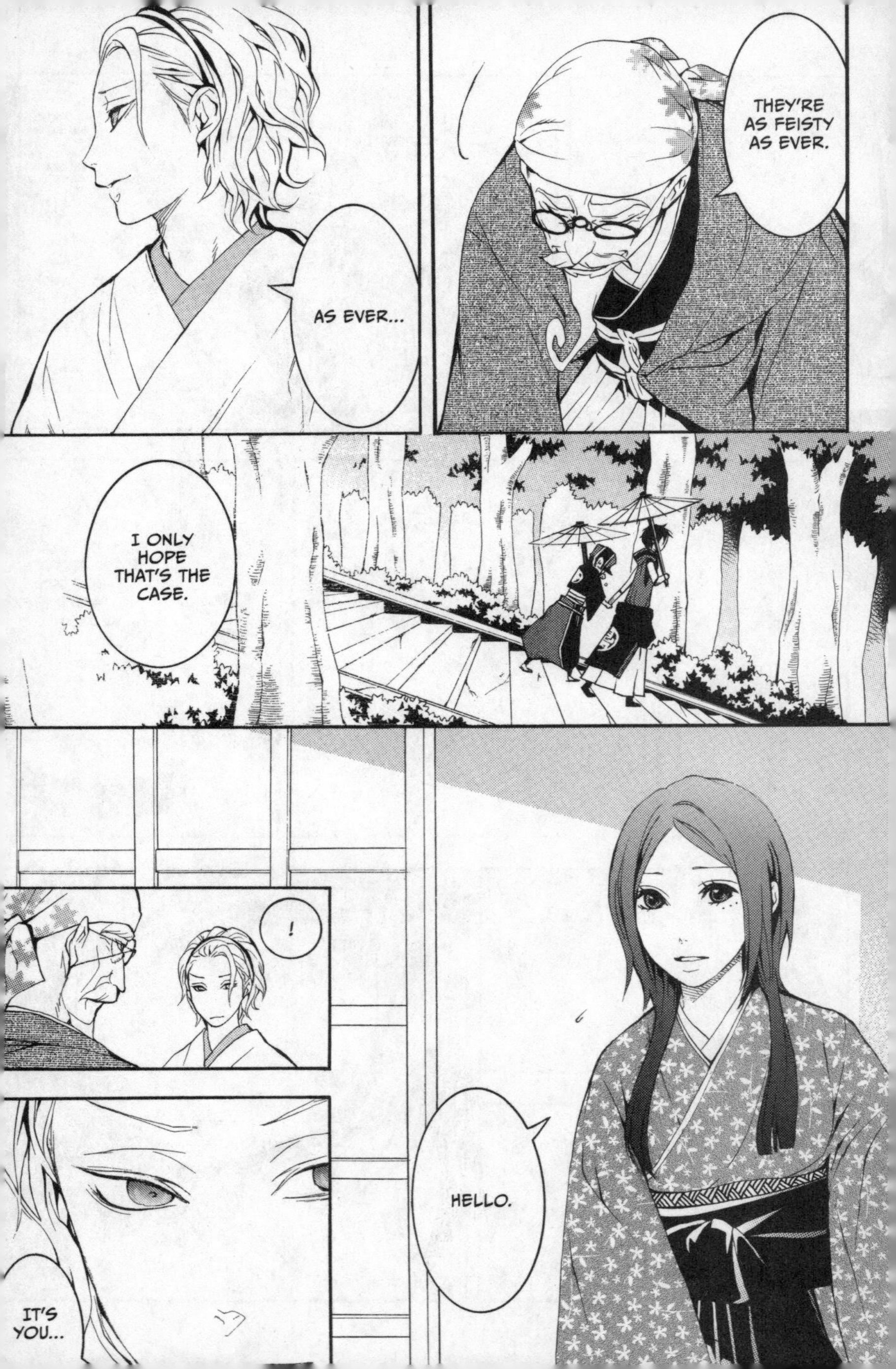

THEY'RE AS FEISTY AS EVER.
AS EVER...
I ONLY HOPE THAT'S THE CASE.
HELLO.
!
IT'S YOU...

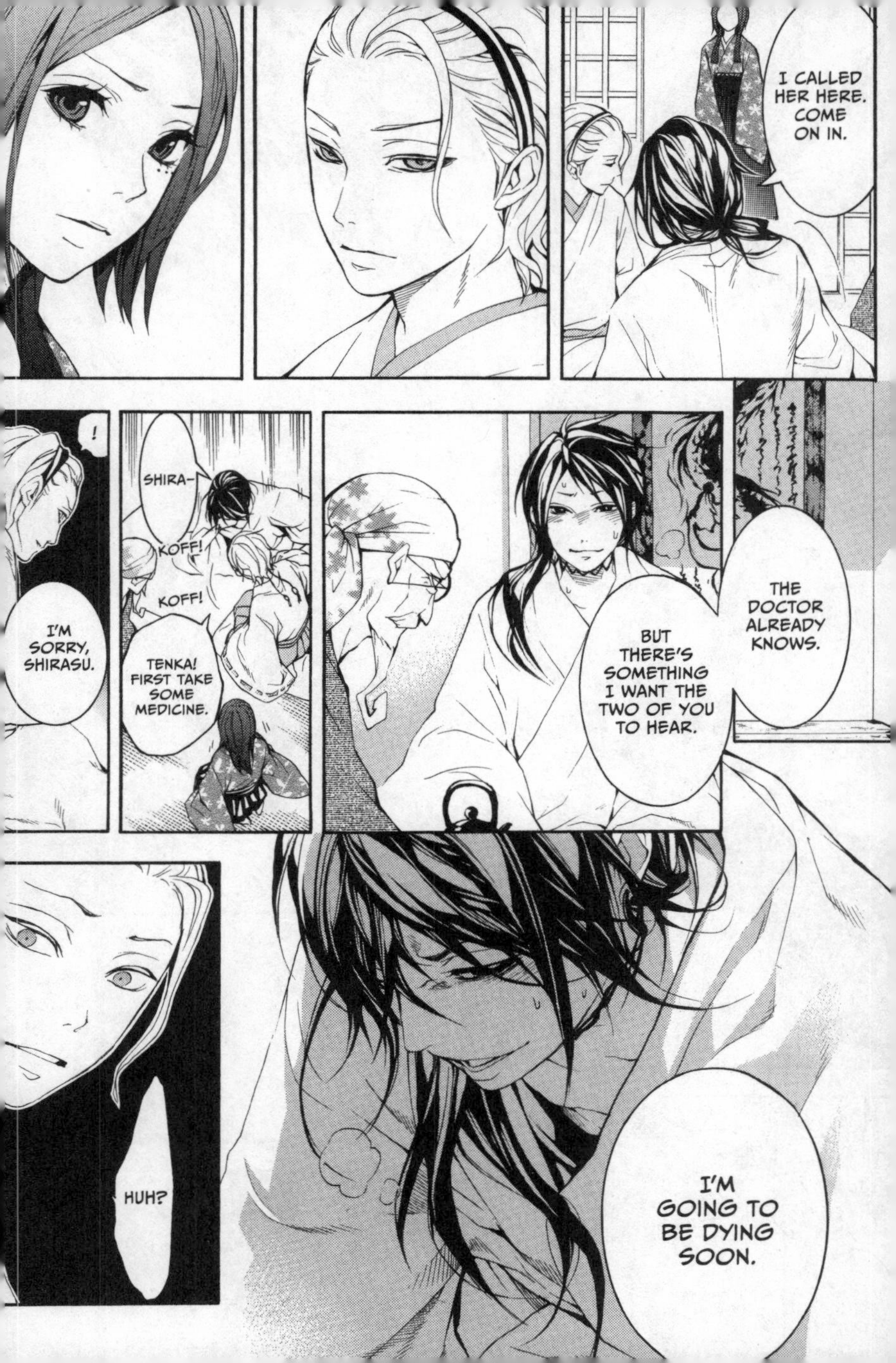
I CALLED HER HERE. COME ON IN.
THE DOCTOR ALREADY KNOWS.
BUT THERE'S SOMETHING I WANT THE TWO OF YOU TO HEAR.
SHIRA—
KOFF!
KOFF!
TENKA! FIRST TAKE SOME MEDICINE.
!
I'M SORRY, SHIRASU.
I'M GOING TO BE DYING SOON.
HUH?

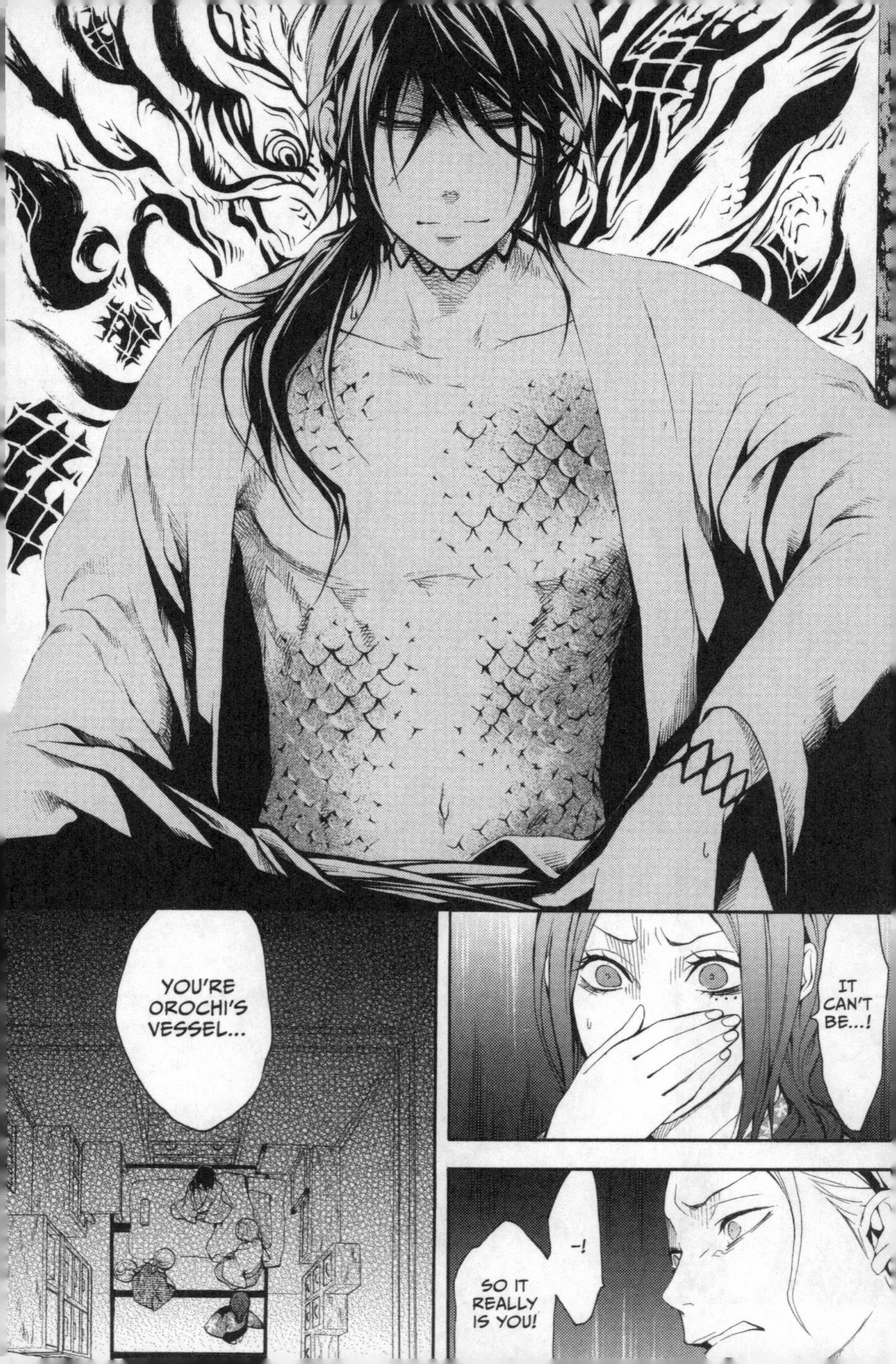
IT CAN'T BE...!
—!
SO IT REALLY IS YOU!
YOU'RE OROCHI'S VESSEL...

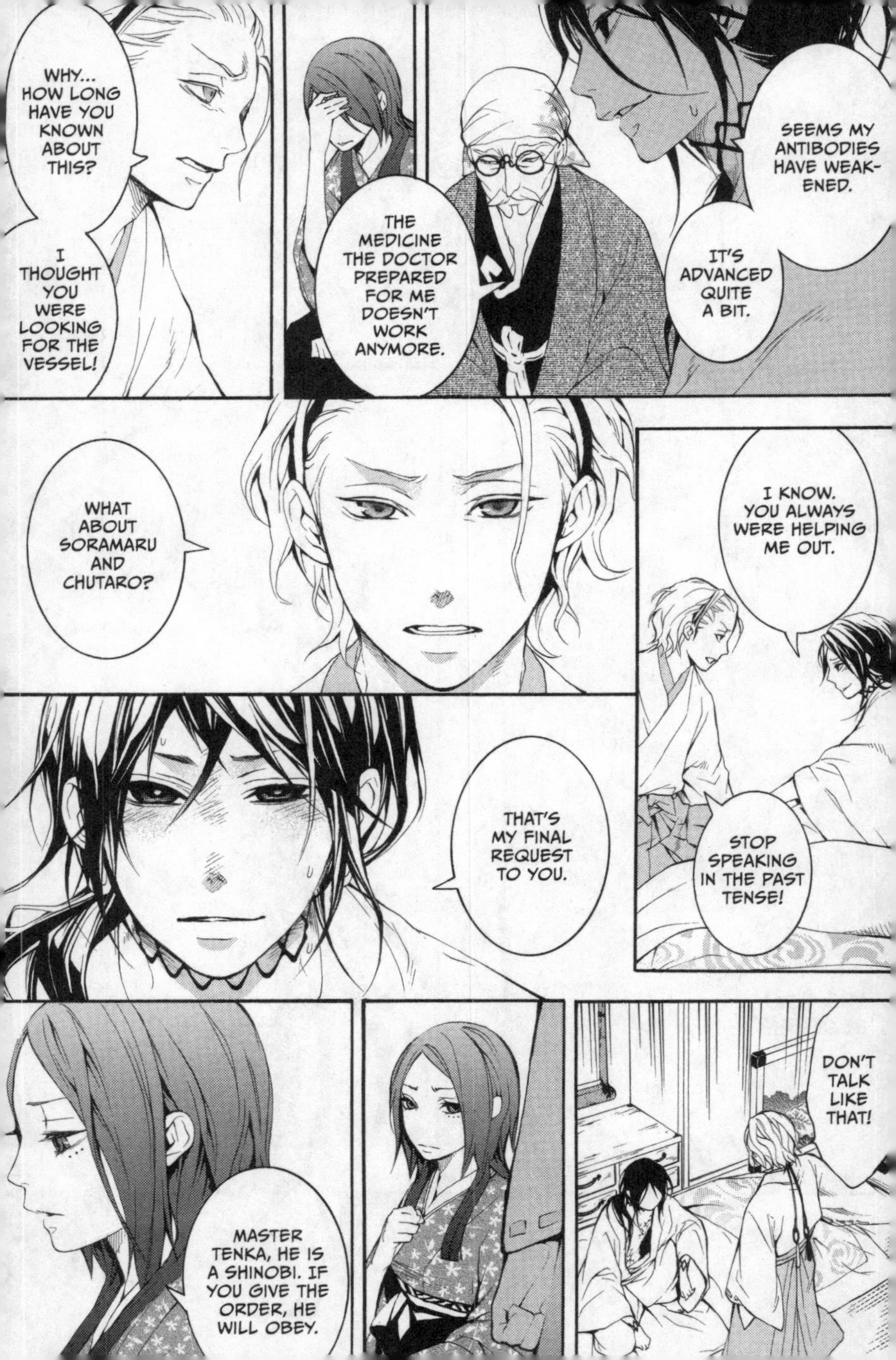
SEEMS MY ANTIBODIES HAVE WEAK-ENED.
IT'S ADVANCED QUITE A BIT.
THE MEDICINE THE DOCTOR PREPARED FOR ME DOESN'T WORK ANYMORE.
WHY... HOW LONG HAVE YOU KNOWN ABOUT THIS?
I THOUGHT YOU WERE LOOKING FOR THE VESSEL!
I KNOW. YOU ALWAYS WERE HELPING ME OUT.
STOP SPEAKING IN THE PAST TENSE!
WHAT ABOUT SORAMARU AND CHUTARO?
THAT'S MY FINAL REQUEST TO YOU.
DON'T TALK LIKE THAT!
MASTER TENKA, HE IS A SHINOBI. IF YOU GIVE THE ORDER, HE WILL OBEY.

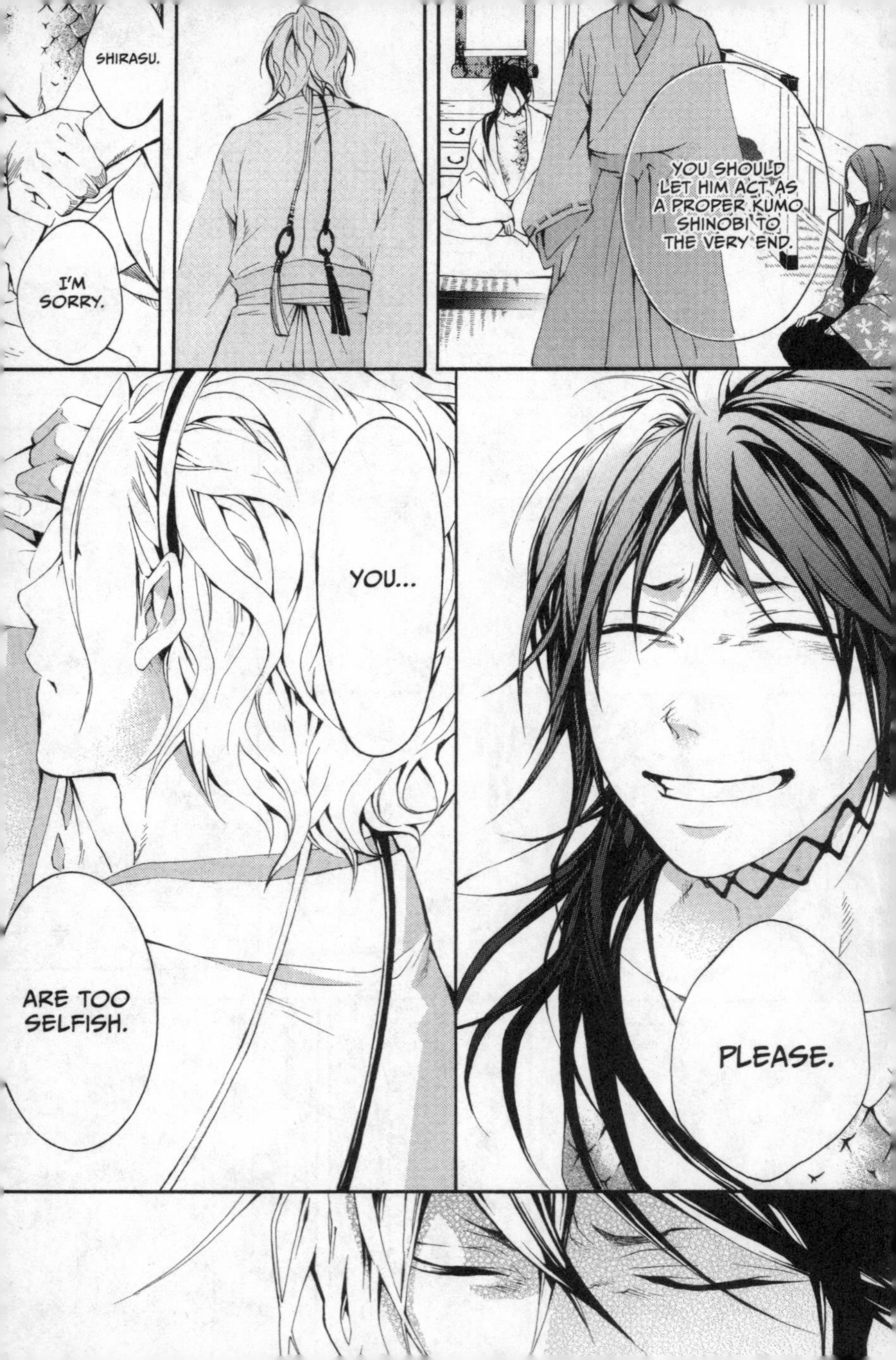
YOU SHOULD LET HIM ACT AS A PROPER KUMO SHINOBI TO THE VERY END.
SHIRASU.
I'M SORRY.
PLEASE.
YOU...
ARE TOO SELFISH.

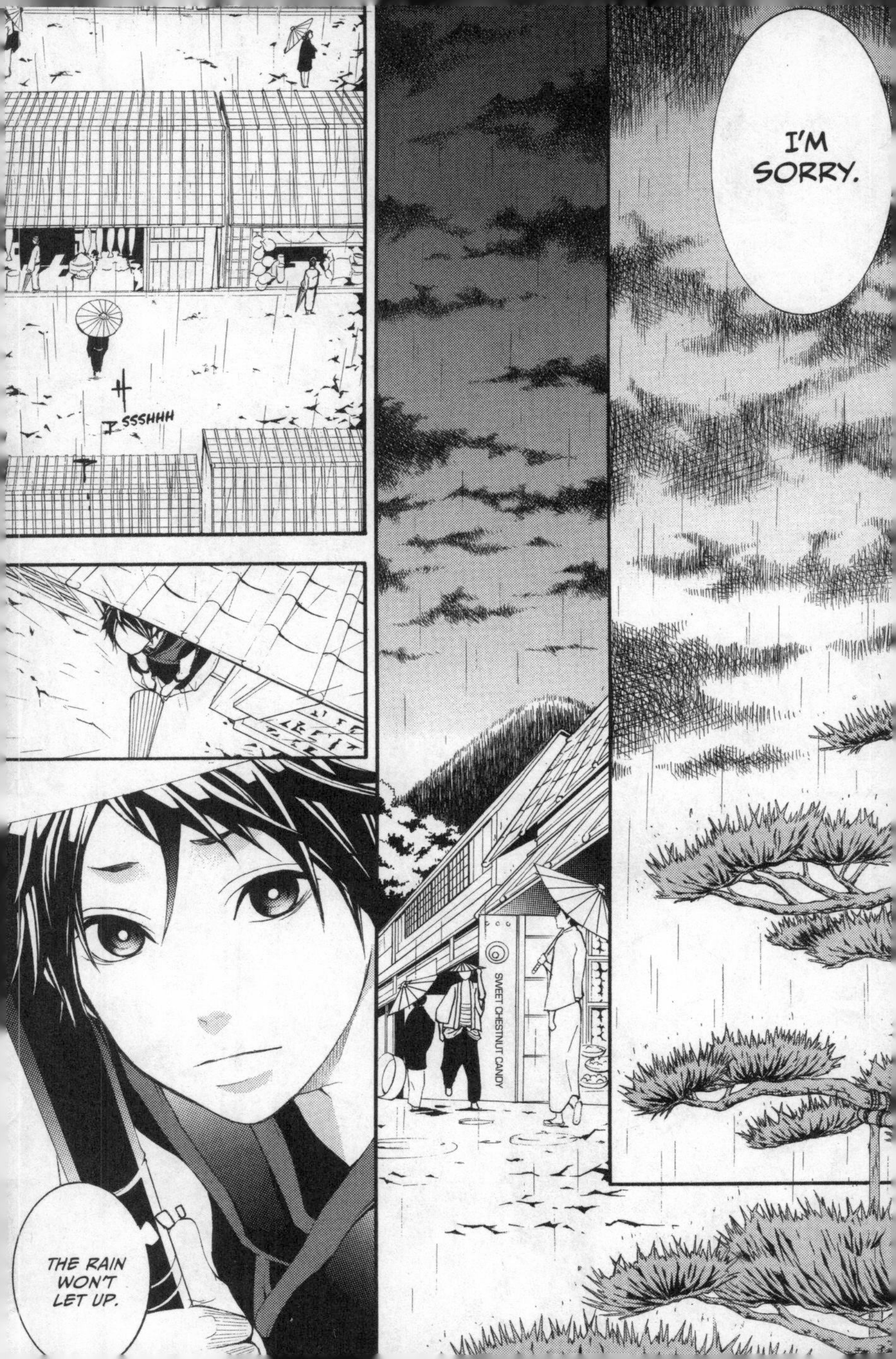
I'M SORRY.
SWEET CHESTNUT CANDY
SSSHHH
THE RAIN WON'T LET UP.

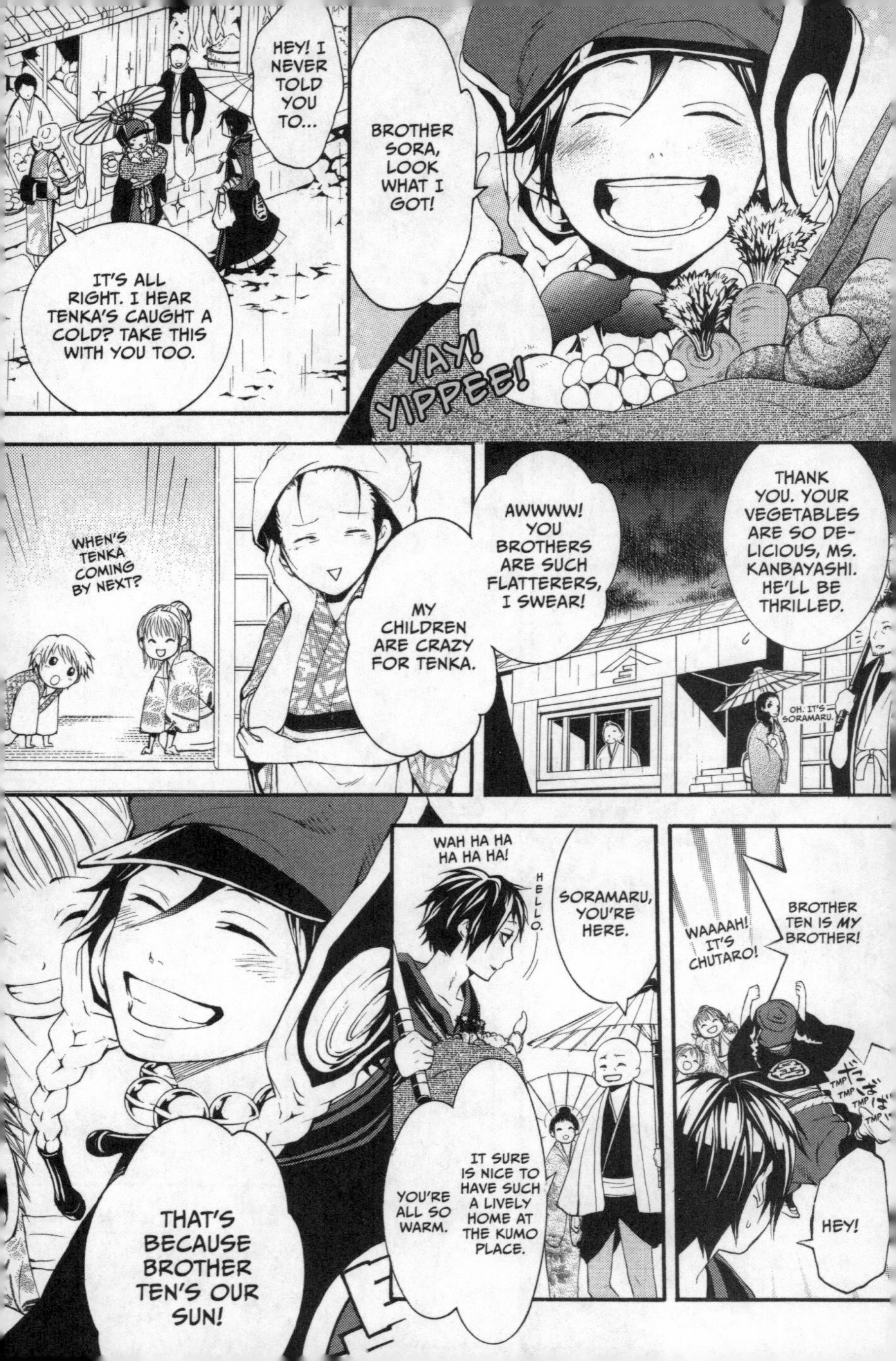
BROTHER SORA, LOOK WHAT I GOT!
YAY! YIPPEE!
HEY! I NEVER TOLD YOU TO...
IT'S ALL RIGHT. I HEAR TENKA'S CAUGHT A COLD? TAKE THIS WITH YOU TOO.
THANK YOU. YOUR VEGETABLES ARE SO DE-LICIOUS, MS. KANBAYASHI. HE'LL BE THRILLED.
OH. IT'S SORAMARU.
AWWWW! YOU BROTHERS ARE SUCH FLATTERERS, I SWEAR!
MY CHILDREN ARE CRAZY FOR TENKA.
WHEN'S TENKA COMING BY NEXT?
BROTHER TEN IS MY BROTHER!
WAAAAH! IT'S CHUTARO!
TMP TMP TMP TMP
HEY!
SORAMARU, YOU'RE HERE.
HELLO.
WAH HA HA HA HA HA!
IT SURE IS NICE TO HAVE SUCH A LIVELY HOME AT THE KUMO PLACE.
YOU'RE ALL SO WARM.
THAT'S BECAUSE BROTHER TEN'S OUR SUN!

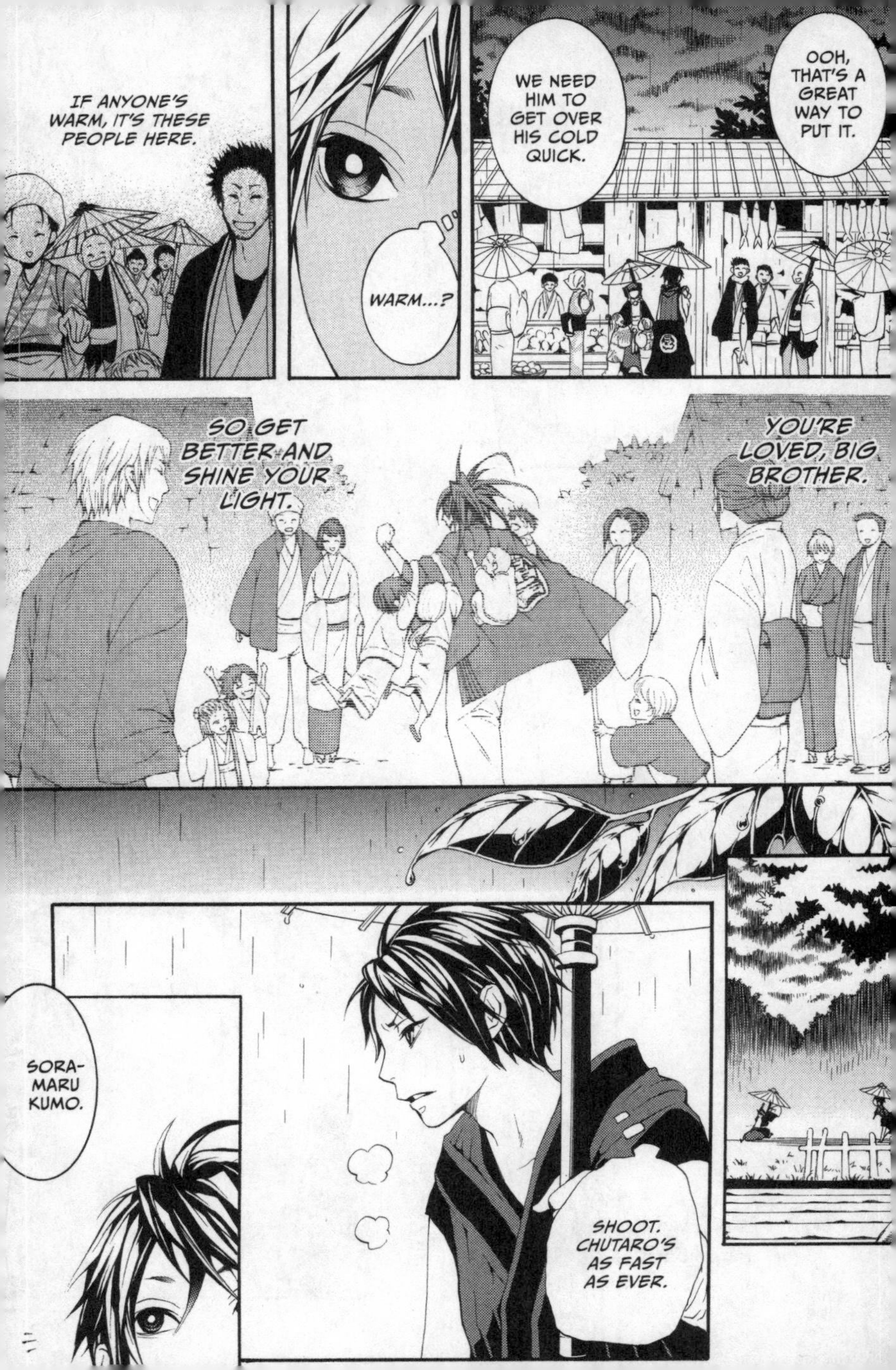
OOH, THAT'S A GREAT WAY TO PUT IT.
WE NEED HIM TO GET OVER HIS COLD QUICK.
WARM...?
IF ANYONE'S WARM, IT'S THESE PEOPLE HERE.
YOU'RE LOVED, BIG BROTHER.
SO GET BETTER AND SHINE YOUR LIGHT.
SHOOT. CHUTARO'S AS FAST AS EVER.
SORA-MARU KUMO.

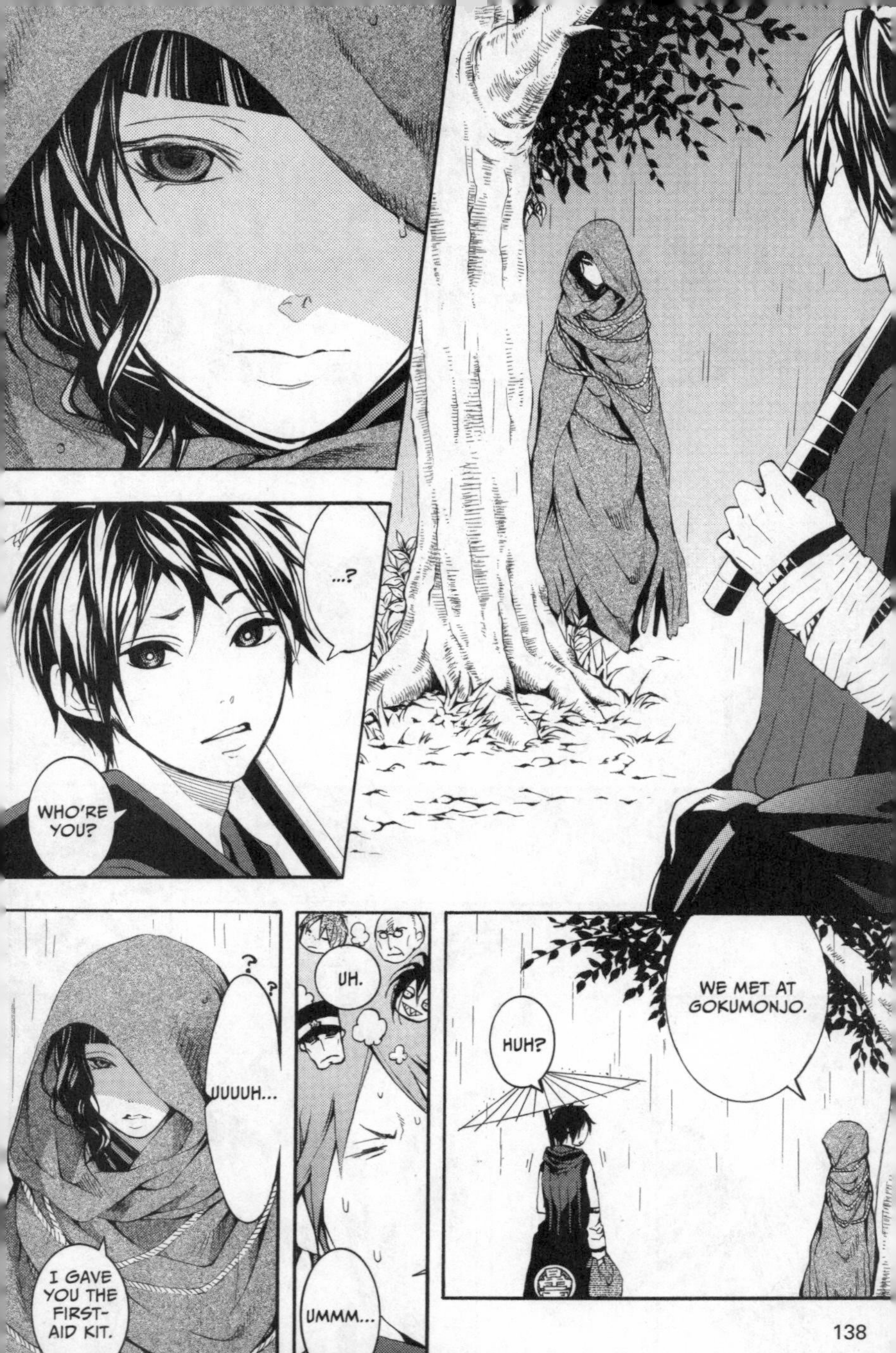
...?
WHO'RE YOU?
WE MET AT GOKUMONJO.
HUH?
UH.
UMMM...
? ?
UUUUH...
I GAVE YOU THE FIRST-AID KIT.

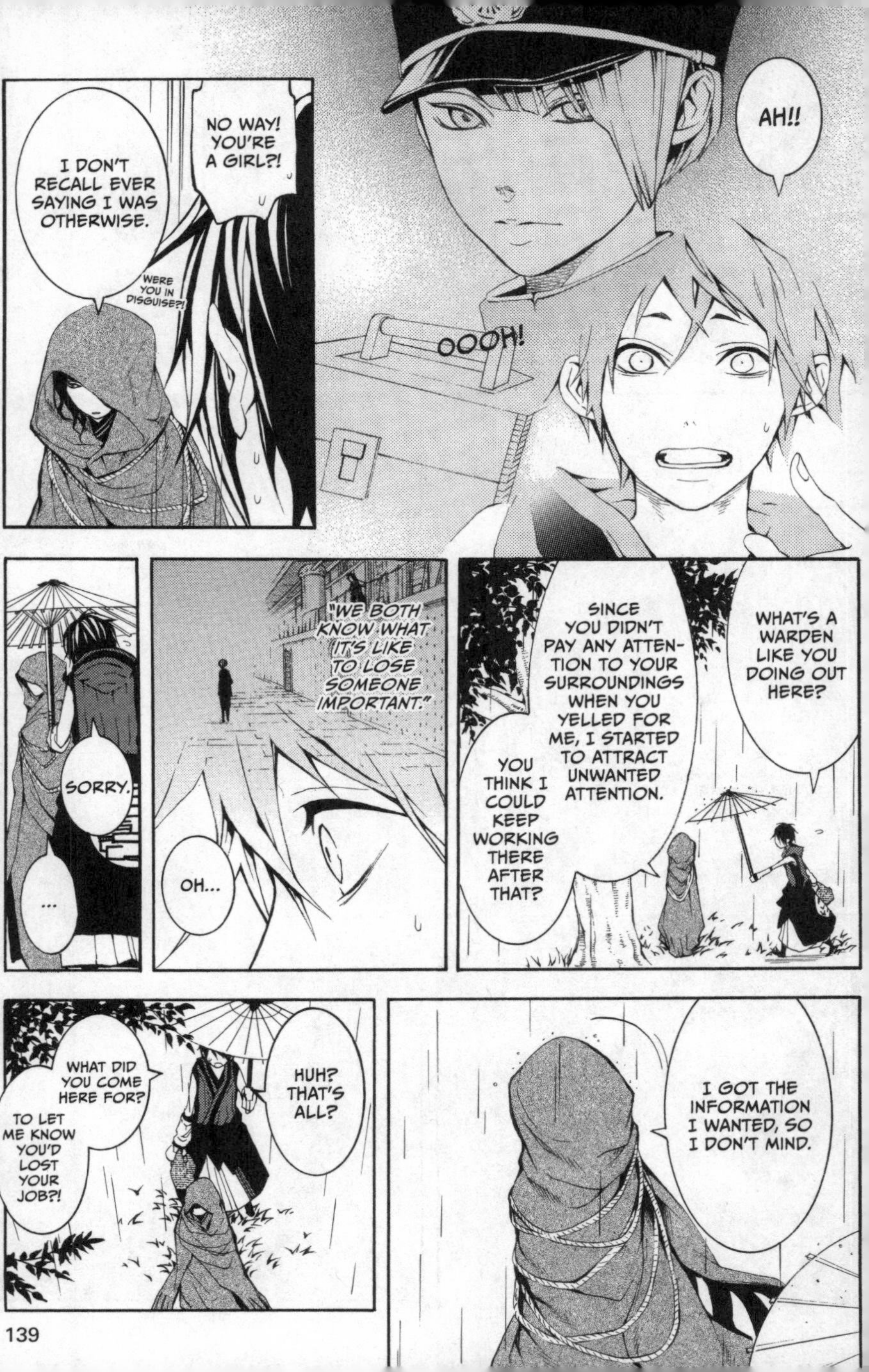
AH!!
OOOH!
NO WAY! YOU'RE A GIRL?!
I DON'T RECALL EVER SAYING I WAS OTHERWISE.
WERE YOU IN DISGUISE?!
WHAT'S A WARDEN LIKE YOU DOING OUT HERE?
SINCE YOU DIDN'T PAY ANY ATTENTION TO YOUR SURROUNDINGS WHEN YOU YELLED FOR ME, I STARTED TO ATTRACT UNWANTED ATTENTION.
YOU THINK I COULD KEEP WORKING THERE AFTER THAT?
"WE BOTH KNOW WHAT IT'S LIKE TO LOSE SOMEONE IMPORTANT."
OH...
SORRY.
...
I GOT THE INFORMATION I WANTED, SO I DON'T MIND.
HUH? THAT'S ALL?
WHAT DID YOU COME HERE FOR?
TO LET ME KNOW YOU'D LOST YOUR JOB?!

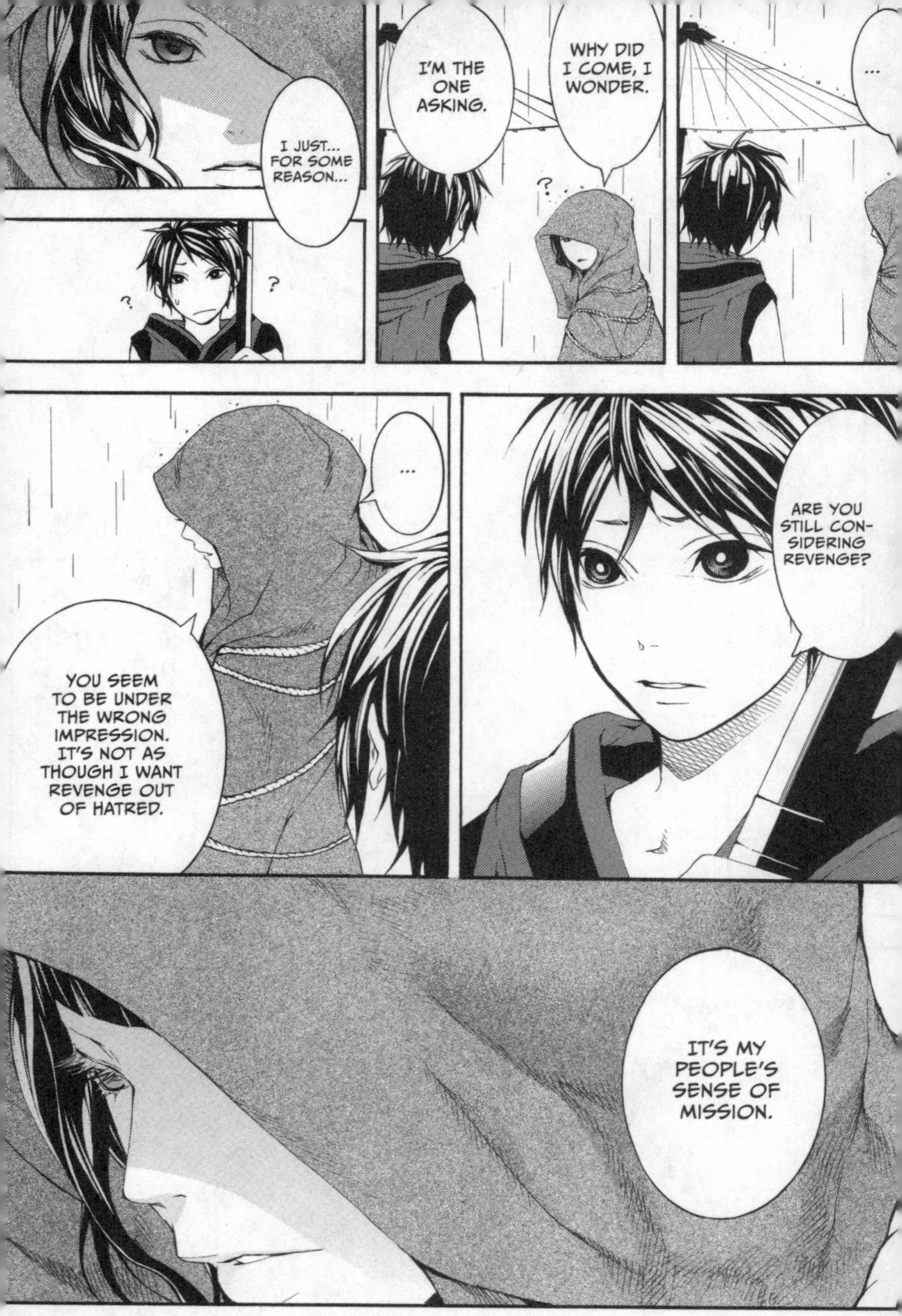
...
WHY DID I COME, I WONDER.
I'M THE ONE ASKING.
I JUST... FOR SOME REASON...
ARE YOU STILL CON-SIDERING REVENGE?
...
YOU SEEM TO BE UNDER THE WRONG IMPRESSION. IT'S NOT AS THOUGH I WANT REVENGE OUT OF HATRED.
IT'S MY PEOPLE'S SENSE OF MISSION.

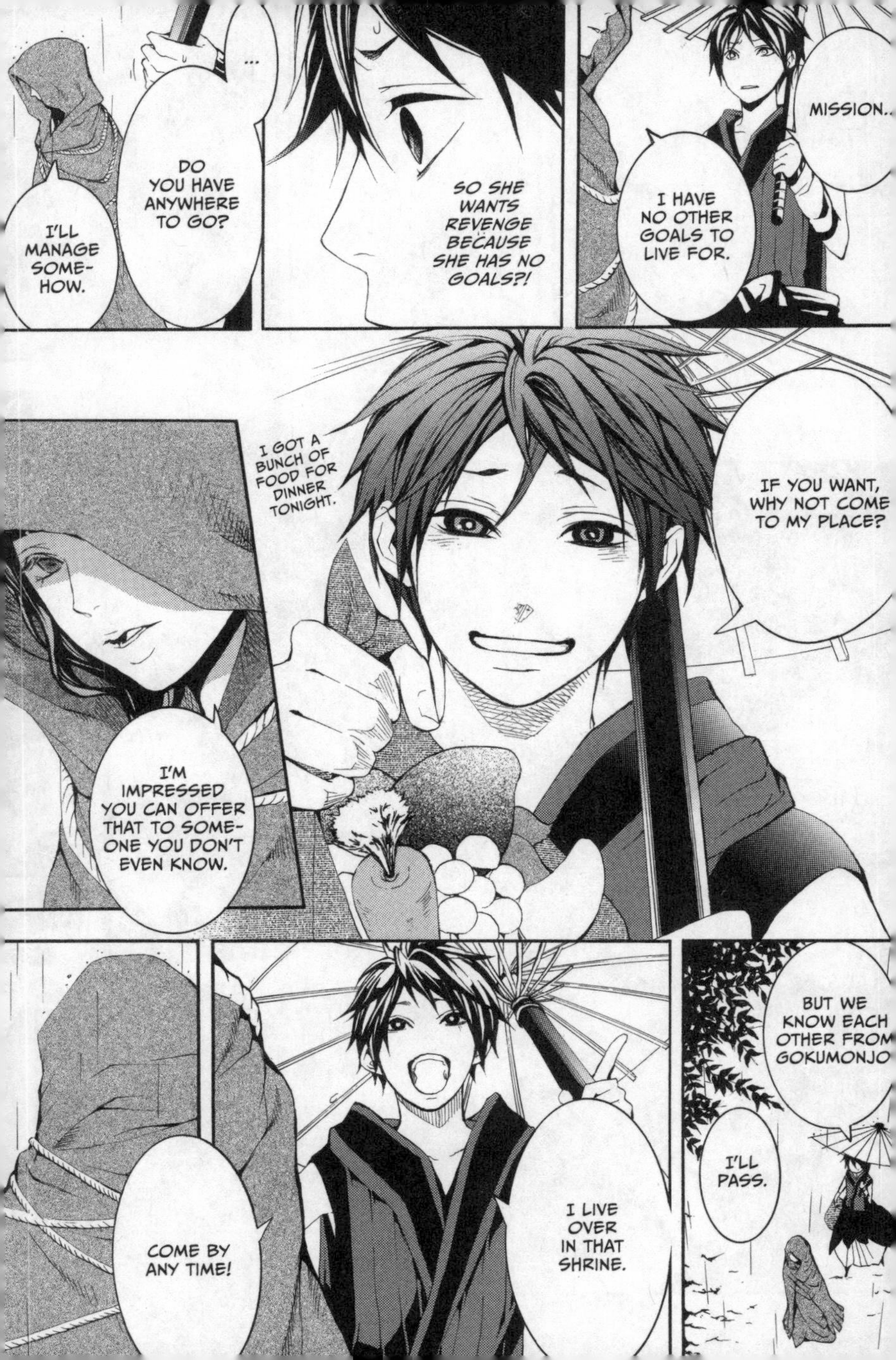
MISSION...
I HAVE NO OTHER GOALS TO LIVE FOR.
SO SHE WANTS REVENGE BECAUSE SHE HAS NO GOALS?!
...
DO YOU HAVE ANYWHERE TO GO?
I'LL MANAGE SOME-HOW.
IF YOU WANT, WHY NOT COME TO MY PLACE?
I GOT A BUNCH OF FOOD FOR DINNER TONIGHT.
I'M IMPRESSED YOU CAN OFFER THAT TO SOME-ONE YOU DON'T EVEN KNOW.
BUT WE KNOW EACH OTHER FROM GOKUMONJO
I'LL PASS.
I LIVE OVER IN THAT SHRINE.
COME BY ANY TIME!

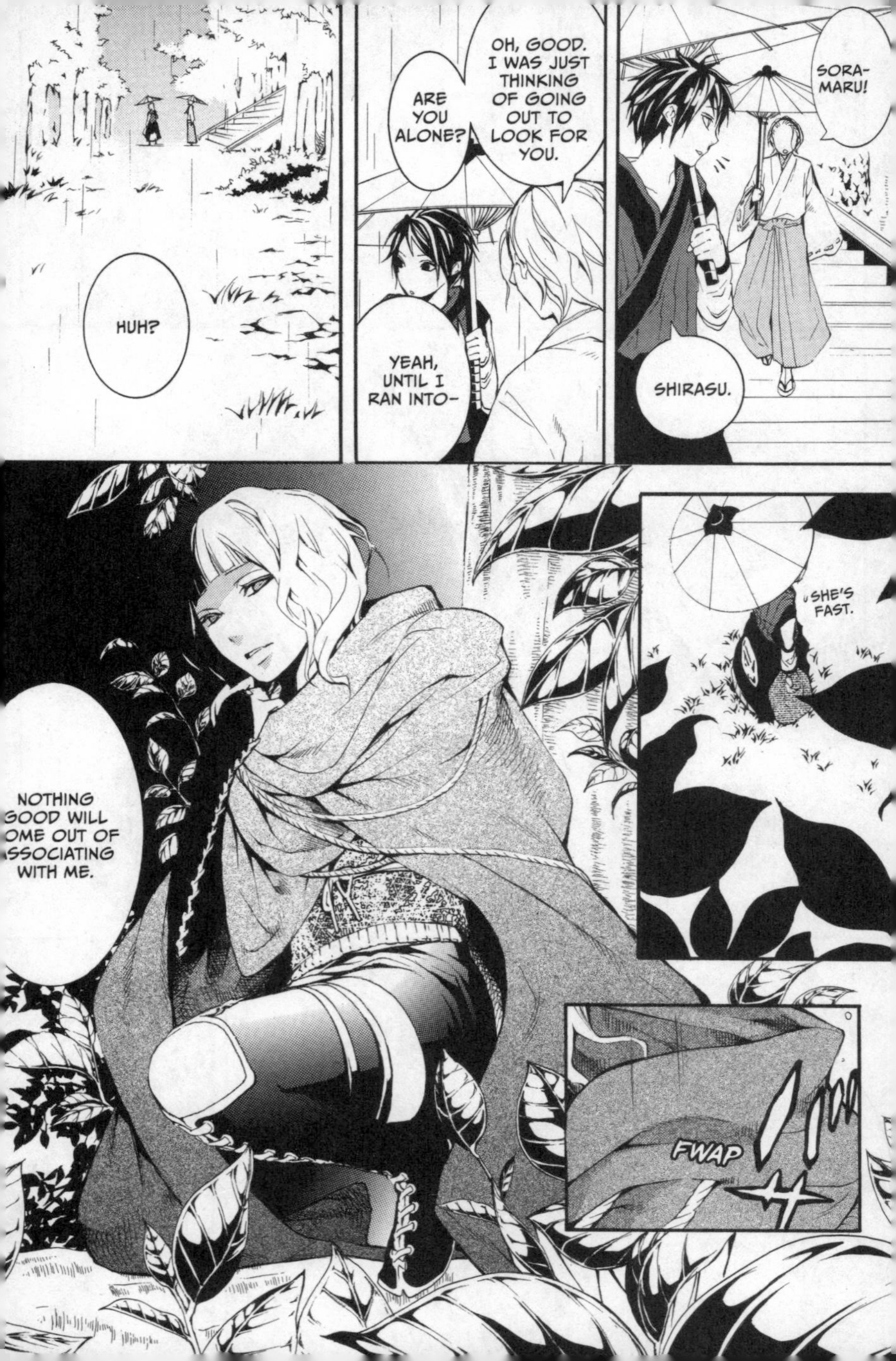
SORA-MARU!
SHIRASU.
OH, GOOD. I WAS JUST THINKING OF GOING OUT TO LOOK FOR YOU.
ARE YOU ALONE?
YEAH, UNTIL I RAN INTO-
HUH?
SHE'S FAST.
FWAP
NOTHING GOOD WILL OME OUT OF SSOCIATING WITH ME.

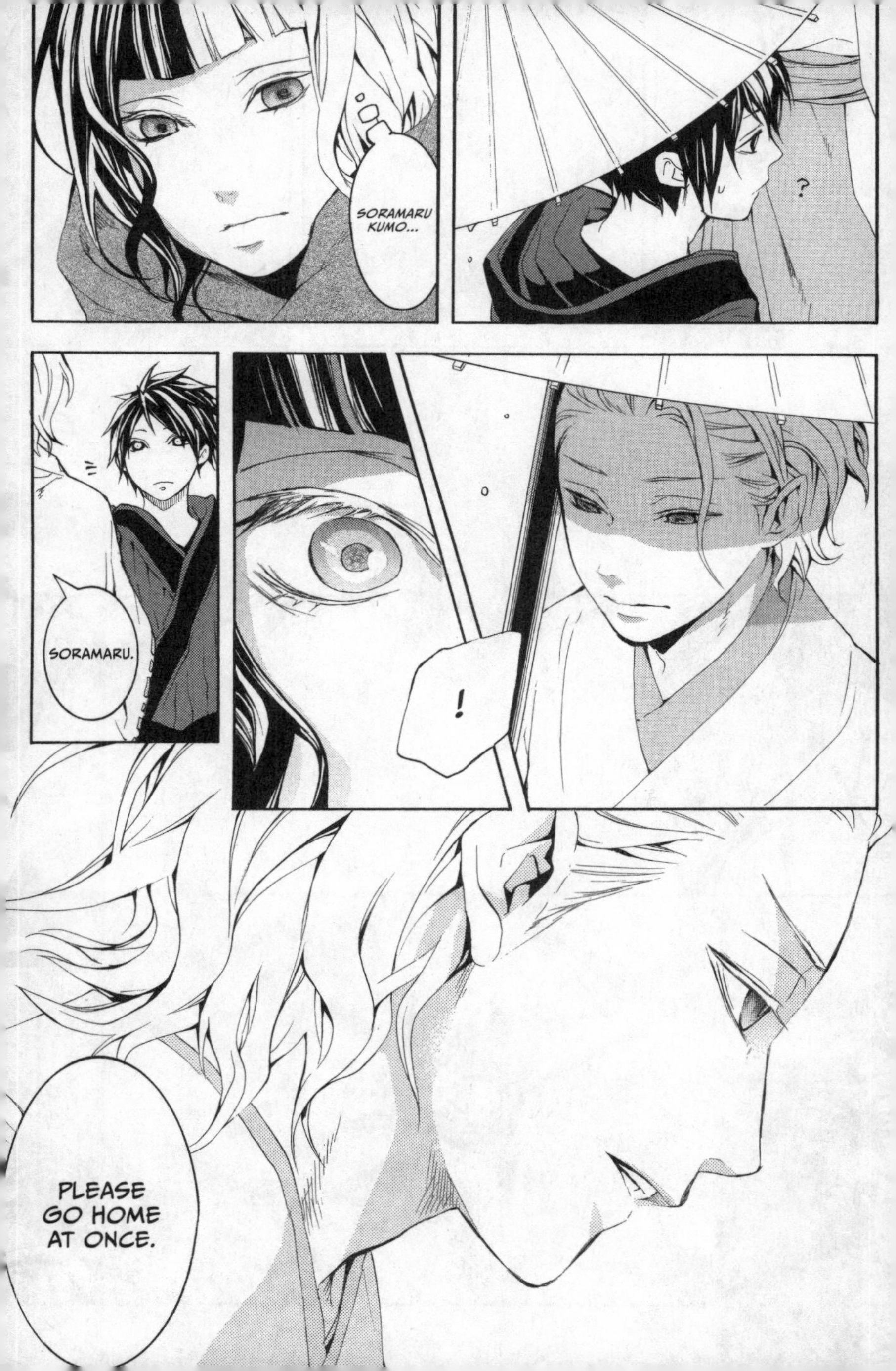
?
SORAMARU KUMO...
!
SORAMARU.
PLEASE GO HOME AT ONCE.

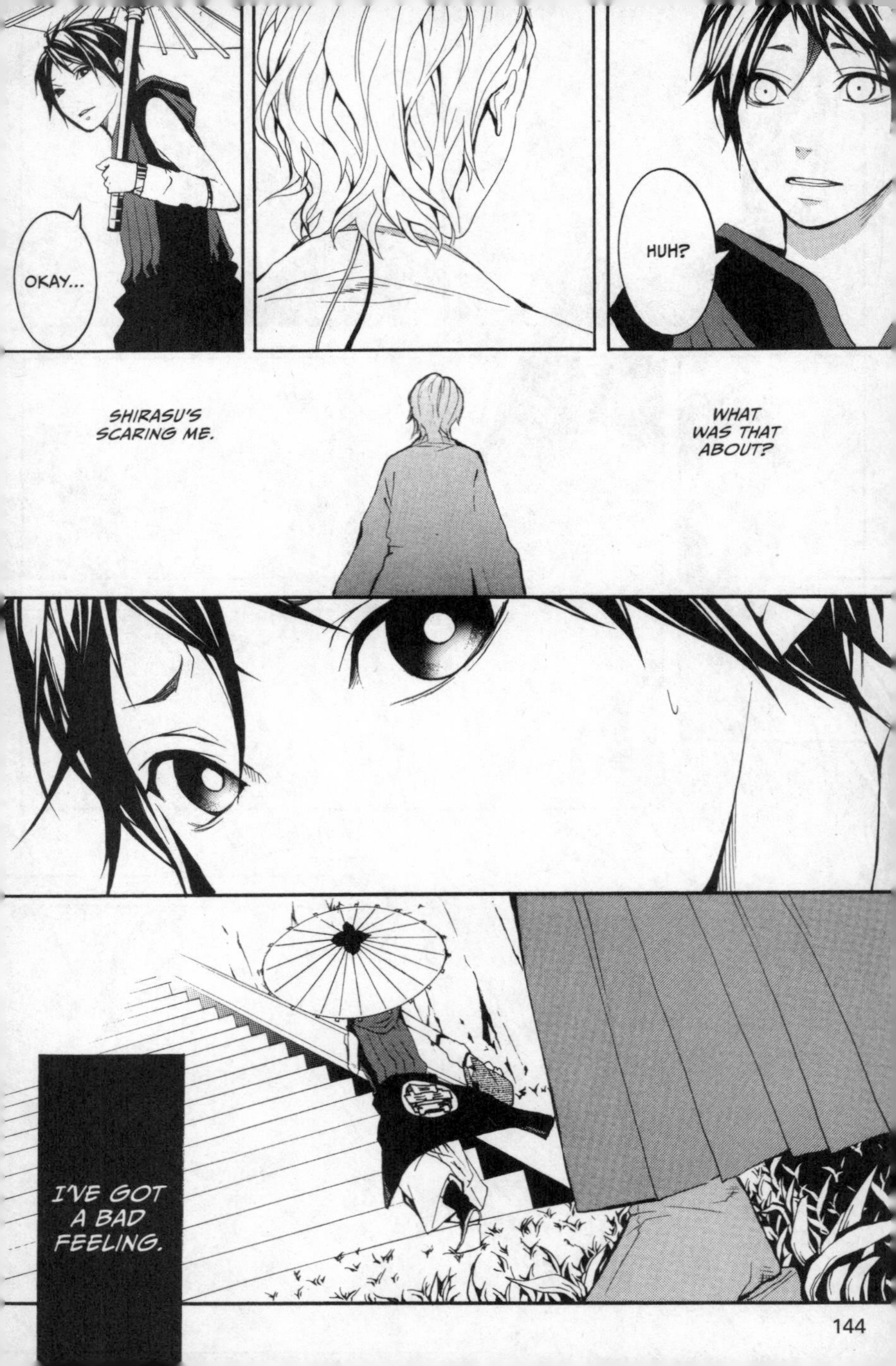
HUH?
OKAY...
WHAT WAS THAT ABOUT?
SHIRASU'S SCARING ME.
I'VE GOT A BAD FEELING.

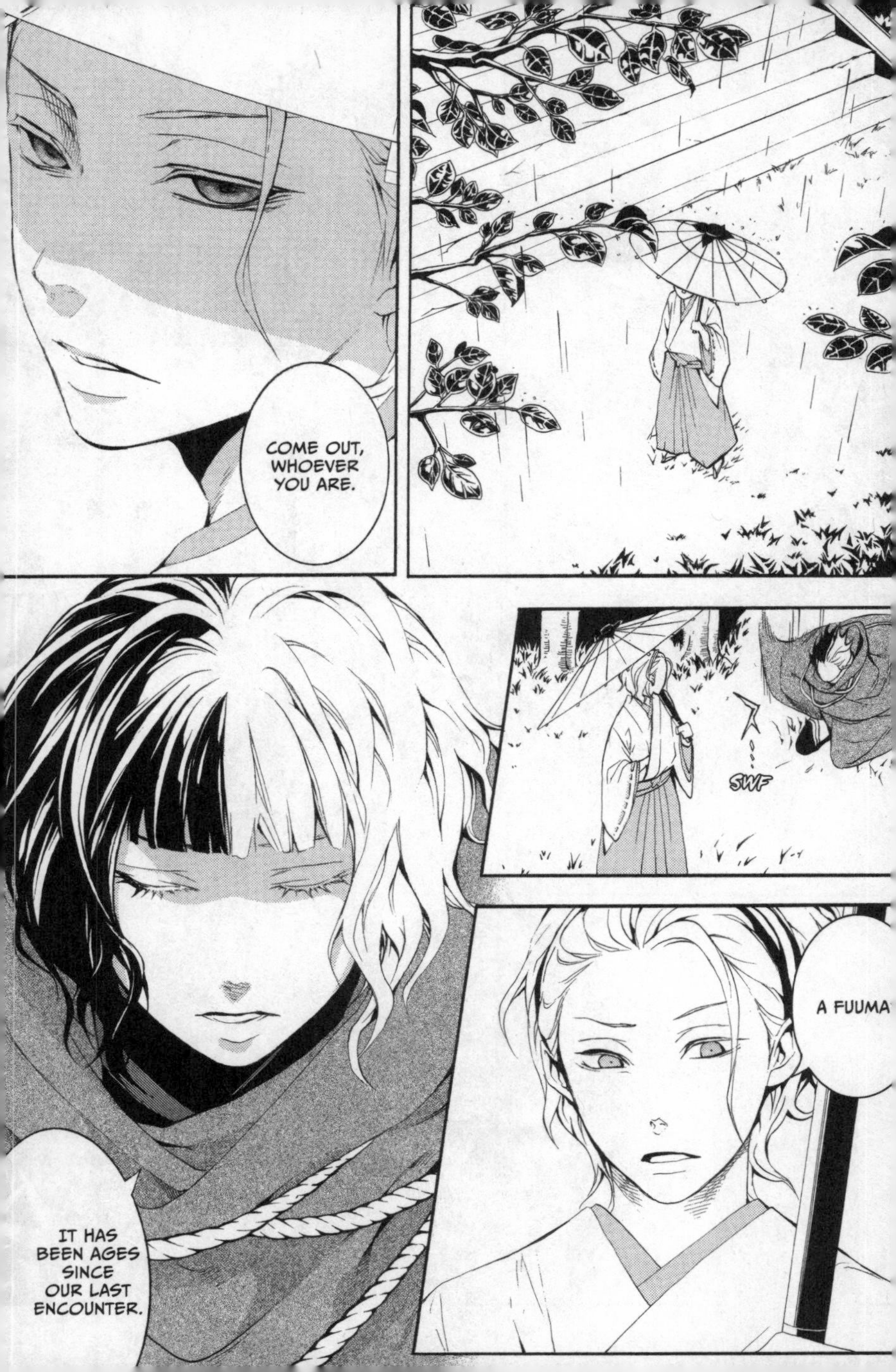
COME OUT, WHOEVER YOU ARE.
SWF
A FUUMA
IT HAS BEEN AGES SINCE OUR LAST ENCOUNTER.

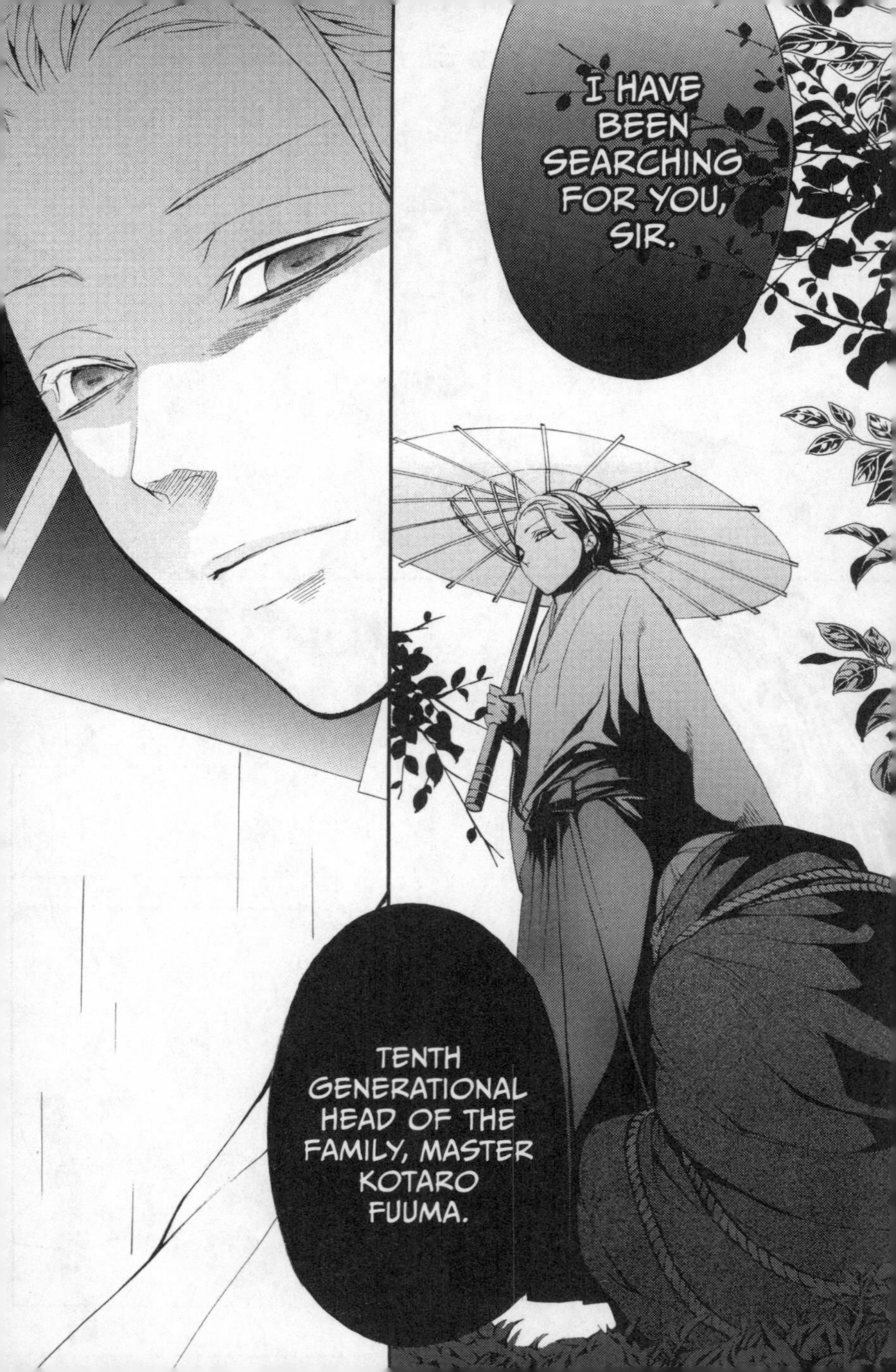
I HAVE BEEN SEARCHING FOR YOU, SIR.
TENTH GENERATIONAL HEAD OF THE FAMILY, MASTER KOTARO FUUMA.

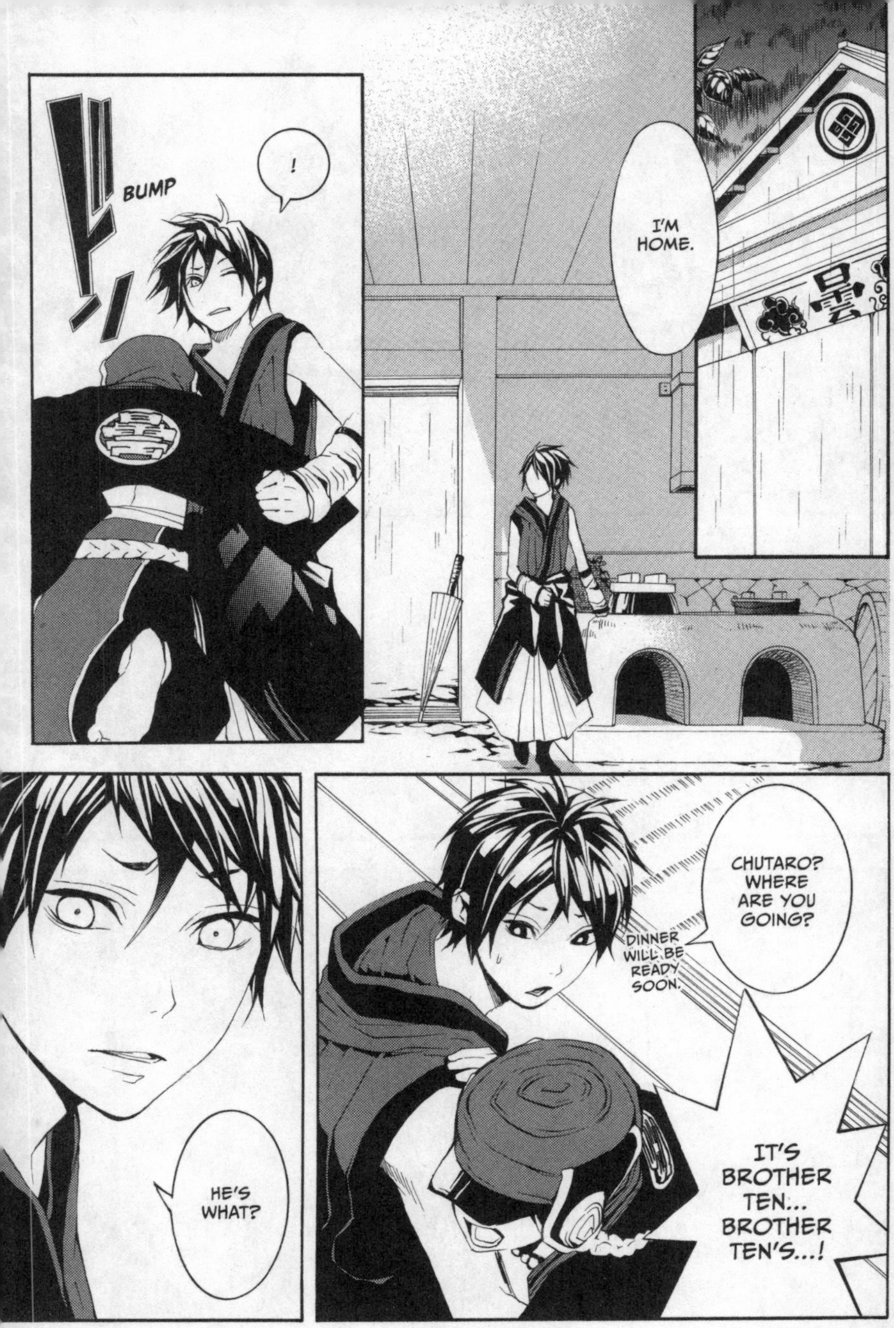
I'M HOME.
!
BUMP
CHUTARO? WHERE ARE YOU GOING?
DINNER WILL BE READY SOON.
IT'S BROTHER TEN... BROTHER TEN'S...!
HE'S WHAT?

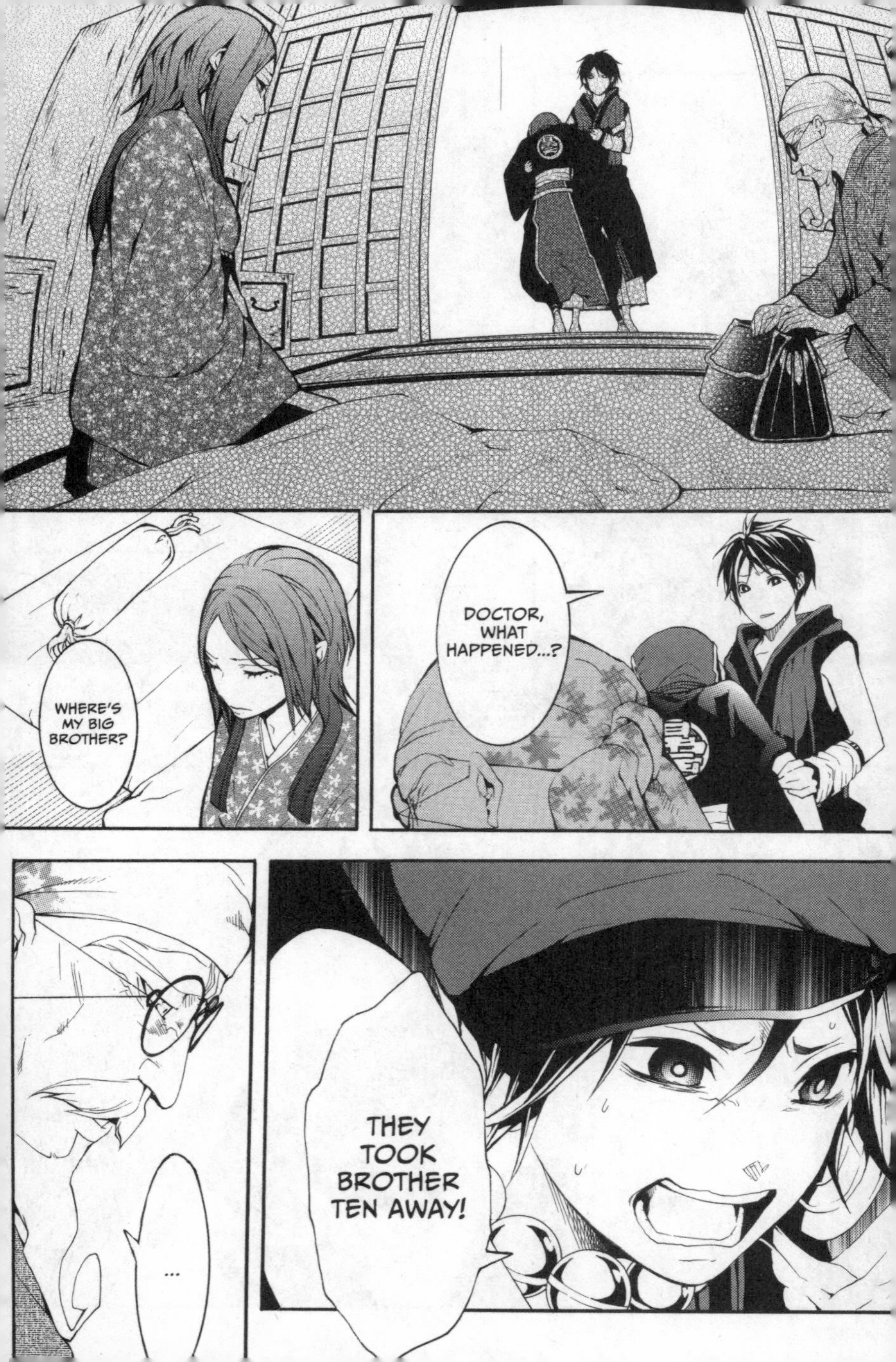
DOCTOR, WHAT HAPPENED...?
WHERE'S MY BIG BROTHER?
THEY TOOK BROTHER TEN AWAY!
...

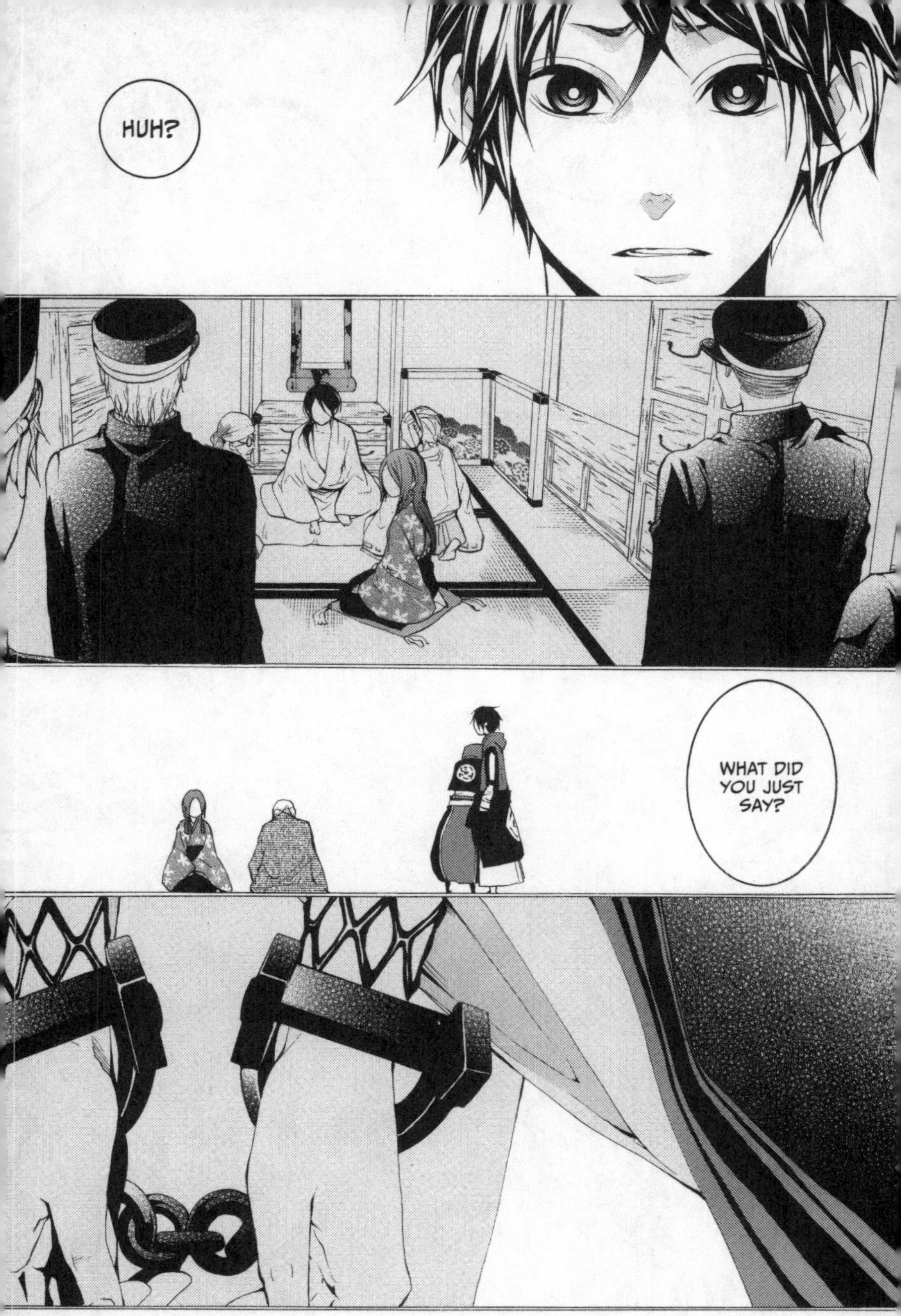
HUH?
WHAT DID YOU JUST SAY?

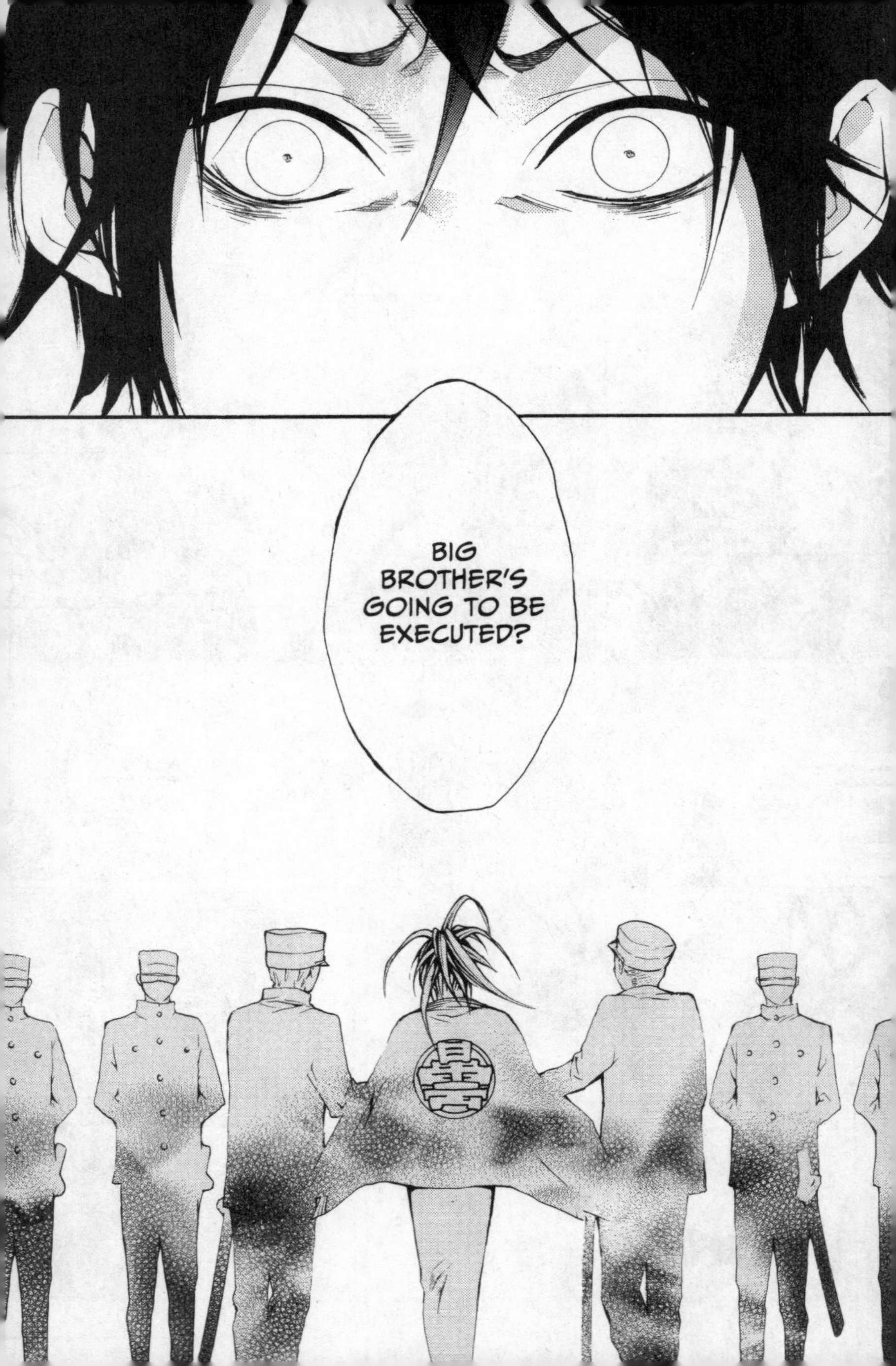
BIG BROTHER'S GOING TO BE EXECUTED?

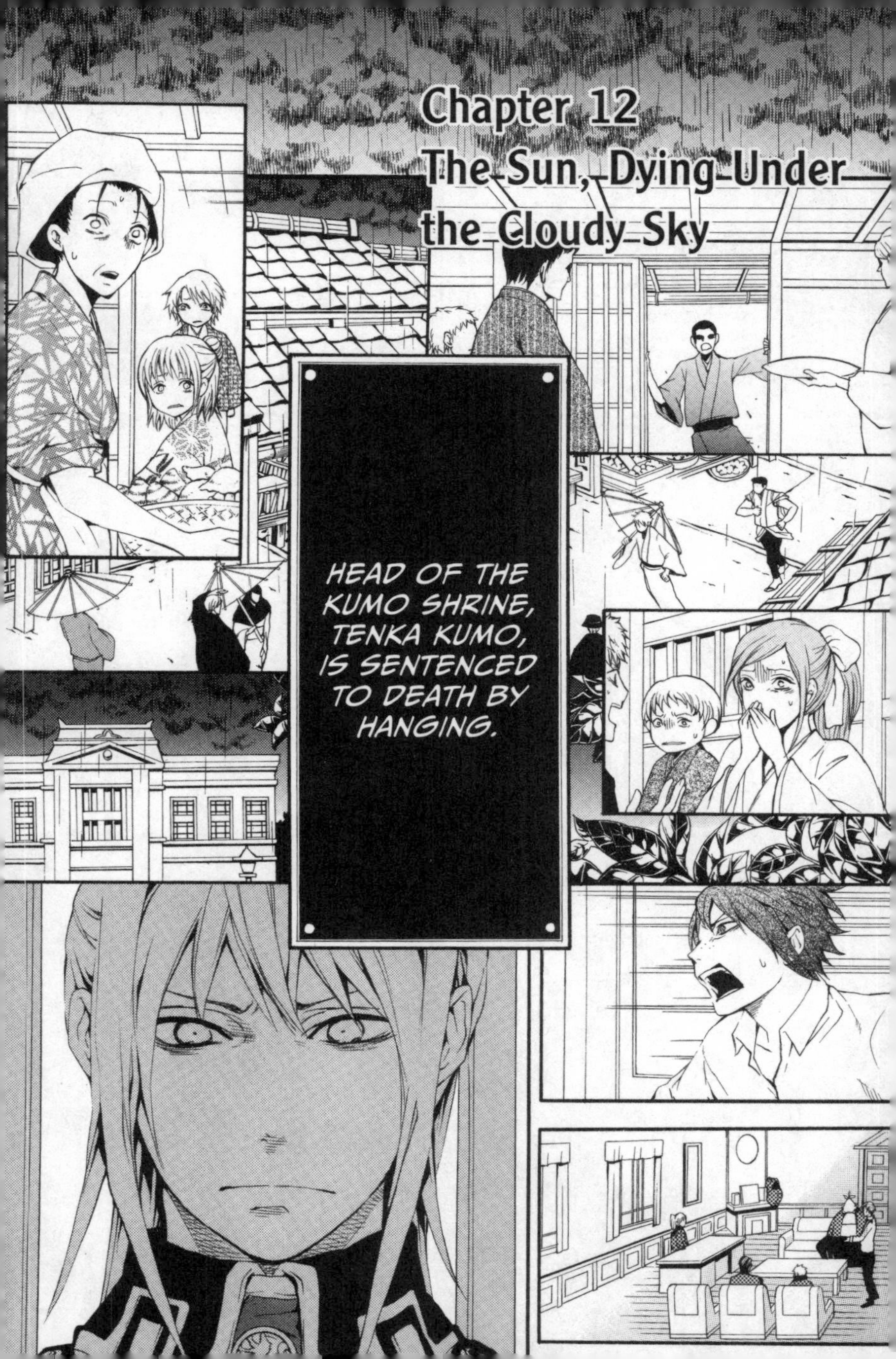

Chapter 12
The Sun, Dying Under the Cloudy Sky
HEAD OF THE KUMO SHRINE, TENKA KUMO, IS SENTENCED TO DEATH BY HANGING.

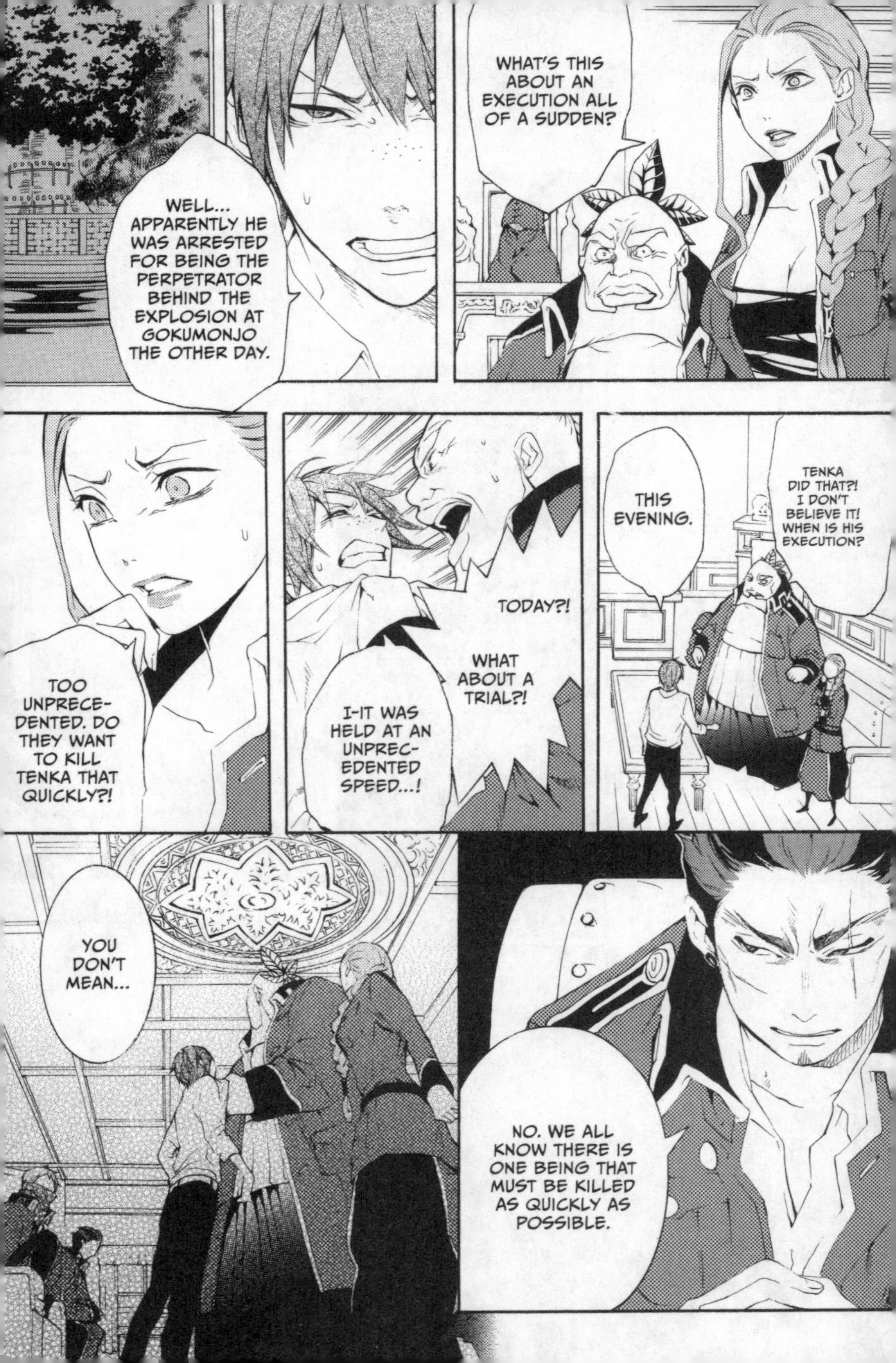
WHAT'S THIS ABOUT AN EXECUTION ALL OF A SUDDEN?
WELL... APPARENTLY HE WAS ARRESTED FOR BEING THE PERPETRATOR BEHIND THE EXPLOSION AT GOKUMONJO THE OTHER DAY.
TENKA DID THAT?! I DON'T BELIEVE IT! WHEN IS HIS EXECUTION?
THIS EVENING.
TODAY?!
WHAT ABOUT A TRIAL?!
I-IT WAS HELD AT AN UNPREC-EDENTED SPEED...!
TOO UNPRECE-DENTED. DO THEY WANT TO KILL TENKA THAT QUICKLY?!
NO. WE ALL KNOW THERE IS ONE BEING THAT MUST BE KILLED AS QUICKLY AS POSSIBLE.
YOU DON'T MEAN...

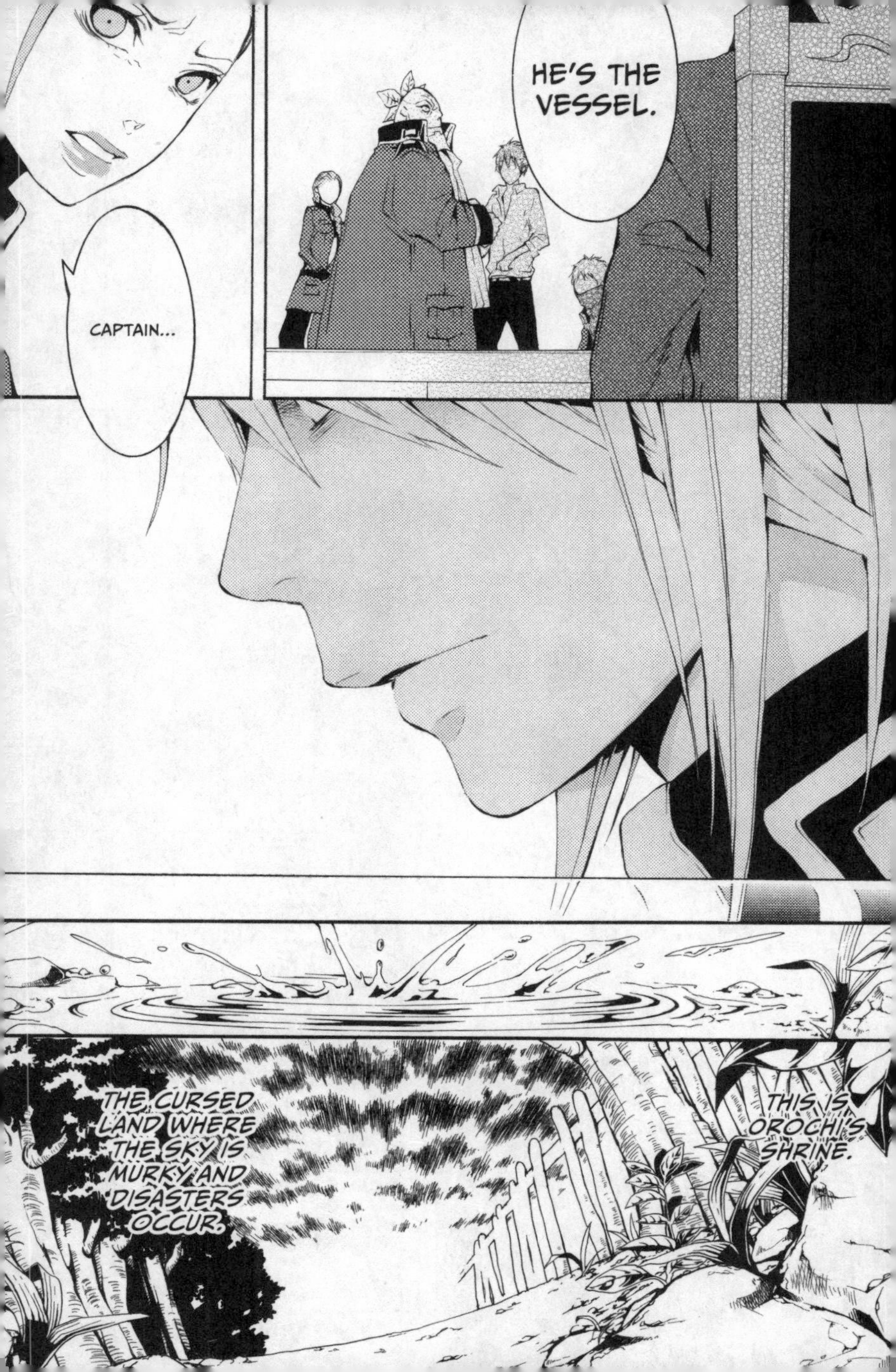

HE'S THE VESSEL.
CAPTAIN...
THIS IS OROCHI'S SHRINE.
THE CURSED LAND WHERE THE SKY IS MURKY AND DISASTERS OCCUR.

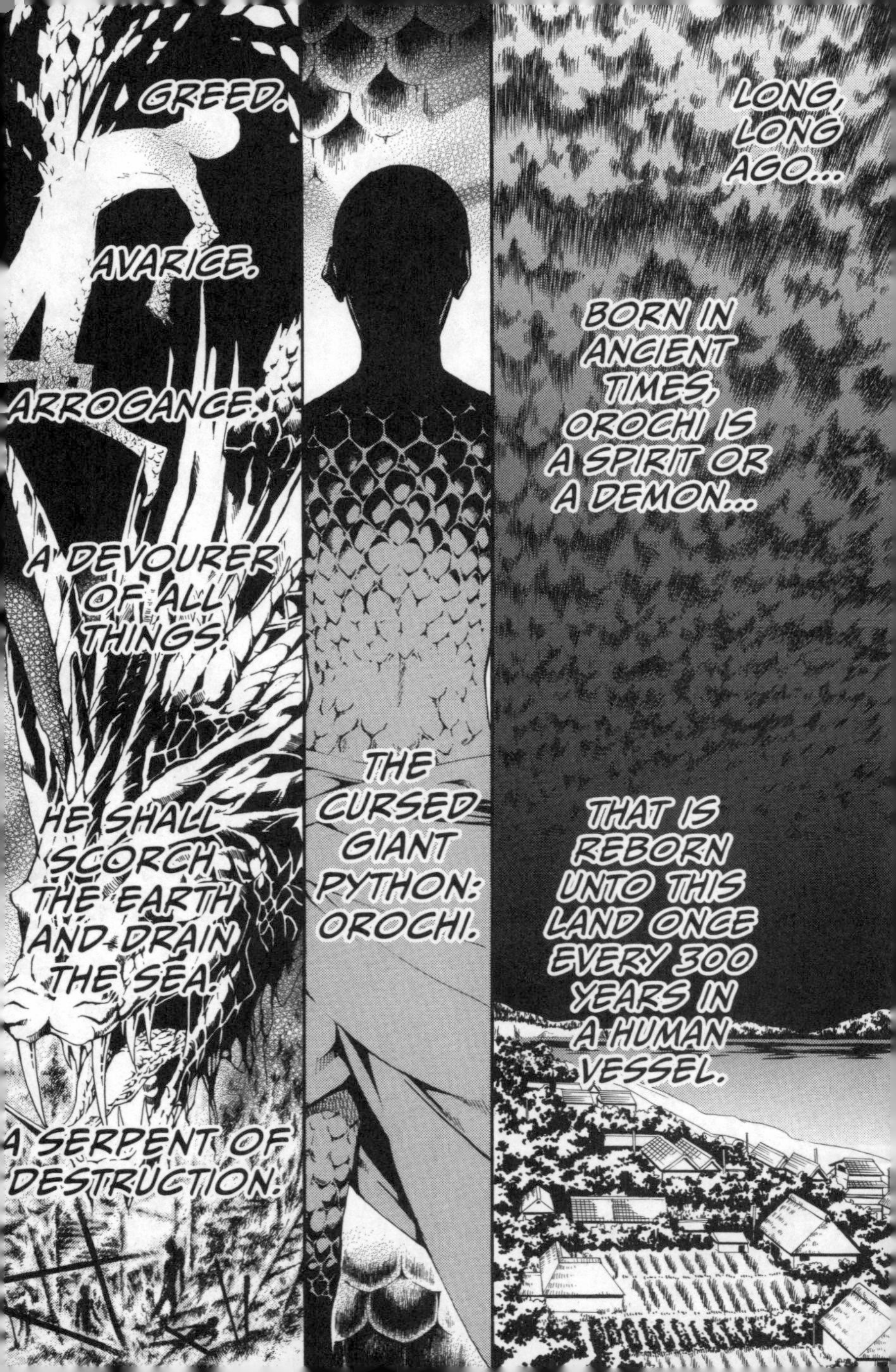
LONG, LONG AGO...
BORN IN ANCIENT TIMES, OROCHI IS A SPIRIT OR A DEMON...
THAT IS REBORN UNTO THIS LAND ONCE EVERY 300 YEARS IN A HUMAN VESSEL.
THE CURSED GIANT PYTHON: OROCHI.
GREED.
AVARICE.
ARROGANCE.
A DEVOURER OF ALL THINGS.
HE SHALL SCORCH THE EARTH AND DRAIN THE SEA.
A SERPENT OF DESTRUCTION.

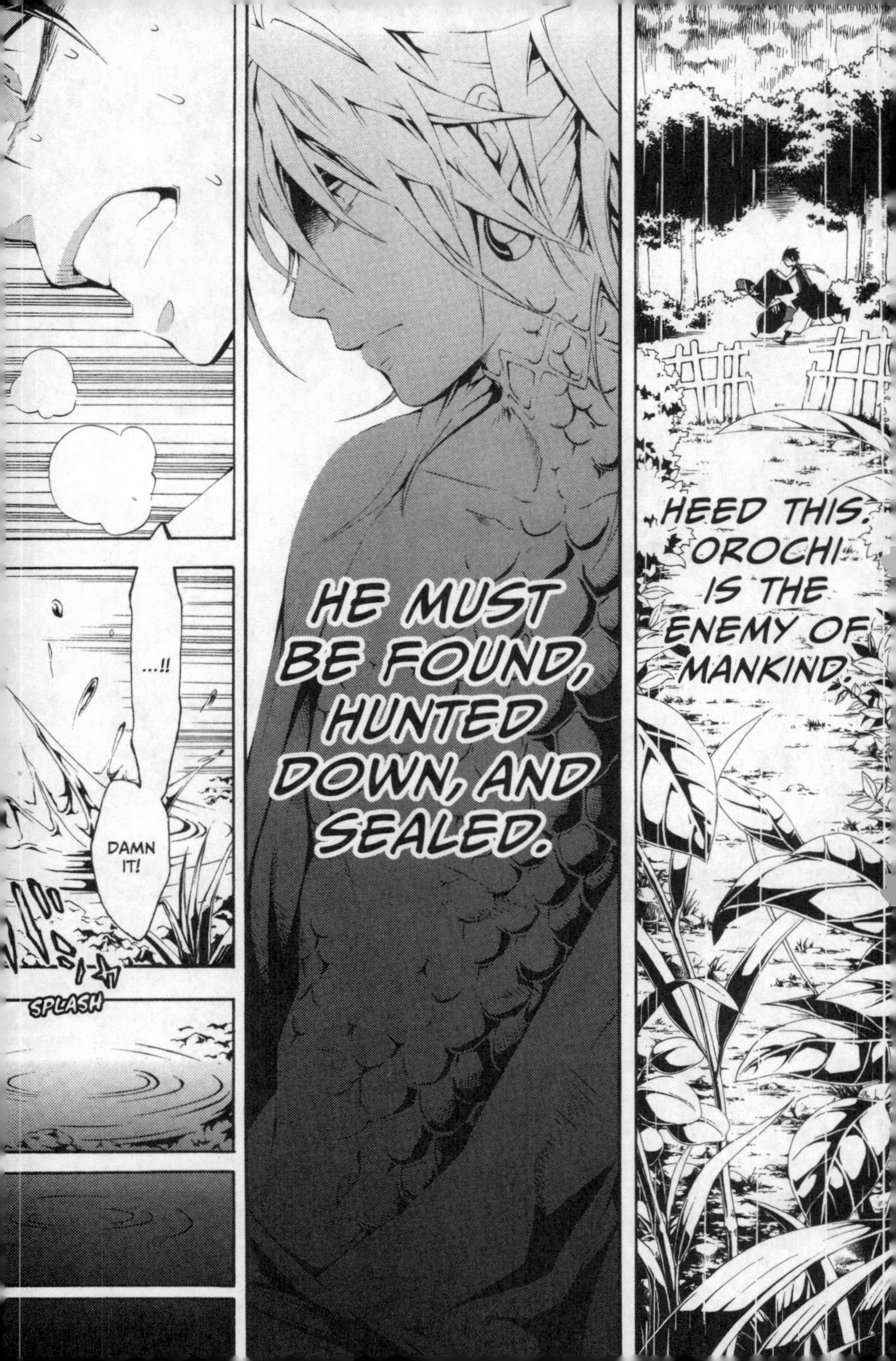
HEED THIS. OROCHI IS THE ENEMY OF MANKIND.
HE MUST BE FOUND, HUNTED DOWN, AND SEALED.
...!!
DAMN IT!
SPLASH

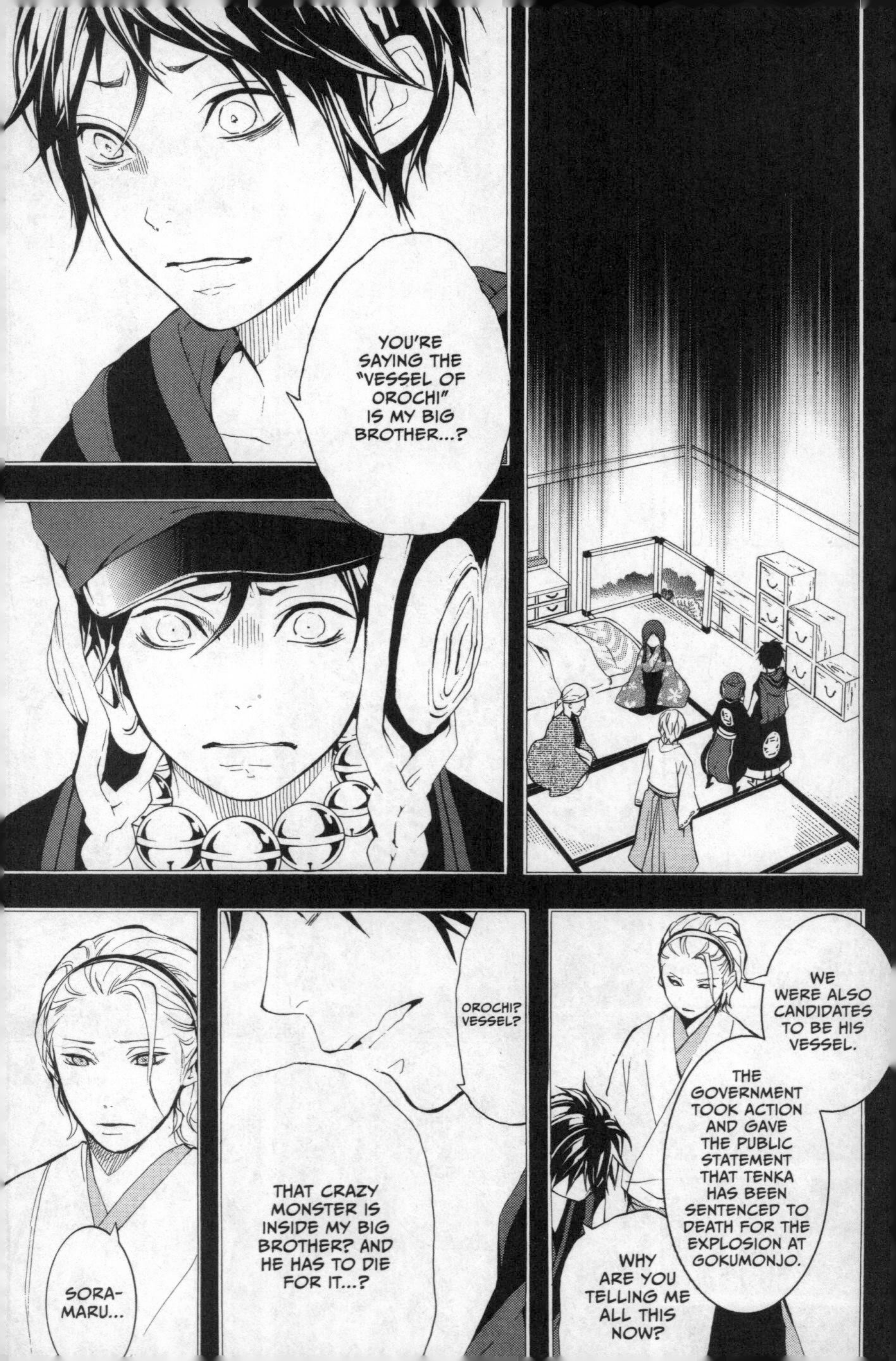
YOU'RE SAYING THE "VESSEL OF OROCHI" IS MY BIG BROTHER...?
WE WERE ALSO CANDIDATES TO BE HIS VESSEL.
THE GOVERNMENT TOOK ACTION AND GAVE THE PUBLIC STATEMENT THAT TENKA HAS BEEN SENTENCED TO DEATH FOR THE EXPLOSION AT GOKUMONJO.
WHY ARE YOU TELLING ME ALL THIS NOW?
OROCHI? VESSEL?
THAT CRAZY MONSTER IS INSIDE MY BIG BROTHER? AND HE HAS TO DIE FOR IT...?
SORA-MARU...

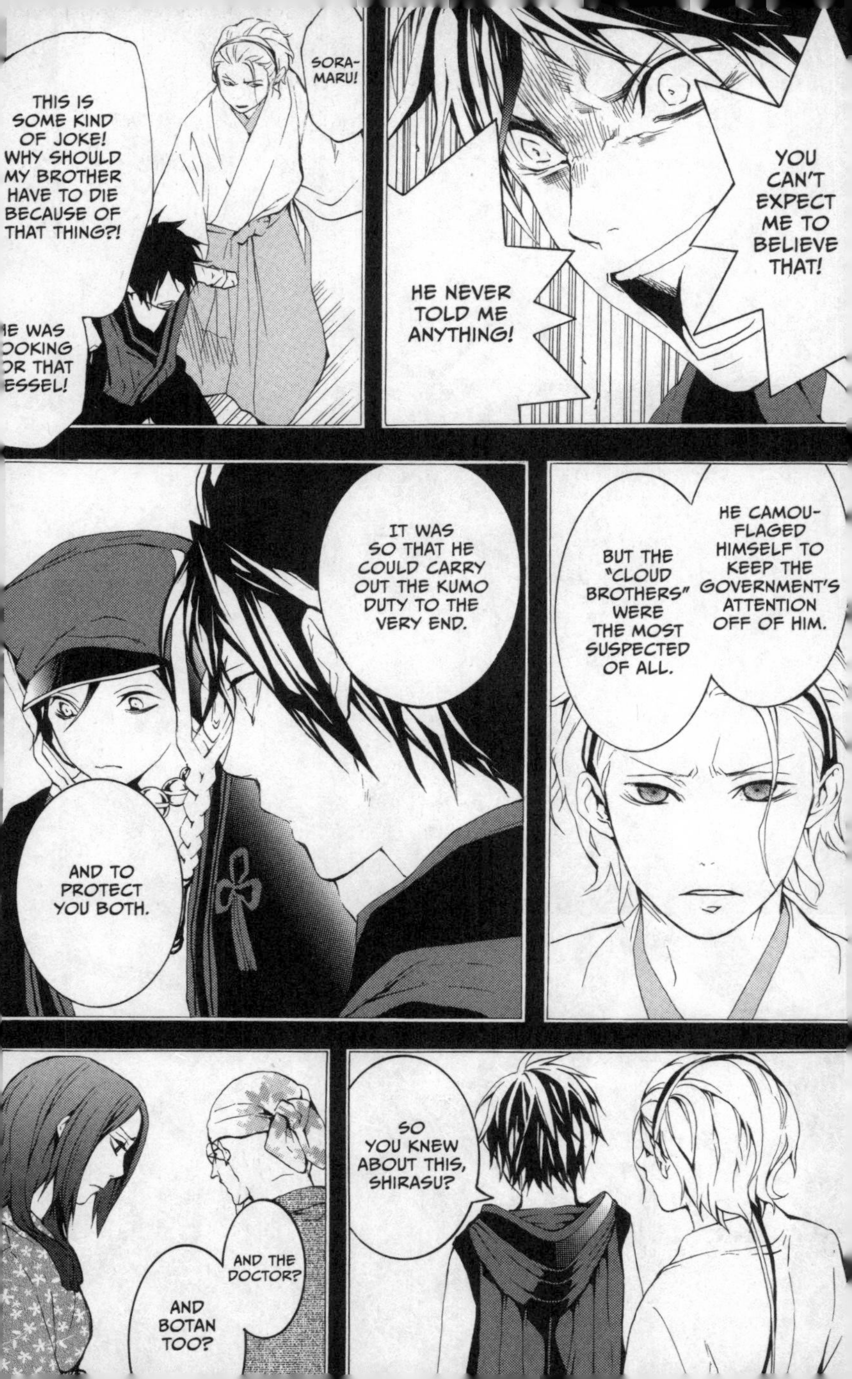
YOU CAN'T EXPECT ME TO BELIEVE THAT!
HE NEVER TOLD ME ANYTHING!
SORA-MARU!
THIS IS SOME KIND OF JOKE! WHY SHOULD MY BROTHER HAVE TO DIE BECAUSE OF THAT THING?!
IE WAS OOKING OR THAT ESSEL!
HE CAMOU-FLAGED HIMSELF TO KEEP THE GOVERNMENT'S ATTENTION OFF OF HIM.
BUT THE "CLOUD BROTHERS" WERE THE MOST SUSPECTED OF ALL.
IT WAS SO THAT HE COULD CARRY OUT THE KUMO DUTY TO THE VERY END.
AND TO PROTECT YOU BOTH.
SO YOU KNEW ABOUT THIS, SHIRASU?
AND THE DOCTOR?
AND BOTAN TOO?

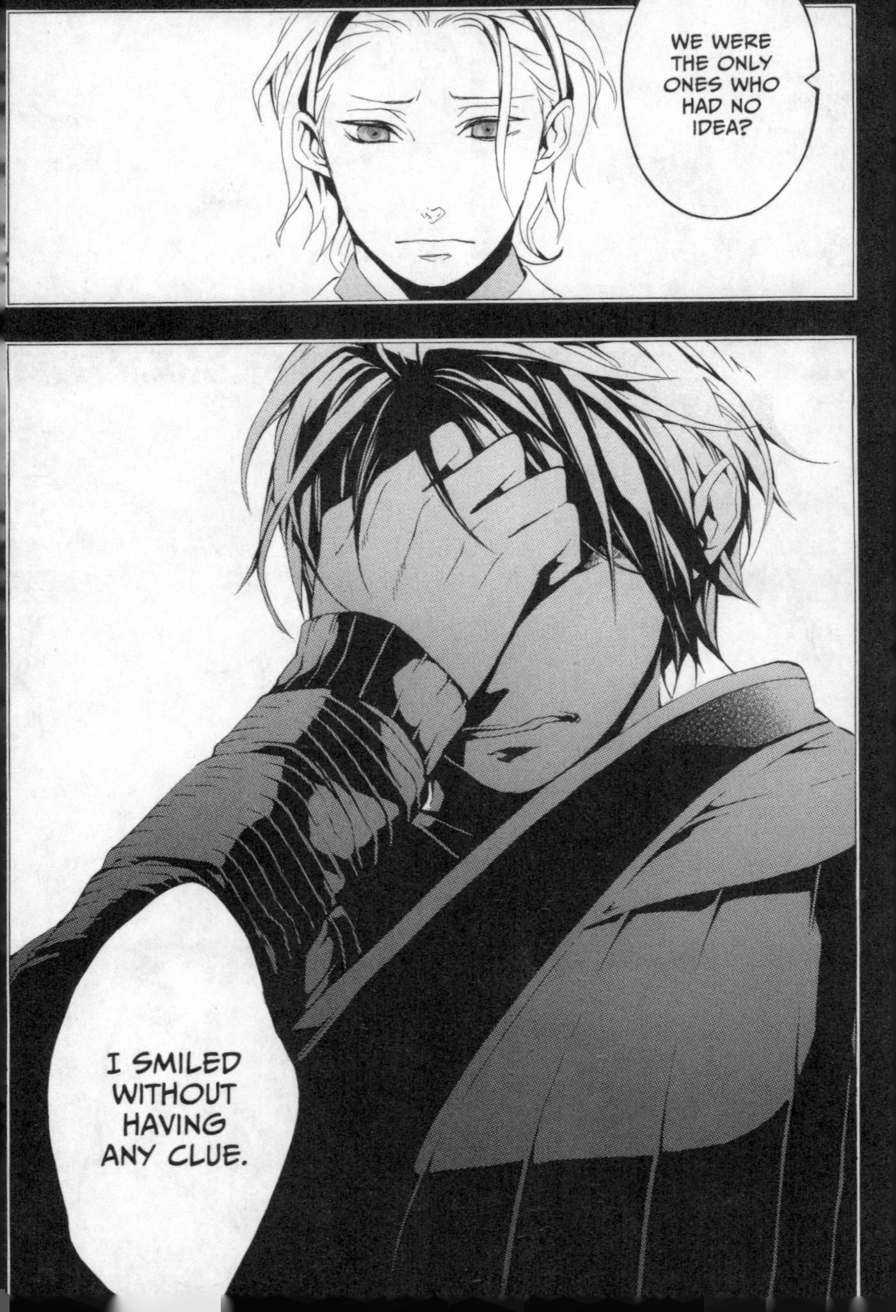
WE WERE THE ONLY ONES WHO HAD NO IDEA?
I SMILED WITHOUT HAVING ANY CLUE.

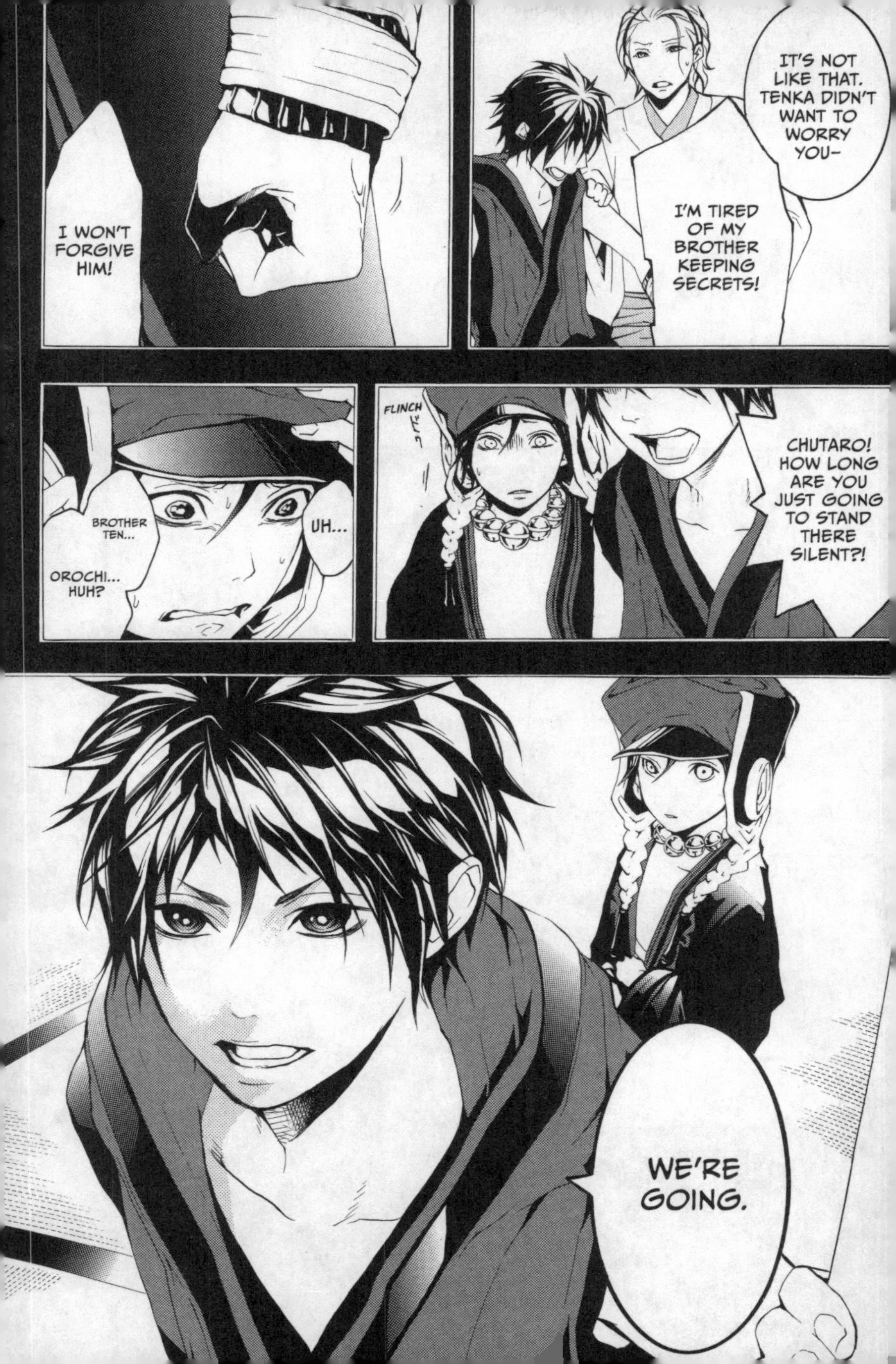
IT'S NOT LIKE THAT. TENKA DIDN'T WANT TO WORRY YOU–
I'M TIRED OF MY BROTHER KEEPING SECRETS!
I WON'T FORGIVE HIM!
CHUTARO! HOW LONG ARE YOU JUST GOING TO STAND THERE SILENT?!
FLINCH
UH...
BROTHER TEN...
OROCHI... HUH?
WE'RE GOING.

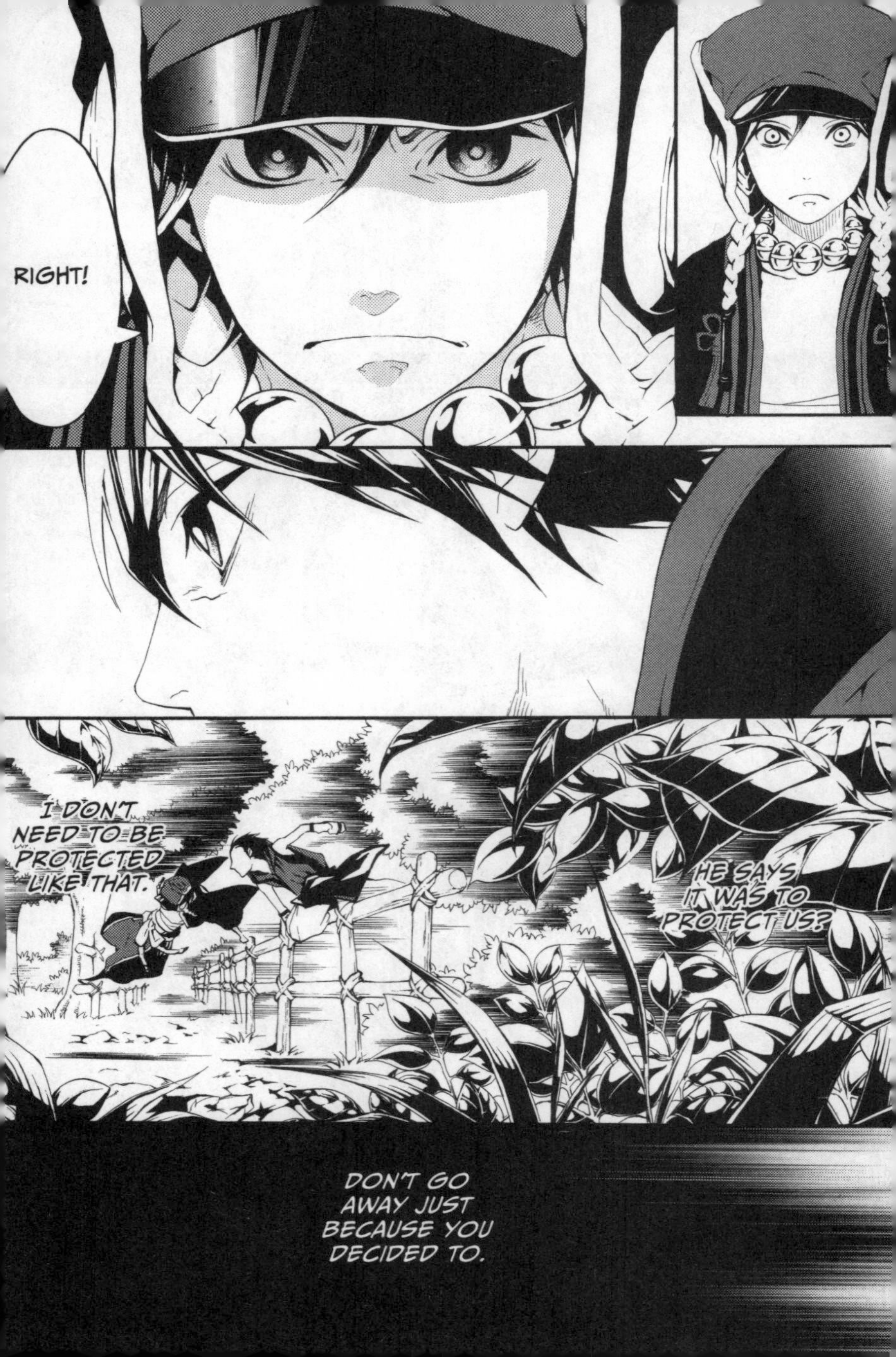
RIGHT!
HE SAYS IT WAS TO PROTECT US?
I DON'T NEED TO BE PROTECTED LIKE THAT.
DON'T GO AWAY JUST BECAUSE YOU DECIDED TO.

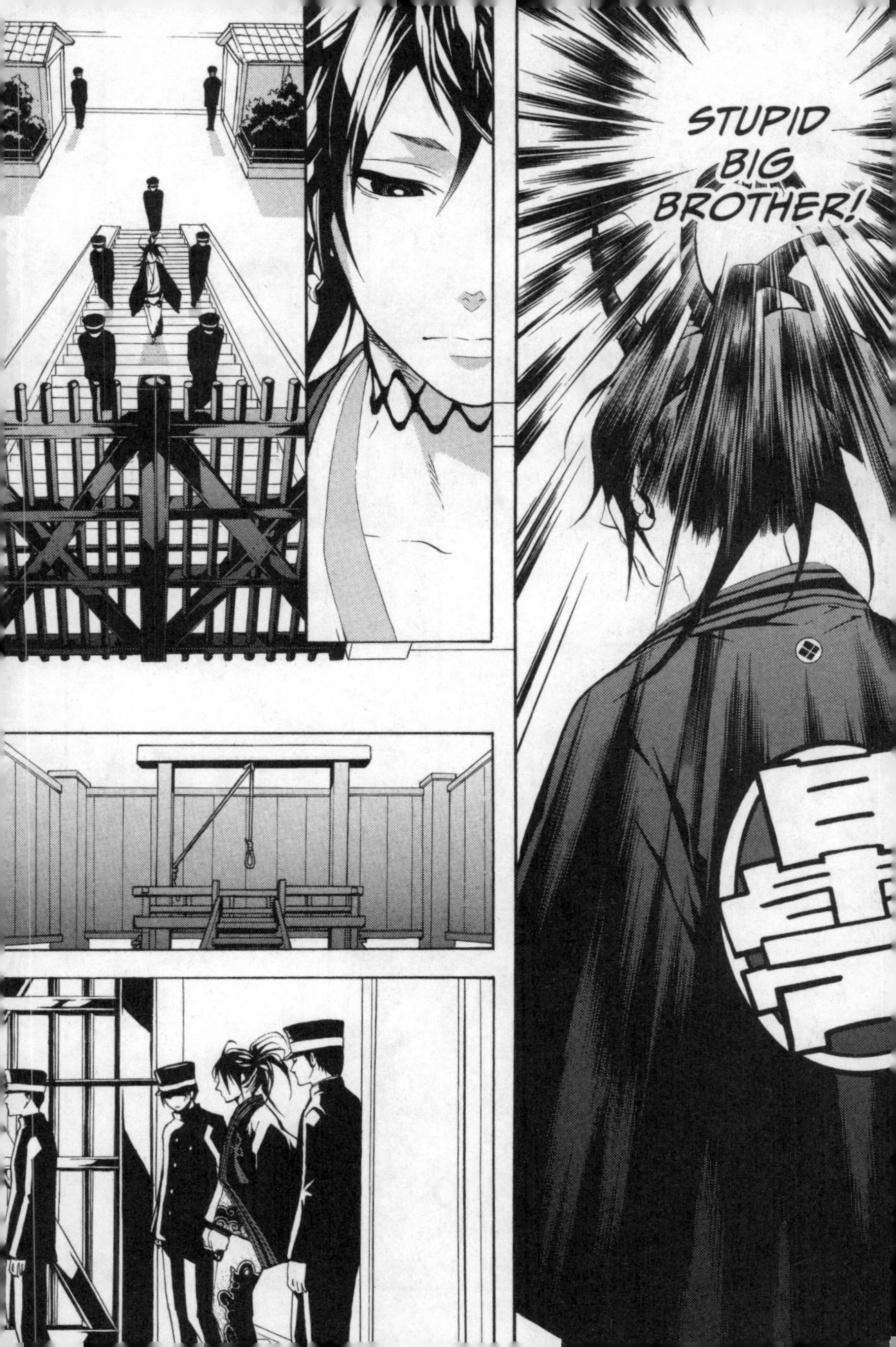
STUPID BIG BROTHER!

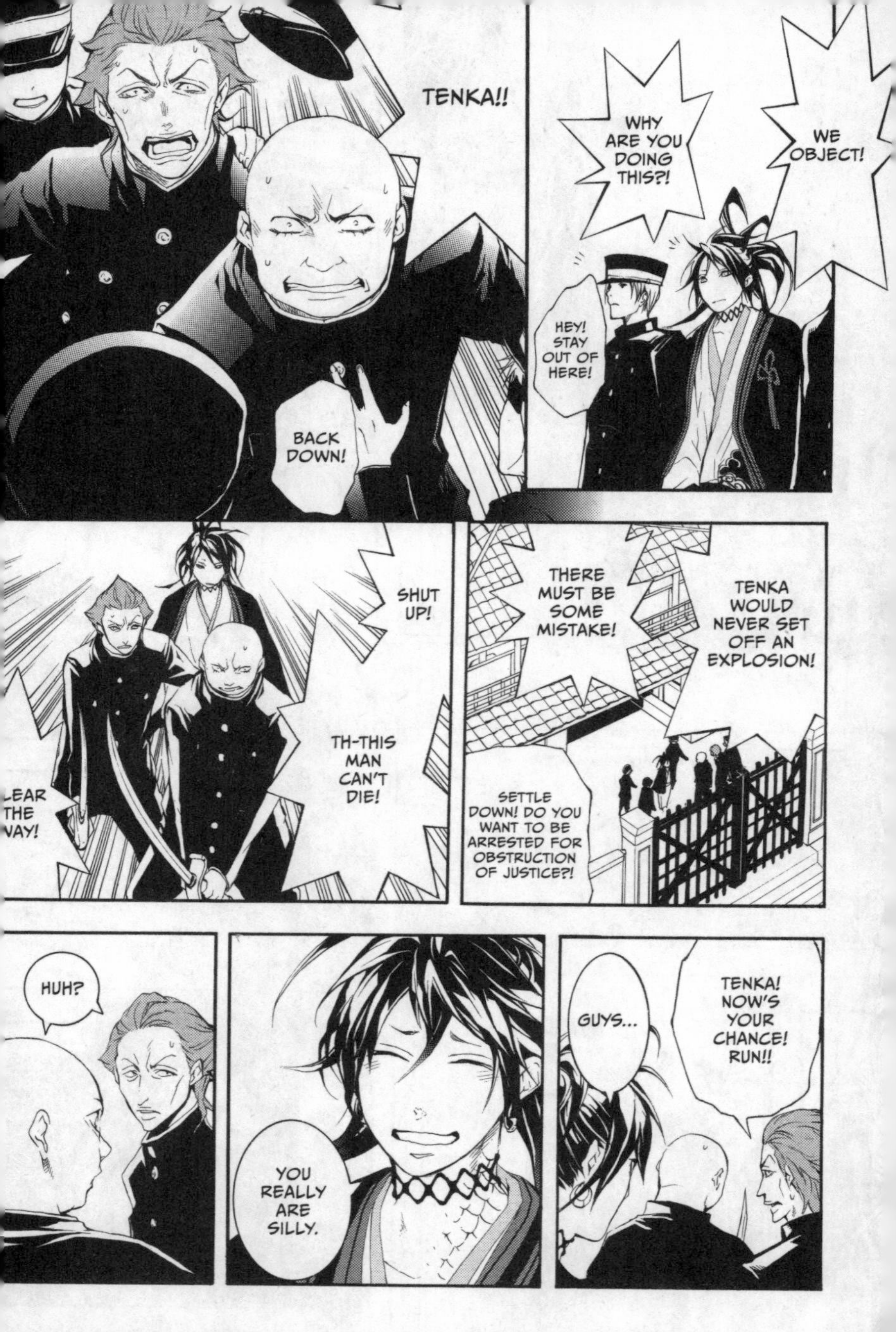
WE OBJECT!
WHY ARE YOU DOING THIS?!
HEY! STAY OUT OF HERE!
TENKA!!
BACK DOWN!
TENKA WOULD NEVER SET OFF AN EXPLOSION!
THERE MUST BE SOME MISTAKE!
SETTLE DOWN! DO YOU WANT TO BE ARRESTED FOR OBSTRUCTION OF JUSTICE?!
SHUT UP!
TH-THIS MAN CAN'T DIE!
TENKA! NOW'S YOUR CHANCE! RUN!!
GUYS...
YOU REALLY ARE SILLY.
HUH?

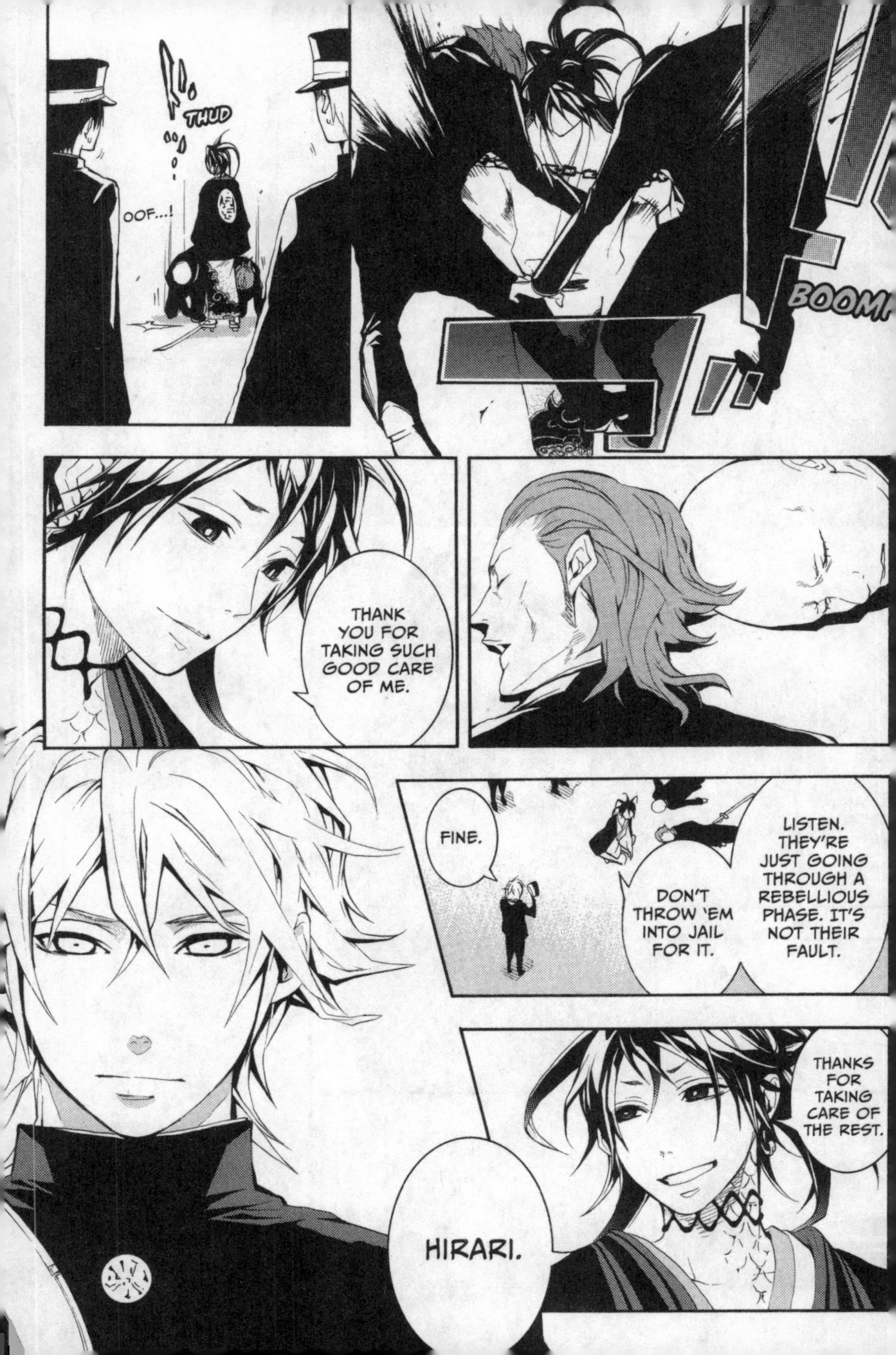

BOOM!
THUD
OOF...!
THANK YOU FOR TAKING SUCH GOOD CARE OF ME.
LISTEN. THEY'RE JUST GOING THROUGH A REBELLIOUS PHASE. IT'S NOT THEIR FAULT.
DON'T THROW 'EM INTO JAIL FOR IT.
FINE.
THANKS FOR TAKING CARE OF THE REST.
HIRARI.

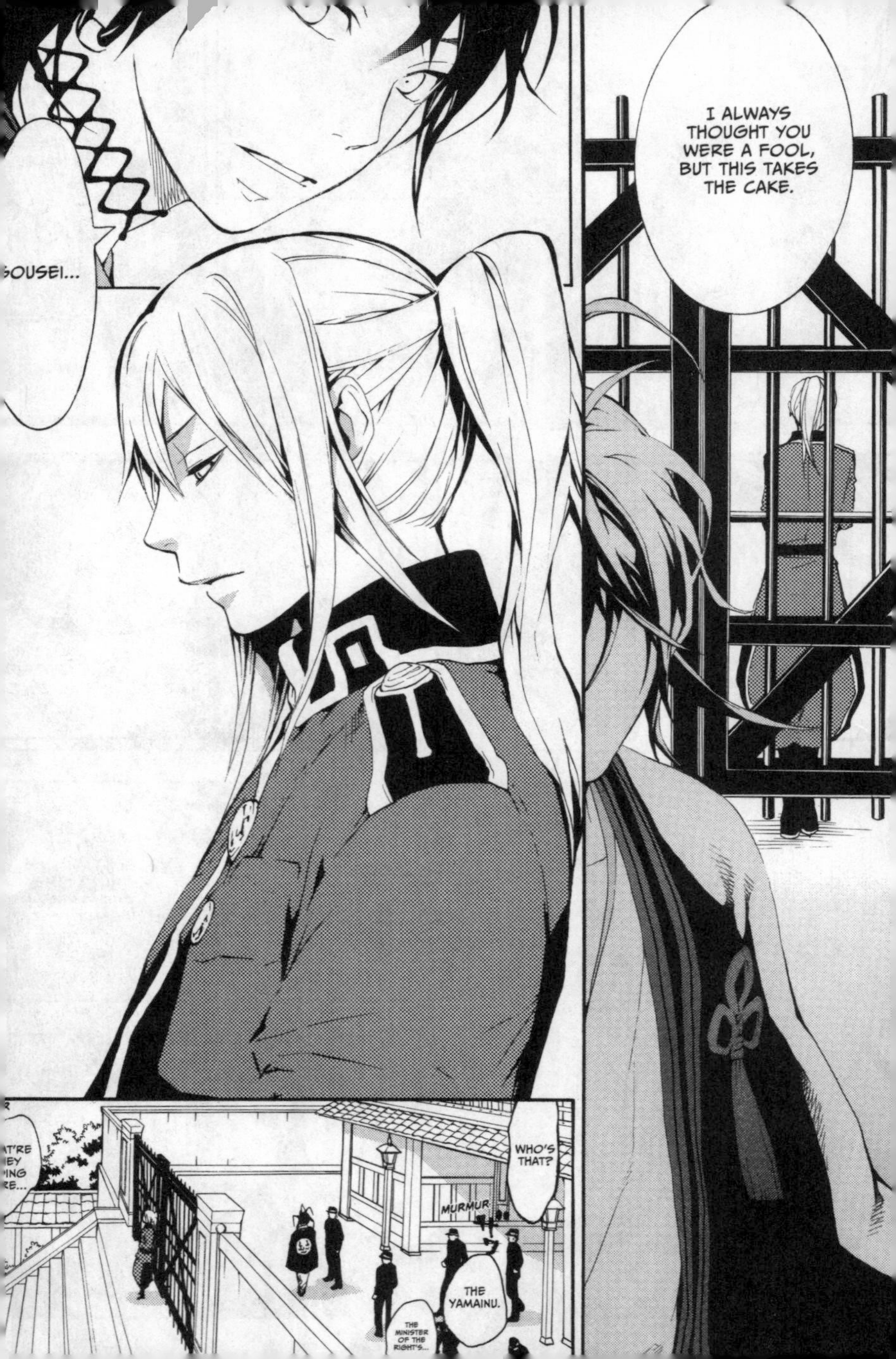
I ALWAYS THOUGHT YOU WERE A FOOL, BUT THIS TAKES THE CAKE.
GOUSEI...
WHO'S THAT?
MURMUR
THE YAMAINU.
THE MINISTER OF THE RIGHT'S...

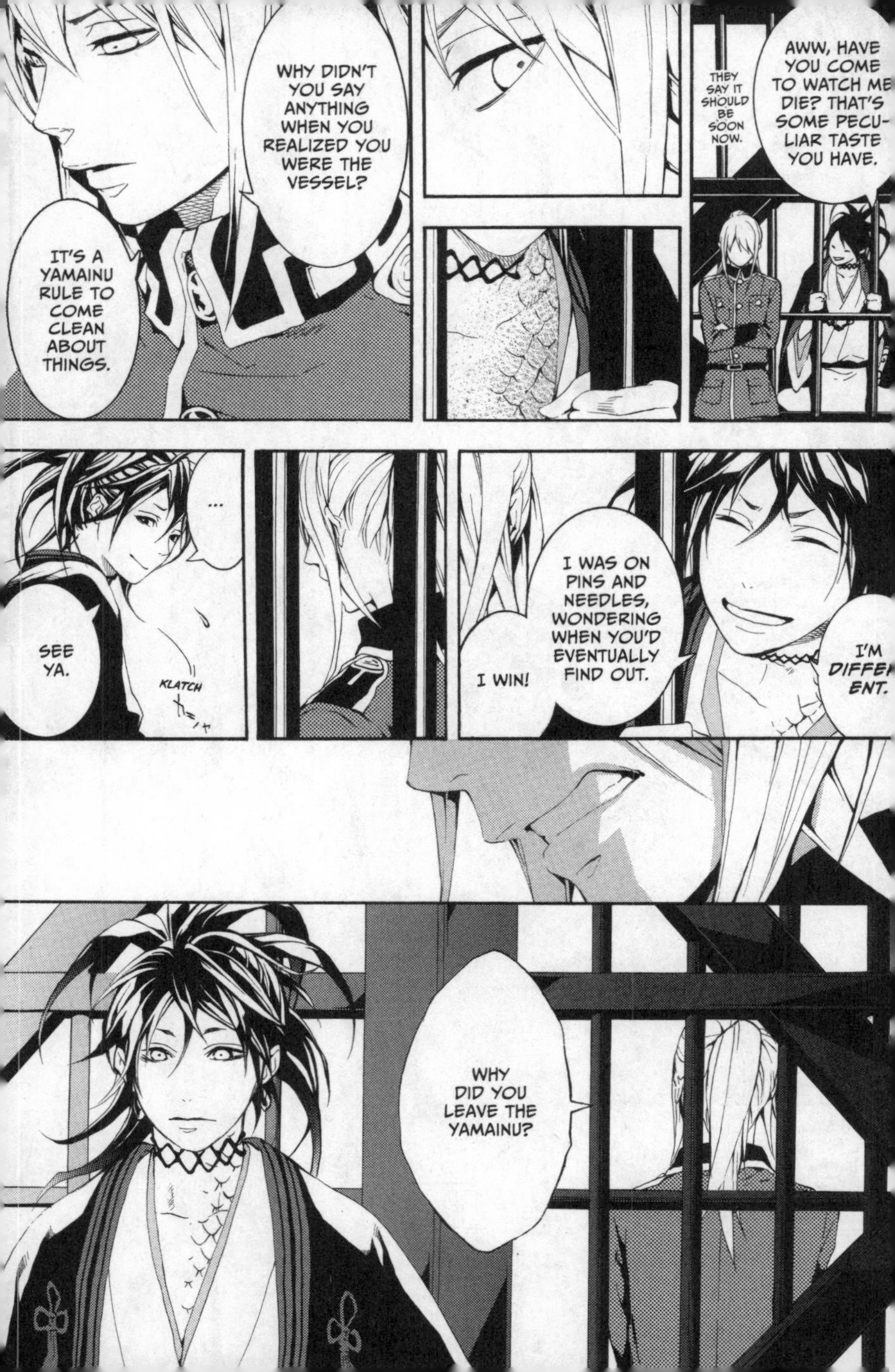
AWW, HAVE YOU COME TO WATCH ME DIE? THAT'S SOME PECULIAR TASTE YOU HAVE.
THEY SAY IT SHOULD BE SOON NOW.
WHY DIDN'T YOU SAY ANYTHING WHEN YOU REALIZED YOU WERE THE VESSEL?
IT'S A YAMAINU RULE TO COME CLEAN ABOUT THINGS.
I'M DIFFE ENT.
I WAS ON PINS AND NEEDLES, WONDERING WHEN YOU'D EVENTUALLY FIND OUT.
I WIN!
...
SEE YA.
KLATCH
WHY DID YOU LEAVE THE YAMAINU?

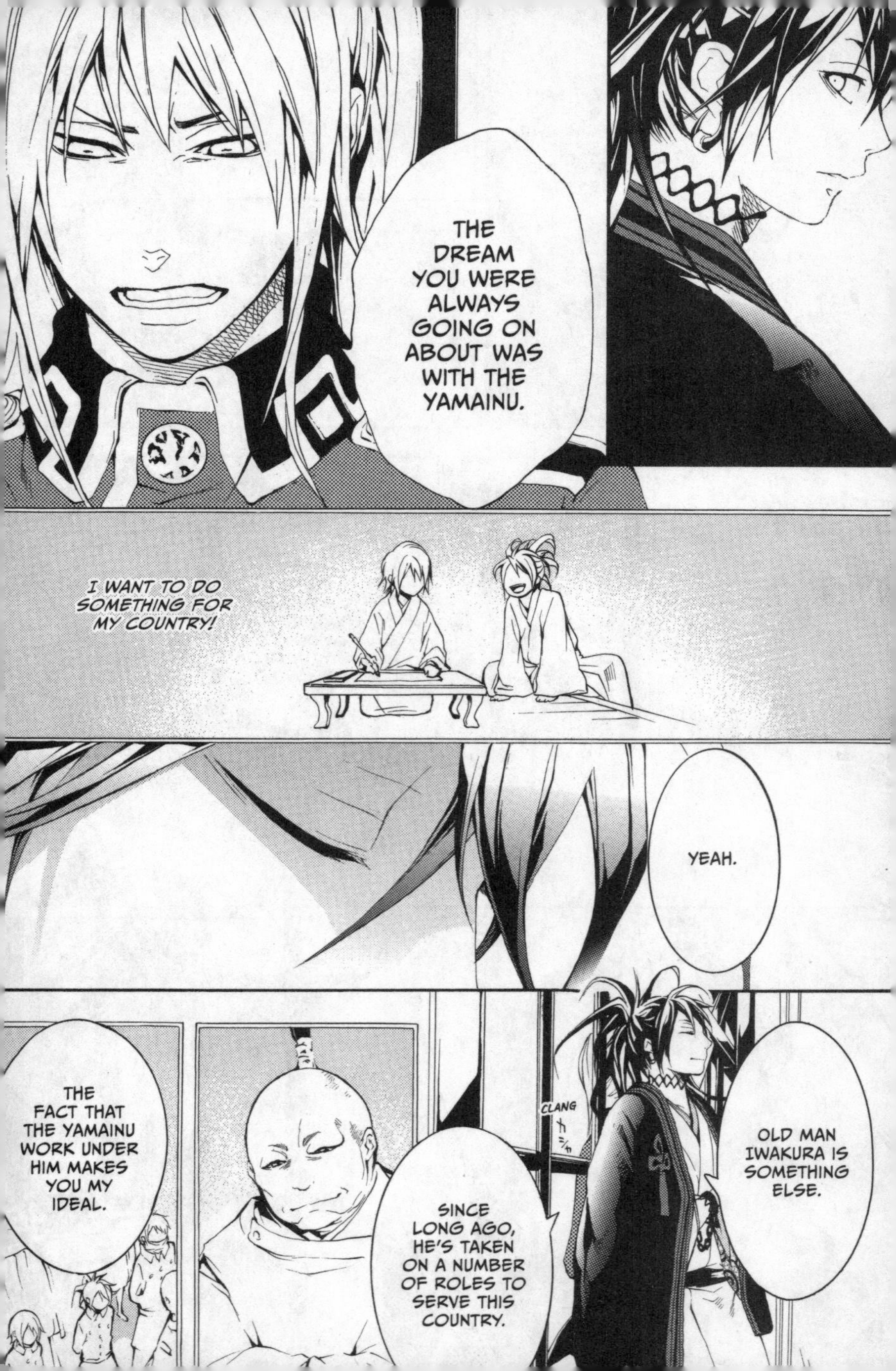
THE DREAM YOU WERE ALWAYS GOING ON ABOUT WAS WITH THE YAMAINU.
I WANT TO DO SOMETHING FOR MY COUNTRY!
YEAH.
OLD MAN IWAKURA IS SOMETHING ELSE.
CLANG
SINCE LONG AGO, HE'S TAKEN ON A NUMBER OF ROLES TO SERVE THIS COUNTRY.
THE FACT THAT THE YAMAINU WORK UNDER HIM MAKES YOU MY IDEAL.

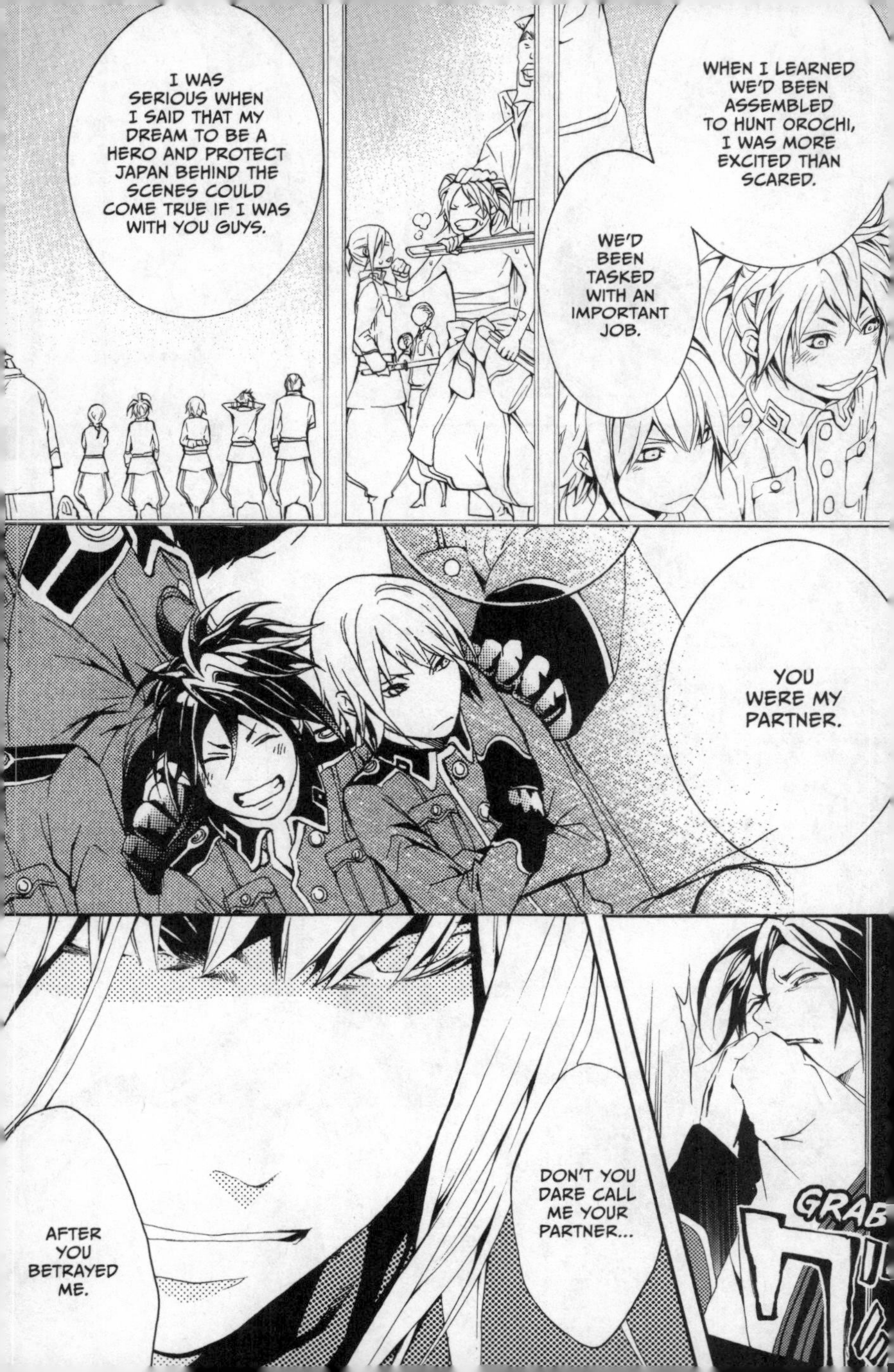
WHEN I LEARNED WE'D BEEN ASSEMBLED TO HUNT OROCHI, I WAS MORE EXCITED THAN SCARED.
WE'D BEEN TASKED WITH AN IMPORTANT JOB.
I WAS SERIOUS WHEN I SAID THAT MY DREAM TO BE A HERO AND PROTECT JAPAN BEHIND THE SCENES COULD COME TRUE IF I WAS WITH YOU GUYS.
YOU WERE MY PARTNER.
GRAB
DON'T YOU DARE CALL ME YOUR PARTNER...
AFTER YOU BETRAYED ME.

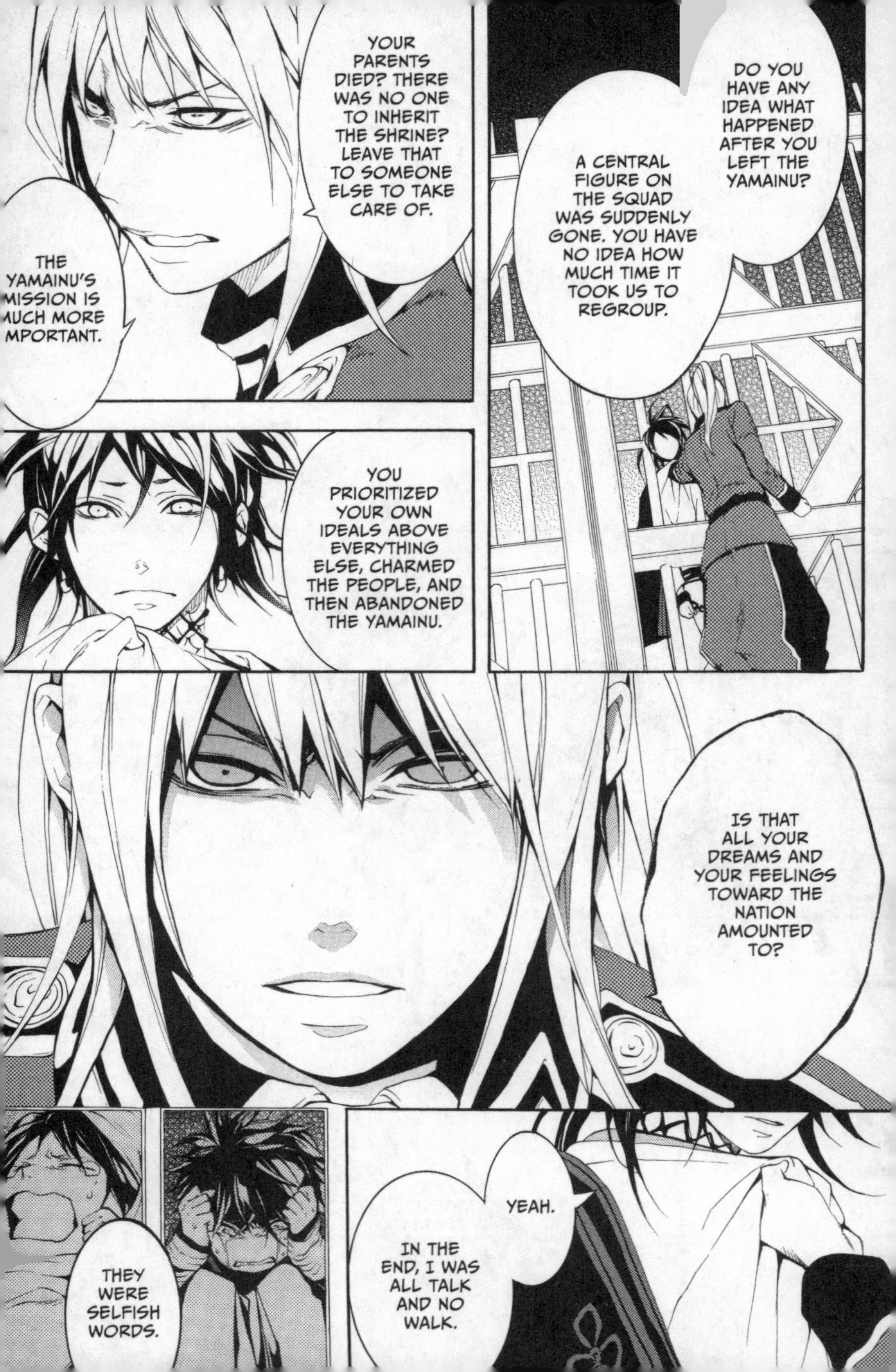
DO YOU HAVE ANY IDEA WHAT HAPPENED AFTER YOU LEFT THE YAMAINU?
A CENTRAL FIGURE ON THE SQUAD WAS SUDDENLY GONE. YOU HAVE NO IDEA HOW MUCH TIME IT TOOK US TO REGROUP.
YOUR PARENTS DIED? THERE WAS NO ONE TO INHERIT THE SHRINE? LEAVE THAT TO SOMEONE ELSE TO TAKE CARE OF.
THE YAMAINU'S MISSION IS MUCH MORE IMPORTANT.
YOU PRIORITIZED YOUR OWN IDEALS ABOVE EVERYTHING ELSE, CHARMED THE PEOPLE, AND THEN ABANDONED THE YAMAINU.
IS THAT ALL YOUR DREAMS AND YOUR FEELINGS TOWARD THE NATION AMOUNTED TO?
YEAH.
IN THE END, I WAS ALL TALK AND NO WALK.
THEY WERE SELFISH WORDS.

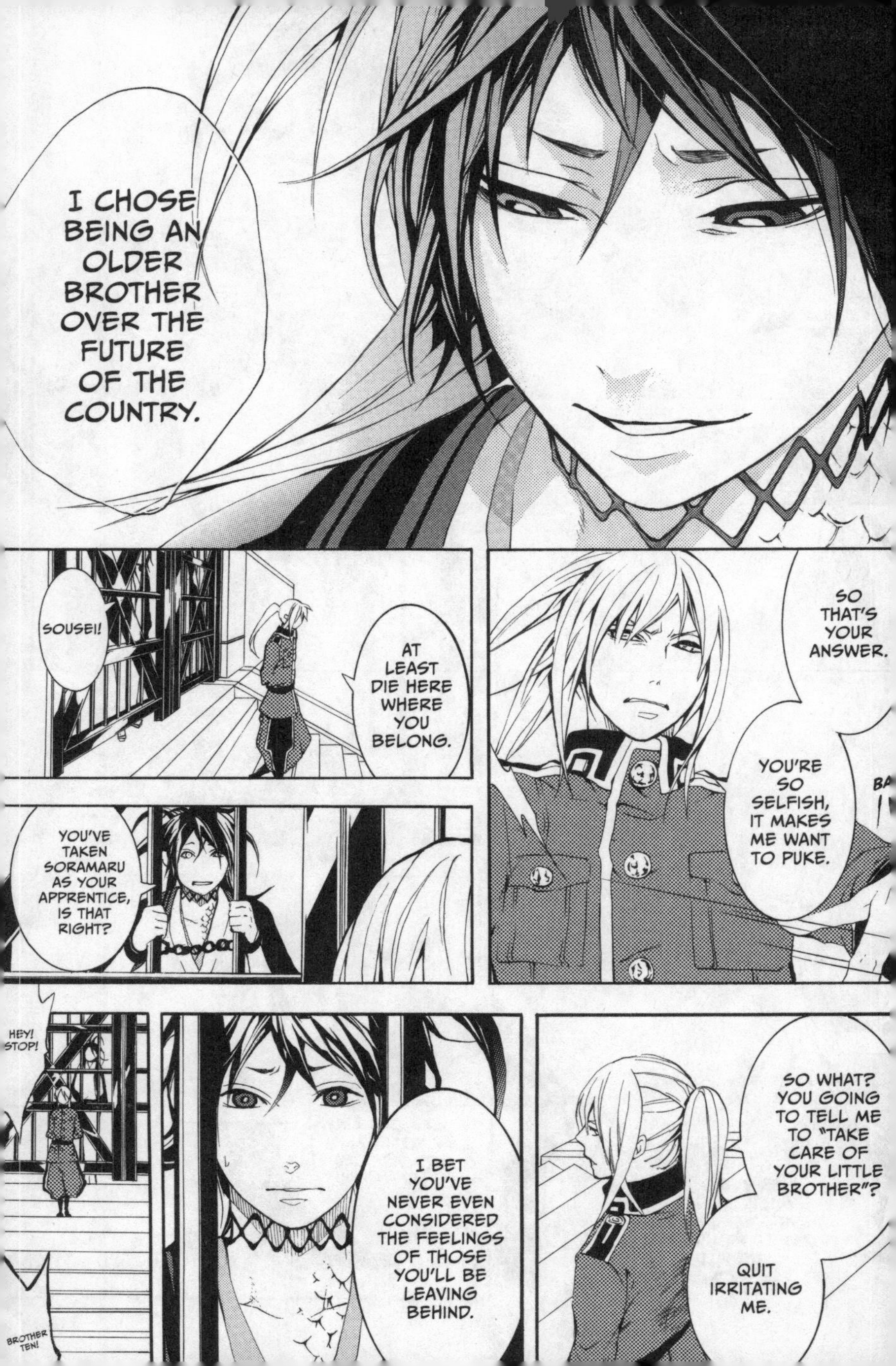
I CHOSE BEING AN OLDER BROTHER OVER THE FUTURE OF THE COUNTRY.
SO THAT'S YOUR ANSWER.
YOU'RE SO SELFISH, IT MAKES ME WANT TO PUKE.
BA
AT LEAST DIE HERE WHERE YOU BELONG.
SOUSEI!
YOU'VE TAKEN SORAMARU AS YOUR APPRENTICE, IS THAT RIGHT?
SO WHAT? YOU GOING TO TELL ME TO "TAKE CARE OF YOUR LITTLE BROTHER"?
QUIT IRRITATING ME.
I BET YOU'VE NEVER EVEN CONSIDERED THE FEELINGS OF THOSE YOU'LL BE LEAVING BEHIND.
HEY! STOP!
BROTHER TEN!

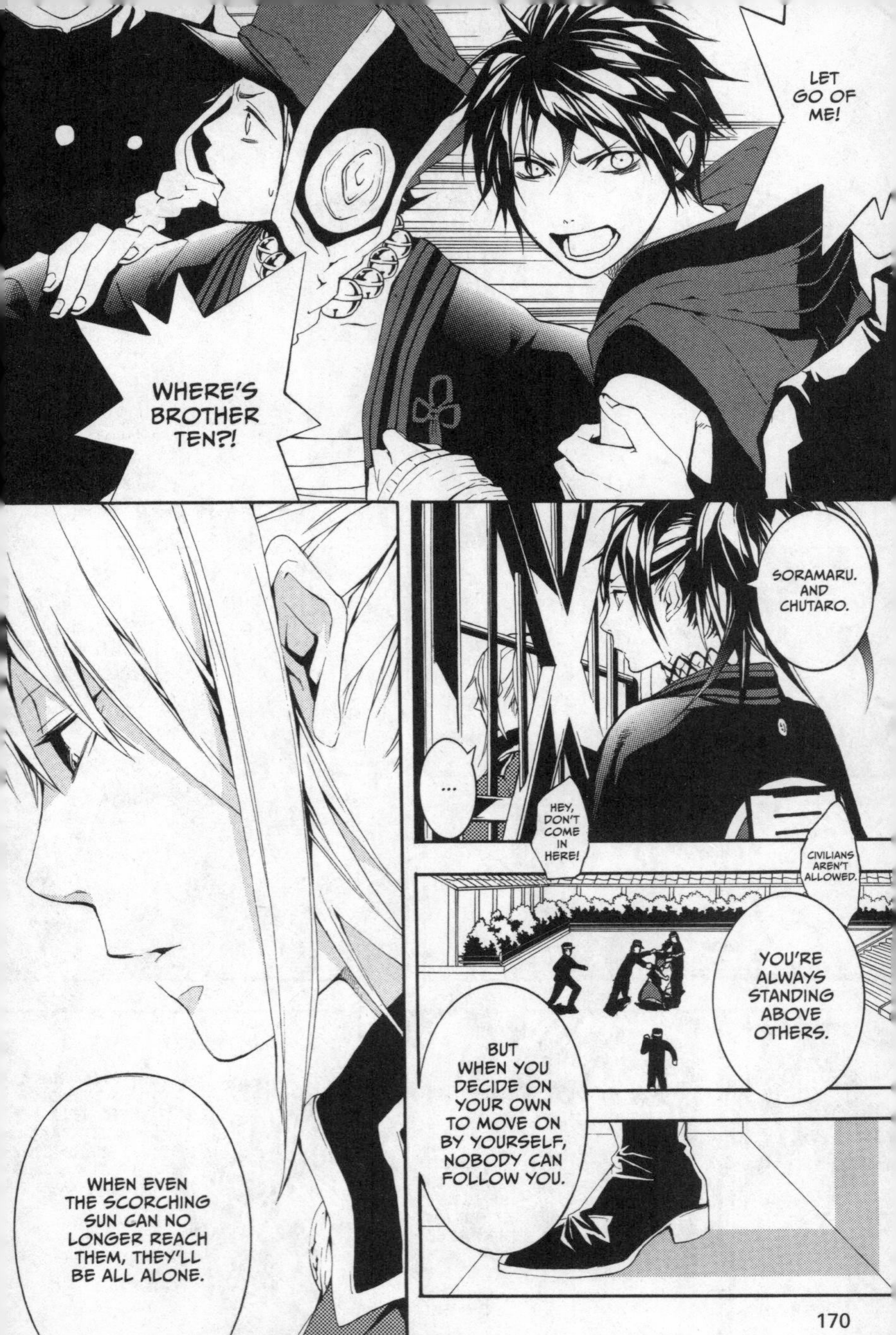

LET GO OF ME!
WHERE'S BROTHER TEN?!
SORAMARU. AND CHUTARO.
...
HEY, DON'T COME IN HERE!
CIVILIANS AREN'T ALLOWED.
YOU'RE ALWAYS STANDING ABOVE OTHERS.
BUT WHEN YOU DECIDE ON YOUR OWN TO MOVE ON BY YOURSELF, NOBODY CAN FOLLOW YOU.
WHEN EVEN THE SCORCHING SUN CAN NO LONGER REACH THEM, THEY'LL BE ALL ALONE.

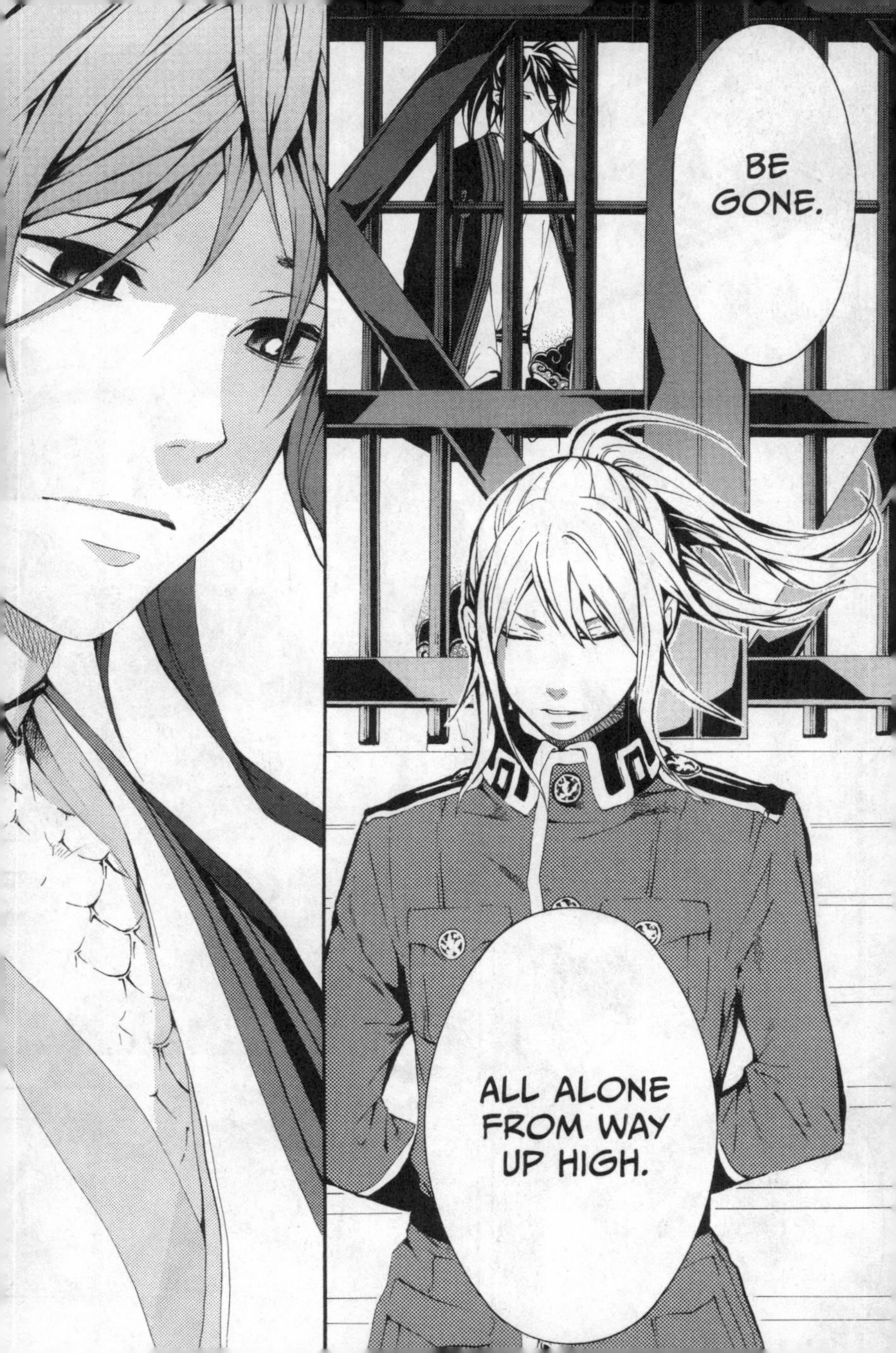
BE GONE.
ALL ALONE FROM WAY UP HIGH.

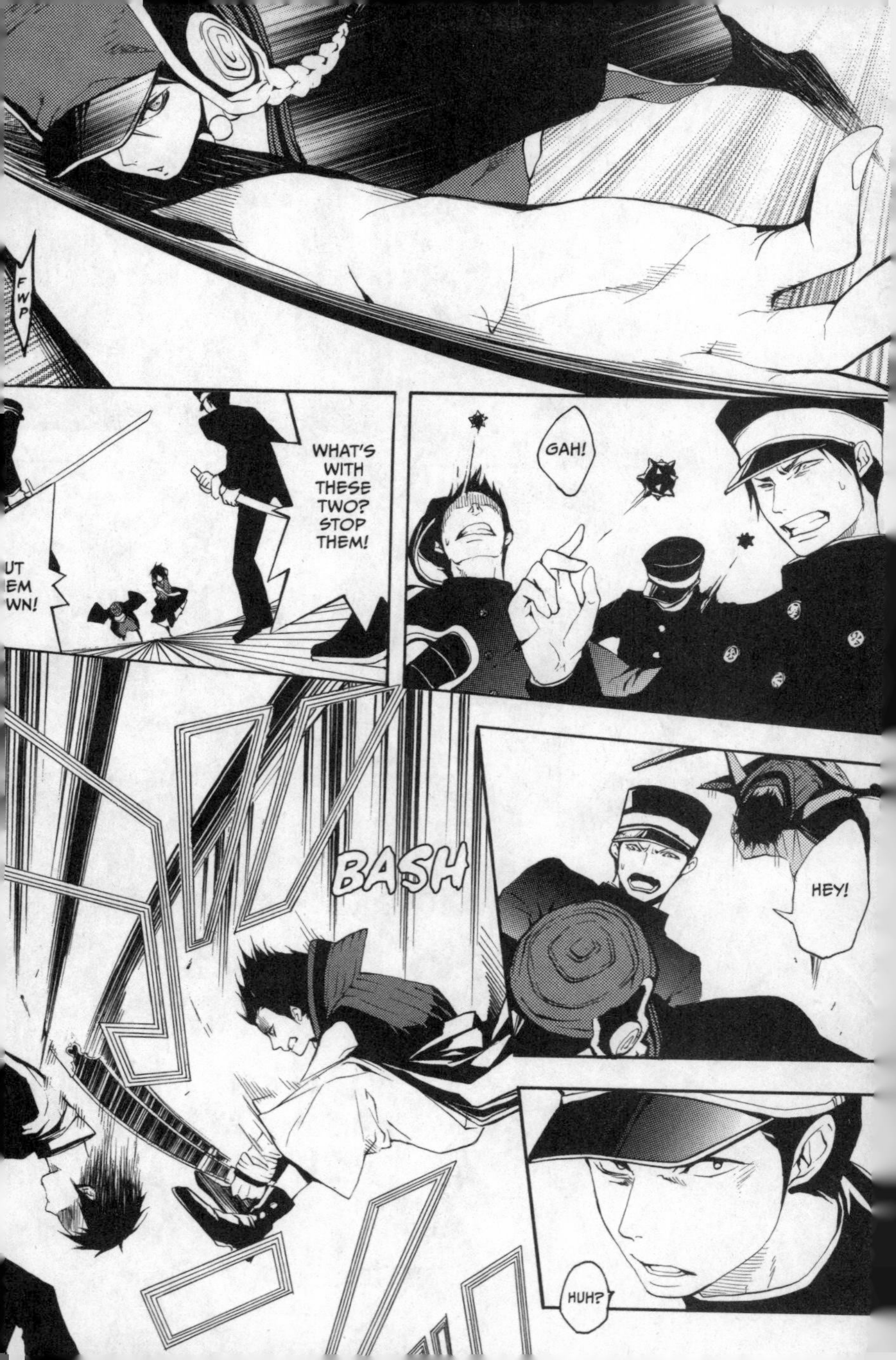
FWP
GAH!
WHAT'S WITH THESE TWO? STOP THEM!
HEY!
HUH?
BASH

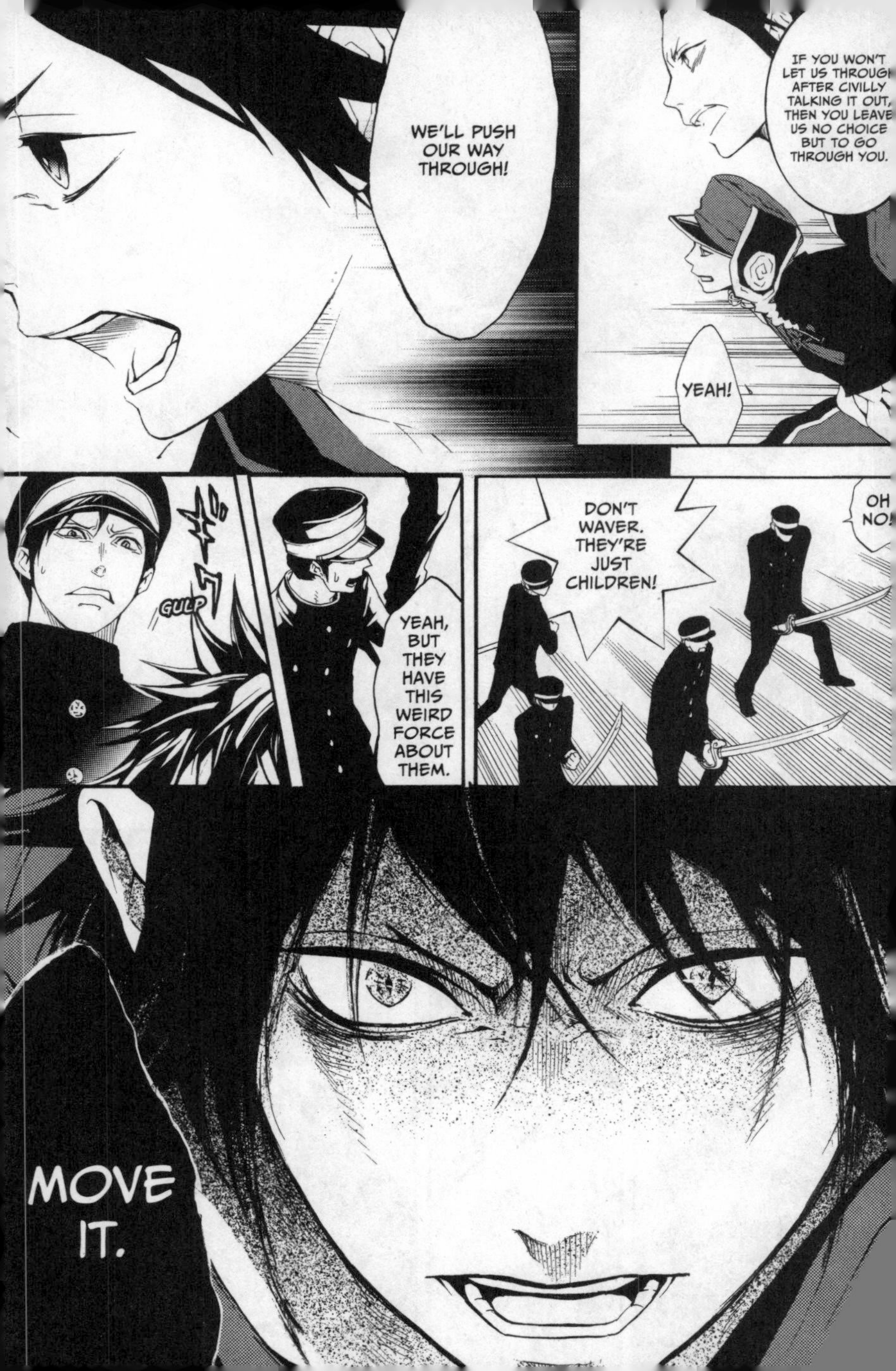

IF YOU WON'T LET US THROUGH AFTER CIVILLY TALKING IT OUT, THEN YOU LEAVE US NO CHOICE BUT TO GO THROUGH YOU.
YEAH!
WE'LL PUSH OUR WAY THROUGH!
OH NO!
DON'T WAVER. THEY'RE JUST CHILDREN!
YEAH, BUT THEY HAVE THIS WEIRD FORCE ABOUT THEM.
GULP
MOVE IT.

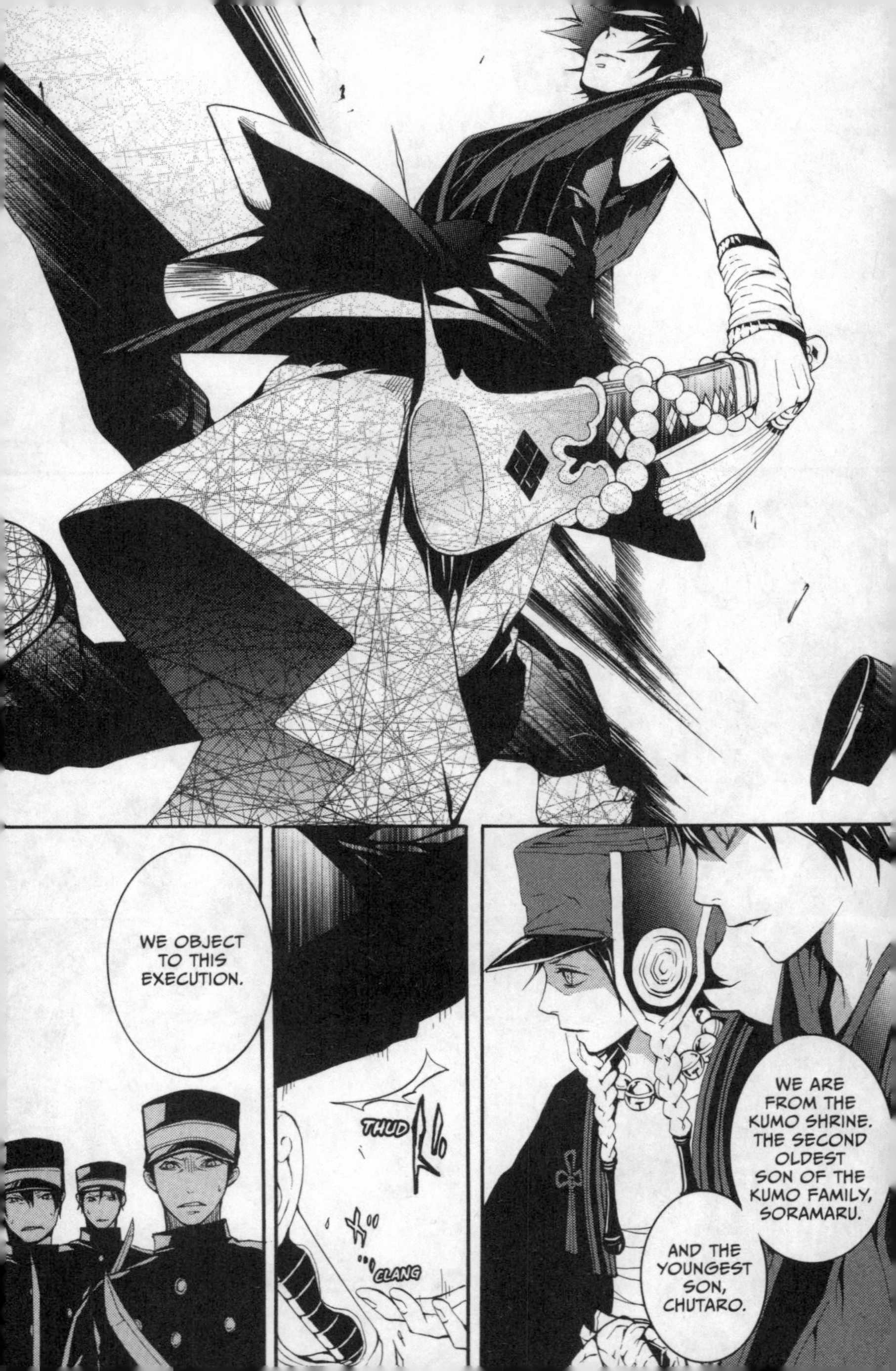
WE ARE FROM THE KUMO SHRINE. THE SECOND OLDEST SON OF THE KUMO FAMILY, SORAMARU.
AND THE YOUNGEST SON, CHUTARO.
THUD
CLANG
WE OBJECT TO THIS EXECUTION.

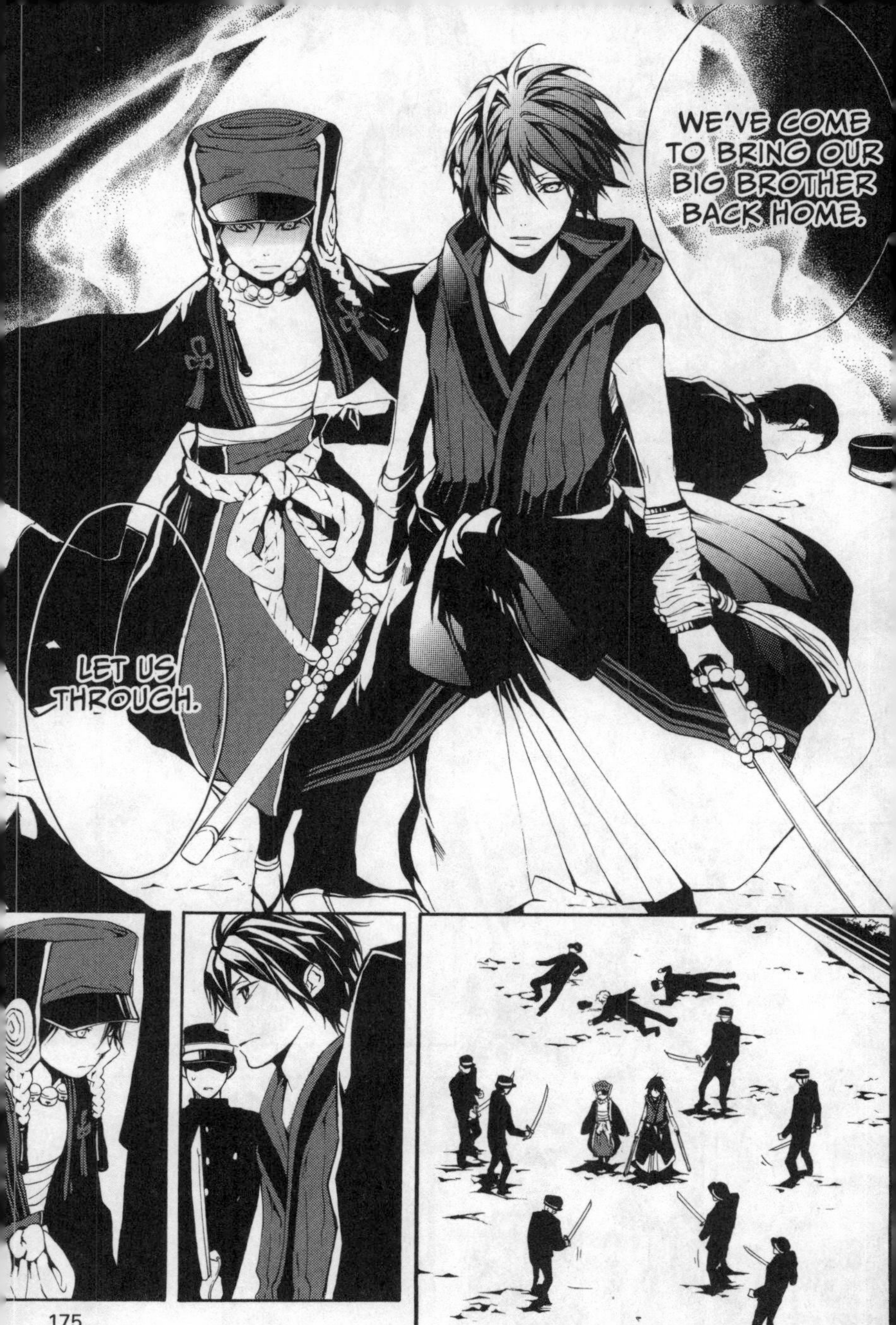
WE'VE COME TO BRING OUR BIG BROTHER BACK HOME.
LET US THROUGH.

WHAT'S GOING ON HERE?!

SORRY. THEY'RE MY LITTLE BROTHERS.

STOP!

BIG BROTHER!

BROTHER TEN!

...I KNOW.

IT'S TIME.

I'M SORRY THIS HAD TO HAPPEN SO SUDDENLY.

WHAT'RE YOU DOING, YOU IDIOT?! WE'RE GOING HOME!

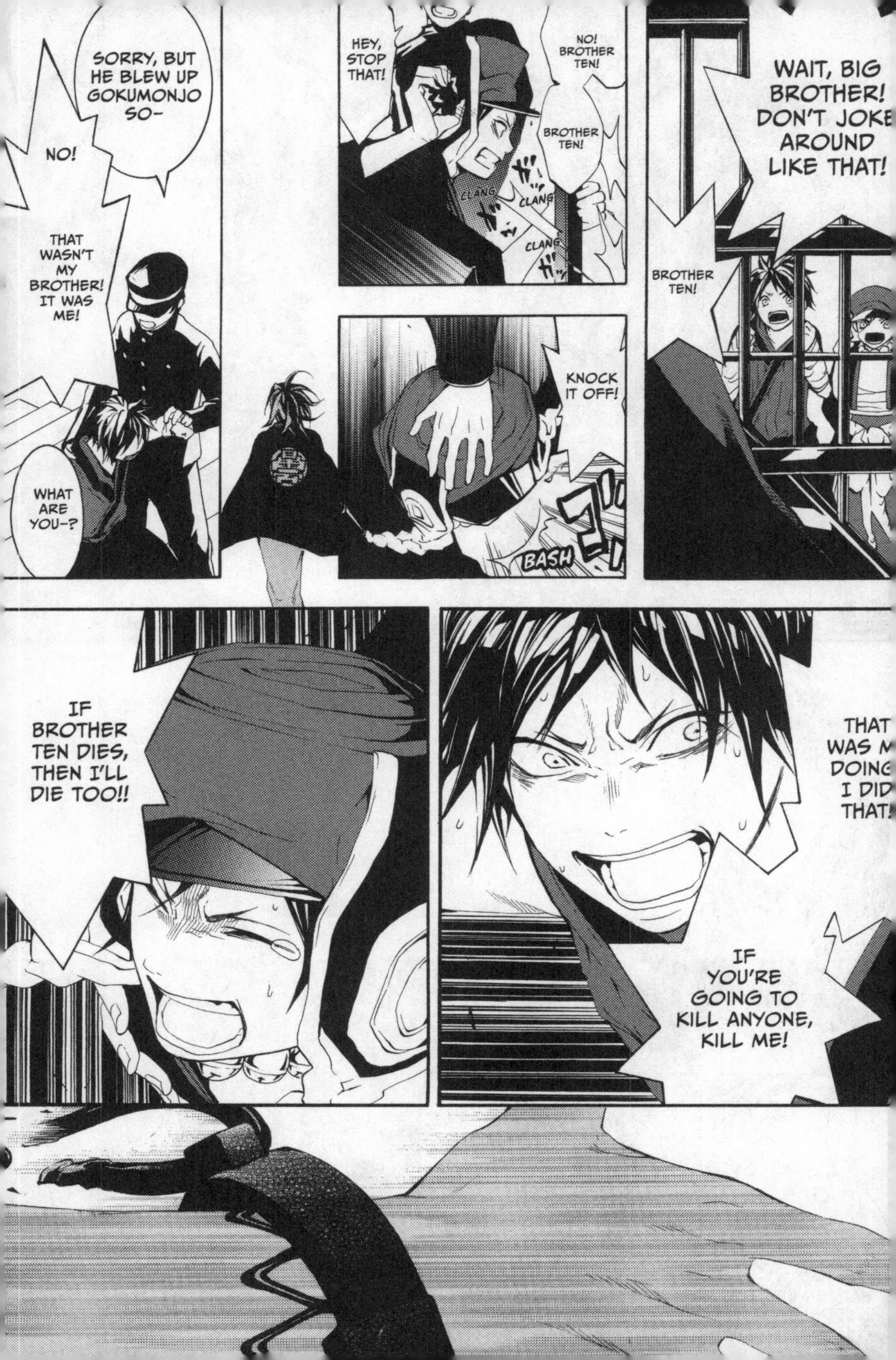
WAIT, BIG BROTHER! DON'T JOKE AROUND LIKE THAT!
BROTHER TEN!
NO! BROTHER TEN!
HEY, STOP THAT!
BROTHER TEN!
CLANG
CLANG
CLANG
KNOCK IT OFF!
BASH
SORRY, BUT HE BLEW UP GOKUMONJO SO-
NO!
THAT WASN'T MY BROTHER! IT WAS ME!
WHAT ARE YOU-?
THAT WAS M DOING I DID THAT!
IF YOU'RE GOING TO KILL ANYONE, KILL ME!
IF BROTHER TEN DIES, THEN I'LL DIE TOO!!

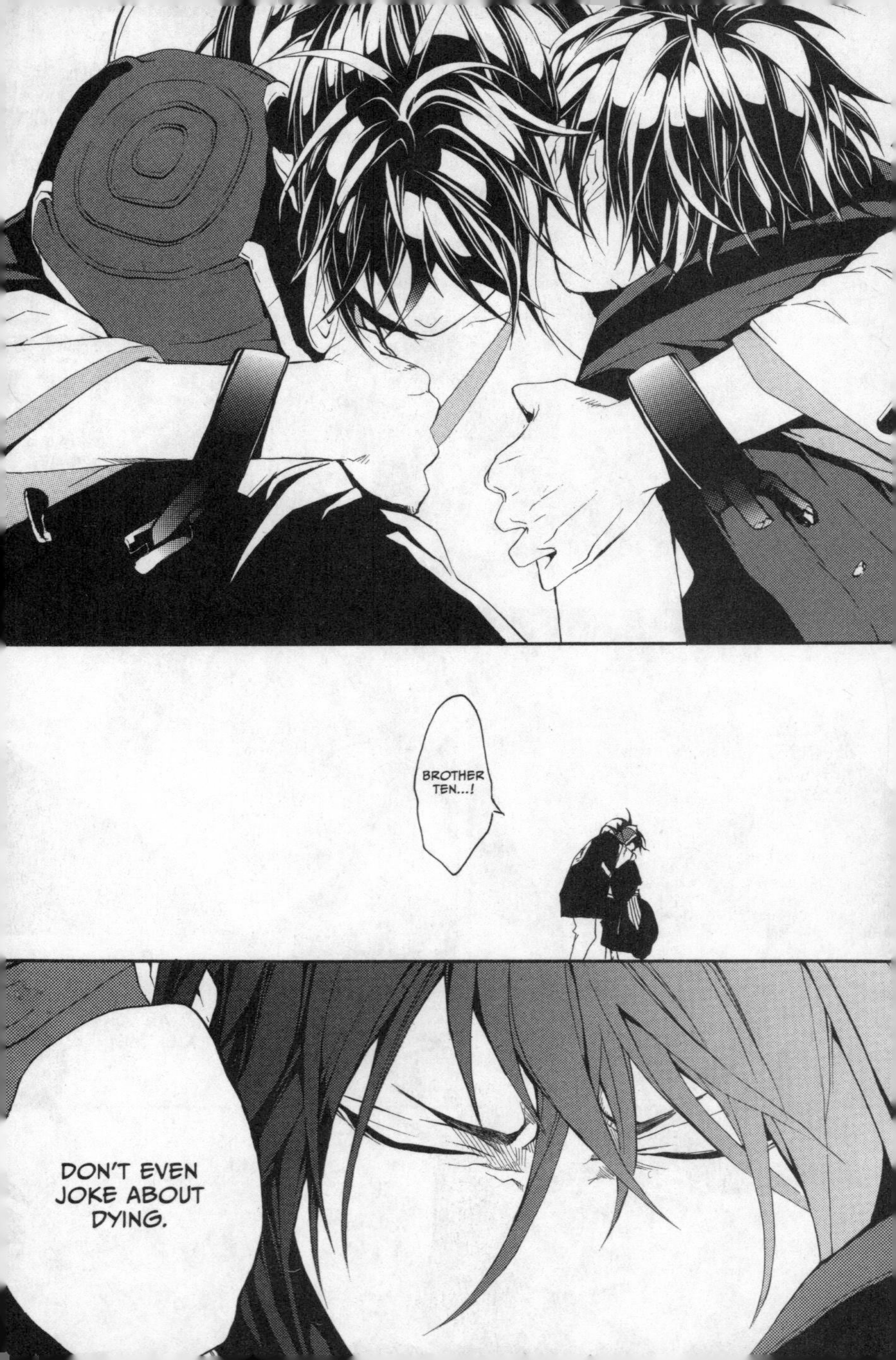
BROTHER TEN...!
DON'T EVEN JOKE ABOUT DYING.

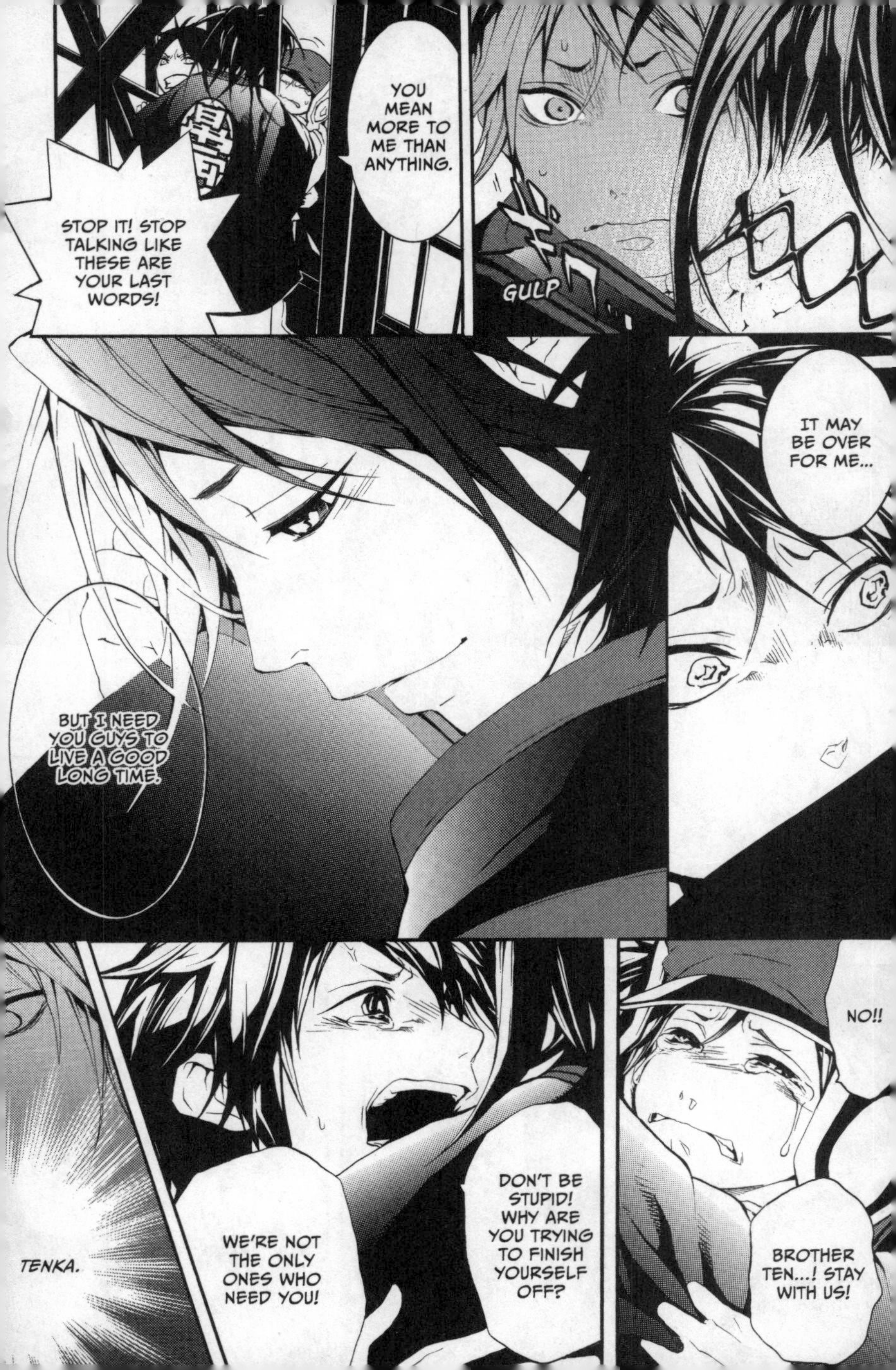
GULP
YOU MEAN MORE TO ME THAN ANYTHING.
STOP IT! STOP TALKING LIKE THESE ARE YOUR LAST WORDS!
IT MAY BE OVER FOR ME...
BUT I NEED YOU GUYS TO LIVE A GOOD LONG TIME.
NO!!
BROTHER TEN...! STAY WITH US!
DON'T BE STUPID! WHY ARE YOU TRYING TO FINISH YOURSELF OFF?
WE'RE NOT THE ONLY ONES WHO NEED YOU!
TENKA.

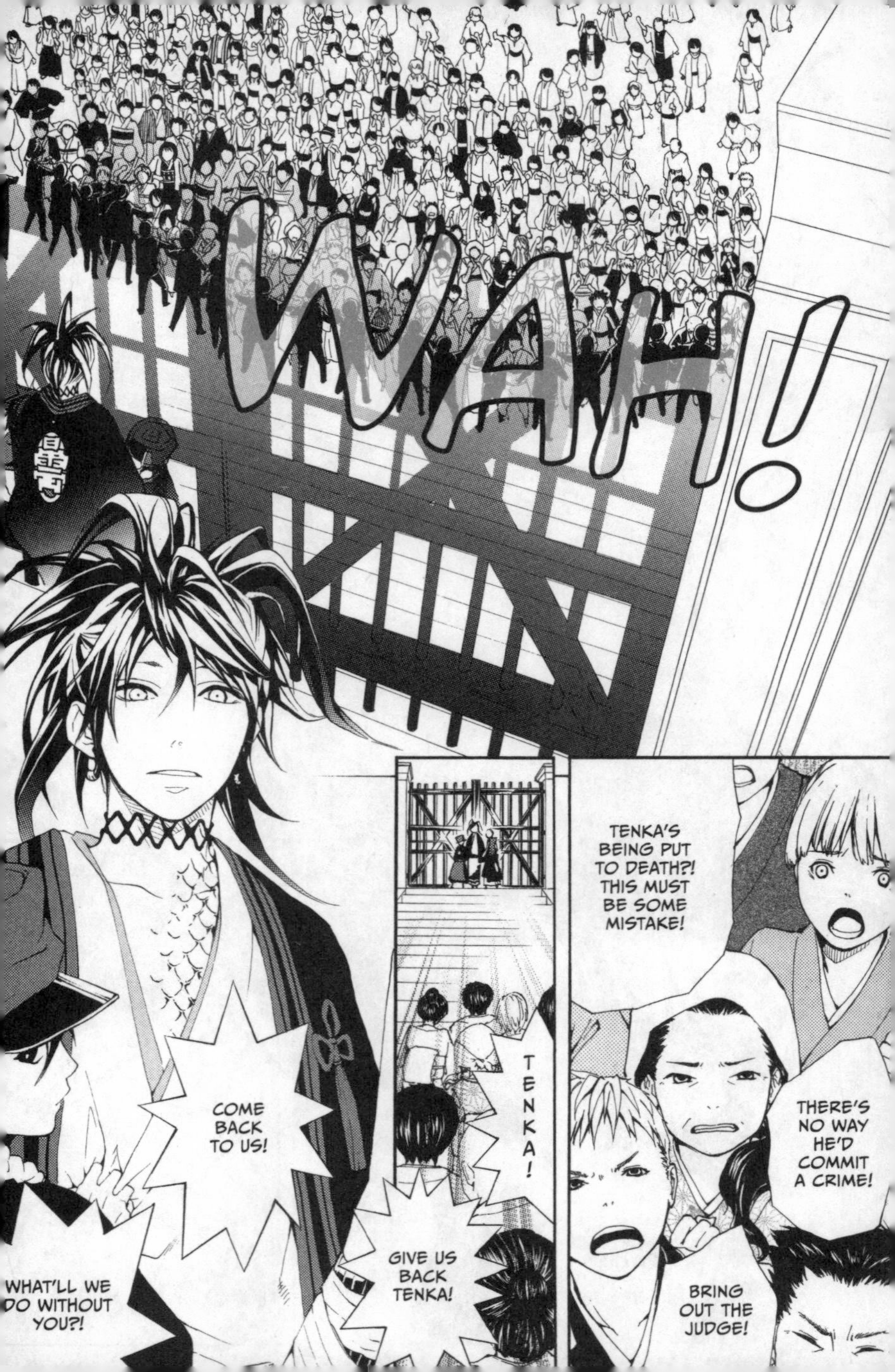
WAH!
COME BACK TO US!
WHAT'LL WE DO WITHOUT YOU?!
TENKA'S BEING PUT TO DEATH?! THIS MUST BE SOME MISTAKE!
THERE'S NO WAY HE'D COMMIT A CRIME!
BRING OUT THE JUDGE!
TENKA!
GIVE US BACK TENKA!

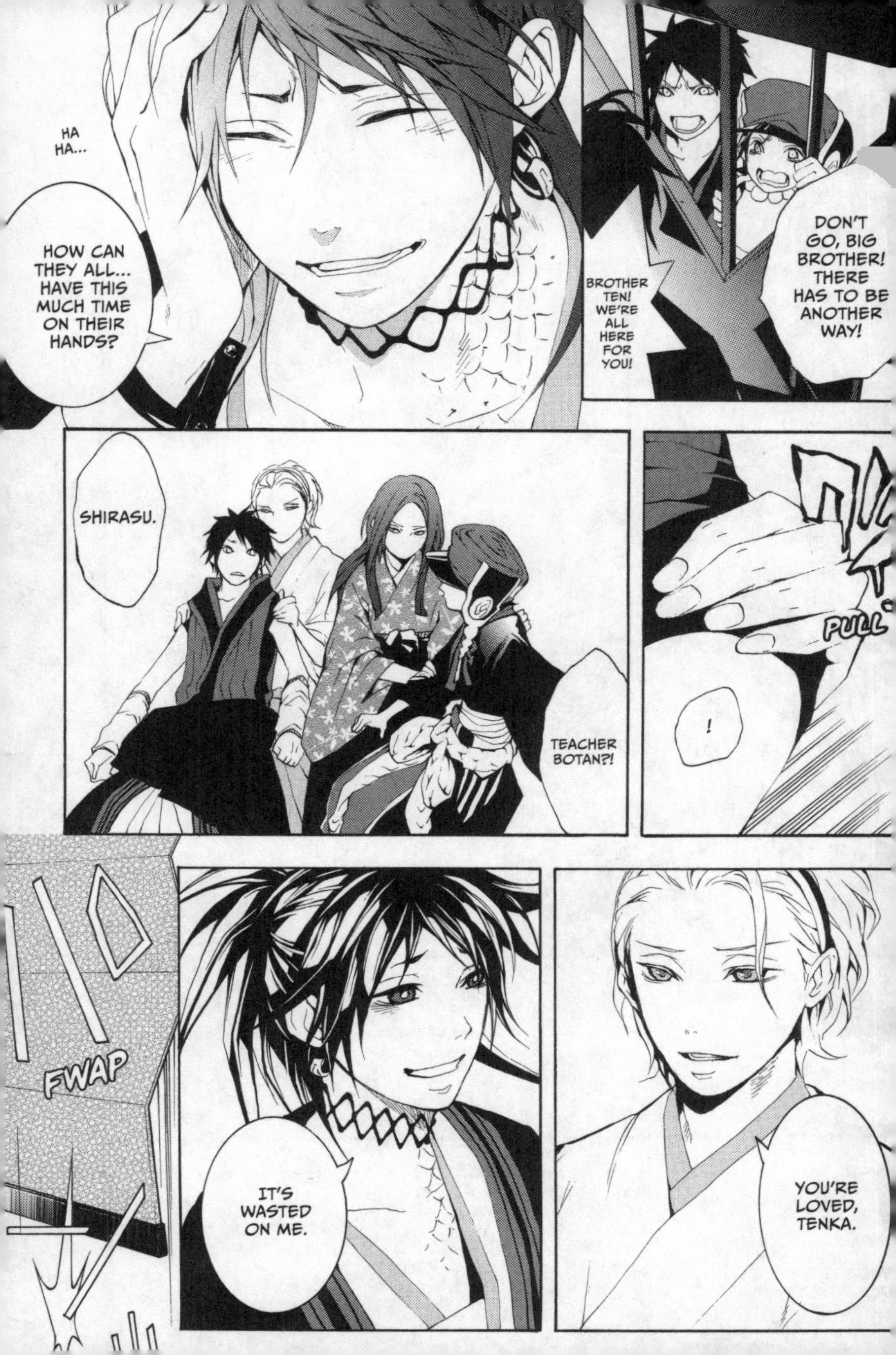
DON'T GO, BIG BROTHER! THERE HAS TO BE ANOTHER WAY!
BROTHER TEN! WE'RE ALL HERE FOR YOU!
HA HA...
HOW CAN THEY ALL... HAVE THIS MUCH TIME ON THEIR HANDS?
PULL
!
TEACHER BOTAN?!
SHIRASU.
YOU'RE LOVED, TENKA.
IT'S WASTED ON ME.
FWAP

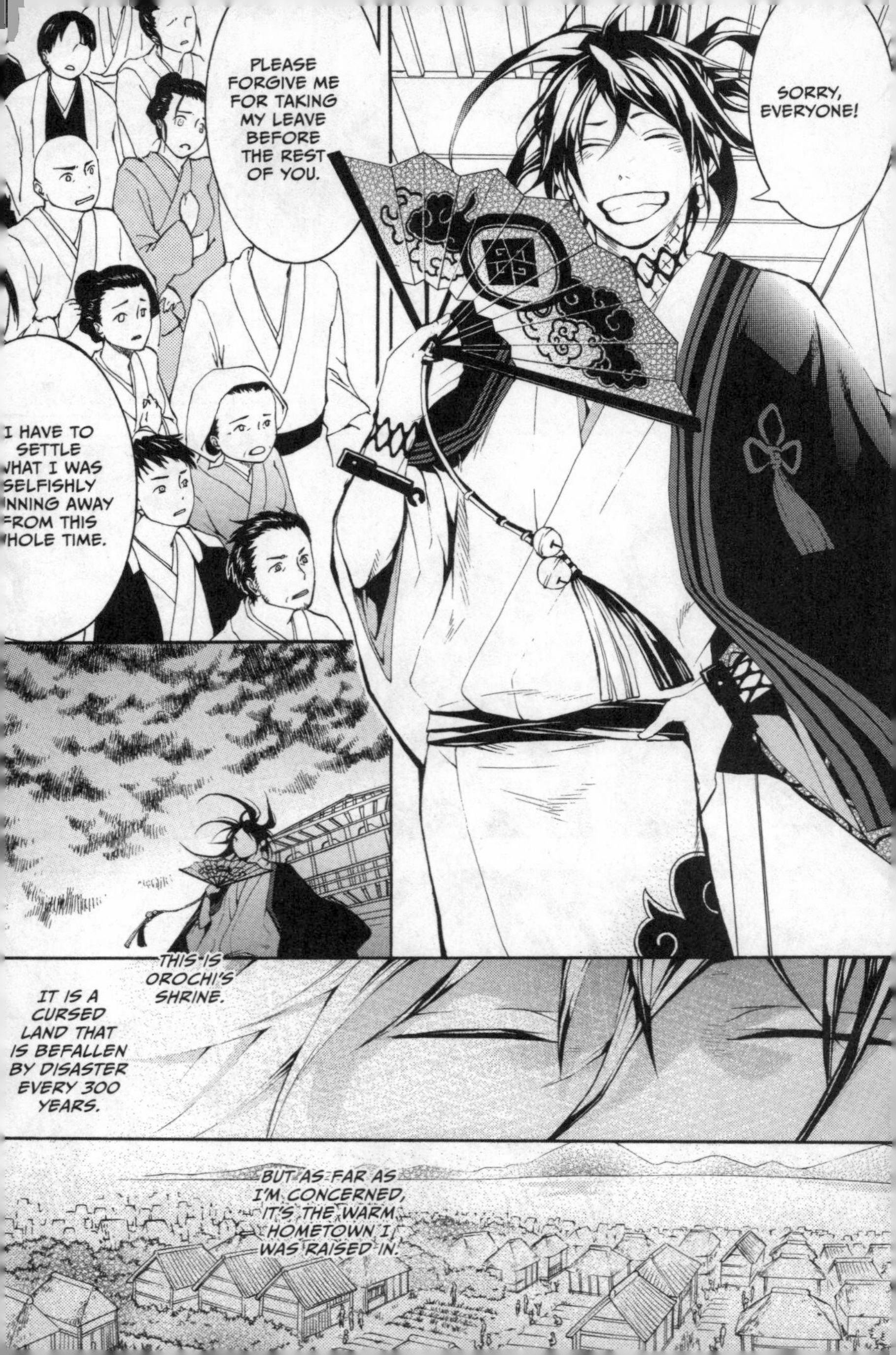
SORRY, EVERYONE!
PLEASE FORGIVE ME FOR TAKING MY LEAVE BEFORE THE REST OF YOU.
I HAVE TO SETTLE HAT I WAS SELFISHLY NNING AWAY FROM THIS HOLE TIME.
THIS IS OROCHI'S SHRINE.
IT IS A CURSED LAND THAT IS BEFALLEN BY DISASTER EVERY 300 YEARS.
BUT AS FAR AS I'M CONCERNED, IT'S THE WARM HOMETOWN I WAS RAISED IN.

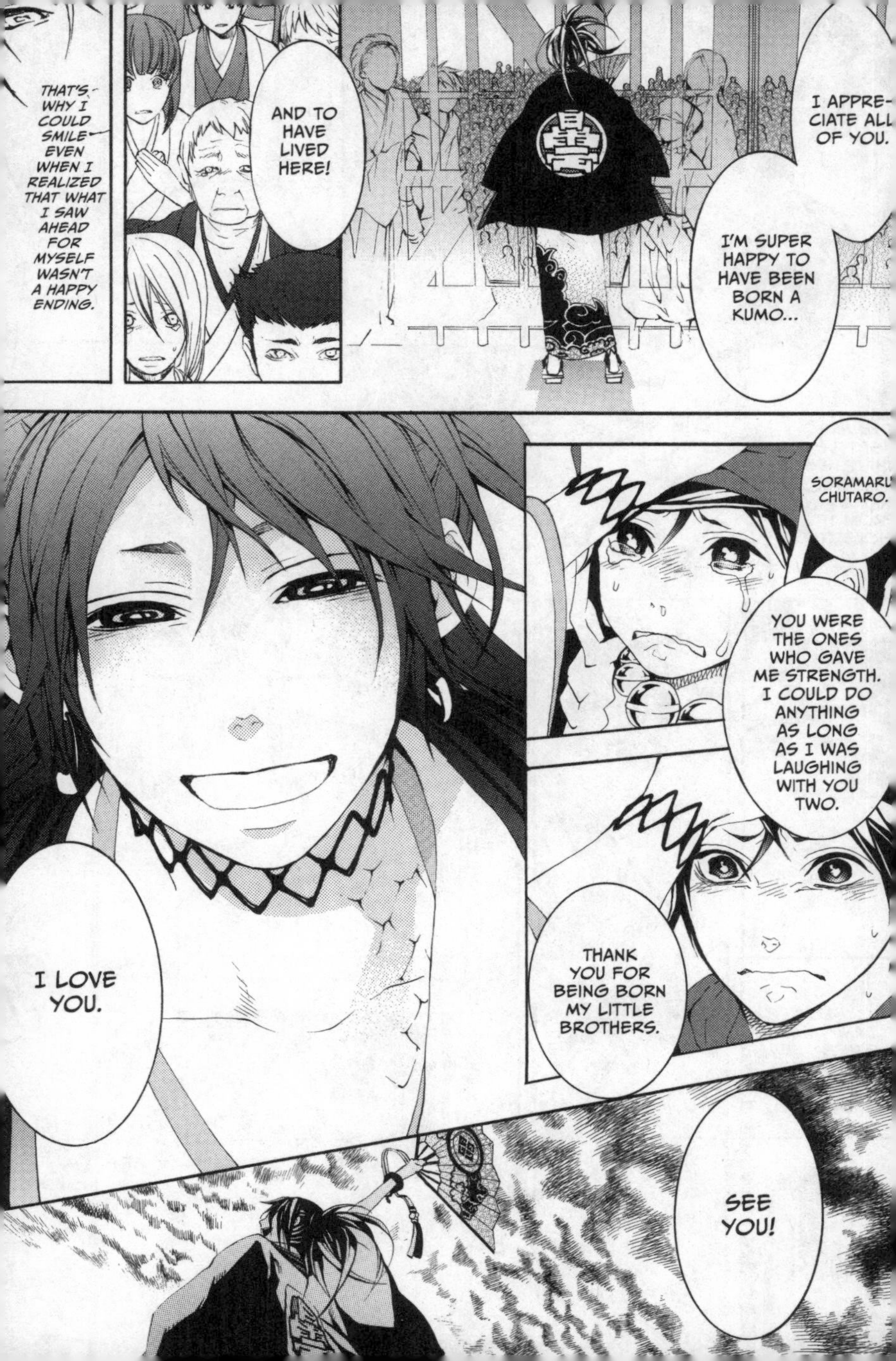
I APPRECIATE ALL OF YOU.
I'M SUPER HAPPY TO HAVE BEEN BORN A KUMO...
AND TO HAVE LIVED HERE!
THAT'S WHY I COULD SMILE EVEN WHEN I REALIZED THAT WHAT I SAW AHEAD FOR MYSELF WASN'T A HAPPY ENDING.
SORAMARU, CHUTARO.
YOU WERE THE ONES WHO GAVE ME STRENGTH. I COULD DO ANYTHING AS LONG AS I WAS LAUGHING WITH YOU TWO.
THANK YOU FOR BEING BORN MY LITTLE BROTHERS.
I LOVE YOU.
SEE YOU!

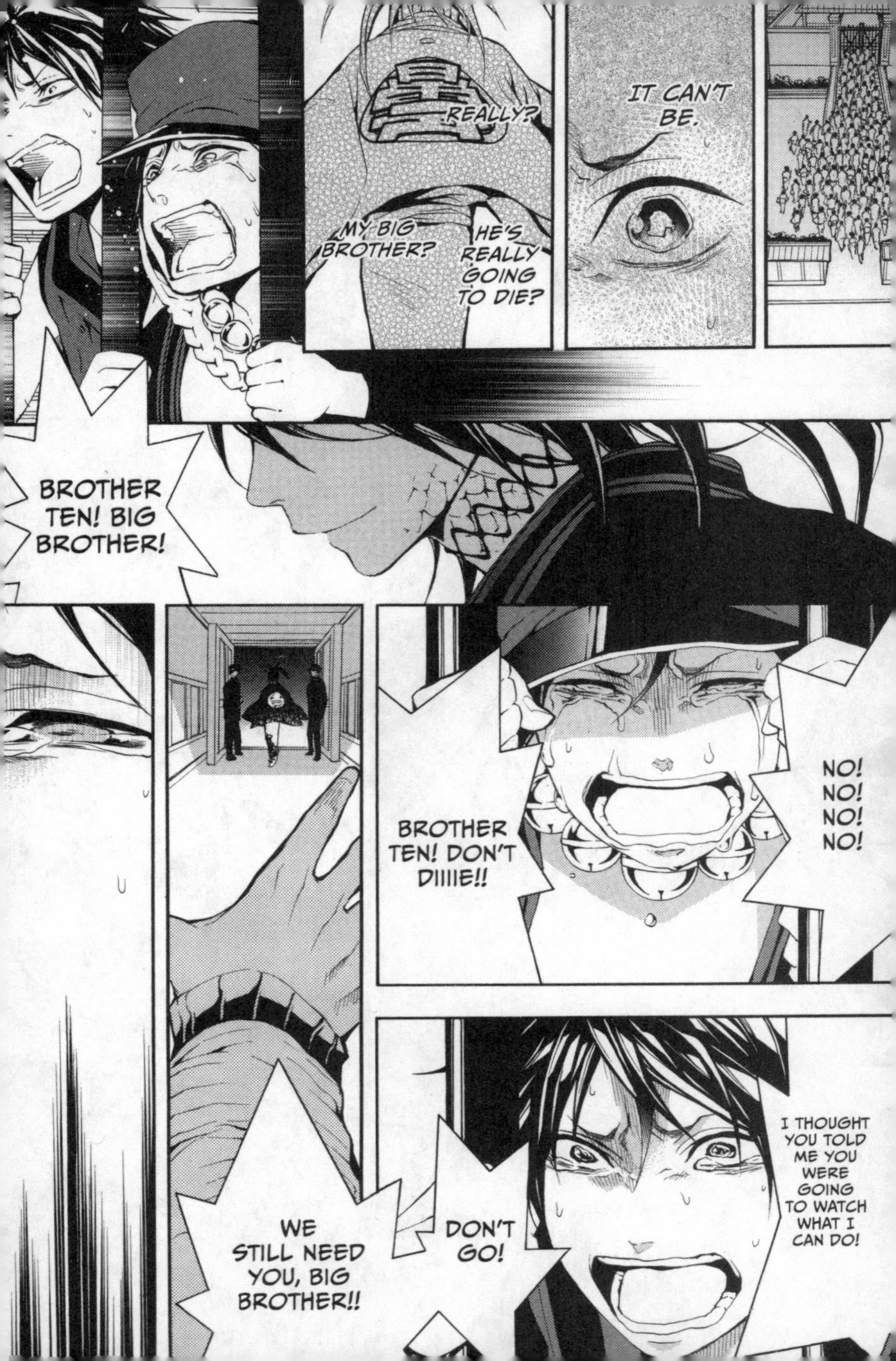
IT CAN'T BE.
REALLY?
MY BIG BROTHER?
HE'S REALLY GOING TO DIE?
BROTHER TEN! BIG BROTHER!
NO! NO! NO! NO!
BROTHER TEN! DON'T DIIIIE!!
I THOUGHT YOU TOLD ME YOU WERE GOING TO WATCH WHAT I CAN DO!
DON'T GO!
WE STILL NEED YOU, BIG BROTHER!!

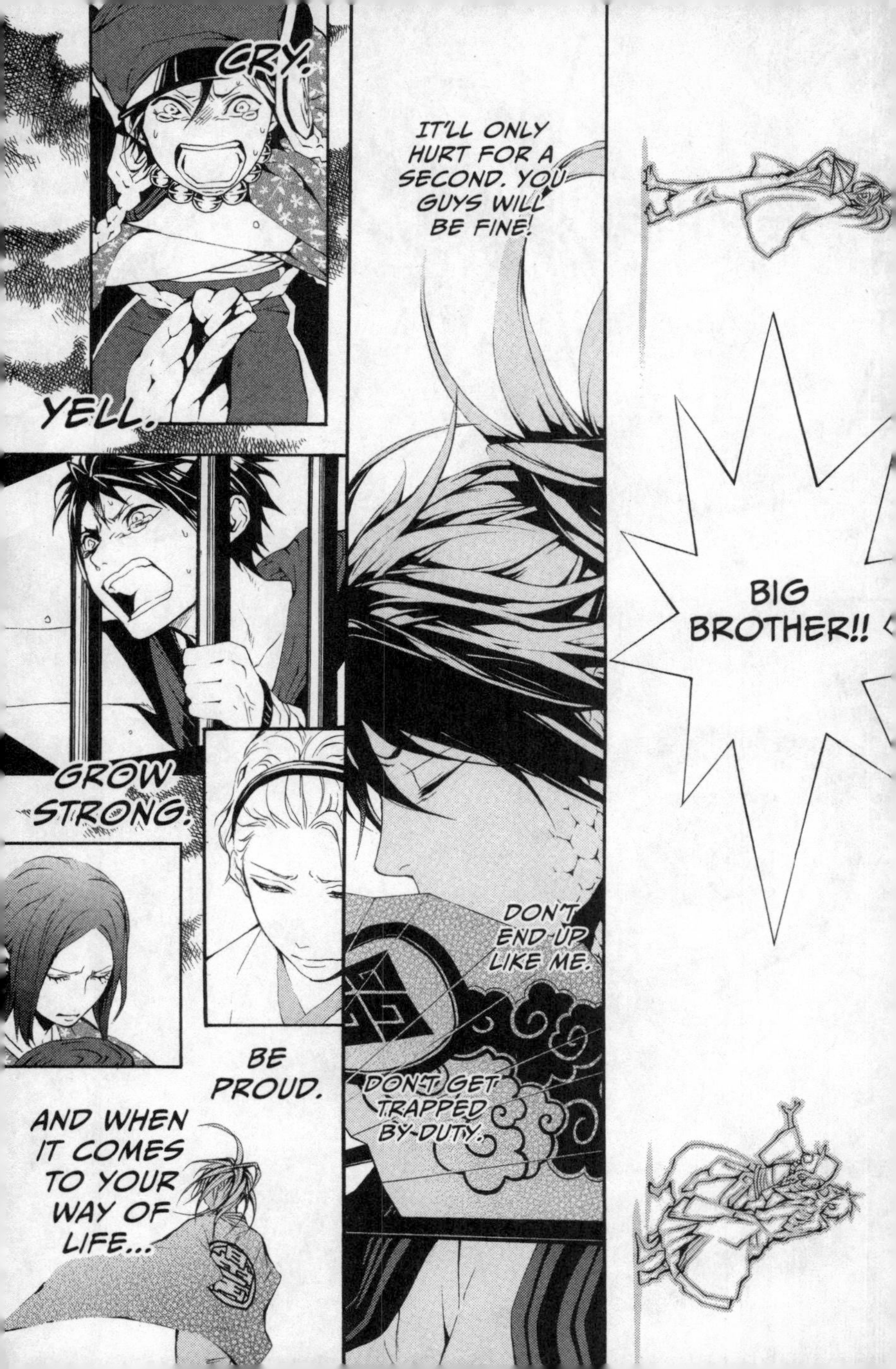
BIG BROTHER!!
IT'LL ONLY HURT FOR A SECOND. YOU GUYS WILL BE FINE!
DON'T END UP LIKE ME.
DON'T GET TRAPPED BY DUTY.
CRY.
YELL.
GROW STRONG.
BE PROUD.
AND WHEN IT COMES TO YOUR WAY OF LIFE...

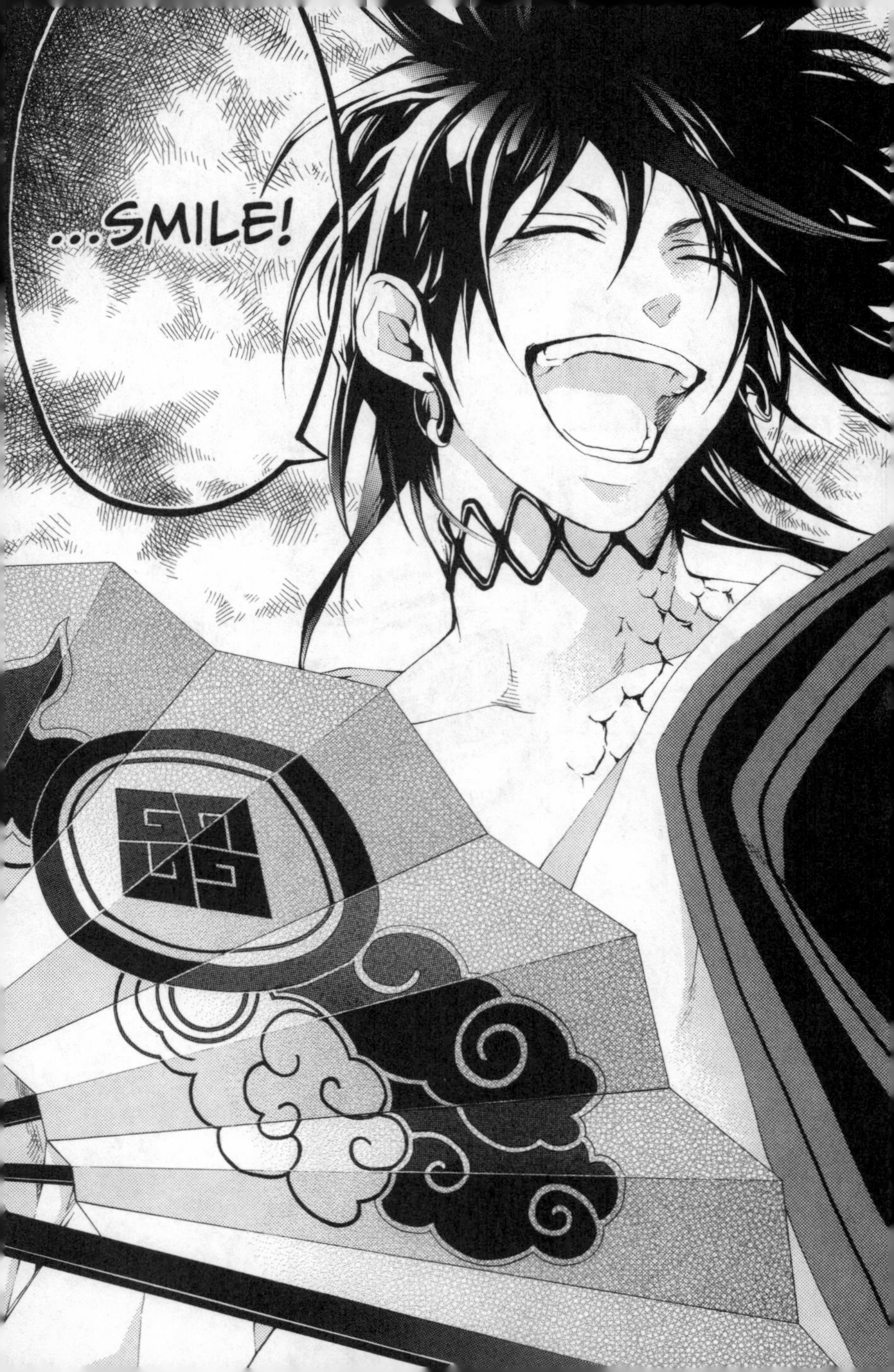
...SMILE!

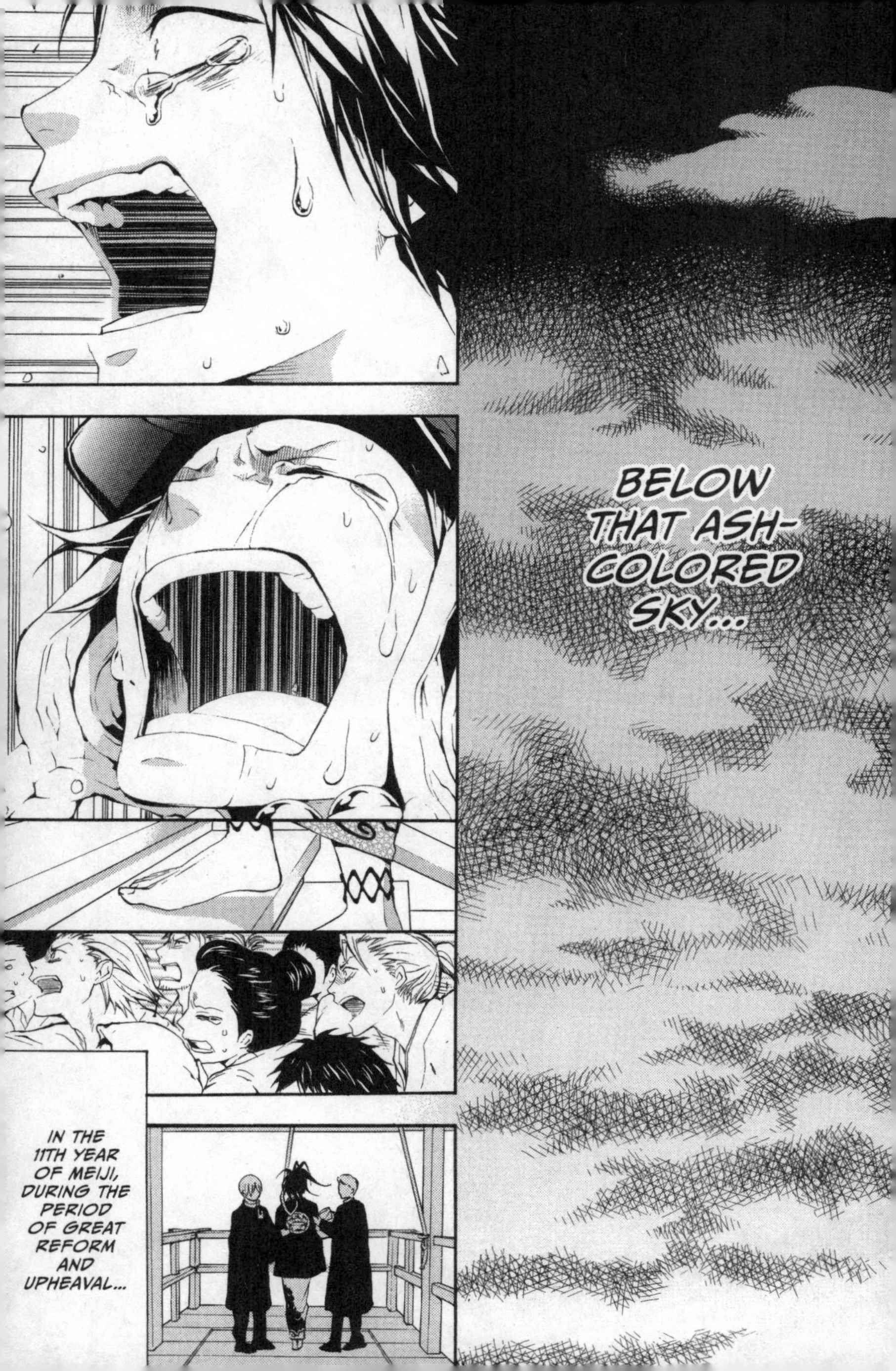
BELOW THAT ASH-COLORED SKY...
IN THE 11TH YEAR OF MEIJI, DURING THE PERIOD OF GREAT REFORM AND UPHEAVAL...

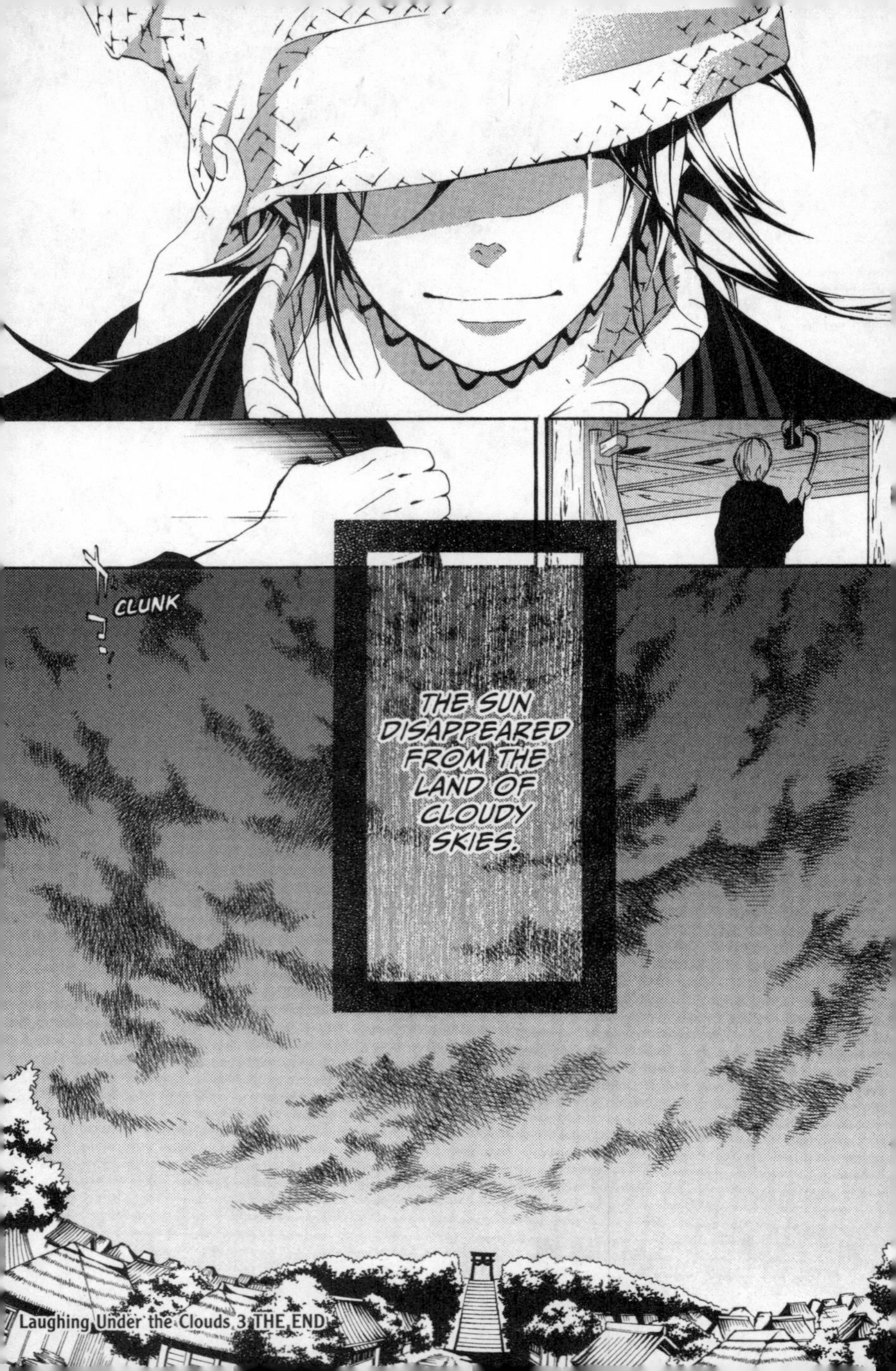
CLUNK
THE SUN DISAPPEARED FROM THE LAND OF CLOUDY SKIES.
Laughing Under the Clouds 3 THE END

LAUGHING UNDER THE CLOUDS

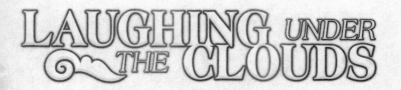

LAUGHING UNDER THE CLOUDS

POKO'S PRAYER

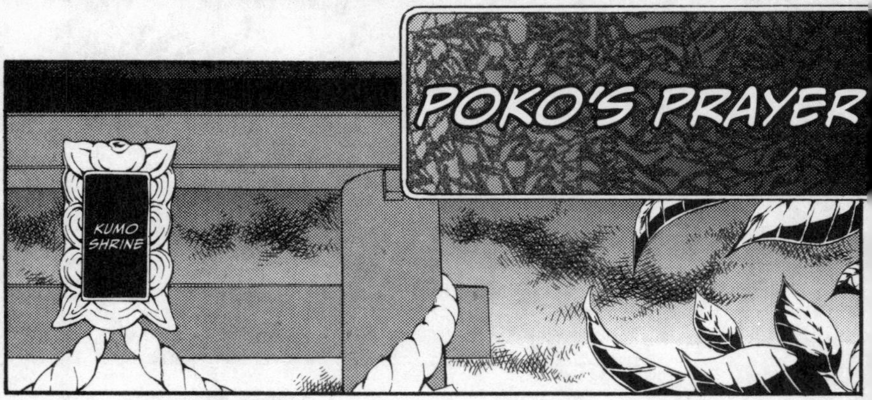
KUMO SHRINE

THE YEAR WAS 1878.

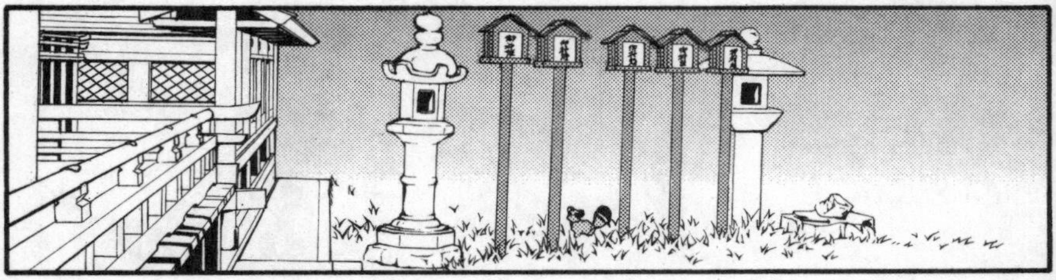

I HAD BEEN LIVING AT THIS SHRINE FOR ABOUT 600 YEARS.

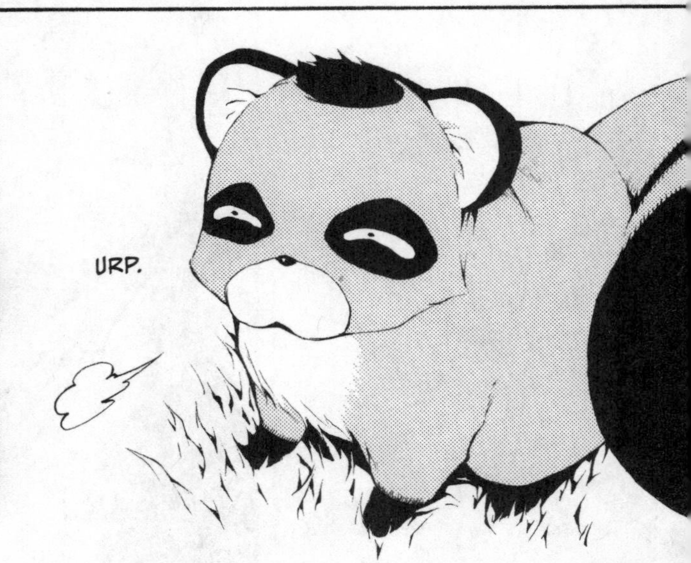
URP.

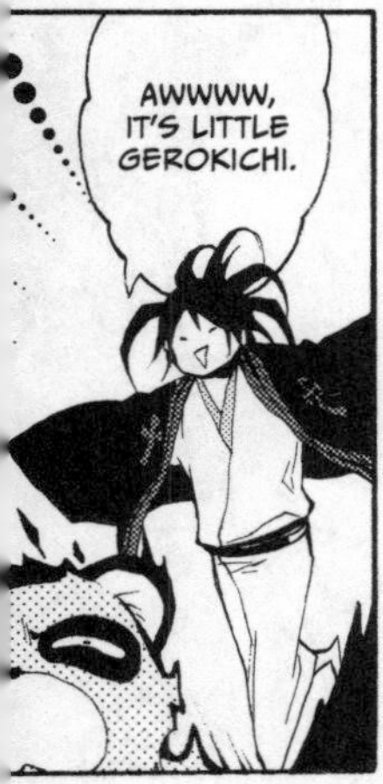
AWWWW, IT'S LITTLE GEROKICHI.

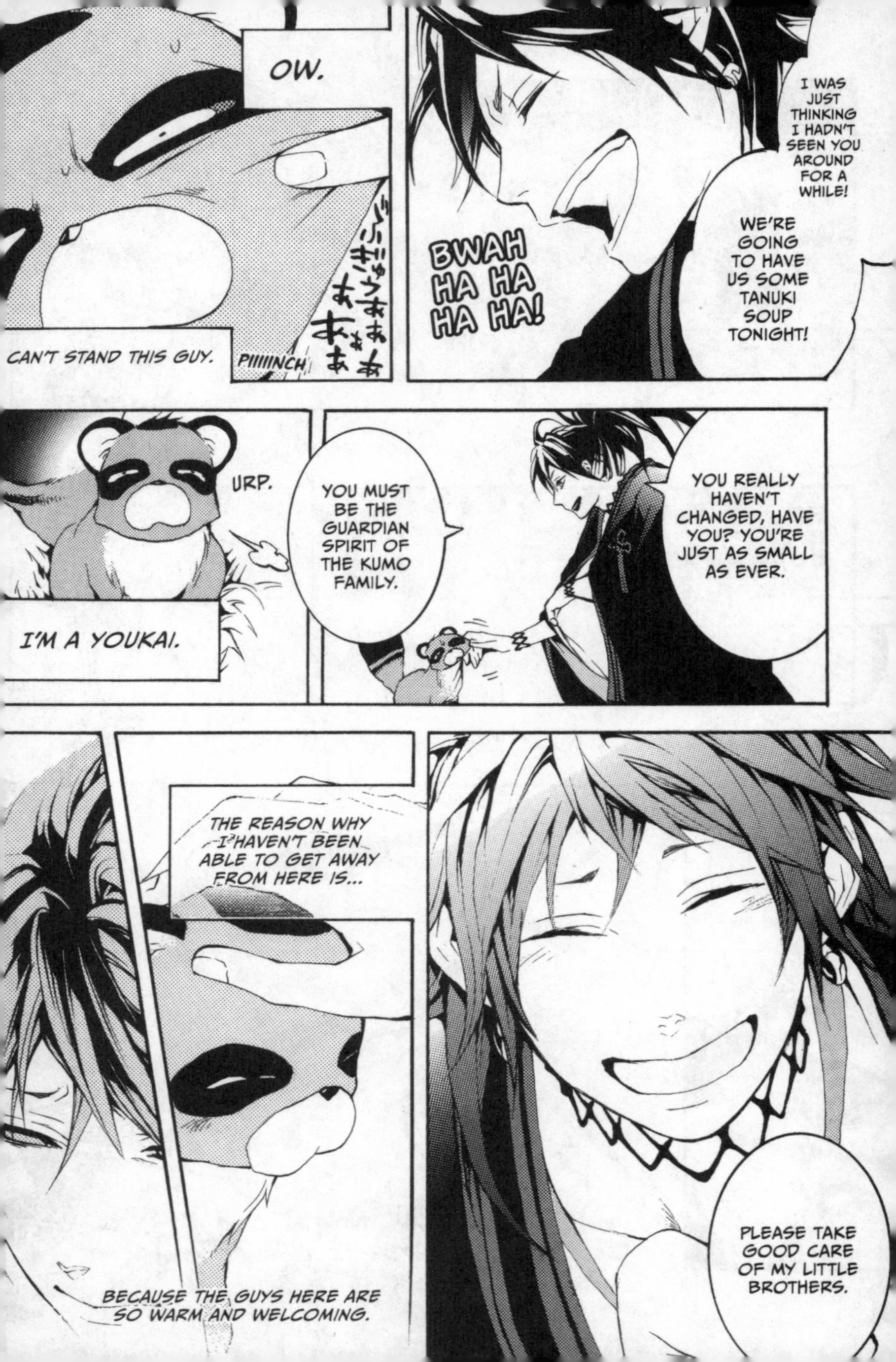
I WAS JUST THINKING I HADN'T SEEN YOU AROUND FOR A WHILE!
WE'RE GOING TO HAVE US SOME TANUKI SOUP TONIGHT!
BWAH HA HA HA HA!
OW.
PIIIIINCH
CAN'T STAND THIS GUY.
YOU REALLY HAVEN'T CHANGED, HAVE YOU? YOU'RE JUST AS SMALL AS EVER.
YOU MUST BE THE GUARDIAN SPIRIT OF THE KUMO FAMILY.
URP.
I'M A YOUKAI.
PLEASE TAKE GOOD CARE OF MY LITTLE BROTHERS.
THE REASON WHY I HAVEN'T BEEN ABLE TO GET AWAY FROM HERE IS...
BECAUSE THE GUYS HERE ARE SO WARM AND WELCOMING.

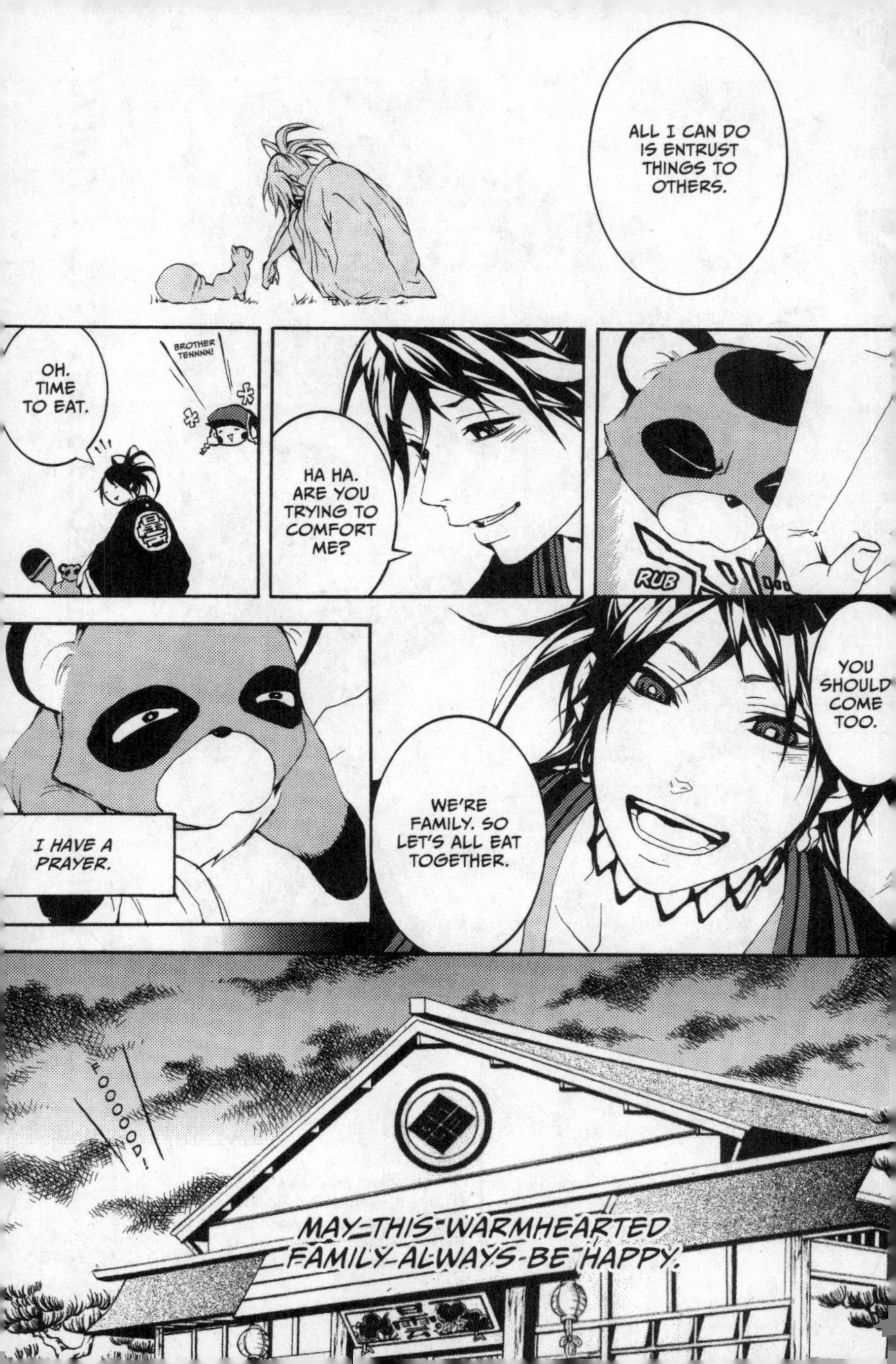
ALL I CAN DO IS ENTRUST THINGS TO OTHERS.
RUB
HA HA. ARE YOU TRYING TO COMFORT ME?
BROTHER TENNNN!
OH. TIME TO EAT.
YOU SHOULD COME TOO.
WE'RE FAMILY. SO LET'S ALL EAT TOGETHER.
I HAVE A PRAYER.
FOOOOOOD!
MAY THIS WARMHEARTED FAMILY ALWAYS BE HAPPY.

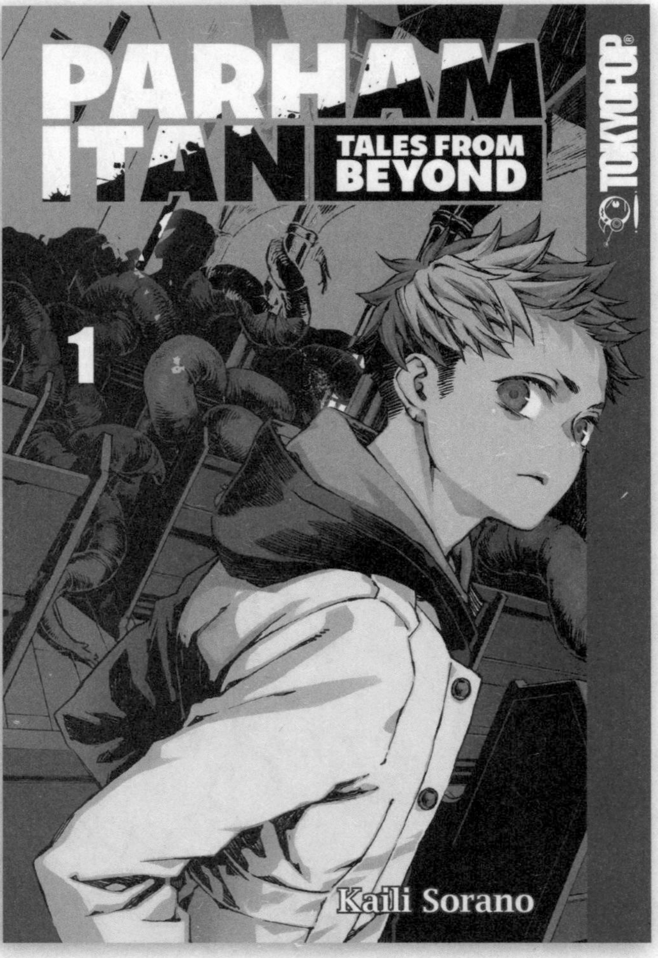
PARHAM ITAN
TALES FROM BEYOND
1
TOKYOPOP
Kaili Sorano

PARHAM ITAN: TALES FROM BEYOND, VOLUME 1

Kaili Sorano

SUPERNATURAL

Yamagishi and Sendo are schoolmates, but that's about all they have in common: one is a down-to-earth guy in the boxing club, while the other is a brainy, bookish conspiracy nut. But when they stumble across something weird and inexplicable after class one evening, it seems they'll have to set their differences aside in order to uncover the truth behind the mysterious creatures and strange figure prowling the school grounds.

TOKYOPOP

When Lizel mysteriously finds himself in a city that bears odd similarities to his own but clearly isn't, he quickly comes to terms with the unlikely truth: this is an entirely different world. Even so, laid-back Lizel isn't the type to panic. He immediately sets out to learn more about this strange place, and to help him do so, hires a seasoned adventurer named Gil as his tour guide and protector. Until he's able to find a way home, Lizel figures this is a perfect opportunity to explore a new way of life adventuring as part of a guild. After all, he's sure he'll go home eventually... might as well enjoy the otherworldly vacation for now!

NO VAMPIRE, NO HAPPY ENDING, VOLUME 1

Shinya Shinya

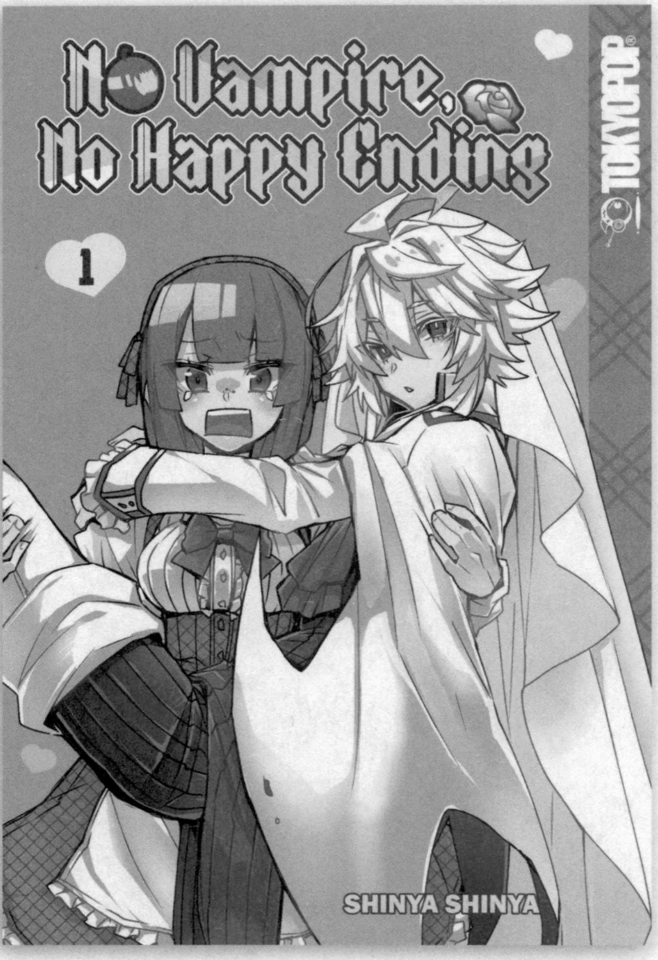
No Vampire, No Happy Ending
1
TOKYOPOP
SHINYA SHINYA

LOVE x LOVE

Arika is what you could charitably call a vampire "enthusiast." When she stumbles across the beautiful and mysterious vampire Divo however, her excitement quickly turns to disappointment as she discovers he's not exactly like the seductive, manipulative villains in her stories. His looks win first place, but his head's a space case. Armed with her extensive knowledge of vampire lore, Arika downgrades Divo to a beta vampire and begins their long, long... long journey to educate him in the ways of the undead.

TOKYOPOP

THE TREASURE OF THE KING AND THE CAT

You Kajika

δLOVE·x·LOVEδ

One day, a large number of people suddenly disappeared in the royal capital. When young King Castio goes out to investigate this occurrence, he comes across the culprit... but the criminal puts a spell on him! To help him out, the king calls the wizard O'Feuille to his castle, along with Prince Volks and his loyal retainer Nios. Together, they're determined to solve this strange, fluffy mystery full of cats, swords and magic!

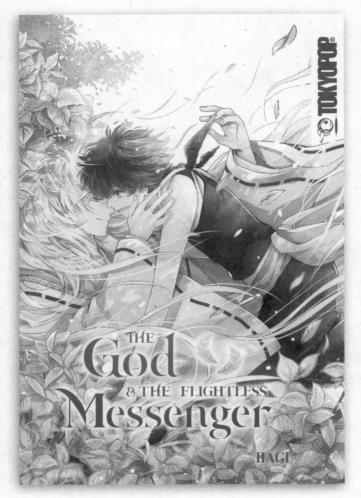

♂LOVE-x-LOVE♂

"My lord, were you the one who stayed by my side?"
Shin is a messenger to the gods, but he's always been alone because of his tiny wings. And when he's finally assigned a god to serve, it turns out to be... a huge ball of fluff?! Stranger still, he feels an odd, nostalgic connection with the funny-looking god.
This is not the story of how a shape-shifting god and an earnest messenger with a short temper meet, but of how they find each other again.

THE CAT PROPOSED

Dento Hayane

The Cat Proposed

Dento Hayane

δLOVE-x-LOVEδ

Matoi Souta is an overworked office worker tired of his life. Then, on his way home from a long day of work one day, he decides to watch a traditional Japanese play. But something strange happens. He could have sworn he saw one of the actors has cat ears. It turns out that the man is actually a bakeneko — a shapeshifting cat from Japanese folklore. And then, the cat speaks: "From now on, you will be my mate."

UNDEAD MESSIAH, VOLUME 1

Gin Zarbo

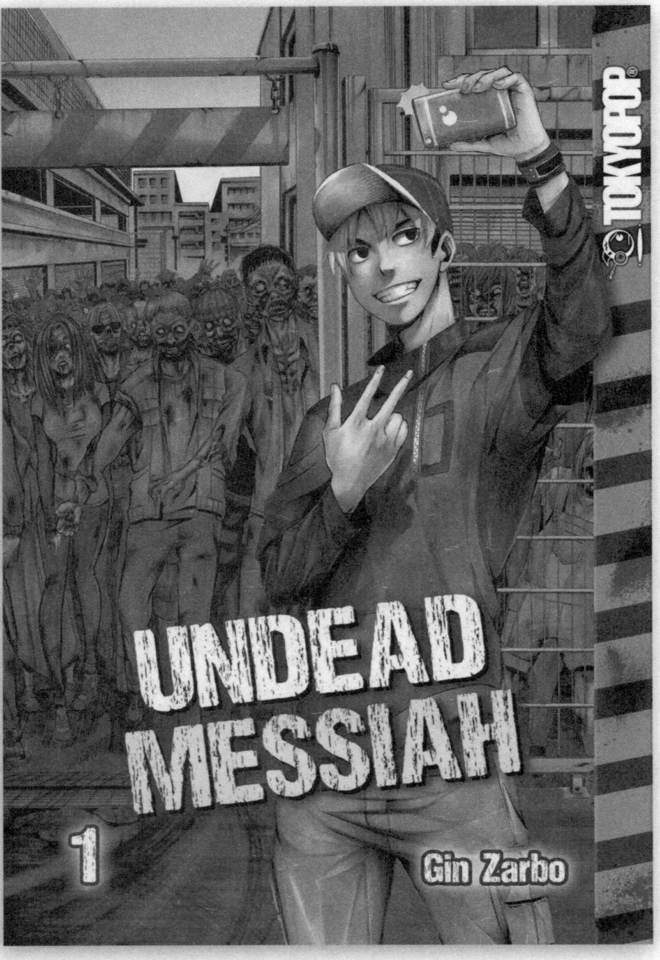
TOKYOPOP
UNDEAD MESSIAH
1
Gin Zarbo

INTERNATIONAL
women of manga

A pregnant woman is pursued by a supernatural creature. On the internet, videos of a bandaged hero surface. 15-year-old Tim Muley makes a terrible discovery in his neighbor's garden. Three seemingly unrelated events, all of which seem to point to an imminent zombie apocalypse! But this time the story's not about the end of mankind; it's about a new beginning...

TOKYOPOP

UNDEAD MESSIAH, VOLUME 2

Gin Zarbo

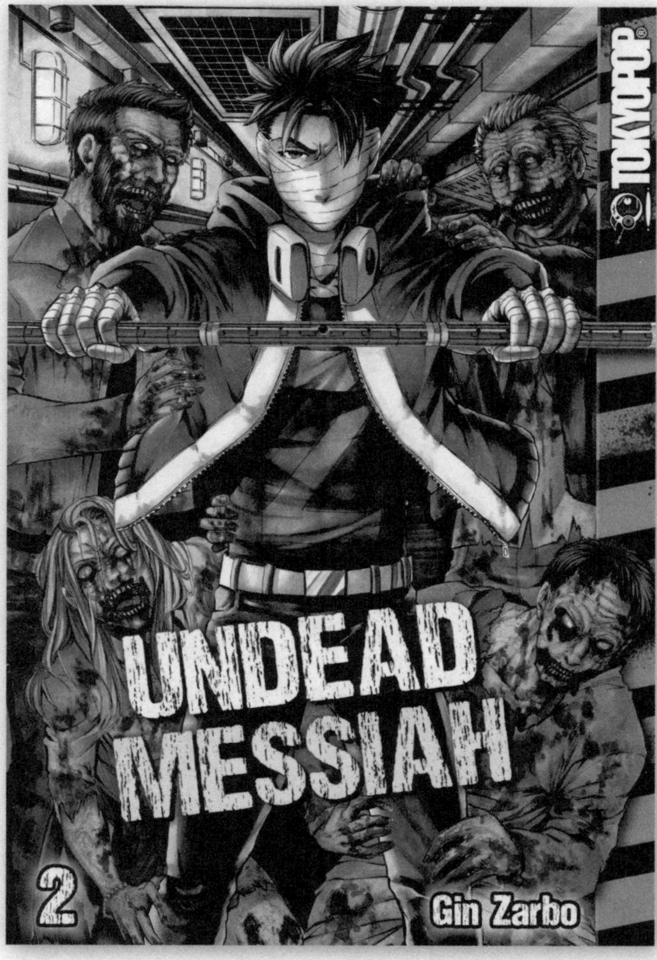
TOKYOPOP
UNDEAD MESSIAH
2
Gin Zarbo

INTERNATIONAL
WOMEN of MANGA

TOKYOPOP

Tim Muley has had a hell of a week: stumbling onto a horde of walking dead, rescuing a baby, escaping the military, and then watching his infected father get murdered by the man everyone else calls a saint. Now, kidnapped by that very same "savior," Tim finds himself surrounded by loyal apostles with unbelievable powers, flesh-eating zombies, and the kind of scientific conspiracy he couldn't have imagined in his wildest nightmares. Who is this secretive, bandaged antihero? What is the truth behind the zombie virus? And what does it have to do with a fantasy-prone teenage gamer?

SCARLET SOUL, VOLUME 1

Kira Yukishiro

KIRA YUKISHIRO

SCARLET SOUL

1

KIRA YUKISHIRO

INTERNATIONAL
WOMEN *of* **MANGA**

Long ago, Eron Shirano used the sacred Sword of a Hundred Souls to seal away the demon underworld Ruhmon. Since then, the Kingdom of Nohmur has enjoyed peace and prosperity with the aid of his descendants, the exorcist clan that protects the barrier. Until one day, for unknown reasons, demons begin slipping through once more...

When Priestess Lys Shirano suddenly vanishes without a trace, it's up to her little sister Rin to take up the sword she left behind. Even though she's an outcast on friendly terms with the mysterious demon Aghyr, Rin sets out to find her missing sister... and try to restore balance to Nohmur before it's far too late.

TOKYOPOP

SCARLET SOUL, VOLUME 2

Kira Yukishiro

INTERNATIONAL
WOMEN of MANGA

After their search for the missing Great Priestess Lys leads Rin and Aghyr into trouble and an unexpected battle at the Water Sanctuary, they take some time to regroup among their friends of the Kaishin Clan. There, they meet up with the Fire Oracles Kara and Koru, who have prophesied the arrival of the Scarlet Soul— none other than Rin Shirano herself. With the Fire Oracles' help, Rin reclaims her sister's sword Hitaken, which has chosen her as its wielder. Whether she feels ready to take on the responsibility or not, she is the only one who can carry the ancient exorcist blade now.

Bizenghast
I
THE COLLECTOR'S EDITION
TOKYOPOP

BIZENGHAST: THE COLLECTOR'S EDITION VOLUME 1

M. Alice LeGrow

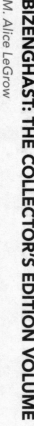

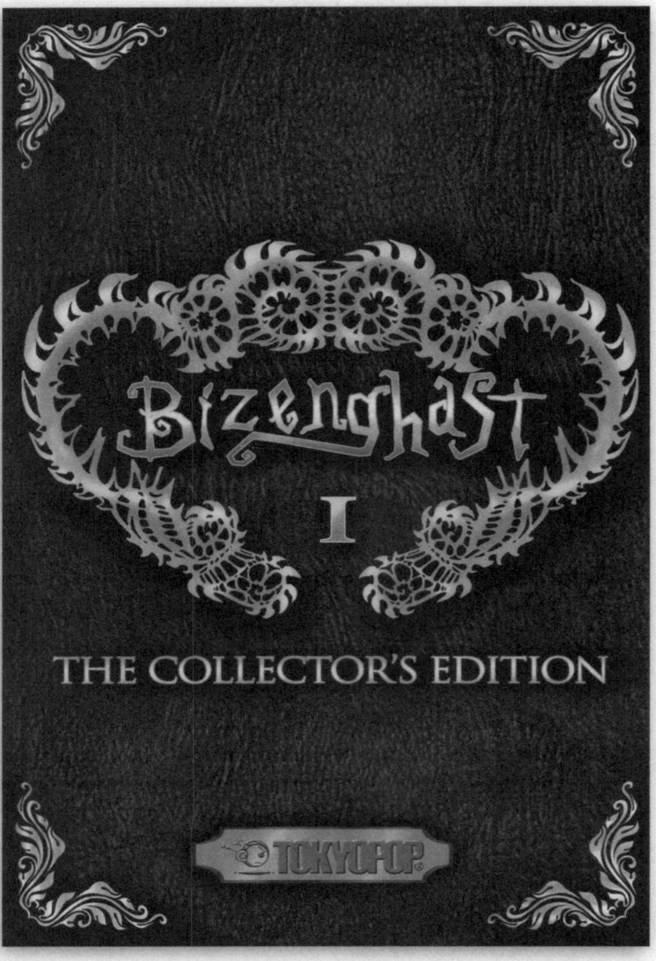

SUPERNATURAL

When a young girl moves to the forgotten town of Bizenghast, she uncovers a terrifying collection of lost souls that leads her to the brink of insanity. One thing that becomes painfully clear: The residences of Bizenghast are just dying to come home. Marty Legrow has crafted an unforgettable Gothic drama that will leave readers haunted long after the last page is turned.

TAROT CAFE: THE COLLECTOR'S EDITION, VOLUME 1

Sang-Sun Park

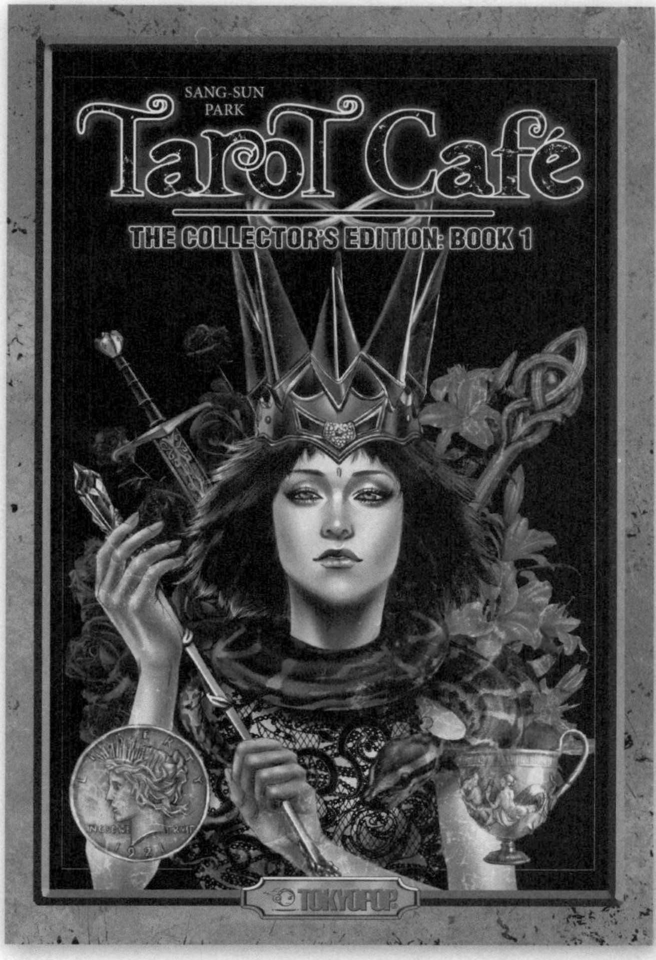
SANG-SUN PARK
Tarot Café
THE COLLECTOR'S EDITION: BOOK 1
TOKYOPOP

FANTASY

Meet Pamela, a tarot card reader who helps supernatural beings living in the human world. She'll help anyone, whether they're a love-stricken cat, a vampire spending eternal life running from his one true love, an unattractive waitress looking for the man of her dreams, or even a magician who creates a humanoid doll to serve the woman he loves. Although she is good-natured, there is a deep dark secret that she must deal with before she can move on to the next life.

TOKYOPOP

Laughing Under the Clouds, Volume 3
Manga by KarakaraKemuri

Editor	- Lena Atanassova
Marketing Associate	- Kae Winters
Translator	- Christine Dashiell
Copy Editor	- M. Cara Carper
Designer	- Sol DeLeo
Editorial Associate	- Janae Young
QC	- Massiel Gutierrez
Licensing Specialist	- Arika Yanaka
Cover Design	- Sol DeLeo
Retouching and Lettering	- Vibrraant Publishing Studio
Editor-in-Chief & Publisher	- Stu Levy

A  Manga

TOKYOPOP inc.
5200 W Century Blvd
Suite 705
Los Angeles, CA 90045 USA

E-mail: info@TOKYOPOP.com
Come visit us online at www.TOKYOPOP.com

f www.facebook.com/TOKYOPOP
🐦 www.twitter.com/TOKYOPOP
p www.pinterest.com/TOKYOPOP
📷 www.instagram.com/TOKYOPOP

ISBN: 978-1-4278-6771-1
First TOKYOPOP Printing: June 2021
Printed in CANADA

STOP

THIS IS THE BACK OF THE BOOK!

How do you read manga-style? It's simple! Let's practice -- just start in the top right panel and follow the numbers below!

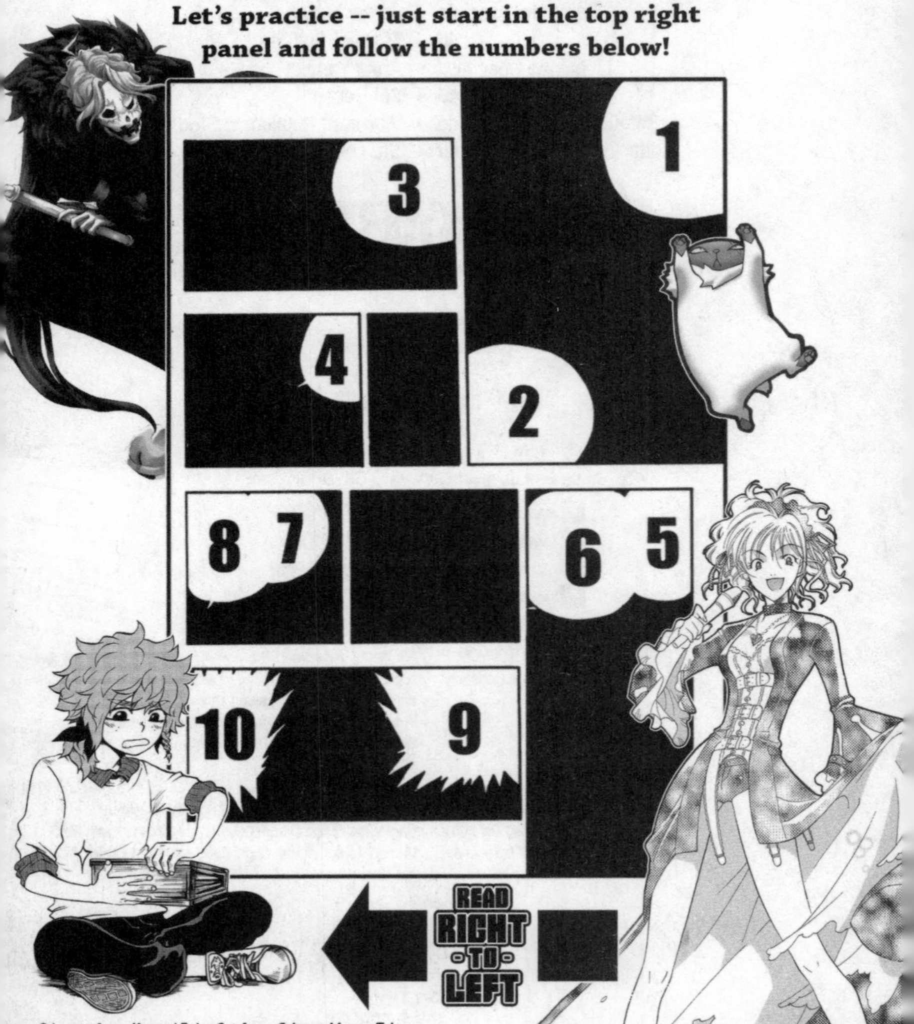
1
2
3
4
5
6
7
8
9
10
READ
RIGHT
-TO-
LEFT

Crimson from ***Kamo*** / Fairy Cat from ***Grimms Manga Tales***
Morrey from ***Goldfisch*** / Princess Ai from ***Princess Ai***